WONDERS

OF THE

EARTH AND THE HEAVENS.

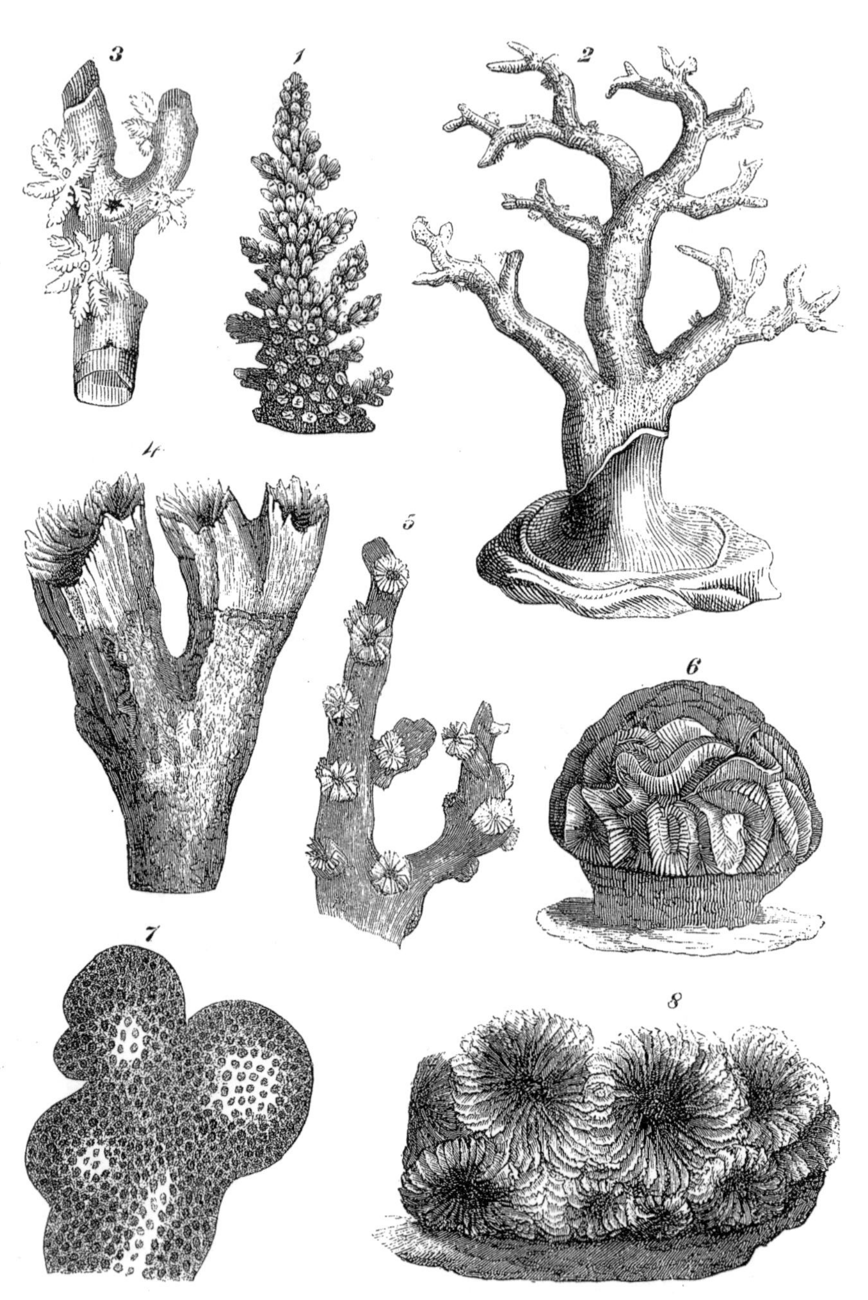

Specimens of the most common genera of corals found in coral reefs. 1. Extremity of branch of *Madrepora muricata*. 2. *Corallium rubrum*. 3. Magnified branch of do. 4. *Caryophyllia fastigiata*. 5. *Oculina hirtella*. 6. *Meandrina labyrinthica*. 7. *Porites clavaria*. 8. *Astrea dipsacea*.

THE

GALLERY OF NATURE;

OR

WONDERS

OF THE

EARTH AND THE HEAVENS

BY

THOMAS MILNER, A.M. F.R.G.S.

WITH

INTERESTING INFORMATION FROM OTHER NATURALISTS.

CONDENSED AND REVISED BY

CALEB WRIGHT, A. M.,

AUTHOR OF "TRAVELS IN INDIA," ETC.

EMBELLISHED WITH NUMEROUS FULL-PAGE ILLUSTRATIONS,

ENGRAVED EXPRESSLY FOR THIS WORK, BY THE BEST ARTISTS.

IN TWO VOLUMES.

VOLUME I.

Third American Edition.

BOSTON:

CALEB WRIGHT, 68 CORNHILL.

SOLD BY SUBSCPIPTION ONLY.

PREFACE.

These volumes, containing a description of some of the most interesting and remarkable of Nature's works as seen within the earth and upon its surface, in the atmosphere and in the regions of infinite space, have been prepared with the hope of awakening a spirit of inquiry and investigation which would lead to more extensive study, not only of the many valuable publications upon the subjects of which they treat, but also of the great volume of Nature. Should this object be obtained, good, not merely scientific, but moral and religious, must result; for the more we become acquainted with Nature's works, the greater will be our reverence for their Author; and the more fully his revelations of himself in his word and in his works are examined, the more beautifully will they be found to harmonize with and illustrate each other.

TESTIMONIALS.

From B. Silliman, LL.D., Professor of Chemistry, Mineralogy and Geology in Yale College.

"'The Gallery of Nature, or Wonders of the Earth and the Heavens,' is a very judicious, interesting and instructive work. The style of publication is rendered very attractive by an open page, with excellent type, paper, and beautiful illustrations, forming an ornament to any library. The publisher is entitled to an extensive patronage from the American public."

From Louis Agassiz, LL.D., Professor of Zoology and Geology, in Harvard University.

"I have looked through the work entitled 'Wonders of the Earth and the Heavens,' and read entirely several of its chapters, and find it to be an interesting popular illustration of the most remarkable features of the physical world, likely to diffuse much valuable information, and to create a desire for more extensive knowledge upon kindred subjects."

From D. Olmsted, A. M., Professor of Natural Philosophy in Yale College.

"From what examination I have been able to give of the 'Wonders of the Earth and Heavens,' I am deeply impressed with the value and interesting nature of the facts it embraces. They appear to me well chosen, happily condensed, and presented in a style at once lucid and attractive."

From J. Brocklesby, A. M., Prof. of Natural Philosophy in Trinity College.

"The work entitled 'Wonders of the Earth and Heavens' I have examined with great interest and pleasure. The author has rendered a valuable service to the community in presenting such a vast collection of facts in so interesting a style and form. It is a rich mine of attractive information on physical subjects, which well repays the exploration in the profit and delight that it affords."

From Wm. B. Rogers, A. M., late Professor of Natural Philosophy, &c., in the University of Virginia.

"I regard the 'Wonders of the Earth and Heavens' as a judicious compilation of useful knowledge and picturesque details on the great natural phenomena to which it refers, and it offers to the general reader much valuable and curious information in an attractive form."

THE NAMES OF

EIGHTY-SEVEN CLERGYMEN OF BOSTON,

Who have given their testimony in favor of the "Wonders of the Earth and the Heavens," by subscribing for a copy.

E. N. KIRK,
R. H. NEALE,
A. L. STONE,
S. K. LOTHROP,
M. EASTBURN (*Bishop*),
W. S. STUDLEY,
E. O. HAVEN,
G. C. BECKWITH,
T. S. KING,
A. A. MINER,
J. B. FITZPATRICK (*Bishop*),
D. WALSH,
P. T. LYNDON,
F. H. BRANAGAN,
B. STOW,
R. ANDERSON,
S. L. POMROY,
I. R. WORCESTER,
J. A. GOODHUE,
R. W. CLARK,
J. B. WATERBURY,
S. H. WINKLEY,
W. H. CUDWORTH,
T. WORCESTER,
T. F. CALDICOTT,
E. A. RENOUF,
S. H. RIDDELL,
I. J. P. COLLYER,
J. C. STOCKBRIDGE,
W. R. CLARK,
W. H. WINES,
S. BLISS,
J. H. TWOMBLY,
A. H. VINTON,
D. S. KING,
G. W. FIELD,
L. COLBY,
P. STOWE,
C. F. BARNARD,
N. M. GAYLORD,
O. A. SKINNER,
D. E. CHAPIN,
J. W. OLMSTEAD,
S. PECK,
J. W. PERKINS,
C. STONE,
J. H. CLINCH,
I. S. KALLOCH,
S. COBB,
W. T. SMITHETT,
W. HEATH,
J. S. CLARK,
W. HOWE,
A. P. CLEVERLY,
L. B. SCHWARZ,
F. BYRNE,
S. B. CRUFT,
J. TRACY,
C. S. PORTER,
S. STREETER,
H. WINSLOW,
N. ADAMS,
S. BARRETT,
E. T. TAYLOR,
W. W. DEAN,
R. W. ALLEN,
J. S. BARRY,
L. BOYDEN,
J. B. FELT,
J. IRWIN,
E. KELLOGG,
D. TENNY,
J. N. SYKES,
C. MASON,
S. MAY, Jr.,
A. RUMPFF,
E. EDMUNDS,
W. THOMPSON,
A. BLAIKIE,
A. BIGELOW,
A. GRIMES,
D. STEELE,
T. DAWES,
C. ROCKWELL,
J. G. WARREN,
D. C. HAYNES.
H. W. WARREN.

CONTENTS

OF THE

WONDERS OF THE EARTH AND THE HEAVENS.

CHAPTER I.

Animals of extinct species, many of them of enormous size and uncouth form, embedded at various depths in the soil, and in the hard rocks which constitute the crust of the earth. — Footprints of quadrupeds and of gigantic birds on the surface and in the interior of rocks. . . . . Page 15

CHAPTER II.

Extensive strata of the earth's crust, composed of the fossil remains of living beings, so small that more than 40,000,000,000 of them are contained in a cubic inch. — Strata composed of various kinds of shells, which in some instances constitute marble of great beauty. 40

CHAPTER III.

Minerals. — Origin of mineral coal. — Fifty-nine forests discovered, embedded one above another in the earth. — Geological discoveries respecting the age of the world consistent with the Mosaic account of creation. 54

CHAPTER IV.

Formation of peat. — Extensive forests converted into peat bogs. — Trees twelve feet in diameter embedded in them. — A house discovered sixteen feet below the surface of a bog. — A village destroyed by the bursting of a bog. — Preservation from decay of human bodies, their costumes, &c., in bogs where for many centuries they had remained embedded. 83

CHAPTER V.

Coral animals, and the beautiful submarine groves and arbors, the islands, atolls, reefs, and other portions of the earth which they have constructed. 96

CHAPTER VI.

Mountains. — Perilous adventures of travellers in ascending high mountains. — Snow fields of the Alps. — Elevated snow plains of Norway. 120

CHAPTER VII.

Glaciers. — The ice of which they are composed from 100 to 600 feet in thickness. — Their deep and dangerous chasms. — The variety and beauty of their colors. — Rocks of vast size transported by them from mountains to distant valleys. — Glaciers in the midst of orchards and fields of ripening corn. 138

CHAPTER VIII.

Village of Bueras, in Switzerland, buried and removed from its site by an avalanche. — A forest transported across a valley by an avalanche. — Village of Randa destroyed by the agitation of the air produced by the fall of an immense mass of ice from a glacier. — Destructive flood caused by fragments of a glacier falling into the River Dranse and forming across its valley a barrier of solid ice one hundred feet in height. . . . 161

CHAPTER IX.

Fall of a part of Mount Carnans, in Switzerland. — Fall of part of Mount Ruffi, burying five villages and twenty square miles of cultivated land. — Fall of part of Mount Conto, burying 2430 persons. — Fall of one of the mountains called "The Devil's Horns." — Fall of a part of Mount Grenier, burying five parishes, and strewing its fragments over nine square miles. — Landslip in the White Mountains. 170

CHAPTER X.

Earthquake of 1755, which destroyed Lisbon and 60,000 of its inhabitants. — Earthquake of 1812, which destroyed Caraccas, and effected great changes in the Mississippi Valley. — The great earthquakes of 1783, 1835, and 1815. — Earthquake in Java in 1822, and the destruction of 114 villages by descending torrents of hot water, boiling mud, and burning brimstone. — Formation by earthquakes of chasms, lakes, islands and mountains. — Location of fields exchanged, and other freaks of earthquakes. — Theory of earthquakes. 183

CHAPTER XI.

Crater of an extinct volcano in Java, containing a lake of sulphuric acid. — Guevo Upas, or Poison Valley. — Volcanoes of boiling mud. — The volcanic matter which buried Pompeii composed in part of animalcules. — Large volumes of water containing fish ejected by volcanoes. — Remarkable volcanic eruptions. — A flood of melted lava fifty miles in extent. — Theory of the origin of volcanic agency. 290

CHAPTER XII.

The table land of Quito the dome of an enormous subterranean vault. — Crystal caves. — Fingal's Cave. — Gurtshellir Cave. — Martin's Hole, and other natural tunnels through mountains. — Cave of Adelsberg. — Peak Cavern. — Cavern of the Guacharo. — Grotto of Antiparos. — Mammoth Cave. — Caverns in which ice accumulates in *summer*, and melts in *winter*. — Caverns containing immense quantities of the bones of animals of extinct species. — Mines remarkable for their depth and extent. 382

Skeleton of a Pterodactyle, found embedded in the interior of a solid rock, at Solenhofen, in Germany. In the rocks of England, one species of these flying reptiles has been found, whose expanded wings must have extended 16 feet.

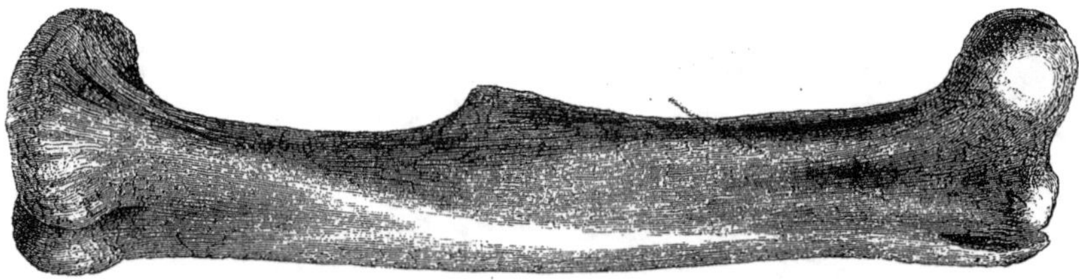

Thigh bone of an Iguanodon, a huge animal, whose fossil remains are found in the rocks of England. Length, 4 feet 8 inches. Length of the animal, 30 feet.

WONDERS

OF THE

EARTH AND THE HEAVENS.

CHAPTER I.

Animals of extinct Species, many of them of enormous Size and uncouth Form, embedded at various Depths in the Soil, and in the hard Rocks which constitute the Crust of the Earth.—Footprints of Quadrupeds and of gigantic Birds on the Surface and in the Interior of Rocks.

In the year 1814, Sir Everard Home published an account of some large and very remarkable bones found in a rock, thirty or forty feet above the sea level, on the English coast, between Lyme and Charmouth. The remains examined were incomplete, and the nature and habits of the animal to which they belonged baffled all inquiry, until the discovery of more perfect skeletons, and the application to them of the great genius of Cuvier, Mr. Conybeare, De la Beche, and others, unfolded a race of water saurians, which received the name of Ichthyosaurus, or fish lizard, from Mr. König, of the British Museum. This strange creature, (see engraving opposite next page,) ranging from five to more than thirty feet in length, of which ten species are enumerated, had the snout of a porpoise, the head of a lizard, the teeth of a crocodile, the vertebræ of a fish, the sternum of an ornithorhynchus, and the paddles of a whale; thus presenting in itself a combination of mechanical contrivances which are now found distributed among three distinct classes of the animal kingdom. "Persons," says Dr. Buckland, "to whom this subject may now be presented for the first time, will receive with much surprise, perhaps almost with incredulity, such statements as are here advanced. It must be admitted that they at first seem much more like the dreams of fiction and romance than the sober results of calm and deliberate investigation; but to those who will examine the evidence of facts upon which our conclusions rest, there can remain no more reasonable doubt of the former existence of these strange and curious creatures, in the times and places we assign to them, than is felt by the antiquary, who, finding the catacombs of Egypt stored with the mummies of men, and apes, and crocodiles, concludes them to be the remains of mammalia and reptiles, that have formed part of an ancient population on the banks of the Nile." The teeth of the ichthyosaurus, in some instances amounting to two hundred and ten, and the length of the jaws to more than six feet, qualified it for predacious habits; and the half-digested remains of fishes and reptiles, found within the skeletons, indicate the precise nature of its food. A single paddle of the four with which the animal was furnished sometimes contains more than a hundred bones, giving it great elasticity and power, and enabling it to proceed at a rapid rate through the water. The eye was enormously large, the orbital cavity, in one species, being fourteen inches in its longest direction. The eye also had a peculiar construction, to make it operate both like a telescope and a microscope, so that the animal could descry its prey by night as well as day, and at great depths in the water. This fish-like lizard in some degree answers to the words of Milton —

"With head uplift above the waves, and eyes
That sparkling blazed, his other parts besides,
Prone on the flood, extended long and large,
Lay floating many a rood, in bulk as huge
As whom the fables name of monstrous size,

Restoration of extinct animals from skeletons found in the interior of solid rocks. — 1. Ichthyosaurus. 2. Plesiosaurus. 3. Pterodactyle.

Titanian, or earth-born, that warred on Jove,
Briarchus, or Typhon, whom the den
By ancient Tarsus held, or that sea beast
Leviathan, which God of all his works
Created hugest that swam the ocean stream."

The ichthyosaurus was an air-breathing, cold-blooded, and carnivorous inhabitant of the ocean, probably haunting principally its creeks and estuaries, fitted by its formidable jaws and teeth, its rapid motion and power of vision, to be the scourge and tyrant of the existing seas of its era, keeping the multiplication of the species of other animals within proper limits. Though essentially marine, and admirably adapted by its organization to cut the waves, certain peculiarities of structure have induced the opinion that the anterior paddles might be subservient to locomotion not only in the water, but on land. Professor Owen thinks it very conceivable that the ichthyosauri, like the existing crocodiles, may have come ashore to sleep, or resorted thither to deposit their eggs, supposing them to have been oviparous, as the sum of the analogies deducible from their osseous texture would indicate. The remains of these animals occur in great abundance in England, at Barrow-on-Soar, in Leicestershire, in the valley of the Avon, between Bath and Bristol, and on the coast of Dorsetshire, where the cliffs appear to be inexhaustible quarries of them.

In the same strata in which the remains of the ichthyosaurus are found, another marine reptile appears, which received its name of Plesiosaurus, signifying akin to the lizard, from its more closely resembling animals of this genus than fishes, especially in the character of the vertebræ. (See engraving.) A similar remarkable combination of forms appears in this animal to that which distinguishes its preceding congener — the head of a lizard, the teeth of a crocodile, a neck resembling the body of a serpent, the trunk and tail of an ordinary quadruped, the ribs of a chameleon, and the paddles of a whale. "Such," writes Dr. Buckland, "are the strange combinations of form and structure in the plesiosau-

3

rus, a genus, the remains of which, after interment for thou sands of years amidst the wreck of millions of extinct inhab itants of the ancient earth, are at length recalled to light by the researches of the geologist, and submitted to our exami nation in nearly as perfect a state as the bones of species that are now existing upon the earth." Its most striking feature is the great length of the neck, which has from thirty to forty vertebræ, a larger number than in any other known animal, those of living reptiles varying from three to six, and those of birds from nine to twenty-three. It has been therefore correctly compared to a serpent, threaded through the body of a turtle. "That it was aquatic," remarks Mr. Conybeare, "is evident from the form of its paddles; that it was marine is almost equally so, from the remains with which it is universally associated; that it may have occasionally visited the shore, the resemblance of its extremities to those of the turtle may lead us to conjecture; its motion, however, must have been very awkward on land; its long neck must have impeded its progress through the water, presenting a striking contrast to the organization of the ichthyosaurus, which so admirably fitted it for that purpose. May it not therefore be concluded (since, in addition to these circumstances, its respiration must have required frequent access of air) that it swam upon or near the surface, arching back its long neck like the swan, and occasionally darting it down at the fish which happened to float within its reach? It may perhaps have lurked in shoal water along the coast, concealed among the sea weed, and raising its nostrils to the surface from a considerable depth, may have found a secure retreat from the assaults of dangerous enemies; while the length and flexibility of its neck may have compensated for the want of strength in its jaws, and its incapacity for swift motion through the water, by the suddenness and agility of the attack which they enabled it to make on every animal fitted for its prey." These remarks are in harmony with the appearance of the animal, which is far less formidable than that of the ichthyosaurus, more adapted to occupy the tranquil waters of sheltered creeks and bays than to brave the rough breakers of the deep, with which its congener might contend. The first almost entire skeleton of plesiosaurus was obtained in January, 1824, from the cliffs of Dorset, England, by Miss Mary Anning; soon afterwards Cuvier demonstrated its existence on the opposite side of the Channel, from an examination of some vertebræ and other bones which had been collected at Honfleur, near the mouth of the Seine; and subsequently, sixteen species have been established. From the connected and almost perfect state of the skeletons of ichthyosauri and plesiosauri, as if prepared by an anatomist, these animals appear to have been suddenly destroyed and immediately embedded. As we know that river fish are sometimes stifled, even in their own element, by muddy water, during floods, it cannot be doubted that the periodical discharge of large bodies of turbid fresh water into the sea may be still more fatal to marine tribes. Large quantities of mud and drowned animals have been swept down into the sea, by rivers, during earthquakes, as in Java, in 1699; and indescribable multitudes of dead fishes have been seen floating on the sea, after a discharge of noxious vapors, during similar convulsions.

Contemporaneously with these strange animals, marine, fresh-water, and terrestrial tortoises flourished, with crocodilians of extinct species, and the pterodactyle, or wing-fingered reptile, perhaps the most singular and monstrous creature of the ancient world, the type of which appears in no living genus. This flying reptile is represented in the engraving, with the ichthyosaurus and plesiosaurus. Naturalists pored over its remains, and were unable to refer it to its true place in the animal kingdom, some pronouncing it a bird, others a reptile, and others a bat, till Cuvier took its skeleton in hand. "Behold," he observes, "an animal, which, in its osteology, from its teeth to the end of its claws, offers all the characters of the saurians; nor can we doubt that those characters existed in its integuments and soft parts—in its scales, its circulation, its generative organs. But it was, at the same time, an animal provided with the means of flight, which, when stationary, could not have made much use of its anterior extremities, even if it did not keep them always folded as birds keep their wings; which, nevertheless, might use its small anterior fingers to suspend itself from the branches of trees, but when at rest must have been ordinarily on its hind feet, like the birds, again; and also, like them, must have carried its neck sub-erect, and curved backwards, so that its enormous head should not interrupt its equilibrium." Pterodactyles had the head and neck of a bird, the mouth and teeth of a reptile, the wings of a bat, the body and tail of a mammifer. Their eyes were enormously large, so that they could seek their prey in the night. They could not only fly, but Dr. Buckland supposes that, like the existing vampire bat, they had the power of swimming. "Thus," says he, "like Milton's fiend, all qualified for all services and all elements, the pterodactyle was a fit companion for the kindred reptiles that swarmed in the seas, or crawled on the shores of a turbulent planet:—

"The Fiend,
O'er bog, or steep, through strait, rough, dense, or rare,
With head, hands, wings, or feet pursues his way,
And swims, or sinks, or wades, or creeps, or flies."

Cuvier, in his great work, pronounces these flying reptiles the most extraordinary of all the beings whose ancient existence is revealed to us; and those which, if alive, would seem most at variance with living forms. Their remains have been found at Lyme Regis and Stonesfield, England, also at Pappenheim and Solenhofen, in Germany. Seventeen species have been determined, most of them varying from the size of a snipe to that of a cormorant. It is estimated that the expanded wings of the *pterodactylus giganteus* measured six feet in width.

Not less remarkable than these inhabitants of the ocean

and the air were the land reptiles of the same period, the iguanodon and megalosaurus. The iguanodon derives its name from the resemblance of its structure to that of the living iguana, especially in the form of the teeth. Although the size and proportions of its body and limbs have been determined from numerous detached bones, and the few specimens in which several are collected in the same block of stone, yet but a vague idea of the form and appearance of the original animal can be derived from the relics hitherto discovered. We may, however, safely conclude that the body of the iguanodon was equal in magnitude to that of the elephant, and as massive in its proportions; for being a vegetable feeder, a large development of the abdominal region may be inferred. Its limbs must have been of a proportionate size to sustain so enormous a bulk; one of the thigh-bones in the British Museum, if covered with muscles and integuments of suitable proportions, would form a limb seven feet in circumference. The hinder extremities, in all probability, presented the unwieldy contour of those of the hippopotamus or rhinoceros, and were supported by very strong, short feet, the toes of which were armed with claws, like those of certain turtles. The fore legs appear to have been less bulky, and were furnished with hooked claws, resembling the unequal phalanges of the iguana. The teeth demonstrate the nature of the food required for the support of this herbivorous reptile, and the power of mastication it enjoyed; and the ferns, cycadeous plants, and coniferous trees, with which its remains are associated, indicate the flora adapted for its sustenance. But the physiognomy of this creature, from the peculiar modification of the skull and jaws required for the attachment and support of the powerful muscles necessary for the trituration of tough vegetable substances, must have differed entirely from that of all known saurians.

The length of the iguanodon has been variously estimated; the difference in the computation depending chiefly on the extent assigned to the tail, which in the iguana and many other lizards is much longer than the body. If the tail of the fossil reptile was slender, and of the same relative proportions as in the iguana, the largest individual would be fifty or sixty feet long; but it is more probable, and in fact almost certain, from the shortness of the bodies of the caudal vertebræ, that the tail was short, and flattened in a vertical direction, as in certain living reptiles — for example, the *doryphorus ;* in that case the length of a full grown iguanodon would but little exceed thirty feet.

The accompanying engraving of the Megalosaurus restored is from a model made by Mr. Hawkins, and exhibited at the London Crystal Palace. In the manner in which the body is placed upon the legs, it is evidently incorrect, for no bulky reptile ever carried its body high upon its legs. The Megalosaurus, as its name implies, was a lizard of great size, and its legs, in their relative position to the body, should be like the legs of other lizards. No skeleton of the Megalosaurus has yet been found entire, but many perfect bones and teeth have been discovered in the same quarries of stone. Its remains have been discovered in Switzerland, also in Stonesfield, Tilgate Forest, near Cuckfield, in Sussex, and in other localities in England.

Baron Cuvier estimated this animal to have been about fifty feet in length. The calculations of Mr. Owen, founded on more complete evidence than had been at the baron's command, reduce its size to about thirty-five feet; but with the superior proportional height and capacity of trunk as contrasted with the largest existing crocodiles, even that length gives a most formidable character to this extinct predatory reptile. Mr. Hawkins's restoration, according to the proportions calculated from the largest portions of fossil bones of the megalosaurus hitherto obtained, yields a total length of the animal, from the muzzle to the end of the tail, of thirty-seven feet, the length of the head being five feet, the length of the tail fifteen feet, and the greatest girth of the body twenty-two feet six inches.

Megalosaurus, restored from portions of its skeleton discovered in the stone quarries of England. Length 37 feet, girth of body, 22½ feet.

As the thigh bone and leg bone measure each nearly three feet, the entire hind leg, allowing for the cartilages of the joints, must have attained a length of two yards; the metatarsal bone was thirteen inches long, and indicated a foot, with the toes and claws entire, of at least three feet in length.

The form of the teeth shows the megalosaurus to have been strictly carnivorous, and their compressed conical crowns, with cutting and finely serrated edges, were fearfully fitted to the destructive office for which they were designed. They appear straight when young, but become slightly bent backwards in the progress of growth, and the fore part of the crown, below the summit, becomes thick and convex. A minute and interesting description of these teeth will be found in Dr. Buckland's Bridgewater Treatise. He remarks that they present a combination of contrivances analogous to those which human ingenuity has adopted in the construction of the knife, the sabre, and the saw.

When the ichthyosaurus and plesiosaurus ceased to rule the ocean and became extinct, the mososaurus took their place, to keep the multiplication of the species of other animals within proper limits. The mososaurus derives its name from the locality, Maestricht, on the River Meuse, in Germany, where its remains have been chiefly discovered, and from the Greek word *sauros*, a lizard, to which tribe of animals it belongs. The occasional discovery of bones and teeth of an unknown animal in the limestone had long since directed the attention of naturalists to the quarries of St. Peter's Mountain. In 1770, M. Hoffmann, who was forming a collection of organic remains, had the good fortune to discover a specimen, which has conferred additional interest on this locality. Some workmen, on blasting the rock in one of the caverns of the interior of the mountain, perceived, to their astonishment, the jaws of an enormous animal attached to the roof of the chasm. The discovery was immediately made known to M. Hoffmann, who repaired to the spot, and for weeks presided over the arduous task of separating from the rock the mass of stone containing these remains. His labors were at length repaid by the successful extrication of the specimen, which he conveyed in triumph to his house. Unfortunately, the canon of the cathedral, which stands on the mountain, claimed the fossil in right of being lord of the manor, and succeeded, by a most unjust and expensive lawsuit, in obtaining this precious relic. It remained in his possession for years, and Hoffmann died without regaining his treasure, or receiving any compensation. The French revolution broke out, and the armies of the republic advanced to the gates of Maestricht; the town was bombarded, but by desire of the committee of *savans*, who accompanied the French troops, the artillery was not allowed to play on that part of the city in which the celebrated fossil was known to be contained. In the mean while, the canon, shrewdly suspecting why such peculiar favor was shown to his residence, concealed the specimen in a secret vault; but when the city was taken, the French authorities compelled him to give up his ill-gotten prize, which was immediately transmitted to the *Jardin des Plantes* at Paris, where it still forms one of the most striking objects in that magnificent collection.

The entire length of the mososaurus has been estimated at from twenty-five to thirty feet; the number of its vertebræ is one hundred and thirty-three. Its skull measures four and a half feet in length, and two and a half feet in width.

A few remains of this reptile have been met with in the English chalk. Dr. Mantell collected three vertebræ, near Lewes, many years since, and has more recently obtained a caudal vertebra from Kemptown; the latter is partially invested with flint, which has consolidated around it without obscuring its essential characters. Fossil bones and teeth of the mososaurus have also been found in the greensand of the State of New Jersey.

In the more recent deposits, the remains of immense mammalia are found in great numbers; among the most remarkable of these is the mammoth or fossil elephant.

There are but two species of existing elephants, namely, the African, which ranges as far south as the Cape of Good Hope, and the Asiatic, which is limited to within thirty-one degrees north latitude. Yet the remains not only of one, but of several distinct species of this family, occur all over Europe and North America, and are embedded in frozen gravel and drift in seventy-two degrees north latitude. They even abound in ice cliffs on the north-west angle of the American continent, near to Behring's Straits. In Russia, and more especially in Siberia, the fossil bones of extinct species of elephants and other mammalia are found in great quantities, and in the sandy plains which extend from the borders of Europe to the nearest extreme point of America, and south and north from the base of the mountains of Central Asia to the shores of the Arctic Sea. Within this space, which is almost equal in extent to the whole of Europe, fossil ivory is every where to be found; and the tusks are so numerous and well preserved, especially in Northern Russia, that thousands are annually collected, and form a lucrative article of commerce. In Siberia alone, the remains of a greater number of elephants have been discovered than are supposed to exist at the present time all over the world. In 1844 a company of merchants was formed to collect teeth and tusks of mammoths from Siberia; for the fossil ivory was found to possess all the qualities of the recent, and at the same time was less liable to turn yellow. During the year, sixteen thousand pounds of jaws and tusks of mammoths were obtained, and these were sold at St. Petersburg, under the denomination of Siberian ivory, at prices from thirty to one hundred per cent. above those of the recent elephantine ivory.

Not only are the bones and tusks found in a beautiful state of preservation, but sometimes even the entire body, with the flesh and skin as fresh as if but recently embedded. In the year 1799 a Tungusian fisherman observed, in a cliff of ice and gravel on the banks of the River Lena, a shapeless mass, the nature of which he was unable to determine. In the course of the next year it was more visible, and on the third, a large tusk was seen projecting from the ice cliff, and at length became detached. On the fifth year, an early thaw set in, and the entire carcass of a mammoth was exposed, and at length fell upon the ground. It was twelve feet high, and about sixteen feet in length; the tusks were nine feet long. The flesh was in such a state of preservation, that it was devoured as it lay by wolves and bears, and the hunters fed their dogs with the remains. The skin was covered with hair, consisting of black bristles, thicker than horse hair, and fifteen inches in length; with wool of a reddish brown, and hair of a fawn color, and with a mane on the neck. The ears were dry and shrivelled; the brain, and even the capsule of the eye, were preserved; the bones and part of the integuments, and a considerable quantity of the hair, upwards of thirty pounds of which were collected, are in the Museum of Natural History at St. Petersburg.

The tusks are curved forward and upward. The teeth differ from those of the two living species of elephants in the disposition of the plates of dentine, and also in their internal microscopic structure; the configuration of the skull is likewise peculiar; and these discrepancies, together with the hairy and woolly skin, led Baron Cuvier to consider the species as having been adapted to exist in a colder climate than the living types.

Although the mastodon is frequently called the mammoth in this country, where the remains of the largest species are abundant, yet it differs generically from the elephant in the form of its teeth.

No less than seven species of mastodon have been discovered in a fossil state, (thirteen species according to Professor Grant,) viz., three in Europe, two in South America, one in the United States, and one in India. The largest species, *M. maximus*, has been found in almost every part of the United States, though most abundantly in the *salt licks* of Kentucky, Ohio, &c. The most easterly point where the bones of these animals have been found is Berlin, in Connecticut. The most remarkable locality in this country is at the Big Bone Lick, in Kentucky, where a vast number of bones of various extinct animals are embedded in dark-colored mud and gravel, which appear to have been formerly the bottom of a marsh. This spot has been examined by William Cooper, Esq., with his usual discrimination and accuracy; and he is of opinion that the deposit containing the bones is to be regarded as drift. He estimates that the bones of one hundred mastodons, twenty elephants, two oxen, two deer, and one megalonyx, have already been carried from this spot.

In 1845 the skeleton of a mastodon, almost entire, was dug up in New Jersey, with skulls and other bones of four or five others. These have been purchased for Harvard College. A more gigantic and perfect skeleton was found the same year, in Orange county, New York, in a peat bog, with marl beneath, where it stood in an erect position, as if the animal lost its life by getting *mired* in search of food. In the place where its stomach and intestines lay was found a large mass of fragments of twigs and grass, hardly fossilized at all. This skeleton was twenty-five feet in length, twelve feet in height, and weighed two thousand pounds, and is perhaps the most perfect and gigantic ever found. It is now owned by Dr. John C. Warren, of Boston.

Until recently the mammoth and the mastodon have been supposed the largest of all the terrestrial mammalia that ever inhabited the earth; but they must give place to the dinotherium, described by Cuvier as a gigantic tapir; but, more recently, by Professor Kaup, a distinguished German naturalist, as a new genus between the tapir and the mastodon. Its remains have been found in the south of France, in Austria, Bavaria, and especially in Hesse Darmstadt. Its length must have been as much as eighteen feet. One of its most remarkable peculiarities consisted in two enormous tusks, at the anterior extremity of the lower jaw, which curved downwards, like those of the walrus. Its general structure seems to have been adapted to digging in the ground; and for this purpose its feet as well as tusks, projecting a foot or two beyond the jaws, which were four feet long, were intended. It lived principally in the water, like the hippopotamus; and it probably used its tusks for tearing up the roots of aquatic vegetables, which, as is shown by its teeth, constituted its food. Dr. Buckland suggests that these tusks might also have been useful as an anchor, fastened into the banks of a river, while the body of the animal floated in the water and slept. They might have been useful also to aid in dragging the body out of the water, and for defence.

Numerous remains of dinotheria, mastodons, elephants, hippopotami, rhinoceroses, horses, camels, antelopes, struthious birds, and crocodilian and chelonian reptiles, are found in various localities in India. The alluvial deposits of the sub-Himmalaya district extend about two hundred miles in length, and seven in breadth, and dip to the north at an angle of twenty-five degrees. Here we have intombed in the same rocky sepulchre bones of the most ancient extinct races of mammalia, with species and genera which still inhabit India.

Among these marvellous relics of the past are the skull and bones of an animal named sivatherium, (from the Indian deity *Siva*,) that requires a passing notice. This creature forms, as it were, a link between the ruminants and the large pachyderms. It was larger than a rhinoceros, had four horns, and was furnished with a proboscis; thus combining the horns of a ruminant with the characters of a pachyderm. When living it must have resembled an immense antelope, or gnu, with a short and thick head and elevated cranium, crested with two pairs of horns; the front pair were small, and the hinder large, and set quite behind, as in the auroch. With the face and figure of the rhinoceros, it had small lateral eyes, great lips, and a nasal proboscis.

Among the reptilian remains are skulls and bones of a Gangetic crocodile, and of a land turtle, which cannot be distinguished from those of a species still living in India.

But the most extraordinary discovery is that of bones, and portions of the carapace of a tortoise of gigantic dimensions. It has been aptly named *colossochelys atlas*. The length of this reptile exceeded *twelve feet*.

The pampas, those vast plains in South America which present a sea of waving grass for nine hundred miles, are principally composed of alluvial loam and sand, containing fresh-water and marine shells, and were once a gulf or arm of the sea. In the most recent of these deposits, bones of enormous extinct mammalia have frequently been discovered. Their occurrence demonstrates that a bay of salt water was gradually encroached upon, and at length became the bed of a muddy estuary, into which floated the carcasses of the animals which then inhabited the neighboring dry land.

The most remarkable of the fossil bones discovered in the pampas belong to several extinct colossal animals of the *edentata*, (so named from having no teeth in the front of the jaws,) an order of which the armadillos, sloths, and ant-eaters are the living representatives. But as the extinct forms differ greatly from the existing ones, in their gigantic proportions, short massy extremities, and thick and strong tail, their mode of life must have been very dissimilar. To impart a clear perception of the peculiar modification of structure which these extinct beings present, it will be necessary to offer some remarks on the existing types — the sloths.

The sloths are arranged by naturalists in a tribe termed *tardigrada*, from their feeble power of progression on the surface of the land; for the same reason they are called *paresseux* by the French, whence the English name *sloth*. They are of slender form and small size; the largest species is but little larger than a cat. They have long toes, and nails which fold up, so as to enable the animal to walk, in the same way as if our fingers were folded under the palms of the hands, but which are not capable of being retracted into a sheath, as in the feline tribes. The arms are double the length of the legs, and, from the construction of the limbs, the animal, when it walks, or rather crawls on the ground, is obliged to drag itself along on its elbows. But these creatures are destined to inhabit trees; their proper element is on the branches, and they can pass from bough to bough, and from tree to tree, with a rapidity which soon enables them to lose themselves in the depths of the forests. They live on the leaves and young shoots, and unless disturbed, never quit a tree till they have stripped off every leaf. To avoid the labor of a descent, they drop to the ground, previously coiling themselves into a round ball, in which state, while attached to the branch, they may be taken alive. Thus the habits and economy of the sloth point out the necessity for a peculiarity in the structure of its claws. The monkey leaps and swings himself from tree to tree, and catches at will the branches or the trunk; but the sloths do not grasp; their claws are mere hooks to hang by, and their great strength is in their arms. They never unfix one set of hooks until they have caught a secure hold with the other, thus hanging by their arms and legs, while their bodies are pendent; and they sleep in the same position. The bones of the arm are constructed to suit these conditions. The humerus has a long internal condyle for the origin of large muscles to move the enormous claws; and there is an opening for the passage of the principal nerves and blood vessels, to protect them from the pressure to which they would be exposed from the powerful muscular action; and the radius (one of the bones of the fore arm,) is constructed to allow of a free rotatory motion to the limb. In the extinct sloths, a similar conformation is maintained, but somewhat modified to suit the different physical conditions under which they existed. There are three genera well established from the fossil remains. The names assigned to them refer to some striking character; as *megalonyx*, from the enormous size of the claw; *megatherium*, or enormous wild animal, from its colossal proportions; *mylodon*, or molar tooth animal, from the peculiarity of its dental organs.

Towards the close of the last century, an almost perfect skeleton of a gigantic animal was dug up, at the depth of one hundred feet, in a bed of clay on the banks of the River Luxan, about four leagues W. S. W. from Buenos Ayres. This skeleton was sent in 1789 to the Museum at Madrid, where it now remains. It is described and figured by Cuvier, under the name of megatherium. The megatherium was armed with claws of enormous length and power, its whole frame possessing an extreme degree of solidity. With a head and neck like those of the sloth, its legs and feet exhibit the character of the armadillo and the anteater. Some specimens of the animal give the measurement of five feet across the haunches, and the thigh bone was nearly three times as thick as that of the elephant. The spinal marrow must have been a foot in diameter, and the tail, at the part nearest the body, twice as large, or six feet in circumference. The girth of the body was fourteen feet and a half, and the length eighteen feet. The teeth were admirably adapted for cutting vegetable substances, and the general structure and strength of the frame for tearing up the ground in search of roots, wrenching off the branches of trees, and uprooting their trunks, on which it principally fed. "Heavily constructed, and ponderously accoutred," says Dr. Buckland, in his eloquent description of the megatherium, "it could neither run, nor leap, nor climb, nor burrow under the ground; and all its movements must have been necessarily slow. But what need of rapid locomotion to an animal whose occupation, of digging roots for food, was almost stationary? And what need of speed, for flight from foes, to a creature whose giant carcass was incased in an impenetrable cuirass, and who, by a single pat of his paw, or lash of his tail, could in an instant have demolished the cougar or the crocodile? Secure within the panoply of his strong armor, where was the enemy that would dare encounter this leviathan of the pampas? or in what more powerful creature can we find the cause that has effected the extirpation of his race? His entire frame was an apparatus of colossal mechanism, adapted exactly to the work it had to do—strong and ponderous in proportion as this work was heavy, and calculated to be the vehicle of life and enjoyment to a gigantic race of quadrupeds, which, though they have ceased to be counted among the living inhabitants of our planet, have in their fossil bones left behind them imperishable monuments of the consummate skill with which they were constructed." Since this passage was written, it has been shown by Professor Owen that the megatherium was nót incased with a bony armor, like the armadillo, as is here assumed, and that the tessellated shell or case, found in one instance with some remains, which led to the surmise, belonged to another contemporaneous extinct animal, nearly as colossal, which he has called the glyptodon, discovered near Monte Video by Sir Woodbine Parish.

The mylodon was nearly as large as the hippopotamus, but shorter. Its hinder extremities are relatively short, and the feet are placed at right angles with the legs, and are as long as the thigh bones. The tail is remarkably thick and strong, and as long as the hinder extremities. The pelvis is very massive and solid. The ribs are as stout and broad as in the elephant. The fore legs or arms are connected to the sternum by powerful clavicles, and are so constructed as to admit of unrestrained motion in every direction. The toes are five in number on each fore foot, and four on the hinder; the two external toes are unarmed; the others have powerful curved nails or claws. The skull is long, narrow, and smaller than that of the ox; it terminates in a flat or truncated muzzle. The bones of the upper part of the cranium are of enormous thickness, large air cells being interposed between the inner and outer table. The teeth, which are implanted in very deep sockets, are of the same form and size throughout, and closely resemble in structure those of the megatherium, but the surface of the crown when worn is flat; there are four on each side in the lower, and five in the upper jaw

The mylodon, like the megatherium, was a vegetable

1. Megatherium, restored from a skeleton discovered 100 feet below the earth's surface, near Buenos Ayres. Length 18 feet.
2. Mylodon, restored from skeletons discovered in South America. Length 13 feet.

feeder, and probably browsed on shrubs and the branches of trees. The arms are especially adapted for grasping and wrenching; and though no trees could support the weight of this enormous creature, there is nothing to forbid the supposition that with its hinder feet it could clasp the trunk of a large tree, and with its fore feet climb to a sufficient height to seize and wrench off the branches.

An enormous curved ungual phalanx or claw bone, and several bones of the arm and sternum, of an animal related to the sloths, and called the megalonyx, were found many years since in Big Bone Cave, one of the numerous saltpetre caverns which occur in the States of Kentucky, Tennessee, and Virginia. Some of these caves extend many miles under ground, passing beneath hills, valleys, and even rivers. In these subterranean retreats are sometimes found Indian mummies, which are simply desiccated human bodies, in a fine state of preservation. Bones of existing species of mammalia, and of mastodons, mammoths, and rarely of extinct gigantic sloths, also occur.

The remains of the megalonyx were first described by President Jefferson; and the claw bones, the largest of which was nearly seven inches long, excited especial attention, from the supposition that they belonged to a carnivorous animal of marvellous size. But Cuvier, in an admirable memoir, proved, from the following circumstances, that they were referable to an extinct form of the edentata. The paws, both of the canine and feline tribes, are armed with claws. In the former the nails are thick and coarse, as in the dog, wolf, &c., and will bear the friction and pressure incident to a long chase; but in the cat tribe they are curved and sharp, and these qualities are preserved by a particular mechanism. The last bone which supports the claw is placed laterally to the penultimate bone of the phalanx, and is so joined to it that an elastic ligament draws it back, and raises the sharp extremity of the claw upwards, and the proximal or nearest extremity of the animal, while the claw is retracted into a sheath; but when the creature makes a spring and strikes, the claws are uncased by the action of the flexors, or bending tendons. In the Bengal tiger the claws are so sharp and strong, and the arms so powerful, that they have been known to fracture the skull of a man by a single touch from the animal in the act of leaping over him. A cat affords a familiar illustration of this peculiarity of structure; when pleased, its claws are retracted, and when angry they are thrown out.

In the claw of the megalonyx there is no such lateral provision for its retraction, and the point could not have been raised vertically, as in the cat, so as to have permitted it to touch the ground without injury. The articulating surface is double; that is, there is a ridge or spine in the middle, and it must, therefore, have moved like a hinge. The bones of the arm present a corresponding configuration with those of the sloth; the humerus is perforated for the passage of the blood vessels, and the radius is constructed for rotation.

The megalonyx resembled the megatherium in its general character, configuration, and habits, but was much smaller.

The glyptodon — so named from the deeply-grooved teeth — was an animal allied to the armadillos, and possessed a carapace, or coat of mail, formed of polygonal bony plates united by suture, which constituted an impenetrable covering over the upper part of the body. The plates of this bony integument were not disposed in rings, as in the armadillo, but were articulated to each other, and formed a tessellated cylinder, or rather arch; the tail was enclosed in a case of this kind like a sword in its scabbard.

Such were the gigantic edentata that inhabited the dry land of South America at a comparatively modern period; and it is worthy of especial remark, that though these beings have long been extinct, sloths, anteaters, and armadillos, but of diminutive size, are still the characteristic animals of that country.

In the year 1828, Dr. Duncan gave an account, with drawings, to the Royal Society of Edinburgh, of the tracks of an animal on new red sandstone, in the quarry of Corn Cockle Muir, in Dumfriesshire, Scotland. The tracks were found there in great abundance, on many successive layers of stone, to the depth of forty-five feet, or as low as the quarry had been opened. After removing a large slab which presented foot prints, perhaps the very next stratum, at the distance of a few feet or inches, exhibited the same phenomenon. Hence the process by which the impressions were made on the sand, and subsequently buried, must have been repeated at successive intervals. In another quarry in similar strata, near the town of Dumfries, the same marks were discovered, and in one instance a track extended from twenty to thirty feet in length. Dr. Buckland refers these impressions to land tortoises. In 1834 an account was published of some remarkable fossil footsteps in the new red sandstone at Hesseburg, near Hildburghausen, in Saxony. The largest track appears to have been made by an animal whose hind foot was eight inches long, the fore foot being much smaller. It received the name of chirotherium, from Professor Kaup, owing to the resemblance of its impressions to the shape of the human hand. Fossil skulls, jaws, teeth, and a few other bones of this animal, have since been discovered, and from some characteristics which they possess,—found at the present day only in frogs and salamanders, and from the proportionate size of its fore and hind feet, also a characteristic of the toad and frog,—this extinct animal is supposed to have been a huge batrachian. It has more recently received the name of labyrinthodon, from the peculiar structure of its teeth, which, under the microscope, present a series of irregular folds, resembling the labyrinthic windings of the human brain. The accompanying pictorial representation is from a model exhibited at the London Crystal Palace.

In the summer of 1838 a variety of tracks, referred to the chirotherium, tortoises, and saurian reptiles, were discovered in the new red sandstone at the quarries of Storeton Hill, in the neighborhood of Liverpool. The largest foot print was nine inches long, and six inches broad, the length of the step approaching to two feet. Abundant foot prints, along with ripple marks, have been found on layers of the forest marble, to the north of Bath. These are conjectured to have been made by crustacea, crawling along the bottom of an estuary; for between the rows of the foot marks the impression of the stomach, or the trail of the tail, is sometimes visible.

A communication made to the American Journal of Science, in January, 1836, by President Hitchcock, brought before the attention of the public some very distinct tracks in the red sandstone of the Connecticut valley, first observed by Dr. Deane, of Greenfield, who immediately noticed their resemblance to the impressions left on the muddy banks of the river by the living aquatic birds common to the locality.

President Hitchcock, in his Elements of Geology, says that he is now acquainted with more than forty species of footmarks along the banks of the Connecticut River, which he supposes were made by as many species of animals. In his Report on the Geology of Massachusetts, in 1841, he figured and described twenty-seven species, which he divided into *ornithoidichnites*, or tracks resembling those of birds, and *sauroidichnites*, or tracks resembling those of saurians. Nine species more have since been described in the Transactions of the Association of American Geologists, and in the American Journal of Science, and several species have more recently been discovered. Five of these are quadrupeds, and probably more; and the rest bipeds, with the exception of two species of annelids, which have left only a trackway or furrow, and three species of a very anomalous character. Some of the foot prints of birds are no less than eighteen inches in length, and the strides from three to five feet.

The slab which first arrested the attention of Dr. Deane is about six feet by eight in dimensions, and contains above seventy-five impressions. There are five rows of the species called by Professor Hitchcock *ornithichnites fulicoides*, of five and six foot marks each; three rows of the medium size, of

Labyrinthodon, an extinct animal whose bones and footprints are found in sandstone.

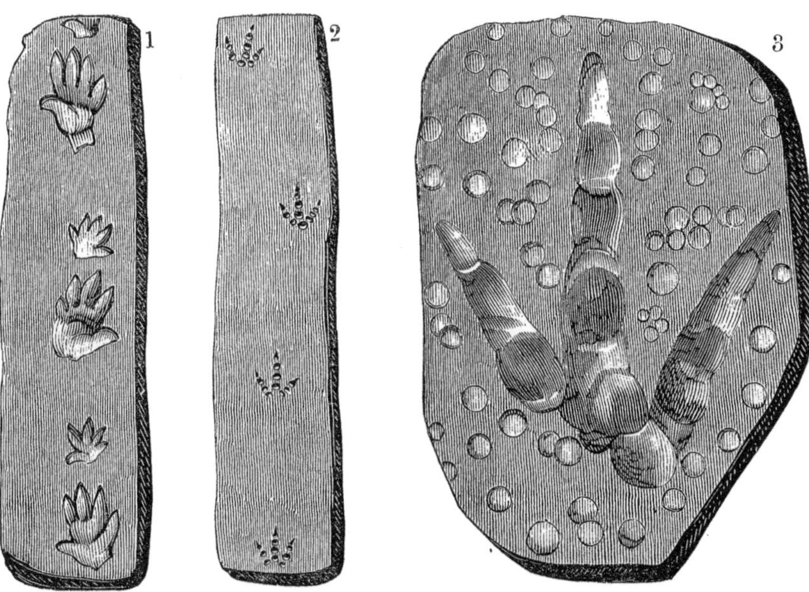

1. Footprints of the Labyrinthodon in sandstone; hind feet eight inches long. From Hildburghausen, Saxony.
2. Footprints of a bird in sandstone. From Turner's Falls, Massachusetts.
3. Footprint of a bird and impressions of rain drops in sandstone. From Massachusetts. Natural size.

four imprints each; one row of the small size, of fourteen consecutive imprints; besides several others, ranging from two to six impressions each. It is worthy of remark, that of these numerous foot prints, with but one or two exceptions, two or more nowhere occur on the same spot.

In his description of these slabs, Dr. Deane says, "It is rare to find a stratum containing these foot prints exactly as they were impressed by the animals; for they are usually more or less distorted and obliterated by the soft nature of the mud, the coarseness of the materials, and other circumstances, which have partially defaced them; so that although the general form of the foot may be apparent, the minute traces of its appendages are almost invariably lost. In general, distinct evidence of the peculiar phalangeal structure of the toes of birds is wanting, and each toe appears to be formed of a single joint, without the terminal claw. But a few specimens have been discovered in which the true characters of the foot are clearly developed, with its rows of joints, and its claws, and integuments. So far as my observations extend, the sharpest impressions are on the shales of the finest texture, with a smooth, glossy surface, such as would retain the impressions of rain drops. The layers of stone do not often present this kind of surface; but recently it has been my good fortune to discover a stratum containing in all more than one hundred most beautiful impressions of the feet of four or five varieties of birds; the whole surface having also been pitted by a shower of rain. The impression of a medallion is not more sharp and clear than are most of these imprints; and I would suggest that their remarkable preservation may probably be ascribed to the circumstance that the entire surface of the stratum was incrusted with a layer of micaceous sandstone, and which adhered so firmly, that it could not be removed without the laborious and skilful application of the chisel. The appearance of this glossy layer, which is of a gray color, while the slab is of a dark red, seems to indicate that it was washed or blown over the latter, while in a state of loose sand;

thus filling up the foot prints and rain drops, and preserving them unchanged in the smallest particular; the form of the nails, or claws, and joints, and the deep impressions of the distal extremity of the tarso-metatarsal or shank bone being exquisitely displayed."

Similar impressions of rain drops occur in the Storeton quarry, near Liverpool, England, where tracks of the chirotherium are found. The under surface of two strata, at the depth of thirty-two or thirty-five feet from the top of the quarry, presents a remarkably blistered or watery appearance, being densely covered by minute hemispheres of the same substance as the sandstone. The impressions are sometimes perfect hemispheres, indicating a vertical fall of rain; but in other cases they are irregular and elongated in a particular direction, as if the drops had struck the surface obliquely, indicating a wind accompanying the rain. The same appearances occur in the formation near Shrewsbury. President Hitchcock mentions specimens of sandstone in his possession, obtained from various parts of the United States, which show foot prints, ripple marks, and rain drops, the latter evincing, by a uniform elongation of shape, the direction of the wind when the rain fell.

Walking along our shores in the present day, we observe a well-defined cast of our own footstep left in the sand still wet from the retreating tide, and similar distinct impressions made by the passage of animals and birds across it, and by the descent of a shower of rain upon it. In the same manner it is probable that the tracks which the new red sandstone presents were formed on the shores of an estuary, or a tidal river, between high and low water mark—then dried and hardened by the action of the sun and air during the recession of the waters—the returning waves washing up silt to cover up the impressions, the two layers uniting, to exhibit, if ever separated, the one a mould, and the other a cast from it, of the forms that have been there. The observation of like phenomena, now, to these unfolded by this geological formation, are of no mean importance and interest to mankind, in every condition of society. Many a depredator has been detected by the correspondence of his foot to its imprint in the snow or loose earth near the place of his crime. The North American Indian finds his enemy by his trail, and can not only distinguish between the elk and the buffalo by the marks of their hoofs, but determine with great exactness the space of time that has elapsed since the animals have passed. In the deserts of Africa the track of the camels proclaims to the Arab whether a heavily or lightly laden caravan has crossed the sands. But from the imprints presented by the sandstone formation, we gather information respecting what transpired many thousands of years ago, catch a glimpse of the gigantic birds and strangely-formed quadrupeds that then existed, and even have indicated to us, in a manner so plain as not to be mistaken, the direction from which the wind blew while a shower of rain was falling.

CHAPTER II.

EXTENSIVE STRATA OF THE EARTH'S CRUST, COMPOSED OF THE FOSSIL REMAINS OF LIVING BEINGS, SO SMALL THAT MORE THAN 40,000,000,000 OF THEM ARE CONTAINED IN A CUBIC INCH. — STRATA COMPOSED OF VARIOUS KINDS OF SHELLS, WHICH IN SOME INSTANCES CONSTITUTE MARBLE OF GREAT BEAUTY.

WE find embedded in the earth the fossil remains of vast quantities of animals no less remarkable for their minuteness than those described in the preceding chapter are for their colossal size. They are called animalcules, or infusoria. Their skeletons constitute nearly the whole mass of some soils and rocks, many feet in thickness, and extending over areas of several miles. Such is the *polirschiefer*, or polishing slate, (Tripoli, or rottenstone,) of Bilin in Bohemia, which occupies a surface of great extent, probably the site of an ancient lake, and forms slaty strata of fourteen feet in thickness, almost wholly composed of the silicified shields of animalcules. The size of a single one, forming the polishing slate, "amounts upon an average, and in the greatest part, to $\frac{1}{288}$ of a line, which equals $\frac{1}{6}$ of the thickness of a human hair, reckoning its average size at $\frac{1}{48}$ of a line. The globule of the human blood, considered at $\frac{1}{300}$, is not much smaller. The blood globules of a frog are twice as large as one of these animalcules. As the polirschiefer of Bilin is slaty, but without cavities, these animalcules lie closely compressed. In round numbers, about 23,000,000 would make up a cubic line, and would in fact be contained in it. There are 1728 cubic lines in a cubic inch; and therefore a cubic inch would contain, on an average, about 41,000,000,000 of these animals. On weighing a cubic inch of this mass, I found it to be about 220 grains. Of the 41,000,000,000 of animals,

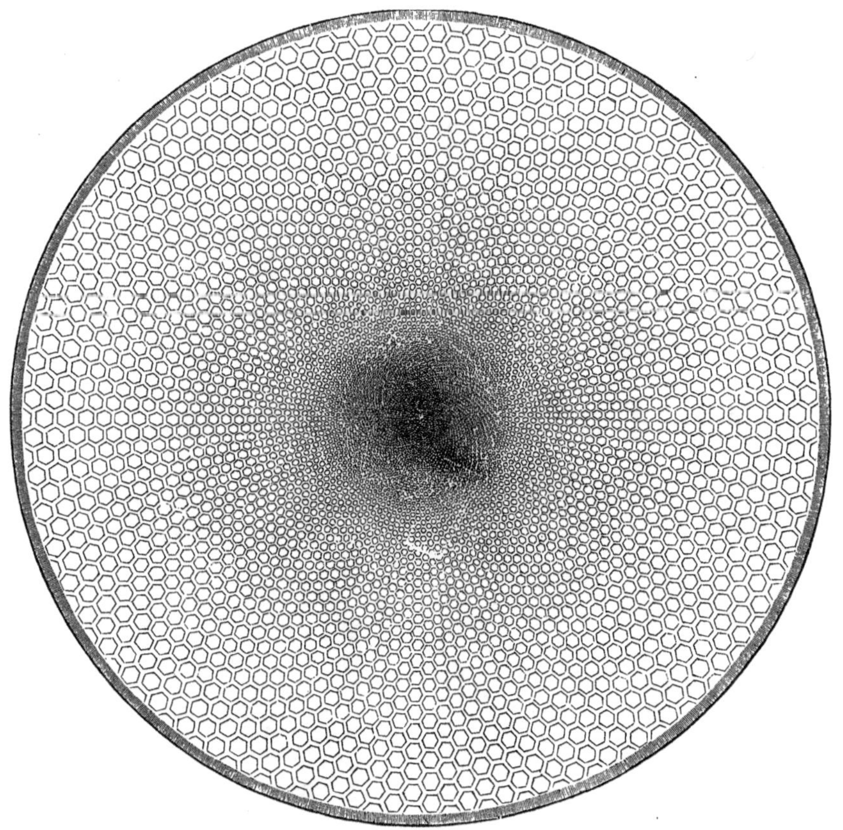

An Animalcule, (*Coscinodiscus*,) from Richmond earth, very highly magnified. Natural size, one thousandth of an inch in diameter.

187,000,000 go to a grain; or the silicious shield of each animalcule weighs about $\frac{1}{187}$ millionth part of a grain." Such is the statement of Ehrenberg, which naturally suggests the reflection of the French philosopher, that if the Almighty is great in great things, he is still more so in those which are minute; and furnishes additional data for the well-known moral argument of the theologian, derived from a comparison of the telescope and the microscope—"The one led me to see a system in every star; the other leads me to see a world in every atom. The one taught me that this mighty globe, with the whole burden of its people and of its countries, is but a grain of sand on the high field of immensity; the other teaches me that every grain of sand may harbor within it the tribes and the families of a busy population. The one told me of the insignificance of the world I tread upon; the other redeems it from all insignificance—for it tells me that in the leaves of every forest, and in the flowers of every garden, and in the waters of every rivulet, there are worlds teeming with life, and numberless as are the glories of the firmament." The composition of the polishing slate of Bilin is far from being unique; for in several other European localities, and very largely in America, strata consisting mainly of fossil animalcules have been observed. This is the case with the infusorial earth of Virginia, a yellowish silicious clay, forming a deposit from twelve to fifteen feet in thickness, upon which the towns of Richmond and Petersburg are built. The surface of the country over which it extends is characterized by a scanty vegetation, owing to the silicious nature of the soil dependent on the minute organisms of which it almost entirely consists. When a few grains of this earth are properly prepared for microscopic examination, immense numbers of the shields or cases of animalcules are visible under a magnifying power of three hundred diameters; in fact, the merest stain left by the evaporation of water in which some of the marl has been mixed, teems with these fossil remains.

These organisms are of exquisite structure, and comprise many species and genera. The most beautiful and abundant are the circular shields termed *coscinodisci*, (sieve-like disks,) which are elegant saucer-shaped cases, elaborately ornamented with hexagonal apertures disposed in curves, somewhat resembling the engine-turned sculpturing of a watch. These shells are from $\frac{1}{1000}$ to $\frac{1}{100}$ of an inch in diameter. The body of the living animalcule was protected and enclosed by a pair of these concave shells, the perforations admitting of the exsertion of filaments or tentacula.

Deposits of this silicious marl are very common in Massachusetts. President Hitchcock has examined specimens from Spencer, Pelham, Barre, Manchester, Fitchburg, Wrentham, North Bridgewater, and Andover, and all contain vast numbers of these relics; indeed they constitute nearly the whole of these deposits. Professor Bailey calculates that a cubic inch of the infusorial deposit from Maidstone, Vermont, contains 15,625,000,000 skeletons.

Beds of a white infusorial earth, resembling magnesia in appearance, occur in Lapland and Finland, where it is called by the natives berghmehl, and is used in seasons of scarcity as food, and considered quite nutritious. At San Fiora in Tuscany, near Egra in Bohemia, in the Bermudas, Barbadoes, &c., similar deposits have been discovered, all being composed of the shields of various kinds of animalcules.

A large proportion of the sand of the Libyan desert consists of microscopic fossil remains; and the marine sands of the Paris basin are in some localities so full of microscopic forms, that it is calculated that a cubic inch of the mass contains sixty thousand. Many of the peat bogs of Ireland contain layers of a white, earthy substance, which when dry is of the appearance and consistence of friable chalk, and this consists of the silicious cases of animalcules.

Infusoria abound also at the present time. They are generally to be found in stagnant pools, and not unfrequently in springs, rivers, lakes, and seas; also in the internal moisture of living plants and animal bodies, and are probably at times carried about in the vapor and dust of the atmosphere.

Unlike the larger animals, throughout the whole of which the comparative anatomist is enabled to trace, by easy gradations, one common type, the forms of the infusoria are varied and singular. Some are egg-shaped, others resemble spheres; others again different kinds of fruit, funnels, tops, cylinders, pitchers, wheels, flasks, eels, serpents, and many classes of the invertebrated animals.

Some of the infusoria are visible to the naked eye, as moving points, though the size of the body does not exceed in any case the one twelfth of an inch, and the smallest are not more than the 24,000th of an inch in diameter; the thickness of the skin of their stomachs is not more than the 50,000,000th part of an inch, a single drop of water having been estimated sometimes to contain 500,000,000 individuals. They were formerly supposed to be little more than mere particles of matter endowed with vitality; but Ehrenberg has discovered in them an apparatus of muscles, intestines, teeth, different kinds of glands, eyes, nerves, and organs of reproduction. They not only propagate by eggs, but by self-division; and are the most reproductive of all organized bodies, an individual of one species increasing in ten days to 1,000,000, on the eleventh day to 4,000,000, and on the twelfth day to 16,000,000; while of another kind, Ehrenberg states that one individual is capable of becoming in four days 170,000,000,000. They possess a comparatively long life, and in general maintain themselves pretty uniformly against all external influence, as do larger animals. As far as is yet known, they appear to be sleepless.

The infusoria are sometimes hurtful by causing the death of fish in ponds, deterioration of clear water, and boggy smells; but not, as has been supposed, in giving rise to malaria, plague, and other maladies. They also form invisible intestinal worms in many animals, and in man, and have sometimes lice and intestinal worms themselves.

The wisdom and goodness of Providence have endowed these living creatures with all that can be needed for their happy existence. What, for instance, can be more admirable in structure than the infusoria of the family *volvocina?* In what class of animals are its members so curiously and so symmetrically associated together? In the *volvocina* innumerable beings are colonized within a simple, delicate, crystal-like shell, whose form, sometimes spherical, at others quadrangular, presents us with examples of perfect harmony and proportion. Who can behold these hollow, living globes, revolving and disporting themselves in their native element with as much liberty and pleasure as the mightiest monster of the deep—and to carry our views a step farther, to speak in detail of series of globes, one within another, alike inhabited, and their occupants alike participating in the same enjoyment—who can behold such evidences of creative wisdom, and not exclaim with the Psalmist, "How wonderful are thy works, O Lord, *sought out* of all them that have *pleasure therein?*"

Again: to take an example from those families of infusoria who possess the power of *changing their forms* at pleasure, the family *astasiœa* are capable of assuming fourteen entirely distinct forms in the short interval of a few seconds, and that under the observer's eye. In the beautiful little creatures of the genus *euglena* you may also perceive a distinct *visual organ*, by which they can steer their course with unerring rectitude. Many of the infusoria do not possess this organ; but those which have it live, for the most part, near the surface of the water, whilst those which have it not locate near the bottom.

Again: look at the graceful forms of the small family *closterina*, which have long riveted the attention of eminent naturalists of modern times, and which have hitherto defied all their powers of investigation, aided by all the refined and searching means which human ingenuity can supply, to determine whether they are animals or plants. No characteristic, at present known, has been found sufficient to satisfy both the zoölogist and botanist.

In short, there is not one species but offers ample scope for the exercise of our deepest reflection, at the same time that it affords an admirable proof of the adaptation and design of creative wisdom.

A well-known substance, called bog iron ore, often met with in peat mosses, has been shown to consist of innumerable articulated threads of a yellow ochre color, composed partly of flint and partly of oxide of iron. These threads are the cases of a minute microscopic body, called *gaillonella ferruginea.* Professor Bailey, of West Point, speaks of the elegant fragile animalcule of the bog iron ore as occurring in immense quantities in the pools of that neighborhood, "the bottoms of which," he states, "are literally covered, in the first warm days of spring, with a ferruginous-colored mucous matter about a quarter of an inch thick, which, on examination by the microscope, proves to be filled with millions and millions of these exquisitely beautiful silicious bodies. Every submerged stone, twig, and spear of grass is enveloped by them; and the waving, plume-like appearance of a filamentous body, covered in this manner, is often extremely elegant. Alcohol completely dissolves the coloring matter of this species; and the silicious shields are left as colorless as glass, and resist the action of fire." The size of the animalcule is $\frac{1}{21}$ of the thickness of a human hair, one cubic inch of the iron ore containing 1,000,000,000,000 of the skeletons of these living beings!

It has been ascertained by Ehrenberg that accumulations of microscopic beings are choking up the harbor of Wismar, in the Baltic, and that similar formations are effecting changes in the bed of the Nile at Dongola, and of the Elbe at Cuxhaven.

The rapid and mysterious transition of color which is observable in lakes, and which has often created an alarm in the timid minds of the superstitious inhabitants on their borders, the microscope has shown to arise from certain changes in the condition of infusoria. Thus a lake of clear, transparent water will assume a green color in the course of a day, when the sun brings these creatures to the surface, and rapidly develops them, or causes their dead bodies to ascend, whilst in the morning and evening it will again be clear.

It is the opinion of geologists that the present continents, except, perhaps, the tops of some of the highest mountains, have for a very long time constituted the bottom of the ocean, and have been subsequently elevated. Two thirds, at least, of these continents are covered with rocks, often several thousand feet thick, abounding in marine organic remains, which must have been quietly deposited, along with the sand, mud, and calcareous or ferruginous matter in which they are enveloped, and which could have accumulated but slowly. In some instances, vast quantities of these remains have been deposited almost entirely separate from other matter. Near Tours in France there is a bed of oyster shells which is twenty-seven miles long, with a corresponding breadth, and twenty feet thick. And in the United States there are beds far exceeding this; a stratum nearly continuous has been traced from the Eutaw Springs in South Carolina to the Chickasaw country—being six hundred miles in length by ten to a hundred miles in breadth.

The chalk formation, comprising strata several hundred feet in thickness, in England and other parts of the world, abounds in marine shells and corals, and in the remains of fishes, crabs, lobsters, and reptiles, all of which differ essentially from living species; although a few of the corals and shells resemble, in some particulars, certain kinds that inhabit the seas of hot climates. These remains are found in so perfect a state—the shells with all their spines and delicate processes, and the fishes with their teeth, scales, and fins entire—that no doubt can be entertained of the animals having been surrounded by the chalk while living in their native sea, and that many of them were intombed in their stony sepulchres suddenly, when the rock was in the state of mud, or like liquid plaster of Paris.

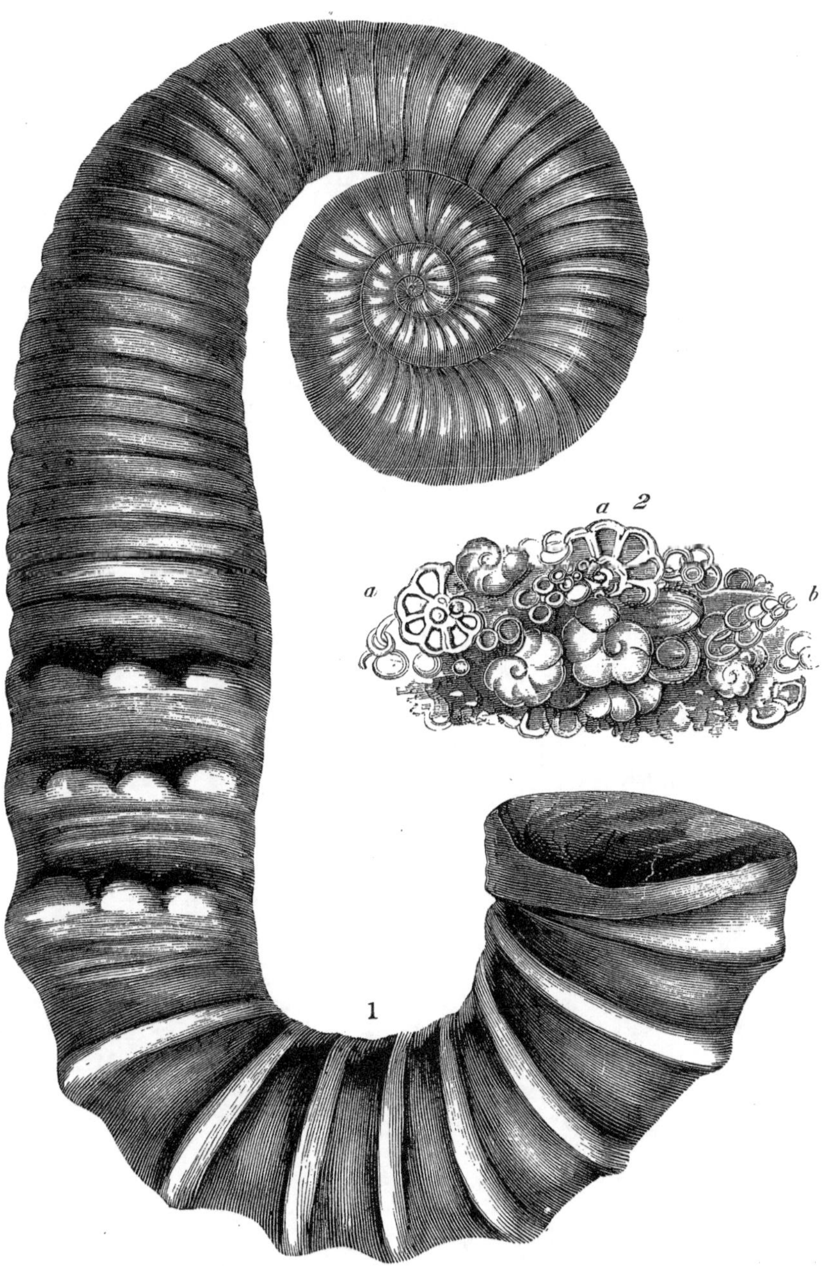

1. Shell of the *Ancyloceras Gigas*, two feet in length, common in chalk cliffs.
2. A few grains of chalk dust, highly magnified and shown to consist of shells, &c. *a, a, rotalia ; b, textularia.*

But besides the fossils which are obvious to the unassisted eye, the chalk teems with myriads of minute forms that may readily be detected with a lens of moderate power; and even when these have been extracted, the residue, which appears to be mere white calcareous earth, is found, when examined under the microscope, to consist almost wholly of bodies yet more infinitesimal—of perfect shells and corals, so minute that a cubic inch of chalk may contain upwards of a million of these organic remains.

The chalk is stratified—that is, divided into *strata*, or layers—as if a certain quantity of mud had sunk to the bottom of the sea, and enveloped the shells, corals, &c., which fell in its way, and had become somewhat solid before another layer was deposited upon it.

The mineral substance termed *silex*, or *flint*, is variously distributed through the chalk. It most commonly occurs in the state of nodules of an irregular spheroidal or globular figure, which are arranged in rows parallel and alternating with the cretaceous strata; it is likewise disposed in continuous thin layers, which are spread over considerable areas; and it often forms horizontal, vertical, and oblique veins, that fill up the fissures and interstices of the chalk. The silicious nodules frequently enclose corals, shells, sponges, and other organic remains; and in many instances these fossils are found partly embedded in the chalk, and partly invested with flint. But though flints contain in abundance relics of the same species of marine animals as the chalk, they are not, like that rock, composed of an aggregation of fossil remains; on the contrary, the silicious earth, which is their constituent substance, was evidently once in a state of complete solution in water, and precipitated into the chalk before the latter was consolidated, the organic bodies serving as centres around which the silex concreted; for the deposition of the flint, like that of the chalk, appears to have taken place periodically.

The composition of the chalk, and the prevalence through out that rock of the relics of animals that can only live in salt water, prove incontestably that the chalk and flint were deposited in the sea; and that the beautiful South Downs of England, now so smooth and verdant, and supporting thousands of flocks and herds, and the rich plains and fertile valleys spread around their flanks, were once the bed of an ocean. It is also evident, not only that such must have been the case, but also that the chalk was deposited in the basin of a very *deep* sea—in the profound abyss of an ocean as vast as the Atlantic. Indeed, this formation constitutes such an assemblage of strata as would probably be presented to observation if a mass of the bed of the Atlantic two thousand feet in thickness were elevated above the waters, and became dry land; the only difference would be in the generic and specific characters of the embedded animal and vegetable remains.

As many other rocks are found on microscopic examination to present similar appearances, it is supposed that not only is the chalk of organic origin, but that a large proportion of the sedimentary strata is derived from the same source, and has passed through the great laboratory of life. This theory of the vital origin of calcareous strata derives confirmation from the operations of nature. Not only is it found that the coral polype is rearing reefs and islands from the bosom of the deep, and uniting them into continents, but on the shores of many of the West India Islands, especially the Bermudas, it is observed that, on the coral formations being exposed to the abrading power of the waves, the sea becomes loaded with calcareous matter, a considerable portion of which is drifted to the shores in the state of fine sand, which, being wafted inland by the winds, becomes consolidated by the percolation of water and the infiltration of carbonate of lime in solution; so that a white calcareous stone is formed of various degrees of hardness, from a coarse friable limestone to the compact rock employed in constructing the fortifications of the islands.

Lieutenant Nelson states that the whole of these islands, comprising a hundred and fifty in number, may be called organic formations, as they present one mass of animal remains, in various stages of disintegration. From the most compact rock to the loose sand of the shore, the materials are fragments of shells, corals, &c.

Towards the centre of France, south of the confluence of the Allier and the Loire, are the sites of a series of lakes, whose waters have been drained off, and their beds elevated, in the course of those physical revolutions which the earth has undergone. The largest of these occupies a considerable part of the valley plain of the Allier, and contains, besides vegetable remains, land and fresh-water shells, with bones of extinct quadrupeds. The most remarkable deposit is an indusial limestone, so called from the Latin *indusium*, a case, because essentially composed of the cases of a species of insect in its larva state, incrusted with travertine, and cemented into a rock. The reader has no doubt often observed, when by the side of a clear and shallow pool of water, little oblong masses moving along the bottom, resembling pieces of straw, wood, or even stones. These are the straw or caddis worms, really the larvæ of a tribe of four-winged insects, of which nothing is seen in the water but the head and legs, by means of which they move, and drag along the case in which the rest of the body is enclosed, and into which, on any alarm, they wholly retire. The construction of these habitations is very various. Some select four or five pieces of the leaves of grass, which they glue together into a shapely polygonal case; others employ portions of the stems of rushes, placed side by side so as to form an elegant fluted cylinder; some arrange round them pieces of leaves like a spirally-rolled ribbon; others enclose themselves in a mass of the leaves of any aquatic plants, united without regularity; and others, again, form their abode of minute pieces of wood, either fresh or decayed. Other species construct houses which may be called alive, forming them of the shells of various aquatic snails, of different kinds and sizes, even while inhabited, all of which are immovably fixed to it, and dragged about at its pleasure—a covering as singular as if a savage, instead of clothing himself with squirrels' skins, should sew together into a coat the animals themselves. (See engraving on oppo site page, Fig. 1.) Even those that are most careless about the nature of the materials of their houses are solicitously attentive to one circumstance respecting them, namely, their specific gravity. Not having the power of swimming, but only of walking at the bottom of the water, by the aid of the six legs attached to the fore part of the body, which is usually protruded out of the case, and the insect itself being heavier than water, it is of great importance that its house should be of a specific gravity so nearly that of the element in which it resides, as, while walking, neither to incommode it by its weight, nor by too great buoyancy; and it is as essential that it should be so equally ballasted in every part as to be readily movable in every position. Under these circumstances the caddis worms evince their proficiency in hydrostatics, selecting the most suitable substances, and, if the cell be too heavy, gluing to it a bit of leaf or straw; or, if too light, a piece of shell or gravel. In a precisely similar way the cases which constitute the indusial limestone are composed. Around the larva dwelling the shells of a small spiral univalve belonging to the genus *paludina*, a tribe of fresh water snails, are aggregated, and both the insects and mollusks must have existed in countless swarms in the ancient lakes of Central France, since ten or twelve cases may be packed within the space of a cubic inch, and some single strata of the indusial limestone are six feet in thickness, and may be traced over an area of several miles.

Extensive beds of marble consist entirely of shells united by a mineral cement, and are indebted to their half-obliterated forms for the beautiful markings with which they are ornamented. An example of this is found in the Purbeck marble, of which many of the monuments in Westminster Abbey, also the cluster columns in the Temple Church, London, and in Chichester Cathedral, are constructed. (See accompanying engraving, Fig. 3.)

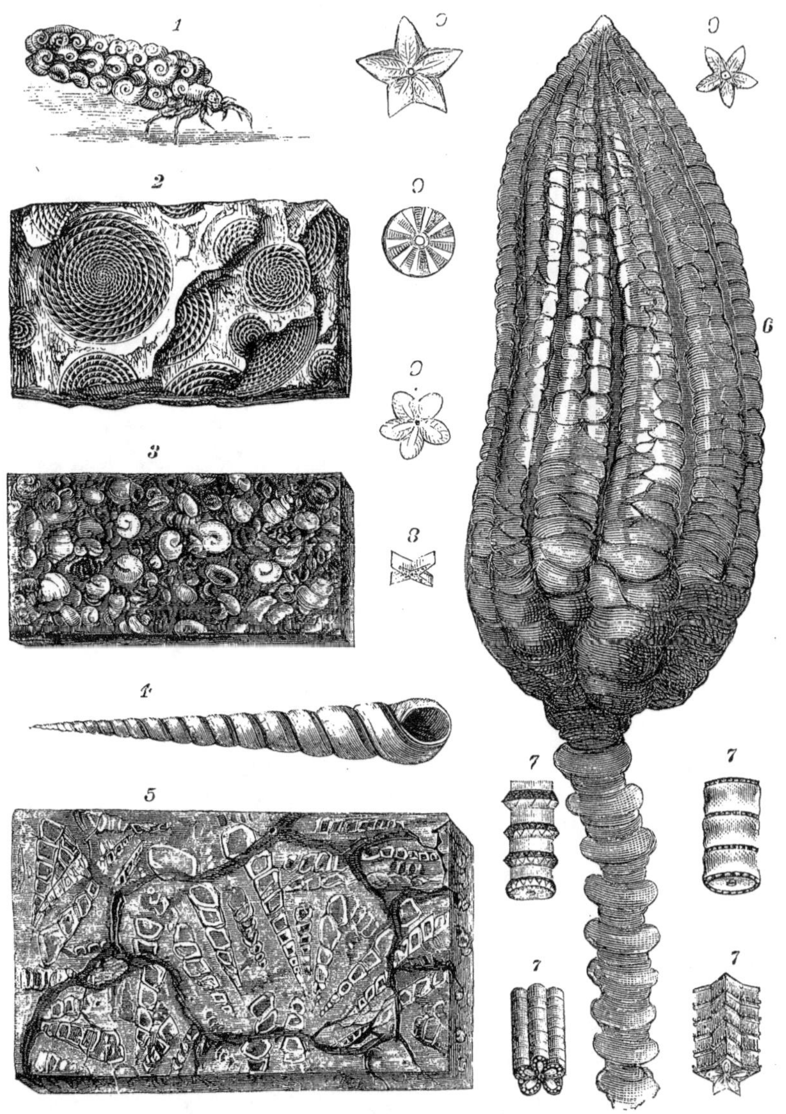

1. Caddis Fly, in its caterpillar state, clad in a garment which it has formed of minute shells, containing their living occupants.
2. Polished slab of marble composed of the shells of nummulites. From the Pyrenees.
3. Polished slab of Purbeck marble, composed of river snail shells. From England.
4. Perfect shell of the *Turritella Conoidea*, natural size
5. Polished slab of marble containing shells of the *Turritella Conoidea* and veins of spar. From Sussex, England.
6. Lily Encrinite, natural size. From Brunswick, England.
7, 7, 7, 7. Portions of the stems of Encrinites and Pentacrinites.
8. Single joint or ossiculum of a Pentacrinite of four angles.
9, 9, 9, 9. Surfaces of the joints or ossicula of Encrinites and Pentacrinites.

The black and dark-brown spots and veins in shelly marbles have originated from the transmutation of the soft bodies of the mollusca into a carbonaceous substance termed *mollusk-ite.* Those shells which were empty at the period of their becoming embedded had their cavities filled with mud, silt, or other detritus, which has subsequently hardened into clay, marl, limestone, &c.; but those which contained the gelatinous bodies of the snails are occupied by a mass consisting of carbon and a large proportion of phosphate of lime.

The nummulites, so called from bearing some resemblance to a coin, are a small shell of a flat discoidal form, slightly convex, and smooth externally. Upon splitting them transversely, or rubbing them down, numerous cells or chambers are exposed, arranged in a discoidal spire, and on the same plane, but having no communication with each other. Aggregations of these minute shells constitute, in some instances, limestones, and occasionally a compact crystalline marble. A specimen of nummulitic marble is represented in the engraving by number 2.

The nummulitic formation often attains a thickness of many thousand feet, and extends from the Alps to the Apennines, is found in the Carpathians and Pyrenees, and in Algeria and Morocco. It has been traced from Egypt into Asia Minor, and across Persia, by Bagdad, to the mouths of the Indus. It also occurs in Cutch, and in the mountain ranges which separate Scinde from Persia, and which form the passes leading to Cabul; and it has been followed still farther eastward into India. The limestone of which the great pyramid of Egypt is in part constructed is an aggregation of nummulites and microscopic animalculites, that serve as a cement to the larger fossils; and it has recently been mentioned as an interesting fact, that the nummulite limestone rocks in the neighborhood of the Nile are in some places washed down and disintegrated, and the loose nummulites re-deposited in the recent detritus or mud of the river. Strabo alludes to the nummulites of the pyramids under the supposition that they are lentils, which had been scattered about by the workmen, and had become converted into stone. This fossil was the subject of many a German legend, under the name of the *bauern-pfennige*, or peasant's penny, and *teufelsgeld*, or devil's money, under which appellation it was equally known.

Formations many miles in extent, and of considerable thickness, consist entirely of the calcareous skeletons of encrinites; and in Derbyshire, England, some of the beds form a compact marble which is largely employed for chimney pieces and other ornamental purposes. These animals derive their name from a resemblance, when in a state of repose, to a closed lily. (See Fig. 6.) They are characterized by having a root or process of attachment, by which they are fixed at the base to a rock; a stem composed of numerous articulations, or separate pieces of a solid calcareous substance; and a cup or vase at the summit of the stem, which contains the body or viscera, and from the upper border of which proceed articulated arms or tentacula. When the animal is alive the skeleton is covered by a soft integument; the mouth is situated on one side of the centre of the receptacle, which is surrounded by the arms that spread out and expand into a net to capture the living prey, and, like the tentacula of the hydra, seize and convey it to the mouth.

The term pentacrinite is applied to a similar animal, whose stem, instead of being circular or elliptical, is made up of angular bones or ossicula. Ossicula of the encrinites and pentacrinites, both single and in connected series, are found in great quantities in some localities in England and Germany. They commonly occur singly in the northern counties of England, and are known there under the denomination of St. Cuthbert's beads, having been strung and used as rosaries in the middle ages; hence the lines in Marmion,—

"On a rock by Lindisfern
St. Cuthbert sits and toils to frame
The sea-born beads that bear his name."

Dr. Mantell states that he has found these circular perforated ossicula, which had been worn as ornaments, in the tumuli of the ancient Britons.

These fossils bore in Germany the several names of *spangensteine*, or bead-stones; *roedersteine*, or wheel-stones; and *Bonifacius-pfennige*, or St. Boniface's pennies, being found in great numbers on a mountain in the neighborhood of Frankenhausen, which obtains its name from that saint; while in Westphalia they are called *hünenthränen*, from being considered the petrified tears of the giants. They are also variously termed mill stones, cheese stones, basket stones, cask stones, &c., from their fancied resemblance to these objects.

The number of ossicula in the skeleton of a single encrinite is computed at thirty thousand; but in the more complicated pentacrinites they exceed one hundred and fifty thousand, and in the plumose encrinites must amount to hundreds of thousands.

CHAPTER III.

Minerals. — Origin of mineral Coal. — Fifty-nine Forests discovered embedded one above the other in the Earth. — Geological Discoveries respecting the Age of the World consistent with the Mosaic Account of Creation.

Minerals are deposited in veins or fissures of rocks, in masses, in beds, and sometimes in gravel and sand. Most of the metals are found in veins; a few, as gold and tin, iron and copper, are disseminated through the rocks, though rarely. Veins are cracks or fissures in rocks, seldom in a straight line; yet they maintain a general direction, though in a zigzag form, striking downwards at a very high angle, seldom deviating from the perpendicular by so much as forty-five degrees, and extending to an unfathomable depth. When cutting through stratified rocks, they are for the most part accompanied by a subsidence of the beds on one side of their course, and by an elevation on the other; the throw, or perpendicular distance between the corresponding strata on the opposite sides of a vein, varies from a few inches to thirty, forty, even a hundred fathoms. A small number of the metals occur pure, but in general they are found in the form of ores, in which the metal is chemically combined with other substances, and the ore is often so mixed with earthy matter and rock that it is necessary to reduce it to a coarse powder in order to separate the ore, which is rarely more than a third or fourth part of the mass brought above ground.

Gold is found in almost every country, but in such minute quantities that it is often not worth the expense of working. It is almost always in a native state, and in the form of crystals, grains, or rolled masses. Sometimes it is combined with silver. It is exhausted in several parts of Europe where it was formerly found. The united produce of the mines in Transylvania, Hungary, the north-western districts of Austria, and the bed of the Danube, is nearly sixty thousand ounces annually. Gold is found in small quantities in Spain, in the Lead Hills in Scotland, and the Wicklow Mountains in Ireland.

Gold abounds in Asia. The deposits at the foot of the Ural Mountains are very rich. In 1826 a piece of pure gold weighing twenty-three pounds was found there, along with others weighing three or four pounds each, together with the bones of elephants. All the diluvium there is ferruginous; and more to the east, a region as large as France has lately been discovered, with a soil rich in gold dust, resting on rocks which contain it. In 1834 the treasures in that part of the Altaï chain, called the Gold Mountains, were discovered, forming a mountain knot nearly as large as England, from which a great quantity of gold has been extracted. Gold is found in Thibet, in the Chinese province of Yunnan, and abundantly in the mountains of the Indo-Chinese peninsula, in Japan, and Borneo. In the latter island it occurs near the surface in six different places.

Africa has long furnished a large supply to Europe. That part of the Kong Mountains west of the meridian of Greenwich was one of the most auriferous regions in the world before the discoveries of California. The gold stratum lies from twenty to twenty-five feet below the surface, and increases in richness with the depth. It is found in particles and pieces in a reddish sand. Most of the streams from the table land bring down gold, as well those that descend to the low ground to the north as those that flow to the Atlantic. On the shores of the Red Sea it was found in sufficient quantity to induce the Portuguese to form a settlement there.

In South America the Western Cordillera is poor in metals, except in New Grenada, where the most westerly of the three chains of the Andes is rich in gold and platinum — a metal found only there, in Brazil, and on the European side of the Ural Mountains — in alluvial deposits. The largest piece of platinum that has been found weighed twenty-one ounces. Gold is found in sand and gravel on the high plains of the Andes, on the low lands to the east of them, and in almost all the rivers that flow on that side. The whole country between Jaen de Bracamoros and the Guaviare is celebrated for its metallic riches. Almost all the Brazilian rivers bring down gold; and the mine of Gongo Soco, in the province of Minas Geraës, is said to yield several varieties of gold ore. Central America, Mexico, and California are auriferous countries. The quantity of gold found near the surface of California is immense, greatly surpassing that of any other country. A considerable quantity is found in Tennessee, in Virginia, the mountains of Georgia, and on one thousand square miles of North Carolina it occurs in grains and masses.

From the similarity of the geological formation of some parts of Australia with that of California, it was believed that gold might be obtained in that country. Search was accordingly made in the year 1851, which proved in the highest degree successful. The total product of the Australian gold fields, during the first sixteen months from their discovery, was five million five hundred and thirty-two thousand four hundred and twenty-two ounces, or one hundred and five tons, ten cwt., and two ounces of gold.

A great deal of silver is raised in Europe. The mines of Hungary are the most productive, especially those in the mountains of Chemnitz. The metalliferous mountains of the Erzgebirge are very rich, also the mines near Christiania in Sweden. Silver is also found in Saxony, Transylvania, and Austria. In no part of the old continent is silver in greater abundance than in the Ural and Altaï Mountains, especially in the district of Kolyvan. There are silver mines in Armenia, Anatolia, Thibet, China, Cochin-China, and Japan.

The richness of the Andes in silver can hardly be conceived; but the mines are frequently on such high ground that the profits are diminished by the difficulty of carriage, the expense of living in a barren country, sometimes destitute of water, where the miners suffer from the cold and snow, and especially the want of fuel. This is particularly the case at the silver mines of Copiapo in Chile, where the country is utterly barren, and not a drop of water is to be found in a circuit of nine miles. These mines were discovered by a poor man in 1832, who hit upon a mass of silver in rooting out a tree. They extend over one hundred and fifty square leagues. Sixteen veins of silver were found in the first four days, and, before three weeks elapsed, forty more, not reckoning smaller ramifications. The rolled pieces which lay on the surface produced a large quantity of pure silver. A single mass weighed five thousand pounds.

In Peru there are silver mines along the whole range of the Andes, from Caxamarca to the confines of the Desert of Atacama. The richest at present are those of Pasco, which were discovered by an Indian in 1630. They have been worked without interruption since the beginning of the seventeenth century, and seem to be still inexhaustible. The soil under the town of Pasco is metalliferous, the ores probably forming a series of beds contemporaneous with the strata. The richness of these beds is not every where the same, but the nests of ore are numerous. The mines of Potosi, sixteen thousand one hundred and fifty feet above the sea level, are celebrated for richness; but the owners had to contend with all the difficulties which such a situation imposes. The ore in the mines at Chota is near the surface over an extent of half a square league, and the filaments of silver are sometimes even entwined with the roots of the grass. This mine is thirteen thousand three hundred feet above the level of the sea, and even in summer the thermometer is below the freezing point in the night. In the district of Huantajaya, not far from the shores of the Pacific, there are mines where masses of pure silver are found, of which one weighed eight hundred pounds.

According to Baron Humboldt, the quantity of the precious metals exported to Europe between the discovery of America and the year 1803 was worth twelve hundred and fifty-seven millions sterling; and the silver alone taken from the mines during that period would form a ball eighty-nine feet in diameter. The disturbed state of the South American republics and the high price of quicksilver have interfered with the working of the mines.

Lead ore is very often combined with silver, and is then called argentiferous galena. It is one of the principal productions of the British mines, especially in the northern mining district, which occupies four hundred square miles at the junction of Northumberland, Cumberland, Westmoreland, Durham, and Yorkshire. It comprises Alston Moor, the mountain ridge of Crossfell, and the dales of Derwent, East and West Allandale, the Wear, and Tees. There are other extensive mining tracts separated from this by cultivated ground. The principal products of this rich district are lead and copper. The lead mines lie chiefly in the upper dales of the Tyne, Wear, and Tees, and all of it contains more or less silver, though not always enough to indemnify the expense of refining or separating the silver. The deleterious vapors resulting from this process are conveyed in a tube along the surface of the ground for fourteen miles; and instead of being, as formerly, a dead loss to the proprietor, they are condensed in their passage, and in one instance yield metal to the annual value of ten thousand pounds sterling. The Hudgillburn lead mine in that district has yielded treasures almost unexampled in the annals of mining. The veins, from ten to twelve, and in some places even twenty feet wide, were filled with ore, which is entirely obtained with the pickaxe, without blasting. In 1821 the galena of this mine yielded thirty-two thousand ounces of silver.

Lead mines are in operation in France, but not to any great amount; those of the south of Spain furnish large quantities of this metal; also in Saxony, Bohemia, and Carinthia, where they are very rich. Lead is not very frequently found in Siberia, though it does occur in the Nerchinsk mining district, in the basin of the River Amur. It is also a production of China, of the peninsula beyond the Ganges, and of North and South America.

The Upper Mississippi Valley is among the most remarkable in the world for the variety and abundance of its mineral deposits, and especially for those which are of most extensive use in the arts. The sulphuret of lead occupies about one degree of latitude, extending north from a point on the Mississippi, about eight miles below Galena, and lying on both sides, varying in width, till it covers as great an extent from east to west. On the east side of the river the lead ore is found principally in a clay matrix, at a depth of sometimes only five or six feet from the surface; on the west side of the river it runs at the depth of one hundred feet or more, overlaid with magnesian limestone. To the south-west of the lead deposit is a very abundant bed of iron, about forty miles long by twenty-five broad. The copper region extends north from the lead deposits to Lake Superior; it embraces about three hundred square miles. To the south of the lead region is a vast bed of bituminous coal of good quality, at no great distance below the surface.

In the mineral district there are about four thousand persons employed in digging lead ore. The value of the lead annually produced is estimated at $1,500,000. A considerable quantity was exported to China before the emigration to California withdrew the miners, and thus diminished the product.

Lead mines have been worked in the United States during more than half a century, the quantity produced constantly increasing. In the year 1839, according to the census returns, it was equal to nearly fourteen thousand tons; and in the year ending June 30, 1844, the quantity exported amounted to nearly eight thousand two hundred tons, valued at $595,238.

The most extensive lead mines known in the world are probably those found in the western section of the United

States, in Washington, Jefferson, and Madison counties, Mis souri; and at Galena, in the northwest part of Illinois; in Iowa, in Wisconsin, and in Michigan. Lead ores also occur at various localities in the States of New York, Pennsylvania, Maine, New Hampshire, Virginia, &c.

Quicksilver—a metal so important in separating silver from its ores, and in various arts and manufactures, as well as in medicine—occurs either liquid in the native state, or combined with sulphur in that of cinnabar. The richest mines of quicksilver are those of California. It is found in the mines of Idria and some other places in the Austrian empire, in the Palatinate on the left bank of the Rhine, and in Spain. The richest quicksilver mines of Europe, at the present day, are those of Almaden, where the quicksilver is found in the state of sulphuret. These mines were worked seven hundred years before the Christian era, and as many as twelve hundred tons of the metal are extracted annually. It occurs in China, Japan, and Ceylon, at San Onofrio in Mexico, and in Peru, at Huancavelica, the mines of which, now almost abandoned, produced, up to the beginning of the present century, the enormous quantity of fifty-four thousand tons of quicksilver.

Copper is of such common occurrence that it would be difficult to enumerate the localities where it is found. It is produced in Africa and America, in Persia, India, China, and Japan. The Siberian mines are very productive both in ore and native copper. Malachite is the most beautiful of the ores, and the choicest specimens come from Siberia. Almost every country in Europe yields copper. The mines in Sweden, Norway, Germany, and Great Britain are very productive. In Cornwall it is very plentiful, and is often associated with tin. The period at which the Cornish mines were first worked goes far beyond history, or even tradition; certain, however, it is, that the Phœnicians came to Britain for tin. Probably copper was also worked very early in small quantities, for its exportation was forbidden in the time of Henry

VIII. It was only in the beginning of the eighteenth century that the Cornish copper mines were worked with success, in consequence of the invention of an improved machine for draining them.

Copper also abounds in several localities in the United States. Some idea of the extent and value of the copper mines of Lake Superior may be formed from the following communication of Mr. J. S. Hodge, at a meeting of the "American Association for the Advancement of Science," held at Cambridge, Mass., August, 1849: —

"The mines are wrought wholly for native copper. The veinstone with scattered particles furnish what is called *stamp work*, which is crushed under heavy stamps and then washed. The lumps are called *barrel ore*, being packed in barrels for transportation; and the masses, after being cut up into pieces not exceeding two tons in weight, are shipped in bulk. The size of some of these masses is so enormous as almost to exceed belief. They have been broken up in the Cliff mine of sixty and even eighty tons in weight. Such pieces are reduced, in the mine, to fragments of seven tons weight and less, and after being hoisted to the surface are still further reduced.

"At the Minnesota mine, near the Ontonagon River, I had an opportunity of examining, in June, the most extraordinary mass yet met with. Two shafts had been sunk on the line of the vein, one hundred and fifty feet apart. At the depth of about thirty feet they struck massive copper, which lay in a huge sheet with the same underlay as that of the vein — about fifty-five degrees towards the north. Leaving this sheet as a hanging wall, a level was run under it connecting the two shafts. For this whole distance of a hundred and fifty feet, the mass appears to be continuous; and how much further it goes on the line of the vein, either way, there is no evidence, nor, besides, to what depth it penetrates in the solid vein. I examined it with care, striking it repeatedly with my hammer, in order to detect, if possible, by the sound, any break or interruption there might be in the mass—for a thin scale of stone incrusted it sometimes, and concealed the face of the metal. Examinations had been made by drilling through this scale, where it attained the thickness of an inch or so; but in no place had any sign of a break been found. It forms the whole hanging wall of the level, showing a width of at least eight feet above the floor in which its lower edge was lost. It has been cut through in only one place, where a partial break afforded a convenient opportunity. Measuring the thickness here as well as the irregular shape of the gap admitted, it was found somewhat to exceed five feet. Assuming the thickness to *average* only one foot, there would be in this mass twelve hundred cubic feet, or about two hundred and fifty tons: still it is not safe to assume even one foot, for the masses vary extremely in thickness.

"The mode adopted to remove these masses is to cut channels through them with cold chisels, after they are shattered by large sand blasts put in behind them. Grooves are cut with the chisels across their smallest places, one man holding and another striking, as in drilling. A chip of copper three quarters of an inch wide, and up to six inches in length, is taken out, and the process is repeated until the groove passes through the mass. The expense of this work is from eight to twelve dollars per superficial foot of the face exposed. Fragments of veinstone enclosed in the copper prevent the use of saws. A powerful machine, occupying little room, is much needed, which would perform more economically this work.

"The greatest thickness of any mass cut through at the Cliff mine has been about three feet. Their occurrence through the vein is not regular. Barren spots alternate with productive portions. The same is the case in all the mines. The total product of the Cliff mine for the year 1848 is estimated at eight hundred and thirty tons, averaging sixty per cent. During the present year more than half this amount has been already sent down, and there is enough more on the surface and in sight in the mine, to warrant the belief that one thousand tons will be the product of the year's work, or six hundred tons of copper. The whole amount of copper annually imported into the United States is about the value of two million dollars, or about fifty-four hundred tons.. But little has been supplied from our own mines. Nine such mines, then, as the Cliff, would render us independent of foreign supplies. From present appearances, after careful examination of the region, and consideration of the progress made in mining since my last visit in 1846, I feel myself warranted in expressing a decided conviction that this amount of copper must be supplied in a very few years, and this metal soon become, as lead already has, one of export instead of import. The recent failures of mining speculations, wildly undertaken and ignorantly and extravagantly conducted, may for a time check the development of these mines; but their wonderfully rich character is now beginning to be properly appreciated, as well as the reliance which may be put in the surface appearance of the veins. Some curious features in their character and distribution have been detected, which have heretofore escaped observation for want of sufficient data, and which will, I believe, be found of great consequence in the selection of the best localities. These, after further examination, I may at another time make public. The history of these mines, so far, has remarkably proved the foresight and excellent judgment of the lamented Dr. Houghton, particularly so in his predictions of the disastrous effects that must result from such speculations as have caused the country to be overrun by hordes of adventurers.

"The silver found associated with the copper has not proved of much importance, perhaps for the reason that the greater part of it is purloined by the miners. The Cliff mine has probably yielded more than thirty thousand dollars worth, of which not more than a tenth part has been secured by the proprietors. I saw myself, the present season, no less than six pounds and eight ounces of lumps and bars of silver seized in the hands of an absconding workman."

In Cornwall, clay slate rests upon granite, and is traversed by porphyritic dikes. The veins which contain copper or tin, or both, run east and west, and penetrate both the granite and the clay slate. The non-metalliferous veins run north and south; and if veins in that direction do contain any metal, it never is tin or copper, but lead, silver, cobalt, or antimony, which, with little exception, are believed to be always in the clay slate. No miner in Cornwall has ever seen the end or bottom of a vein; their width varies from the thickness of a sheet of paper to thirty feet; the average is from one to three feet. It rarely happens that either tin or copper is found nearer the surface than eighty or one hundred feet. If tin be first discovered, it sometimes disappears after sinking the mine one hundred feet deeper, when copper is found; and in some instances tin is found one thousand feet deep, without a trace of copper; but if copper is first discovered, it is very rarely succeeded by tin. Tin is found in rolled pieces, in horizontal beds of sand and gravel, and is called stream tin. The most valuable tin mines on the continent of Europe are those in Saxony; it also occurs in France, Bohemia, and Spain. One of the richest deposits of tin known is in the province of Tenasserim, on the east side of the Gulf of Martaban, in the Malayan peninsula. These deposits occur in several parts of that country; the richest is a layer eight or ten feet thick of sand and gravel, in which masses of oxide of tin are sometimes the size of a pigeon's egg. The best of all comes from the Island of Banca, at the extremity of the peninsula of Malacca; a large portion of it is imported into Britain, and much goes to China. It is found in the alluvial tracts through every part of the island, rarely more than twenty-five feet below the surface. Great deposits occur also in the Siberian mining district of Nerchinsk, near the Desert of the Great Gobi, and in Bolivia, near Oruro.

Arsenic, used in the arts and manufactures, is found combined with other metals in many countries. Manganese, zinc, bismuth, and antimony are raised to a considerable amount. As the qualities of the greater part of the more rare metals are little known, they have hitherto been interesting chiefly to the mineralogist.

The mines of rock salt in Cheshire, England, seem to be inexhaustible. Enormous deposits of salt extend six hundred miles on each side of the Carpathian Mountains, and throughout wide districts in Austria, Gallicia, and Spain. It would not be easy to enumerate the places in Asia where rock salt has been found. Armenia, Syria, and extensive tracts in the Punjab abound in it, also China and the Ural district; and the Andes contain vast deposits of rock salt, some at great heights.

Volcanic countries in both continents yield sulphur. Sicily, where it is found in the tertiary marine strata, unconnected with the volcanic district, is the magazine which supplies the greater part of the manufactures of Europe. It is often found beautifully crystallized. Asphalt, nitre, alum, and naphtha are found in various parts of Europe and Asia, and natron is procured from small lakes in an oasis on the west of the Valley of the Nile.

The diffusion of precious stones is very limited. Diamonds are mostly found in a soil of sand and gravel, and in the beds of rivers. Brazil furnishes most of the diamonds in commerce; they are the produce of tracts on each side of the Sierra Espenhaço, and of a district watered by some of the affluents of the Rio San Francisco. During the century ending in 1822, diamonds were collected in Brazil to the value of three millions sterling, one of which weighed a hundred and thirty-eight and one half carats. The celebrated mines of Golconda have produced many splendid diamonds; they are also found in Borneo, which produced one weighing three hundred and sixty-seven carats, valued at two hundred and sixty-nine thousand three hundred and seventy-eight pounds. The eastern parts of the Thian-Tchan, on the great platform of Asia, and a wide district of the Ural Mountains, yield diamonds.

The ruby and sapphire, which have the same crystalline form, are found in Ceylon, in the gravel of streams. The rubies at Gharan, near to the River Oxus, are found in beds of limestone. The gravel of rivulets in the Burman empire contains the oriental, star, and opalescent rubies. The spinelle also occurs in that country in a district five days' journey from Ava. The Hungarian rubies are of inferior value. The blue, green, yellow, and white sapphires are the produce of the Burman empire, and the spinelle is not uncommon in Brazil.

The finest emeralds come from veins in a blue slate, in the Valley of Muso, in New Grenada. Beryls are found in Brazil, and in the old mines in Mount Zebarah, in Upper Egypt. Those of Hungary and of the Heubach Valley, near Saltzburg, are very inferior in color and quality.

Mexico, Hungary, and Bohemia yield the finest opals; the most esteemed are opaque, of a pale brown, and shine with the most brilliant iridescence; some are white, transparent, or semi-transparent, and radiant in colors. The most beautiful garnets come from Bohemia and Hungary; they are found in the Hartz Mountains, Ceylon, and many other localities. The turquoise is a Persian gem, of which there are two varieties; one is supposed to be the enamel of the tooth of a fossilized mastodon, the other a mineral; it is also found in Thibet, and in the Belor-Tagh in Badakshan, which is the country of the lapis lazuli, mined by heating the rock, and then throwing cold water upon it. This beautiful mineral is also found in several places of the Hindoo Coosh, in the hills of Istalif north of Cabul, in Thibet, and in the Baikal Mountains in Siberia.

The cat's-eye is peculiar to Ceylon; the King of Kandy had one two inches broad. Topaz, beryl, and amethyst are of very common occurrence, especially in Brazil and Siberia. They are little valued, and scarcely accounted gems. Agates are so beautiful on the table land of Thibet, and in some parts of the Desert of the Great Gobi, that they form a considerable article of commerce in China; and some are brought to Rome, where they are cut into cameos and intaglios. But the greater part of the agates, cornelians, and chalcedonies used in Europe are found in the trap-rocks of Oberstein, in the Palatinate.

It is remarkable that iron, the metal most useful to man, is by far the most abundant. As it is chiefly found in the same strata from which coal is obtained, it will be most convenient to treat of these minerals in the same connection.

The mines of iron and coal which are wrought are chiefly in the north temperate zone, and occur abundantly in Asia, Europe, and America.

In Asia the ores are very rich in the eastern mining district of Siberia, and are also very abundant in many parts of the Altaï and Ural. In the latter, the mountain of Blagod, at fifteen hundred and thirty-four feet above the sea, is one mass of magnetic iron ore. Coal and iron are worked in so many parts of Northern China, Japan, India, and Eastern Asia, that it would be tedious to enumerate them.

In Europe the richest mines of iron, like those of coal, lie chiefly north of the Alps. Sweden, Norway, Russia, Germany, Styria, Belgium, and France, all contain it plentifully. In Britain many of the coal fields contain subordinate beds of a rich argillaceous iron ore, interstratified with coal, worked at the same time and in the same manner; besides, there is a substratum of limestone, which serves as a flux for melting the metal. The principal mines lie round Birmingham, in the Staffordshire coal field, and the great coal basin of South Wales, about Pontypool and Merthyr Tydvil. There are extensive iron mines in Staffordshire, Shropshire, North and South Wales, Yorkshire, Derbyshire, and Scotland. Altogether there are about two hundred and twenty mines, which yield iron sufficient for home consumption and for exportation. These productive mines would have been of no avail had it not been for the abundance of fuel with which the greater part of them in the north of England, Scotland, and Wales are associated — the great source of national wealth, more precious than mines of gold. Most of the coal mines would have been inaccessible but for the means which their produce affords of draining them at a small expense. A bushel of coals, which costs only a few pence, in the furnace of a steam engine generates a power which in a few minutes will raise twenty thousand gallons of water from a depth of three hundred and sixty feet — an effect which could not be accomplished in a shorter time than a whole day by the continuous labor of twenty men working with the common pump. Yet this circumstance, so far from lessening the demand for human labor, has caused a greater number of men to be employed in the mines.

The coal strata lie in basins, dipping from the sides towards the centre, which is often at a vast depth below the surface of the ground. The centre of the Liege coal basin is twenty-one thousand three hundred and fifty-eight feet, or three and a half geographical miles deep, which is easily estimated from the dip, or inclination, of the strata at the edges, and the extent of the basin. The coal lies in strata of small thickness and great extent. It varies in thickness from three to nine feet, though in some instances several layers come together, and then it is twenty, and even thirty, feet thick; but these layers are interrupted by frequent dislocations, which raise the coal seam towards the surface. These fissures, which divide the coal field into insulated masses, are filled with clay, so that an accumulation of water takes place which must be pumped up.

There are three immense coal fields in England. The first lies north of the Trent, and occupies an area of three hundred and sixty square miles; and although the quantity of coal annually raised in Northumberland and Durham amounts to upwards of three millions of tons, there is enough to last a thousand years. London is chiefly supplied from it. The second or central coal field, which includes Leicester, Worcester, Stafford, and Shropshire, has an area of fourteen hundred and ninety-five square miles, and supplies the manufactories round it, and the midland counties south and east of Derbyshire. The third or western coal field includes South Wales, Gloucestershire, and Somersetshire. The coal field of South Wales alone is one hundred miles long, and eighteen or twenty broad. The Workington and Whitehaven coal mines extend a mile under the sea; several shafts in the latter are a hundred fathoms deep; and it is one of the finest in England for extent and thickness of strata, some of the seams being nine feet thick.

The Scotch coal field occupies the great central low land of Scotland, lying between the southern high lands and the Highland Mountains; the whole of that wide tract is occupied by it, besides which there are others of less extent. Coal has been found in seventeen counties in Ireland, but the island contains only four principal coal districts — Leinster, Munster, Connaught, and Ulster.

The carboniferous strata are enormously developed in the United States. The Appalachian coal field extends without interruption seven hundred and twenty miles, with a maximum breadth of two hundred and eighty miles, from the northern border of Pennsylvania to near Huntsville, in Alabama, occupying an area of sixty-three thousand square miles. It is intersected by three great navigable rivers, — the Monongahela, the Alleghany, and the Ohio, — which expose to view the seams of coal on their banks. The Pittsburg seam, ten feet thick, exposed on the banks of the Monongahela, extends, horizontally, two hundred and twenty-five miles in length and one hundred in breadth, and covers an area of fourteen thousand square miles; so that this seam of coal may be worked for ages almost on the surface, and in many places literally so.

The Illinois coal field, which occupies part of Illinois, Indiana, and Kentucky, is as large as England, and consists of horizontal strata, with numerous seams of rich bituminous coal. There is a vast coal field also in Michigan. Large areas in New Brunswick and Nova Scotia abound in coal. Iron is worked in many parts of the United States, from Connecticut to South Carolina.

In the year 1820 the anthracite coal trade in the United States commenced with 365 tons; in 1827, it reached 48,047 tons; in 1837, 881,026 tons; in 1847, 3,000,000 tons, and in 1851, 4,383,667 tons.

In 1845, the number of tons of coal raised in Great Britain was 31,500,000; in Belgium, 496,077; in the United States, 4,000,000; in France, 4,141,617; in the Russian states, 3,500,000; and in the Austrian states, 659,340.

The tropical regions of the globe have been so little explored, that no idea can be formed of the quantity of coal or iron they contain; but as iron is so universal, it is probable that coal is not wanting. It is found in Formosa. Both abound in Borneo, and in various parts of tropical Africa and America. There is comparatively so little land in the southern temperate zone, that the mineral produce must be more limited than in the northern; yet New Holland, Van Diemen's Land, and New Zealand are rich in coal and iron.

Coal is the result of the mineralization of vegetable remains. This is proved, both by the numerous impressions of plants found in connection with it, and by the traces of organization which are still discoverable in it. By cutting the different varieties of bituminous coal into thin slices, and submitting them to the microscope, the elementary tissue of the plants which produced them can be distinctly recognized.

In general the impressions of plants occur chiefly in the shale of the coal measures; that is, in the mud which separates the seams of coal, or in the sandstone or ironstone associated with the coal formation; and as such impressions are much more distinct than any that occur in the coal itself, it is chiefly from them that our ideas of the vegetation from which coal has been produced have been derived. They are often present in inconceivable beauty and abundance, as may be imagined from Dr. Buckland's graphic account of those in the coal mines of Bohemia. In his Bridgewater Treatise he says, "The finest example I have ever witnessed of distinctly preserved vegetable remains is that of the coal mines of Bohemia. The most elaborate imitations of living foliage upon the painted ceilings of Italian palaces bear no comparison with the beauteous profusion of extinct vegetable forms with which the galleries of these instructive coal mines are overhung. The roof is covered as with a canopy of gorgeous tapestry, enriched with festoons of most graceful foliage, flung in wild, irregular profusion over every portion of its surface. The effect is heightened by the contrast of the coal-black color of these vegetables with the light groundwork of the rock to which they are attached. The spectator feels himself transported, as if by enchantment, into the forests of another world; he beholds trees of forms and characters now unknown upon the surface of the earth, presented to his senses almost in the beauty and vigor of their primeval life; their scaly stems and bending branches, with their delicate apparatus of foliage, are all spread forth before him, little impaired by the lapse of countless ages, and bearing faithful records of extinct systems of vegetation, which began and terminated in times of which these relics are the infallible historians."

Such remains consist chiefly of impressions of leaves, separated from their branches, and of casts of trunks in a more or less broken state; and with them occur occasionally pieces of wood or remains of trees, in which the vegetable texture is to some extent preserved. "Some of the plants of our coal," says Dr. Buckland, "grew on the identical banks of sand, silt, and mud, which, being now indurated to stone and shale, form the strata that accompany the coal; whilst other portions of these plants have been drifted to various distances from the swamps, savannas, and forests that gave them birth, particularly those that are dispersed through the sandstones, or mixed with fishes in the shale beds." "At Balgray, three miles north of Glasgow," says the same author, "I saw, in the year 1824, an unequivocal example of the stumps of several stems of large trees standing close together in their native place, in a quarry of sandstone of the coal formation."

Between the years 1837 and 1840, six fossil trees were discovered in the coal fields of Lancashire, England, where it is intersected by the Bolton Railway. They were all in a vertical position with respect to the plane of the bed, which dips about fifteen degrees to the south. The dimensions of one of the trees is fifteen and a half feet in circumference at the base, seven and a half feet at the top, its height being eleven feet. All the trees have large spreading roots, solid and strong, sometimes branching, and traced to a distance of several feet, and presumed to extend much farther. In the same plane with the roots is a bed of coal eight or ten inches thick, which has been ascertained to extend across the railway, or to the distance of at least ten yards.

In a deep valley near Capel-Coelbren, branching from the higher part of the Swansea Valley, four stems of upright *sigillariæ* were seen, in 1838, piercing through the coal measures of South Wales. One of them was two feet in diameter, another thirteen and a half feet in height, and they were all found to terminate downwards in a bed of coal. "They appear," says Sir H. de la Beche, "to have constituted a portion of a subterranean forest at the epoch when the lower carboniferous strata were formed."

If, instead of working in the dark, the miner was accustomed to remove the upper covering of rock from each seam of coal, and to expose to the day the soils on which ancient forests grew, the evidence of their former growth would be obvious. Thus in South Staffordshire a seam of coal was laid bare in the year 1844, in what is called an open work, at Parkfield Colliery, near Wolverhampton. In the space of about a quarter of an acre the stumps of no less than seventy-three trees, with their roots attached, appeared, some of them more than eight feet in circumference. The trunks, broken off close to the root, were lying prostrate in every direction, often crossing each other. One of them measured fifteen, another thirty feet in length, and others less. They were invariably flattened to the thickness of one or two inches, and converted into coal. Their roots formed part of a stra-

Trees and plants of extinct species, restored from leaves, branches, and trunks, found embedded in coal, sandstone, and other rocks. — 1. *Casuerina.* 2. *Neuropteris.* 3 *Asterophyllites.* 4. *Araucaria.* 5. *Lepidodendron.* 6. *Pecopteris.* 7. Arborescent Fern. 8. *Calamites.* 9. *Palmi.* 10. Arborescent Fern, peculiar species. 11. *Zamia* 12. *Pandanus* 13. *Cycas.*

tum of coal ten inches thick, which rested on a layer of clay two inches thick, below which was a second forest, resting on a two foot seam of coal. Five feet below this, again, was a third forest, with large stumps of *lepidodendra*, *calamites*, and other trees.

One of the finest examples in the world of a succession of fossil forests of the carboniferous period laid open to view in a natural section, is that seen in the lofty cliffs bordering the Chignecto Channel, a branch of the Bay of Fundy, in Nova Scotia. Mr. Logan, who made a survey of this line of cliffs, found erect trees at seventeen levels, extending through a vertical thickness of four thousand five hundred and fifteen feet of strata; and he estimated the total thickness of the carboniferous formation, with and without coal, at no less than fourteen thousand five hundred and seventy feet. He counted nineteen seams of coal, varying in thickness from two inches to four feet. The high tides of the Bay of Fundy, rising more than sixty feet, are so destructive as to undermine and sweep away continually the whole face of the cliffs, and thus a new crop of erect trees is brought into view every three or four years. They are known to extend over a space of between two and three miles from north to south, and more than twice that distance from east to west, being seen in the banks of streams intersecting the coal field.

In the Sydney coal field in Cape Breton, Mr. Richard Brown has observed a total thickness of coal measures, without including the underlying millstone grit, of eighteen hundred and forty-three feet, dipping at an angle of eight degrees. He has published minute details of the whole series, showing at how many different levels erect trees occur, consisting of *sigillaria*, *lepidodendra*, *calamites*, and other genera. In one place, eight erect trunks, with roots and rootlets attached to them, were seen at the same level, within a horizontal space eighty feet in length. Beds of coal of various thickness are interstratified. Some of the associated strata are ripple-marked, with impressions of rain drops. Taking into account

10

forty-one clays filled with roots of *stigmaria* in their natural position, and eighteen layers of upright trees at other levels, there is, on the whole, clear evidence of at least fifty-nine fossil forests ranged one above the other, in this coal field, in the above-mentioned thickness of strata.

The time requisite for the growth of this succession of forests, and for the deposition of the strata between them, must have been inconceivably great; yet it is short when compared with the time required for the deposition of the numerous strata which lie above and below the coal. It is the opinion of President Hitchcock, of Professor Silliman, and of most other geologists, that the earth must have been created millions of years previous to its renovation about six thousand years ago, as recorded in the first chapter of Genesis, commencing with the second verse. "Geology," says President Hitchcock, in his highly interesting work entitled Religion of Geology, "places the time when the matter of the universe was created out of nothing at an epoch indefinitely but immensely remote. Since that epoch, this matter has passed through a multitude of changes, and been the seat of numerous systems of organic life, unlike one another, yet all linked together into one great system by a most perfect unity; each minor system being most beautifully adapted to its place in the great chain, and yet each successive link becoming more and more perfect. Nor does geology admit that any evidence exists of the future annihilation of the material universe, but rather of other changes, by which new and brighter displays of divine wisdom and benevolence shall be brought out, it may be in endless succession. Geology is not indeed insensible to the displays of the divine character which are exhibited on the present theatre of the world. Indeed, she distinctly recognizes the act which is now passing as the most perfect of all. Yet this scene of the great drama she regards as only one of the units of a similar series of changes that have gone by, or will hereafter come; the chain stretching so far into the eternity that is past and the eternity that is to come, that the extremities are lost to mortal vision. Do any shrink back from these immense conclusions because they so much surpass the views they have been accustomed to entertain respecting the beginning and the end of the material universe? But why should they be unwilling to have geology liberalize their minds as much in respect to duration as astronomy has done in respect to space? Perhaps it is a lingering fear that the geological views conflict with revelation. Such fears formerly kept back many from giving up their souls to the noble truths of astronomy. But they learned at length that astronomy merely illustrates, and does not oppose revelation. It showed men how to understand certain passages of sacred writ respecting the earth and heavenly bodies, which they had before misinterpreted. Just so it is with geology. There is no collision between its statements and revelation. It only enables us more correctly to interpret some portions of the Bible; and then, when we have admitted the new interpretation, it brings a flood of light upon the plans and attributes of Jehovah. Geology therefore should be viewed, as it really is, the auxiliary both of natural and revealed religion. And when its religious relations are fully understood, theology, I doubt not, will be as anxious to cultivate its alliance as she has been fearful of it in days past."

The Mosaic narrative commences with a declaration, that "In the beginning God created the heaven and the earth." These few first words of Genesis may be fairly appealed to by the geologist, as containing a brief statement of the creation of the material elements at a time distinctly preceding the operations of the first day. It is nowhere affirmed that God created the heaven and the earth in the *first day*, but in the *beginning;* this beginning may have been an epoch at an unmeasured distance, followed by periods of undefined duration, during which all the physical operations disclosed by geology were going on.

The first verse of Genesis, therefore, seems explicitly to assert the creation of the universe; "the heaven" including the sidereal systems, "and the earth" more especially specifying our own planet, as the subsequent scene of the operations of the six days about to be described. No information is given as to events which may have occurred upon this earth unconnected with the history of man, between the creation of its component matter recorded in the first verse, and the era at which its history is resumed in the second verse; nor is any limit fixed to the time during which these intermediate events may have been going on. Millions of millions of years may have occupied the indefinite interval between the beginning, in which God created the heaven and the earth, and the evening, or commencement of the first day of the Mosaic narrative.

The second verse may describe the condition of the earth on the evening of this first day; (for in the Jewish mode of computation used by Moses, each day is reckoned from the beginning of one evening to the beginning of another evening.) This first evening may be considered as the termination of the indefinite time which followed the primeval creation announced in the first verse, and as the commencement of the first of the six succeeding days, in which the earth was to be fitted up and peopled in a manner fit for the reception of mankind. We have in this second verse a distinct mention of earth and waters as already existing and involved in darkness. Their condition also is described as a state of confusion and emptiness, (*tohu bohu,*) words which are usually interpreted by the vague and indefinite Greek term "chaos," and which may be geologically considered as designating the wreck and ruins of a former world. At this intermediate point of time the preceding undefined geological periods had terminated, a new series of events commenced, and the work of the first morning of this new creation was the calling forth of light from a temporary darkness which had overspread the ruins of the ancient earth.

We have further mention of this ancient earth and ancient sea in the ninth verse, in which the waters are commanded to be *gathered together* into one place, and the dry land to *appear;* this dry land being the same earth whose material creation had been announced in the first verse, and whose temporary submersion and temporary darkness are described in the second verse. The *appearance* of the land and the *gathering together* of the waters are the only facts affirmed respecting them in the ninth verse, but neither land nor waters are said to have been *created* on the third day.

A similar interpretation may be given of the fourteenth and four succeeding verses. What is herein stated of the celestial luminaries seems to be spoken solely with reference to our planet, and more especially to the human race, then about to be placed upon it. We are not told that the substance of the sun and moon was first called into existence upon the fourth day; the text may equally imply that these bodies were then prepared, and appointed to certain offices of high importance to mankind—"to give light upon the earth, and to rule over the day and over the night;" "to be for signs, and for seasons, and for days, and for years." The fact of their creation had been stated before in the first verse. The stars also are mentioned (Gen. i. 16) in three words only, almost parenthetically, as if for the sole purpose of announcing that they also were made by the same Power as those luminaries which are more important to us, the sun and moon. This very slight notice of the countless host of celestial bodies, all of which are probably suns, the centres of other planetary systems, whilst our little satellite, the moon, is mentioned as next in importance to the sun, shows clearly that astronomical phenomena are here spoken of only according to their relative importance to our earth and to mankind, and without any regard to their real importance in the boundless universe. It seems impossible to include the fixed stars among those bodies which are said (Gen. i. 17) to have been set in the firmament of the heaven to give light upon the earth, since without the aid of telescopes by far the greater number of them are invisible. The same principle seems to pervade the description of creation which concerns our planet; the creation of its component matter having been announced in the first verse, the phenomena of geology, like those of astronomy, are passed over in silence, and the narrative proceeds at once to details of the actual creation which have more immediate reference to man.

The interpretation here proposed seems moreover to solve the difficulty which would otherwise attend the statement of the appearance of light upon the first day, while the sun, and moon, and stars are not made to appear until the fourth. If we suppose all the heavenly bodies and the earth to have been created at the indefinitely distant time designated by the word "beginning," and that the darkness described on the evening of the first day was a temporary darkness, produced by an accumulation of dense vapors "upon the face of the deep," an incipient dispersion of these vapors may have readmitted light to the earth upon the first day, whilst the exciting cause of light was still obscured; and the further purification of the atmosphere, upon the fourth day, may have caused the sun, and moon, and stars to reappear in the firmament of heaven, to assume their new relations to the newly-modified earth and to the human race.

We have evidence of the presence of light during long and distant periods of time in which the many extinct fossil forms of animal life succeeded one another upon the early surface of the globe; this evidence consists in the petrified remains of eyes of animals, found in geological formations of various ages.

The eyes of the ichthyosaurus contained an apparatus so like one in the eyes of many birds as to leave no doubt that these fossil eyes were optical instruments calculated to receive in the same manner impressions of the same light, which conveys the perception of sight to living animals. This conclusion is further confirmed by the general fact, that the heads of all fossil fishes and fossil reptiles, in every geological formation, are furnished with cavities for the reception of eyes, and with perforations for the passage of optic nerves, although the cases are rare in which any part of the eye itself has been preserved. The influence of light is also so necessary to the growth of existing vegetables, that we cannot but infer that it was equally essential to the development of the numerous fossil species of the vegetable kingdom, which are coextensive and coeval with the remains of fossil animals.

It is probable that light is not a material substance, but only an effect of undulations of ether; that this infinitely subtile and elastic ether pervades all space, and even the interior of all bodies; so long as it remains at rest there is total darkness; when it is put into a peculiar state of vibration the sensation of light is produced; this vibration may be excited by various causes — by the sun, by the stars, by electricity, combustion, &c. If then light be not a substance, but only a series of vibrations of ether, i. e., an effect produced on a subtile fluid by the excitement of one or many extraneous causes, it can hardly be said, nor is it said in Gen. i. 3 to have been *created*, though it may be literally said to be called into action.

In the reference made in the fourth commandment, Exod. xx. 11, to the six days of the Mosaic creation, the word translated "made" is the same which is used in Gen. i. 7 and Gen. i. 16, and which has been shown to be less strong and less comprehensive than the one rendered "created;" and as it by no means necessarily implies creation out of nothing, it may be here employed to express a new arrangement of materials that existed before.

After all, it should be recollected that the question is not respecting the correctness of the Mosaic narrative, but of our interpretation of it; and still further it should be borne in mind that the object of this account was, not to state *in what manner*, but *by whom*, the world was made. As the prevailing tendency of men in those early days was to worship the most glorious objects of nature, namely, the sun, and moon, and stars, it should seem to have been one important point, in the Mosaic account of creation, to guard the Israelites against the polytheism and idolatry of the nations around them, by announcing that all these magnificent celestial bodies were no gods, but the works of one almighty Creator, to whom alone the worship of mankind is due.

The comparatively modern period of the creation of man is a fact revealed by Scripture, and confirmed by science. The same internal evidence which convinces us of the antiquity of our planet, affords satisfactory proof of the modern origin of our species. The whole vast series of aqueous deposits are crowded with fragments of plants, corals, shells, crustacea, fish, reptiles, birds, and mammalia; but no fossil remains of man have been discovered, except in those accumulations of silt or mud which belong to the modern era — the yesterday, as it were, in the history of the past. It is only in these accumulations that we discover the remains of even the most ancient races; that in England we meet with the implements of our British ancestors, or the coins and weapons of their Roman invaders; that in Italy we find the Cyclopean structures and works of art of the Etruscans, while vestiges of the Pelasgi are alike discoverable in similar deposits in Greece; and in the new world traces exist of the Tulteques, a people who were the predecessors of the Mexicans, and their superiors in knowledge. Had man existed in primeval times, his remains would have been found scattered through the various deposits from the oldest to the most recent. No impediment exists to their conservation; his bones, composed of the same elements as those of animals, are equally capable of being kept from destruction; the same battle field has preserved the bones of the horse and his rider; the same cavern, which in earlier eras gave shelter to the hyena and the bear, has retained their skeletons, and alike preserved the remains of those human occupants, who, at a later period, found in this retreat a refuge and a tomb. Still stronger proof of the modern origin of our species exists in the fact that if man had been an inhabitant of the earth during its early history, his skeleton would have constituted the least of those relics which he would have bequeathed to the soil. We should have discovered his works of art, which so far transcend in duration his own ephemeral existence: we should have found his cities overwhelmed in the waters of ancient seas, or buried beneath the ejections of primeval volcanoes; his majestic pyramids sunk in the bed of early rivers; his mountain temples hewn on the surface of the oldest rocks: we should have encountered his bridges of granite and of iron; his palaces of limestone and of marble; the tombs which he reared over the objects of his affection; the shrines which he erected in honor of his God. But in the absence of these, in any save the most superficial deposits, we recognize the complete accordance of science with revelation. It is impossible to form a more magnificent conception of infinite wisdom than that which geology exhibits, representing the Supreme Being as first elaborating and perfecting our earth into one sphere of blessings; erecting on a foundation of granite a vast superstructure of sandstones, limestones, clays, coal, and the varied substances known as rocks; injecting their fissures with minerals and metallic ores, then, by volcanic agency, bringing those varied deposits near the surface, and so diversifying the soil as to present every variety of condition required for its mineral, agricultural, and economical cultivation; tempering the climate to the degree best adapted for human existence, peopling it with animals suited to the use of men, for supplying him with food and assisting him in his labors; and, finally, calling him into existence to take possession of a world which had been prepared for his reception and enjoyment.

It is a prevalent opinion that death did not enter the animal kingdom until after man's disobedience. "Such a conclusion," says Rev. S. Comfort, "is reached by a misinterpretation of those passages of Scripture which clearly refer to the subject. The great apostle of the Gentiles affirms the contrary. He limits his own meaning when he says, 'By one man sin entered into the world, and death by sin; and so death passed upon all men, for that all have sinned.' Rom. v. 12. The extent to which sin obtained, thus introduced, could not be more definitely expressed. It 'passed upon all *men*.' Hence, animals are excluded. On the contrary, the current theory involves an absolute impossibility. It was not possible for either man or animals to have lived and moved before the fall without destroying myriads of insects and animalcules. To exonerate the Creator from the imputation of partiality in thus subjecting *some* of his creatures to inevitable death, while others were not so exposed, should it be replied that life is relatively more important to some species than to others, we reply, that this is the same as to say there *may* be reasons why death is allowed to some creatures. And why not to others? Hence this is to give up the argument. For who shall draw the line between those which may be thus subjected and those which should be exempted?"

CHAPTER IV.

Formation of Peat. — Extensive Forests converted into Peat Mosses or Bogs. — Trees twelve Feet in Diameter embedded in them. — A House discovered sixteen Feet below the Surface of a Bog. — A Village destroyed by the bursting of a Bog. — Preservation from Decay of Human Bodies, their Costumes, &c., in Bogs where for many Centuries they had remained embedded.

The generation of peat, when not completely under water, is confined to moist situations, where the temperature is low, and where vegetables may decompose without putrefying. It may consist of any of the numerous plants which are capable of growing in such places; but a species of moss (*sphagnum*) constitutes a considerable part of the peat found in marshes of the north of Europe; this plant having the property of throwing up new shoots in its upper part, while its lower extremities are decaying. Reeds, rushes, and other aquatic plants may usually be traced in peat; and their organization is often so entire that there is no difficulty in discriminating the distinct species.

In general, one hundred parts of dry peat contain from sixty to ninety-nine parts of matter destructible by fire; and the residuum consists of earths usually of the same kind as the substratum of clay, marl, gravel, or rock, on which they are found, together with oxide of iron. From the researches of Dr. McCulloch, it appears that peat is intermediate between simple vegetable matter and lignite, the conversion of peat to lignite being gradual, and being brought about by a prolonged action of water.

Peat is sometimes formed on a declivity in mountainous regions, where there is much moisture; but in such situations it rarely, if ever, exceeds four feet in thickness. In bogs, and in low grounds into which alluvial peat is drifted, it is found forty feet thick, and upwards; but in such cases it generally owes one half of its volume to the water which it contains. It has seldom, if ever, been discovered within the tropics; and it rarely occurs in the valleys, even in the south of France and Spain. It abounds more and more in proportion as we advance farther from the equator, and becomes not only more frequent, but more inflammable, in northern latitudes.

The same phenomenon is repeated in the southern hemisphere. No peat is found in Brazil, nor even in the swampy parts of the country drained by the La Plata on the east side of South America, or in the Island of Chiloe on the west; yet when we reach the forty-fifth degree of latitude, and examine the Chonos Archipelago or the Falkland Islands, and Tierra del Fuego, we meet with an abundant growth of this substance. Almost all plants contribute here by their decay to the production of peat, even the grasses; but it is a singular fact, says Mr. Darwin, as contrasted with what occurs in Europe, that no kind of moss enters into the composition of the South American peat, which is formed by many plants, but chiefly by that called by Brown *astelia pumila.*

Water charged with vegetable matter in solution does not throw down a deposit of peat in countries where the mean temperature of the year is above forty-three or forty-four degrees Fahrenheit. Frost causes the precipitation of such peaty matter; but in warm climates the attraction of the carbon for the oxygen of the air mechanically mixed with the water increases with the increasing temperature, and the dissolved vegetable matter or humic acid, (which is organic matter in a progressive state of decomposition,) being converted into carbonic acid, rises and is absorbed into the atmosphere, and thus disappears.

Vast peat districts occur in France, the Netherlands, Germany, Prussia, the Canadas, Scotland, and Ireland, and are found in insulated situations in Iceland, the Shetlands, and the Falkland Islands. In Ireland, the prevailing humidity and low temperature of the climate is especially favorable to the growth of peat, which covers nearly one tenth of the surface; or, excluding some small mountainous and detached patches, the total quantity of bog has been estimated at two million eight hundred and thirty-one thousand acres, of which one million five hundred and seventy-six thousand acres are flat red bog, capable of being reclaimed, and one million two hundred and fifty-five thousand are mountain bog, mostly convertible into pasture land. One of the mosses on the Shannon is described as being fifty miles long, by two or three broad; and the great marsh of Montoire, near the mouth of the Loire, is mentioned, by Blavier, as being more than fifty leagues in circumference. It is a curious and well-ascertained fact, that many of these mosses of the north of Europe occupy the place of forests of pine and oak, which have, many of them, disappeared within the historical era. Such changes are brought about by the fall of trees and the stagnation of water, caused by their trunks and branches obstructing the free drainage of the atmospheric waters, and giving rise to a marsh. In a warm climate, such decayed timber would immediately be removed by insects, or by putrefaction; but, in the cold temperature now prevailing in Great Britain, many examples are recorded of marshes originating in this source. Thus, in Mar forest, in Aberdeenshire, large trunks of Scotch fir, which had fallen from age and decay, were soon immured in peat, formed partly out of their perishing leaves and branches, and in part from the growth of other plants. We also learn that the overthrow of a forest by a storm, about the middle of the seventeenth century, gave rise to a peat moss near Lochbroom, in Ross-shire, where, in less than half a century after the fall of the trees, the inhabitants dug peat. Dr. Walker mentions a similar change, when, in the year 1756, the whole wood of Drumlanrig, in Dumfries-shire, was overset by the wind. Such events explain the occurrence, both in Britain and on the continent, of mosses where the trees are all broken within two or three feet of the original surface, and where their trunks all lie in the same direction.

It may, however, be suggested in these cases, that the soil had become exhausted for trees, and that, on the principle of that natural rotation which prevails in the vegetable world, one set of plants died out and another succeeded. It is certainly a remarkable fact, that in the Danish islands, and in Jutland and Holstein, fir wood of various species, especially Scotch fir, is found at the bottom of the peat mosses, although it is well ascertained that for the last five centuries no coniferæ have grown wild in these countries; the coniferous trees which now flourish there having been all planted towards the close of the last century.

Nothing is more common than the occurrence of buried trees at the bottom of the Irish peat mosses, as also in most of those of England, France, and Holland; and they have been so often observed with parts of their trunks standing erect, and with their roots fixed to the subsoil, that no doubt can be entertained of their having generally grown on the spot. They consist, for the most part, of the fir, the oak, and the birch; where the subsoil is clay, the remains of oak are the most abundant; where sand is the substratum, fir prevails. In the marsh of Curragh, in the Isle of Man, vast trees are discovered standing firm on their roots, though at the depth of eighteen or twenty feet below the surface. Some naturalists have desired to refer the embedding of timber in peat mosses to aqueous transportation, since rivers are well known to float wood into lakes; but the facts above mentioned show that, in numerous instances, such an hypothesis is inadmissible. It has, moreover, been observed, that in Scotland, as also in many parts of the continent, the largest trees are found in those peat mosses which lie in the least elevated regions, and that the trees are proportionally smaller in those which lie at higher levels; from which fact De Luc and Walker have both inferred that the trees grew on the spot, for they would naturally attain a greater size in lower and warmer levels. The leaves, also, and fruits of each species, are continually found immersed in the moss, along with the parent trees; as, for example, the leaves and acorns of the oak, the cones and leaves of the fir, and the nuts of the hazel.

In Hatfield moss, in Yorkshire, which appears clearly to have been a forest eighteen hundred years ago, an oak was found, four yards across at the base, three and a half yards in the middle, and two yards across the top, which was broken off, the length of the trunk remaining being forty yards. A fir tree also was thirty-six yards long, and estimated to be deficient at least fifteen yards, making in the whole fifty-one yards, or a hundred and fifty-three feet.

In the same moss of Hatfield, as well as in that of Kincardine, in Scotland, and several others, Roman roads have been found covered to the depth of eight feet by peat. All the coins, axes, arms, and other utensils found in British and French mosses, are also Roman; so that a considerable portion of the peat in European peat bogs is evidently not more ancient than the age of Julius Cæsar. Nor can any vestiges of the ancient forests described by that general, along the line of the great Roman way in Britain, be discovered, except in the ruined trunks of trees in peat.

De Luc ascertained that the very site of the aboriginal forests of Hercinia, Semana, Ardennes, and several others, are now occupied by mosses and fens; and a great part of these changes have, with much probability, been attributed to the strict orders given by Severus, and other emperors, to destroy all the wood in the conquered provinces. Several of the British forests, however, which are now mosses, were cut at different periods by order of the English Parliament, because they harbored wolves or outlaws. Thus the Welsh woods were cut and burned, in the reign of Edward I., as were many of those in Ireland, by Henry II., to prevent the natives from harboring in them and harassing his troops.

It is curious to reflect that considerable tracts have, by these accidents, been permanently sterilized, and that, during a period when civilization has been making great progress large areas in Europe have, by human agency, been rendered less capable of administering to the wants of man. Rennie observes, with truth, that in those regions alone which the Roman eagle never reached—in the remote circles of the German empire, in Poland and Prussia, and still more in Norway, Sweden, and the vast empire of Russia—can we see what Europe was before it yielded to the power of Rome. Desolation now reigns where stately forests of pine and oak once flourished, such as might now have supplied all the navies of Europe with timber.

Of the pauses in the accumulation of bogs sufficient to permit a growth of trees upon them, as also a surface upon which habitations may be constructed, perhaps as good an example as any is that of an ancient wooden house discovered in 1833, in Drumkelin bog, on the north-east of Donegal. It was sixteen feet below the surface of the bog, before the upper part was taken off, and four feet beneath the cuttings of the time, standing itself upon fifteen feet more of bog, so that the total thickness at that place had been thirty-one feet. The house was a square of twelve feet sides, and nine feet high, and was formed of two floors; the roof was constructed of thick planks of oak, the wood employed for the whole dwelling, upon which no iron had been used. Upon clearing away the bog from the level of the house, a paved pathway was discovered, extending several yards from it, to a hearth-stone covered with ashes, some bushels of half-burned charcoal, some nutshells, and blocks of wood partly burned. Near the house there were stumps of oak trees, which grew at the time it was inhabited. A layer of sand had been spread over the ground before the erection of the house. All seems to have marked a state of repose in the growth of this part of the bog, so that a change of conditions affecting the drainage would seem needful, to account for the accumulation of sixteen feet more above the surface, after the time when the house was constructed. It may have been that a bursting of

A tree 36 feet in circumference, found below the surface of the earth. See page 87.

part of a bog had overwhelmed this locality, soft, boggy matter having gradually accumulated to a higher level under favorable circumstances in some place adjacent.

Peat bogs have long been remarked for their antiseptic properties, or the power of preserving animal substances from putrefaction, some striking instances of which are on record. Two human bodies, buried in moist peat, in Derbyshire, in 1674, about a yard below the surface, were found, nearly twenty-nine years afterwards, with the color of the skin fair and natural, and the flesh as soft as that of persons newly deceased. In June, 1747, a Lincolnshire laborer, digging peat on one of the moors, discovered the body of a woman, a lady of the olden time, at the depth of six feet. The head and feet were nearly bent together, and the skin, nails, and hair were in a high state of preservation. She wore leather shoes, or sandals, each cut out of a single piece of tanned ox hide, folding about the foot and heel, and piked with iron. Chaucer mentions these piked shoes as part of the costume in his time; and in the reign of Edward IV. they had so increased in length, that all who wore them beyond a certain length were to be mulcted, or have them cut shorter, in passing in or out of the city gates of London. For several centuries, therefore, the body had certainly lain in the peat.

On the estate of the Earl of Moira, in Ireland, a human body was dug up, a foot deep in gravel, covered with eleven feet of moss; the body was completely clothed and the garments seemed all to be made of hair. Before the use of wool was known in that country, the clothing of the inhabitants was made of hair, so that it would appear that this body had been buried at that early period; yet it was fresh and unimpaired. In a peat bog in Jutland there was found the mummy of a female, completely sunk in the ground, and fastened to a stake by means of clamps and hooks. The fragments of clothing that remained enabled the antiquaries to decide with tolerable certainty that it belonged to the last period of paganism, and M. Peterson has endeavored to prove, in an able historical essay, that it was the body of Gunhilda, queen of Norway, whom King Harold, by a promise of marriage, enticed to Denmark, A. D. 965, and put to death by sinking her in a bog. Among other analogous facts we may mention, that in digging a pit for a well near Dulverton, in Somersetshire, many pigs were found in various postures, still entire. Their shape was well preserved, the skin, which retained the hair, having assumed a dry, membranous appearance. They were converted into a white, friable, laminated, inodorous, and tasteless substance, but which, when exposed to heat, emitted an odor precisely similar to broiled bacon. This antiseptic property of peat has been attributed by some to the carbonic and gallic acids which issue from decayed wood, as also to the presence of charred wood in the lowest strata of many peat mosses; for charcoal is a powerful antiseptic, and capable of purifying water already putrid. Vegetable gums and resins also may operate in the same way.

The tannin occasionally present in peat is the produce, says Dr. McCulloch, of tormentilla, and some other plants; but the quantity he thinks too small, and its occurrence too casual, to give rise to effects of any importance. He hints that the soft parts of animal bodies, preserved in peat bogs, may have been converted into adipocere by the action of water merely; an explanation which appears clearly applicable to some of the cases above enumerated.

The manner, however, in which peat contributes to preserve, for indefinite periods, the harder parts of terrestrial animals, is a subject of more immediate interest to the geologist. There are two ways in which animals become occasionally buried in the peat of marshy grounds; they either sink down into the semifluid mud, underlying a turfy surface upon which they have rashly ventured, or at other times a bog "bursts," and animals may be involved in the peaty alluvium.

In the extensive bogs of Newfoundland cattle are sometimes found buried with only their heads and necks above ground; and after having remained for days in this situation, they have been drawn out by ropes and saved. In Scotland, also, cattle venturing on the "quaking moss" are often mired, or "laired," as it is termed; and in Ireland, Mr. King asserts that the number of cattle which are lost in sloughs is quite incredible.

The description given of the Solway moss will serve to illustrate the general character of these boggy grounds. That moss, observes Gilpin, is a flat area, about seven miles in circumference, situated on the western confines of England and Scotland. Its surface is covered with grass and rushes, presenting a dry crust and a fair appearance; but it shakes under the least pressure, the bottom being unsound and semifluid. The adventurous passenger, therefore, who sometimes in dry seasons traverses this perilous waste, to save a few miles, picks his cautious way over the rushy tussocks as they appear before him, for here the soil is firmest. If his foot slip, or if he venture to desert this mark of security, it is possible he may never more be heard of.

At the battle of Solway, in the time of Henry VIII., (1542,) when the Scotch army, commanded by Oliver Sinclair, was routed, an unfortunate troop of horse, driven by their fears, plunged into this morass, which instantly closed upon them. The tale was traditional, but it is now authenticated; a man and horse, in complete armor, having been found by peat diggers, in the place where it was always supposed the affair happened. The skeleton of each was well preserved, and the different parts of the armor easily distinguished.

The same moss, on the 16th of December, 1772, swelled to an unusual height above the surrounding country, and then burst. It occupied an area of thirteen hundred acres, stretching along an eminence elevated from fifty to eighty feet above the fertile plain between it and the River Esk. The surface, of some consistency, vibrated to the tread, and might be easily pushed through with a pole, which descended without difficulty from fifteen to twenty feet, showing the soft and watery state of the subjacent matter. After greater rains than had happened for nearly two centuries, the surface of the moss rose, owing to the waters accumulated in it not being able to find a vent, and at length broke, discharging itself upon the hapless valley of the Esk—an entirely new phenomenon in the life of its simple shepherds. What added to their terror and danger was the hour of the eruption, about eleven on the night of the 15th, when the inhabitants of the farms and hamlets of Eskdale had retired to their beds. Some were awakened by the strange noise of the eruption, others by the cry of alarm which speedily rang through the valley; and all awoke from their sleep to encounter in their cottages, or immediately upon opening their doors, a slowly rolling, resistless, and inexplicable deluge of black mud. The members of thirty-five families saved their lives with difficulty, but lost their agricultural produce, with many of their cattle; and when the morning shed light upon the scene, instead of fields, hedgerows, and cottage gardens, there was a dark, slimy torrent of half-consolidated peat earth, almost wholly covering some of the houses, and reaching up to the thatch of others. About four hundred acres were buried; and but for the crawling motion of the semi-solid mass, and the occurrence of an intervening "gap" or broad gully, which diverted into an opposite direction a large quantity of the invading matter, but few of the Eskdale shepherds would have survived the calamity. Though these sudden inroads are few and far between, yet the peat mosses steadily advance in extent and thickness by natural increase, where the conditions essential to their growth remain unaltered; and in a series of years great changes are effected in particular localities. This is observable in the neighborhood of lakes, upon which the peat gains, altering their limits—a process which may be remarked at the upper end of Derwentwater, and around all the small mountain lakes of Wales, the completion of which appears in many of the Irish bogs, which were once lakes, in process of time conquered by the vegetable formations, and supplanted by spongy carbonaceous masses.

A recent inundation in Sligo (January, 1831) affords another example of this phenomenon. After a sudden thaw of snow, the bog between Bloomfield and Geevah gave way, and a black deluge, carrying with it the contents of a hundred acres of bog, took the direction of a small stream, and rolled on with the violence of a torrent, sweeping along heath, timber, mud, and stones, and overwhelming many meadows and cultivated fields. On passing through some boggy land, the flood swept out a wide and deep ravine, and part of the road leading from Bloomfield to St. James's Well was completely carried away from below the foundation for the breadth of two hundred yards.

The "Great Dismal," an extensive swamp, or morass, situated partly in Virginia and partly in North Carolina, offers an exception to a general rule before alluded to, that such peaty accumulations seldom occur so far south as latitude thirty-six degrees, or in any region where the summer heat is so great as in Virginia. This swamp is forty miles long from north to south, and twenty-five wide, and has somewhat the appearance of an inundated river plain covered with aquatic trees and shrubs, the soil being as black as that of a peat bog. It is higher on all sides except one than the surrounding country, towards which it sends forth streams of water to the north, east, and south, receiving a supply from the west only. In its centre it rises twelve feet above the flat region which bounds it. The soil, to the depth of fifteen feet, is formed of vegetable matter without any admixture of earthy particles. In digging canals through the morass for the purpose of obtaining timber, much of the black soil has been thrown out from time to time, and exposed to the sun and air, in which case it soon rots away, so that nothing remains behind, showing clearly that it owes its preservation to the shade afforded by a luxuriant vegetation, and to the constant evaporation of the spongy soil by which the air is cooled during the hot months. The surface of the bog is carpeted with mosses, and densely covered with ferns and reeds, above which many evergreen shrubs and trees flourish, especially the white cedar, which stands firmly supported by its long taproots in the softest parts of the quagmire. Over the whole the deciduous cypress is seen to tower with its spreading top, in full leaf in the season when the sun's rays are hottest, and when, if not intercepted by a screen of foliage, they might soon cause the fallen leaves and dead plants of the preceding autumn to decompose, instead of adding their contributions to the peaty mass. On the surface of the wide morass lie innumerable trunks of large and tall trees, while thousands of others, blown down by the winds, are buried at various depths in the black mire below. They remind the geologist of the prostrate position of large stems of sigillaria and lepidodendron, converted into coal in ancient carboniferous rocks.

The antlers of large and full-grown stags are amongst the most common and conspicuous remains of animals in peat. They are not horns which have been shed; for portions of the skull are found attached, proving that the whole animal perished. Bones of the ox, hog, horse, sheep, and other herbivorous animals, also occur. M. Morren has discovered in the peat of Flanders the bones of otters and beavers; but no remains have been met with belonging to those extinct quadrupeds, of which the living congeners inhabit warmer latitudes, such as the elephant, rhinoceros, hippopotamus, hyena, and tiger, though these are so common in superficial deposits of silt, mud, sand, or stalactite, in various districts throughout Great Britain. Their absence seems to imply that they had ceased to live before the atmosphere of this part of the world acquired that cold and humid character which favors the growth of peat.

From the facts before mentioned, that mosses occasionally burst, and descend in a fluid state to lower levels, it will readily be seen that lakes and arms of the sea may occasionally become the receptacles of drift peat. Of this, accordingly, there are numerous examples; and hence the alternations of clay and sand with different deposits of peat so frequent on some coasts, as on those of the Baltic and German Ocean.

We are informed by Deguer that remains of ships, nautical instruments, and oars have been found in many of the Dutch mosses; and Gerard, in his History of the Valley of the Somme, mentions that in the lowest tier of that moss was found a boat loaded with bricks, proving that these mosses were at one period navigable lakes and arms of the sea, as were also many mosses on the coast of Picardy, Zealand, and Friesland, from which soda and salt are procured. The canoes, stone hatchets, and stone arrow heads found in peat in different parts of Great Britain, lead to similar conclusions.

CHAPTER V.

CORAL ANIMALS, AND THE BEAUTIFUL SUBMARINE GROVES AND ARBORS, THE ISLANDS, ATOLLS, REEFS, AND OTHER PORTIONS OF THE EARTH WHICH THEY HAVE CONSTRUCTED.

A SINGULAR degree of obscurity has been thrown around the growth of coral zoophytes and coral formations, through the various speculations which have been offered in place of facts; and to the present day the subject is seldom mentioned without the qualifying adjective *mysterious* expressed or understood. Some writers, scouting the idea that reefs of rocks can be due in any way to "animalcules," talk of electrical forces, the first and last appeal of ignorance. Others call in the fishes of the seas, suggesting that they are the masons, and work with their teeth in the accumulation of the calcareous material. Very many of those who discourse quite learnedly on zoophytes and reefs, imagine that the polyps are mechanical workers, heaping up these piles of rock by their united labors; and science still retains such terms as polypary, polypidom, as if each coral were the constructed hive or house of a swarm of polyps, like the honeycomb of the bee, or the hillock of a colony of ants.

It is vain to hope to understand fully the works of Him who is himself infinite and incomprehensible. The scrutinizing eye of science penetrates with far-reaching sight the system of things about us, and in the dim limits of vision reads every where the word mystery. All life, animal and vegetable, and all that is inanimate, declare it; surely there is no special reason, except such as may arise from want of study and consideration, for attributing it preëminently to the humblest grades of existence.

An Atoll, or Lagoon Island. Myriads of these beautiful rings adorn the Pacific and Indian Oceans. The Maldive Archipelago consists of atolls, and each of the larger is composed of a series, in some instances exceeding one hundred in number, of smaller atolls.

It is not more surprising, nor a matter of more difficult comprehension, that the polyp should form coral, than that the quadruped should form its bones, or the mollusk its shell. The processes are similar, and so the result: in each case it is a simple animal secretion, a formation of stony matter from the aliment which the animal receives, produced by certain parts of the animal fitted for this secreting process. This power of secretion is the first and most common of those that belong to living tissues; and though differing in different organs according to their end or function, it is all one process, in nature or cause, whether in the animalcule or in man. Coral is never, therefore, an agglutination of grains made by the handiwork of the many-armed polyps; for it is no more an act of labor than bone-making in ourselves. And again, it is not a collection of cells into which the coral animals may withdraw for concealment, any more than the skeleton of a dog is its house or cell; for every part of the coral of a polyp in most reef-making species is enclosed *within* the polyp, where it was formed by the secreting process.

A good idea of a coral polyp may be had from comparison with the garden aster; for the likeness in external form and delicacy of coloring is singularly close. The aster consists of a tinted disk bordered with one or more series of petals; and in exact analogy, the polyp flower, in its most common form, has a disk often richly colored, fringed around with petal-like organs called tentacles. Below the disk, in contrast with the slender pedicel of the plant, there is a stout cylindrical pedicel or body, often as broad as the disk itself, and usually not much longer, which contains the *stomach* and internal cavity of the polyp; and the *mouth*, which opens into the stomach, is placed at the centre of the disk. Here, then, the flower animal and the garden flower diverge in character, the difference being required by the different modes of nutrition in the two kingdoms of nature.

There are many species of polyps, which have all the external and internal characters of coral polyps, yet secrete no lime or coral. Our descriptions of structure may be best drawn from them, and afterwards the single peculiarity of the coral-making polyp—its secretion of coral—will come under consideration. The species here referred to are called *actiniæ* in science, in allusion to the radiated or aster-like flower which forms the summit of the animal. There is the same allusion in the common appellation *sea anemone.* The richest anemones, daisies, and tulips of our gardens would not rival them in beauty, neither will they exceed them in the size of their flowers; for a breadth of two and three inches is common. The polyps here alluded to, along with the coral polyps allied, constitute the order or division of zoophytes called *actinoidea.*

The actiniæ are entirely fleshy, and usually live attached by their lower extremity to the submerged rocks of the shores. The mouth, at the centre of the flower-like disk forming the summit of the animal, is a simple opening without teeth or appendages of any kind. The tentacles—the petals of the flower—are tubular organs, and communicate internally with the interior cavity of the animal. The animal contracts, when disturbed, and conceals the flower by rolling inward over it the margin bearing the tentacles; and in this state it seems like a lifeless lump of animal matter. Left quiet for a while, it again expands and appears as before. This expansion is produced by receiving water into the interior from without, mostly through the mouth, and thus filling the tentacles and swelling out its fleshy body. They are generally found expanded, with the mouth wide open to receive their prey. As they are fixed to the rocks, they must wait for their food to come to them. When a crab, shell fish, or any thing alive, within the capabilities of their bodies, comes within reach, they usually secure it by closing upon the victim the tentacles, (which often have a stinging power,) and pushing it into the mouth. In many species the tentacles are too short to aid in capturing food; and they can then subserve only the purpose of aerating the blood—a function in which all parts of the body are more or less concerned.

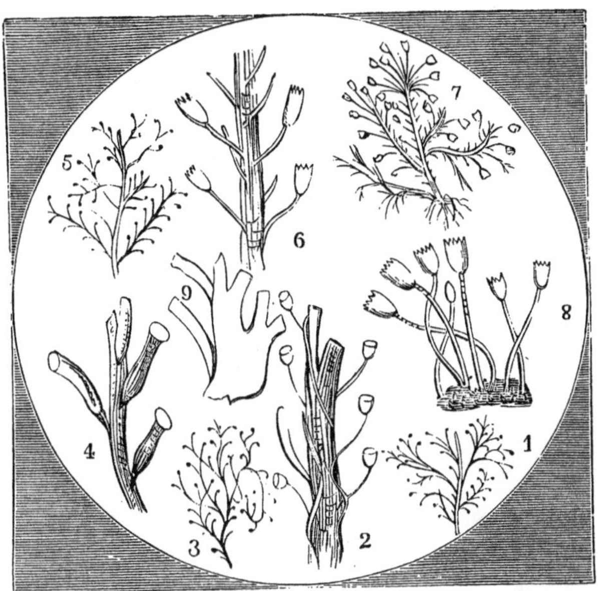

Specimens of corals and coral polyps. Figure 1. A Small branch of *Campanularia integra*, natural size. 2. Portion of do., magnified, exhibiting six cup-shaped polyps. 3. *C. dumosa*, nat. size. 4. Portion of do., magnified, exhibiting four polyps. 5. *C. verticillata*, nat. size. 6. Portion of do., magnified. 7. *C. volubilis*, nat. size. 8. Portion of do., magnified. 9. Outline of a piece of coral.

Specimens of corals and coral polyps. Figure 1. A piece of coral, natural size, with polyps projecting from its surface. 2. One of the polyps magnified. 3. The same partly withdrawn into its cell. 4. *Corynactis vividis*. 5. Extremity of branch of *Pavonaria*, nat. size. 7. Side view of one of the polyps from do., magnified. 6. Tentacula of the polyp, magnified. 8, 9. A different species of the polyp, the *Tubularia gracialis*, magnified. 10, 11. A head of the *Tubularia indivisa* magnified. 12. Fragment of *Plumularia*, magnified.

The interior of the actinia contains a cylindrical stomach suspended from the disk, which opens at bottom into the general cavity of the body. This general cavity, below the stomach and around it, is divided into compartments by radiating fleshy lamellæ, the larger of which, in their upper part, connect the stomach with the sides of the animal. The most important function of these lamellæ is that of reproduction, some being spermatic, and the others bearing clusters of ova. These ova leave the body by passing out through the stomach and mouth; but in many instances this does not take place till the young animal has proceeded from them. The refuse from the food after digestion in the stomach is also ejected by the mouth, as this is the only opening to the alimentary cavity. Other excrementitious matters, separated on the final elaboration of the chyle and its assimilation, may escape through the sides of the animal, the openings at the extremities of the tentacles, or in general by whatever pores or passages water may be ejected in the contraction of the animal.

One of the most singular peculiarities of polyps is their ready restoration of a lost part. Even a fragment will go on to complete the entire animal again. As with the fabled hydra of old, the knife is used but to multiply, for every section becomes a new animal.

In all the points mentioned in the description here given, the polyp of ordinary coral and the actinia are identical.

There is one mode of reproduction which, although having no necessary connection with coral secretions, belongs almost exclusively to coral polyps. This is *reproduction by buds;* and the process is so similar to the production of buds in vegetation, that a remembrance of the latter will aid much in conceiving of it. The bud generally commences as a slight prominence on the side of the parent: the prominence enlarges, and soon a circle of tentacles grows out, with a mouth at the centre; enlargement goes on, till the young finally equals the parent in size. Thus, by budding, a compound group is commenced; and it is evident that if the parent and the new polyp go on budding again, and so on, the compound group may continue to enlarge. This is the fact in nature. The polyps, one and all, continue propagating by buds until in some instances thousands, or hundreds of thousands, have proceeded from a single one, and the colony has spread to a large size. Such are the madrepora and astræa. There are modifications of this process, analogous to those in vegetation, but we need not dwell upon them in this place.

It is obvious that the connection of the polyps in such a compound group must be of the most intimate kind. The several polyps have separate mouths and tentacles, and separate stomachs; but beyond this, there is no individual property. They coalesce, or are one, by intervening tissues, and there is a free circulation of fluids through the many pores or lacunes. The zoophyte is like a living sheet of animal matter, fed and nourished by numerous mouths and as many stomachs. In some species the coalescence is confined to the lower half of the polyps, or to a still less part; and in this case the animals project above the general living surface. Polyps thus clustered, spreading at summit a star of tentacles, constitute the flowering zoophytes of coral reefs.

Those coral animals which do not bud are to all external appearance true actiniæ. The existence of coral in the living coral zoophyte is nowhere apparent, and would not be suspected if not previously known; for, as before stated, it is wholly internal, and the visible exterior is the fleshy skin of the polyp.

We have already remarked on the general nature of coral secretions. These secretions, it should be further observed, increase within simultaneously with growth, and every new animal adds to those previously formed. They go on throughout the sides and base of each polyp, excepting generally the exterior skin, as above stated; and the whole forms a calcareous framework penetrated by the animal tissues, some of these tissues corresponding to and occupying the cellules of the corallum, and others penetrating the solid parts in minute ramifications. Coral is also secreted between the radiating fleshy lamellæ of the internal cavity of the polyp, producing the radiated calcareous lamellæ which constitute the star of a cell. In the corallum of a madrepora or an astræa, each surface cell or star belonged to a separate polyp, and the star was formed as here explained.

It would lead to too long a digression from the main topic before us to explain the principles upon which the forms of zoophytes depend. We may briefly allude to the principal varieties of form proceeding from the budding process, and to a single point in their mode of growth, upon which much of their importance in reef-making depends.

Zoophytes imitate nearly every variety of vegetation. Trees of coral are well known; and although not emulating in size the oaks of our forests—for they do not exceed six or eight feet in height—they are gracefully branched, and the whole surface blooms with coral polyps in place of leaves and flowers. Shrubbery, tufts of rushes, beds of pinks, and feathery mosses are most exactly imitated. Many species spread out in broad leaves or folia, and resemble some large-leaved plant just unfolding: when alive, the surface of each leaf is covered with the polyp flowers. The cactus, the lichen clinging to the rock, and the fungus in all its varieties, have their representatives as regards external form. Besides these forms imitating vegetation, there are gracefully modelled vases, some of which are three or four feet in diameter, made up of a network of branches and branchlets, and sprigs of flowers. There are also solid coral domes among the vases and shrubbery, occasionally ten or even twenty feet in diameter, whose regularly arched surface is gorgeously decked with polyp stars of purple and emerald green.

All the many shapes proceed in each instance from a single germ, which grows and buds under a few simple laws of development, and thus gives origin either to the branch, the broad leaf, the column, or the hemisphere.

But the more massy forms would not exist, and others would

be of diminutive size, were it not for a peculiar mode of growth which characterizes most coral zoophytes.

Life and death are here in concurrent or parallel progress —a condition favored by the existence of coral secretions. In some instances a simple polyp, while growing at top and constantly lengthening itself upward, is dying at its lower extremity, leaving the base of the coral bare, and destitute of any living tissues. The polyp thus continues rising in height, and death progresses below at the same rate, till at last the live polyp may be at the extremity of a coral stem many times its own length.

In species which bud and form large groups, the same operation takes place. In some instances the summit polyp or polyps bud and grow, while at a certain distance below the summit the work of death is going on, and polyps are gradually disappearing. There is thus a certain interval of life, the length of which interval is different for different species. There are zoophytes which grow to a height of several feet, and still only the upper one or two inches are living. The recent polyps at the top of the column are active with life and vigorous in reproduction, while the more aged below, having reached the fixed limits of their existence, are disappearing. The enduring coral remains, and constitutes the basement or stage of action for future generations of polyps.

But this death is not in progress alone at the base of the column or branch. Generally the *whole interior* of a corallum is dead—a result of the same process, as just explained. Thus a madrepora, although the branch may be an inch in diameter, is alive only to a depth of a line or two, the growing polyps of the surface having progressively died at their lower or inner extremity as they increased outward.

The large domes of astræas, which have been stated to attain sometimes a diameter of ten or twenty feet, and are alive over the whole surface, owing to a symmetrical and unlimited mode of budding, are nothing but lifeless coral throughout the interior. Could the living portion be separated, it would form a hemispherical shell of polyps, in most species about half an inch thick. In some porites of the same size, the whole mass is lifeless, excepting the exterior for a sixth of an inch in depth.

With such a mode of increase, there is no necessary limit to the growth of zoophytes. The rising column may grow upward indefinitely, until it nears the surface of the sea, when death ensues simply from exposure, and not from any failure in its powers of life. The huge domes may enlarge till the same exposure just mentioned causes the death of the summit, and leaves only the sides to grow, which may increase indefinitely. Moreover, it is evident that if the land supporting the growing coral were very gradually sinking, the upward increase of the coral might still be without limit.

There is hence sufficient means provided for the production of coral material for islands, however numerous. These humble ministers of creative power might, without other attributes than those they now possess, have even laid the foundations of continents, and covered them with mountain ranges. This remark requires no limitation, if we allow the requisite time, and connect with the power of growth such other agencies, soon to be explained, as have been at work in the Pacific since the reefs were there in progress.

The death of the polyps about the base of a coral tree would expose it seemingly to immediate wear from the waters around it, and especially as the texture is usually porous. But nature is not without an expedient to prevent a catastrophe that would be destructive to a large part of growing zoophytes, and would prevent the indefinite increase just explained. The dead surface becomes the resting place of numberless small incrusting species of corals, besides nullipores, serpulas, and some mollusks. In many instances the lichen-like nullipore grows at the same rate with the rate of death in the zoophyte, and keeps itself up to the very limit of the living part. The dead trunk of the forest becomes covered with lichens and fungi, or, in tropical climes, with other foliage and various foreign flowers; so among the coral productions of the sea, there are other forms of life which replace the dying polyp. The process of wear is thus entirely prevented.

The older polyps, before death, often increase their coral secretions within, filling the pores occupied by the tissues, and rendering the corallum more solid; and this is another means by which the trees of coral growth, though of slender form, are increased in strength and endurance.

The facility with which polyps repair a wound aids in carrying forward the results above described. The breaking of a branch is no serious injury to a zoophyte. There is often some degree of sensibility apparent throughout a clump, even when of considerable size, and the shock, therefore, may occasion the polyps to close. But in an hour, or perhaps much less time, their tentacles will have again expanded; and such as were torn by the fracture will be in the process of complete restoration to their former size and powers. The fragment broken off, dropping in a favorable place, would become the germ of another coral plant, its base cementing, by means of coral secretions, to the rock on which it might rest; or if still in contact with any part of the parent tree, it would be reunited and continue to grow as before. The coral zoophyte may be levelled by transported masses swept over by the waves; yet, like the trodden sod, it sprouts again, and continues to grow and flourish as before. The sod, however, has roots which are still unhurt; while the zoophyte, which may be dead at base, has a root—a source or centre of life—in every polyp that blossoms over its surface. Each animal might live and grow if separated from the rest, and would ultimately produce a mature zoophyte.

We close this review of the characters of coral animals, by alluding briefly to one division of the actinoidea not yet touched upon, and also to the hydroidea and bryozoa, which are likewise coral-making animals.

The polyps of the group among the actinoidea, called alcyonacea, differ from those which have been occupying us, in having but eight tentacles, and these are fringed with minute papillæ. The organ-pipe coral (tubipora) is of this kind. When expanded in the sea, a clump resembles a bed of pinks, or looks like a lilac cluster that had been dropped in the water; and this resemblance extends to color and size as well as form.

Some of these zoophytes secrete lime and form a tube; and of this kind is the tubipora. Others secrete only scattered granules of lime through the tissues; and still others are fleshy throughout. Many of them, besides forming granular calcareous secretions within the body of the polyp, give origin to a horny secretion at base, analogous to the epidermic secretions (hair, nails) of other animals; and this secretion receiving constant additions from the polyps as they are successively budded out, forms the axis of the growing branch. Of this character is the horny axis of the gorgonia or sea fan, which was long taken for a vegetable production. The crust which covers the axis consists of united polyps, which expand over its surface; and when expanded, each branch becomes a spike of flowers.

The hydroidea constitute the second grand division of zoophytes, corresponding in rank with actinoidea. While the actinoidea have a radiated interior cavity with internal organs of reproduction, and eject their ovules through the mouth, the hydroidea have greater simplicity of structure—the internal cavity being a simple tube, without organs of reproduction, and the ovules pullulating, (or growing out,) singly or in clusters, from the sides of an animal. The polyps are with few exceptions quite minute, and the zoophytes act no important part in reef making. A coronet of tentacles surrounds the mouth, as in the actiniæ, though somewhat different in character.

This order includes the hydræ, the sertulariæ, and the tubulariæ. Some species form thready tufts and plumes of extreme delicacy, and others (the hydræ) are simple polyps. The fine branchlets of the feathery species consist, when dead, of one or two series of microscopic cells; and when alive each cell is the site of a minute flower animal. The hydra, an animal a line or less in length, consists of a tubular body, with a mouth at one extremity surrounded by a circle of tentacles; and the structure of the animal is so simple that it may be turned inside out, and still live and eat; it may be cut into forty or more parts, and from the dissected body will grow as many distinct hydræ.

The bryozoa are other coral-making species; but they are related to certain mollusks called ascidiæ, rather than to zoophytes. In habit and size they much resemble the hydroidea. From a minute cabin-like cell, they extend a circlet of slender arms or tentacles, and expand into a delicate goblet-shape flower, seldom over a line in diameter. These polyps differ both from the actinoidea and hydroidea in having two extremities to the alimentary canal—an anus, as well as a mouth; the intestine curves around and terminates in the disk. They are widely removed from true zoophytes, both by this character, and also by having the tentacles furnished with vibratile cilia—that is, minute appendages resembling short hairs, which are kept in nearly constant vibration.

Some species of bryozoa form thin crusts over rocks or sea weeds, consisting of united cells, scarcely distinguishable unless magnified. The coralla of other species are branching or thin foliaceous; and these also consist of series of minute cells.

The *texture* of calcareous corals is in general quite porous or cellular. Small stars or rounded depressions are scattered over the surface, and sometimes these stars form the centres of small prominences, called calicles, (little cups.) Besides these polyp cells, which mark the position each of a separate polyp, there are pores or cellules penetrating the texture of the coral mass; yet in some zoophytes, the coral secretions continue increasing in the animal till the pores are almost or quite obliterated, and the texture is nearly compact, the polyp cells alone remaining. In many species, wherever there are concavities of much depth in the surface of a zoophyte, the coral of these concavities is looser or more spongy than elsewhere, for the reason, apparently, that the polyps in such parts have a poorer chance for securing food and fresh portions of water.

In the gorgoniæ, and other species forming a distinct axis to the branches, this axis is solid, without a trace of a cell, and usually with faint evidences of a concentric structure. It is thus that the red coral of commerce, used in jewelry, differs from the madrepore or common white coral; it is the *axis* of a species of corallium; and the polyps constituted a layer about it, in the same manner as the polyps of a gorgonia cover the horny axis of these species.

In *hardness*, the common calcareous corals are a little above ordinary limestone or marble, the degree being represented in the mineralogical scale of Mohs by 3.5 to 4, while, in limestone, it is about 3. The ringing sound given when coral is struck with a hammer indicates this superior hardness. It is a common error of old date to suppose that coral, when first removed from the water, is soft, and afterwards hardens on exposure. In fact, there is scarcely an appreciable difference; the live coral has a slimy feel in the fingers; but if washed clear of the animal matter, it is found to be quite firm. The waters with which it is penetrated may contain a trace of lime in solution, which evaporates on drying, and adds slightly to the strength of the coral; but the change is hardly appreciable. A branched madrepore rings, on being struck, when first collected; and a blow in any part puts in hazard every branch throughout it, on account of its elasticity and brittleness.

The common reef corals, of which the branching madrepora and the massive astræas are good examples, consist almost wholly of carbonate of lime—the same ingredient which constitutes ordinary limestone. In a hundred parts, ninety to ninety-six parts are of this constituent; of the remainder, there are three to eight parts of organic matter, with some earthy ingredients, amounting in certain species to two parts, though often less than one.

The horny corals (axes of gorgoniæ and antipathi) were found by Hatchett to have nearly the constitution of ordinary horn.

The sea water and the ordinary food of the polyps are evidently the source from which the ingredients of coral are obtained. As coral is an animal secretion, there is no good reason for the surprise with which this subject is sometimes approached. The same powers of elaboration which exist in other animals belong to polyps; for this function, as we have remarked, is the lowest attribute of vitality.

There are four different kinds of coral formations in the Pacific and Indian Oceans, namely, lagoon islands or atolls, encircling reefs, barrier reefs, and coral fringes. They are all nearly confined to the tropical regions; the atolls to the Pacific and Indian Oceans alone.

An atoll or lagoon island * consists of a chaplet or ring of coral, enclosing a lagoon or portion of the ocean in its centre. The average breadth of the part of the ring above the surface of the sea is about a quarter of a mile, oftener less, and it seldom rises higher than from six to ten or twelve feet above the waves. Hence the lagoon islands are not discernible, even at a very small distance, unless when they are covered with cocoa nut, palm, or the pandanus, which is frequently the case. On the outer side this ring or circlet shelves down to the distance of a hundred or two hundred yards from its edge, so that the sea gradually deepens to twenty-five fathoms, beyond which the sides plunge at once into the unfathomable depths of the ocean, with a more rapid descent than the cone of any volcano. Even at the small distance of some hundred yards no bottom has been found with a sounding line a mile and a half long. All the coral at a moderate depth below water is alive—all above is dead, being the detritus of the living part, washed up by the surf, which is so tremendous on the windward side of the tropical islands of the Pacific and

* See engraving opposite page 96.

Indian Oceans, that it is often heard miles off, and is frequently the first warning to seamen of their approach to an atoll.

On the lagoon side, where the water is calm, the bounding ring or reef shelves into it by a succession of ledges, also of living coral, though not of the same species with those which build the exterior wall and the foundations of the whole ring. The perpetual change of water brought into contact with the external coral by the breakers probably supplies them with more food than they could obtain in a quieter sea, which may account for their more luxuriant growth. At the same time they deprive the whole of the coral in the interior of the most nourishing part of their food, because the still water in the lagoon, being supplied from the exterior by openings in the ring, ceases to produce the hardier corals; and species of more delicate forms, and of much slower growth, take their place. The depth of the lagoon varies, in different atolls, from twenty to fifty fathoms, the bottom being partly detritus and partly live coral. By the growth of the coral some few of the lagoons have been filled up; but the process is very slow, from the causes assigned, and also because there are marine animals that feed on the living coral, and prevent its indefinite growth. In all departments of nature the exuberant increase of any one class is checked and limited by others. The coral is of the most varied and delicate structure, and of the most beautiful tints; dark brown, vivid green, rich purple, pink, deep blue, peach color, yellow, with dazzling white, contrasted with deep shadows, shine through the limpid water; while fish of the most gorgeous hues swim among the branching corals, which are of many different kinds, though all combine in the structure of these singular islands. In fine, these ocean depths exhibit the scene so vividly portrayed by Percival:—

"THE CORAL GROVE.

"Deep in the waves is a coral grove,
Where the purple mullet and goldfish rove,
Where the seaflower spreads its leaves of blue,
That never are wet with the falling dew,

But in bright and changeful beauty shine,
Far down in the deep and glassy brine.
The floor is of sand like the mountain drift,
And the pearl shells spangle the flinty snow;
From coral rocks the sea plants lift
Their boughs, where the tides and billows flow;
The water is calm and still below,
For the winds and the waves are absent there,
And the sands are bright as the stars that glow
In the motionless fields of upper air:
There with its waving blade of green,
The seaflag waves through the silent water,
And the crimson leaf of the dulse is seen
To blush like a banner bathed in slaughter.
There, with a light and easy motion,
The fan coral sweeps through the clear deep sea;
And the yellow and scarlet tufts of ocean
Are bending like corn on the upland lea;
And life, in rare and beautiful forms,
Is sporting amidst those bowers of stone."

Lagoon islands are sometimes circular, but more frequently oval or irregular in their form. Sometimes they are solitary or in groups, but they occur most frequently in elongated archipelagoes, with the atolls elongated in the same direction. The grouping of atolls bears a perfect analogy to the grouping of the archipelagoes of ordinary islands.

The size of these fairy rings of the ocean varies from two to ninety miles in diameter, and islets are frequently formed on the coral rings by the washing up of the detritus, for they are so low that the waves break over them in high tides or storms. They have openings or channels in their circuit, generally on the leeward side, where the tide enters, and by these, ships may sail into the lagoons, which are excellent harbors; and even on the surface of the circlet or reef itself there are occasionally boat channels between islets.

Dangerous Archipelago, lying east of the Society Islands, is one of the most remarkable assemblages of atolls in the Pacific Ocean. There are eighty of them, generally in a circular form, surrounding very deep lagoons, and separated from each other by profound depths. The reefs or rings are about half a mile wide, and seldom rise more than ten feet above the edge of the surf, which beats upon them with such violence that it may be heard at the distance of eight miles; and yet on that side the coral insects build more vigorously, and vegetation thrives better, than on the other.

The Caroline Archipelago, the largest of all, lies north of the equator, and extends its atolls in sixty groups over one thousand miles. Many are of great size, and all are beaten by a tempestuous sea and occasional hurricanes. The atolls in the Pacific Ocean and China Sea are beyond enumeration. Though less frequent in the Indian Ocean, none are more interesting, or afford more perfect specimens of this peculiar formation, than the Maldive and Laccadive Archipelagoes, both nearly parallel to the coast of Malabar, and elongated in that direction. The former is four hundred and seventy miles long and about fifty miles broad, with atolls arranged in a double row, separated by an unfathomable sea, into which their sides descend with more than ordinary rapidity. The largest atoll is eighty-eight miles long, and somewhat less than twenty broad; Suadiva, the next in size, is forty-four miles by twenty-three, with a large lagoon in its centre, to which there is access by forty-two openings. There are inhabited islets on most of the chaplets or rings, not higher than twenty feet, while the reefs themselves are nowhere more than six feet above the surge.

The Laccadives run to the north of this archipelago in a double line of nearly circular atolls, on which are low inhabited islets.

Encircling reefs differ in no respect from atoll reefs, except that they have one or more islands in their lagoon. They commonly form a ring round mountainous islands, at a distance of two or three miles from the shore, rising on the outside from a very deep ocean, and separated from the land by a lagoon or channel two or three hundred feet deep. These reefs surround the submarine base of the island, and, rising by a steep ascent to the surface, they encircle the island itself. The Caroline Archipelago exhibits good examples of this structure in the encircled islands of Hogoleu and Siniavin; the narrow ring or encircling reef of the former is one hundred and thirty-five miles in its very irregular circuit, on which are a vast number of islets; six or eight islands rise to a considerable height from its lagoon, which is so deep, and the opening to it so large, that a frigate might sail into it. The encircling reef of Siniavin is narrow and irregular, and its lagoon is so nearly filled by a lofty island, that it leaves only a strip of water round it from two to five miles wide and thirty fathoms deep.

Tahiti, the largest of the Society group, is another instance of an encircled island of the most beautiful kind; it rises in mountains seven thousand feet high, with only a narrow plain along the shore, and, except where cleared for cultivation, it is covered with forests of cocoa nut, palms, bananas, bread fruit, and other productions of a tropical climate. The lagoon, which encompasses it like an enormous moat, is thirty fathoms deep, and is hemmed in from the ocean by a coral band of the usual kind, at a distance varying from half a mile to three miles.

Barrier reefs are of precisely the same structure as the two preceding classes, from which they only differ in their position with regard to the land. A barrier reef off the north-east coast of the continent of Australia is the grandest coral formation existing. Rising at once from an unfathomable ocean, it extends one thousand miles along the coast, with a breadth varying from two hundred yards to a mile, and at an average distance of from twenty to thirty miles from the shore, increasing in some places to sixty and even seventy miles. The great arm of the sea included between it and the land is nowhere less than ten, occasionally sixty fathoms deep, and is safely navigable throughout its whole length, with a few transverse openings by which ships can enter. The reef is really twelve hundred miles long, because it stretches nearly across Torres Straits. It is interrupted off the southern coast of New Guinea by muddy water, which destroys the coral animals, probably from some great river on that island. There are also extensive barrier reefs on the Islands of Louisiade and New Caledonia, which are exactly opposite to the great Australian reef; and as atolls stud that part of the Pacific which lies between them, it is called the Coralline Sea. The rolling of the billows along the great Australian reef has been admirably described. "The long ocean swell, being suddenly impeded by this barrier, lifted itself in one great continuous ridge of deep-blue water, which, curling over, fell on the edge of the reef in an unbroken cataract of dazzling white foam. Each line of breaker ran often one or two miles in length, with not a perceptible gap in its continuity. There was a simple grandeur and display of power and beauty in this scene that rose even to sublimity. The unbroken roar of the surf, with its regular pulsation of thunder, as each succeeding swell fell first on the outer edge of the reef, was almost deafening, yet so deep toned as not to interfere with the slightest nearer and sharper sound. Both the sound and sight were such as to impress the spectator with the consciousness of standing in the presence of an overwhelming majesty and power."

Coral reefs are distinct from all the foregoing; they are merely fringes of coral along the margin of a shore, and, as they line the shore itself, they have no lagoons. A vast extent of coast, both on the continents and islands, is fringed by these reefs, and, as they frequently surround shoals, they are very dangerous.

Lagoon islands are the work of various species of coral animals; but those particular zoophytes which build the external wall, the foundation and support of the whole ring or reef, are most vigorous when most exposed to the breakers; they cannot exist at a greater depth than twenty-five or thirty fathoms at most, and die immediately when left dry; yet the coral wall descends precipitously to unfathomable depths; and although the whole of it is not the work of these animals, yet the perpendicular thickness of the coral is known to be very great, extending hundreds of feet below the depth at which these polypi cease to live. From an extensive survey of the coralline seas of the tropics, Mr. Darwin has found an explanation of these singular phenomena in the instability of the crust of the earth.

Since there are certain proofs that large areas of the dry land are gradually rising, and others sinking down, so the bottom of the ocean is not exempt from the general change that is slowly bringing about a new state of things; and as there is evidence, on multitudes of the volcanic islands in the Pacific, of a rise in certain parts of the basis of the ocean, so the lagoon islands indicate a subsidence in others — changes arising from the expansion and contraction of the strata under the bed of the ocean.

There are strong reasons for believing that a continent once occupied a great part of the tropical Pacific, some part of which subsided by slow and imperceptible degrees. As portions of it gradually sank down below the surface of the deep, the tops of mountains and table lands would remain as islands of different magnitude and elevation, and would form archipelagoes elongated in the direction of the mountain chains. Now, the coral animal which constructs the outward wall and mass of the reefs, never builds laterally, and cannot exist at a greater depth than twenty-five or thirty fathoms. Hence, if it began to lay the foundation of its reef on the submerged flanks of an island, it would be obliged to build its wall upwards in proportion as the island sank down, so that at length a lagoon would be formed between it and the land. As the subsidence continued, the lagoon would increase, the island would diminish, and the base of the coral reef would sink deeper and deeper, while the animal would always keep its top just below the surface of the ocean, till at length the island would entirely disappear, and a perfect atoll would be left. If the island were mountainous, each peak would form a separate island in the lagoon, and the encircled islands would have different forms, which the reefs would follow continuously. This theory perfectly explains the appearances of the lagoon islands and barrier reefs, the continuity of the reef, the islands in the middle of the lagoons, the different distances of the reefs from them, and the forms of the archipelago, so exactly similar to the archipelagoes of ordinary islands, all of which are but the tops of submerged mountain chains, and generally partake of their elongated forms.

Every intermediate form between an atoll and an encircling reef exists: New Caledonia is a link between them. A reef runs along the north-west coast of that island four hundred miles, and for many leagues never approaches within eight miles of its shore, and the distance increases to sixteen miles near the southern extremity. At the other end the reefs are continued on each side one hundred and fifty miles beyond the submarine prolongation of the land, marking the former extent of the island. In the lagoon of Keeling Atoll, situate in the Indian Ocean, six hundred miles south of Sumatra, many fallen trees and a ruined storehouse show that it has subsided: these movements take place during the earthquakes at Sumatra, which are also felt in this atoll. Violent earthquakes have lately been felt at Vanikora, (celebrated for the wreck of La Pérouse,) a lofty island of the Queen Charlotte group, with an encircling reef in the western part of the South Pacific, and on which there are marks of recent subsidence. Other proofs are not wanting of this great movement in the beds of the Pacific and Indian Oceans.

The extent of the atoll formations, including under this name the encircling reefs, is enormous. In the Pacific, from the southern end of Low Archipelago to the northern extremity of Marshall or Radick Archipelago, a distance of forty-five hundred miles, and many degrees of latitude in breadth, atolls alone rise above the ocean. The same may be said of the space in the Indian Ocean, between Saya de Matha and the end of the Laccadives, which include twenty-five degrees of latitude—such are the enormous areas that have been, and probably still are, slowly subsiding. Other spaces of great extent may also be mentioned, as the large archipelago of the Carolinas, that in the Coralline Sea, off the north-west coast of Australia, and an extensive one in the China Sea.

The following beautiful lines, descriptive of corals and coral building, are from the pen of G. F. Richardson, Esq., the English poet and geologist: —

"THE CORALS.

"Beneath the realm which the waves o'erwhelm,
In the seas of the torrid zone,
Our ancient race have a dwelling-place,
In a world that is all our own.

Earth boasts no spots like the fairy grots
Where we build our sparry cell;
Nor can its bowers produce such flowers
As in depths of ocean dwell.

And our forms so strange we ever change,
As over the deep we roam;
And our varied hue is ever new,
As we vary our ocean home.

In tranquil calms we wave like palms,
Or bend like the drooping willow;
Or we climb to the verge of the foaming surge,
And dash to the winds its billow.

In peaceful haunts, like tender plants
We twine our fragile forms;
Or we build a rock to the tempest's shock,
That mocks its fiercest storms.

And we rear the walls of those marble halls
As a precipice high and steep,
Till a new-found isle is seen to smile
Like a beacon o'er the deep.

By viewless hands those new-born lands
Are strewn with blessings rife;
Till man appears, and claims the spheres
To being raised and life.

And we join the piles of these fossil isles
Till they spread from shore to shore;
And we build from the caves of the ocean waves
A world unknown before.

Then say, proud man, how poor the plan
 Of thy pyramids, castles, and towers;
How vain the boasts of thy mightiest hosts
 Or their labors, compared with ours.

Though such our lot, yet we are — what,
 In the scale of being vast?
The meanest germs of life's poor worms,
 The lowest and the last!

Yet though obscure, and low, and poor,
 And lost in distance dim,
We still can raise our Maker's praise,
 And pour our thanks to him."

The coral island in its best condition is but a miserable residence for man. There is poetry in every feature; but the natives find this a poor substitute for the bread fruit and yams of more favored lands. The cocoa nut and pandanus are, in general, the only products of the vegetable kingdom afforded for their sustenance, and fish and crabs from the reefs their only animal food. Scanty too is the supply; and infanticide is resorted to in self-defence, where but a few years would otherwise overstock the half a dozen square miles of which their little world consists.

Yet there are more comforts than might be expected on a land of so limited an extent — without rivers, without hills, in the midst of salt water, with the most elevated point but ten feet above high tide, and no part more than three hundred yards from the ocean. Though the soil is light and the surface often strewed with blocks of coral, there is a dense covering of vegetation to shade the native villages from a tropical sun. The cocoa nut, the tree of a thousand uses, grows luxuriantly on the coral-made land, after it has emerged from the ocean; and the scanty dresses of the natives, their drinking vessels and other utensils, mats, cordage, fishing lines and oil, besides food, drink, and building material, are all supplied from it. The pandanus or screw pine flourishes well, and is exactly fitted for such regions: as it enlarges and spreads its branches, one prop after another grows out from the trunk, and plants itself in the ground; and by this means its base is widened and the growing tree supported. The fruit, a large ovoidal mass, made up of oblong dry seed, diverging from a centre, each near two cubic inches in size, affords a sweetish husky article of food, which, though little better than prepared corn stalks, admits of being stored away for use when other things fail. The extensive reefs abound in fish, which are easily captured, and the natives, with wooden hooks, often bring in larger kinds from the deep waters. From such resources a population of ten thousand persons is supported on the single Island of Taputeouea, whose whole habitable area does not exceed six square miles. There are a few islands better supplied with vegetable food, though the above statements are literally true of a large majority.

Water is usually to be found in sufficient quantities for the use of the natives, although the land is so low and flat. They dig wells five to ten feet deep in any part of the dry islets, and generally obtain a constant supply. These wells are sometimes fenced around with special care; and the houses of the villages, as at Fakaafo, are often clustered about them. The Tarawan Islands are generally provided with a supply sufficient for bathing, and each native takes his morning bath in fresh water—esteemed by them a great luxury.

The only source of this water is the rains, which, percolating through the loose surface, settle upon the hardened coral rock that forms the basis of the island. As the soil is white, or nearly so, it receives heat but slowly, and there is consequently but little evaporation of the water that is once absorbed.

An occasional log drifts to their shores, and at some of the more isolated atolls, where the natives are ignorant of any land but the spot they inhabit, they are deemed direct gifts from a propitiated deity. These drift logs were noticed by Kotzebue, at the Marshall Islands, and he remarked also that they often brought stones in their roots. Similar facts have been observed at the Tarawan group, and also at Enderby's Island and elsewhere.

The stones at the Tarawan Islands are generally basaltic, and they are highly valued for whetstones, pestles, and hatchets. The logs are claimed by the chiefs for canoes. Some of the logs on Enderby's Island were forty feet long, and four in diameter.

The language of the natives indicates their poverty, as well as the limited productions and unvarying features of the land. All words like those for "mountain," "hill," "river," and many of the implements of their ancestors, as well as the trees and other vegetation of the land from which they are derived, are lost to them; and as words are but signs for ideas, they have fallen off in general intelligence. It would be an interesting inquiry for the philosopher, to what extent a race of men placed in such circumstances are capable of mental improvement. Perhaps the query might be best answered by another: How many of the various arts of civilized life could exist in a land where shells are the only cutting instruments — the plants in all but twenty-nine in number — but a single mineral — quadrupeds none, with the exception of foreign mice — fresh water barely enough for household purposes — no streams, nor mountains, nor hills? How much of the poetry or literature of Europe would be intelligible to persons whose ideas had expanded only to the limits of a coral island — who had never conceived of a surface of land above half a mile in breadth — of a slope higher than a beach — of a change of seasons beyond a variation in the prevalence of rains? What elevation in morals should be expected upon a contracted islet, so readily over-peopled that threatened starvation drives to infanticide, and tends to cultivate the extremest selfishness? Assuredly there is not a more unfavorable spot for moral or intellectual development in the wide world than the coral island, with all its beauty of grove and lake.

CHAPTER VI.

MOUNTAINS. — PERILOUS ADVENTURES OF TRAVELLERS IN ASCENDING HIGH MOUNTAINS. — SNOW MOUNTAINS. — ELEVATED SNOW PLAINS OF NORWAY.

THE term "mountain" is used with a very equivocal meaning, being applied alike to single eminences and to an entire group. It denominates, also, in one country, elevations which, in another district abounding with those of a superior class, would be regarded as mere hillocks. It has been proposed to confine the term to eminences ranging a thousand feet and upwards above the general surface land, and to regard those which are below that standard as simple hills or slopes. The slighter acclivities, whether crowned with grove and forest, whether planted with vegetable productions by the cultivating hand of man, or left to the natural grasses, form the most pleasing features of the soil; while the loftier projections of the superficies, stamped with an air of dignity, and indicating an upheaving power of irresistible might in their construction, present to the eye a thousand imposing combinations. Fringed with the dark-green pine, and spotted with the lighter mosses, with naked heads, as if in reverence of an invisible Superior, the mountains captivate while impressing the imagination. They are specimens of the fine arts of nature, the gems of continents, wonderful examples of the diverse forms by which the ideas of beauty, majesty, and power may be expressed.

The high lands occur in isolation, or in groups, ridges, and chains. Groups of mountains have sometimes the appearance of elevations radiating from a central point where the height is the greatest, forming a kind of circular cluster; but clusters of very irregular form occur without any principal eminence. The most general arrangement of mountains is in chains and ridges; a ridge being simply an inferior chain. To this class those elevations belong which are so distributed as to form a kind of zone or band, the breadth bearing little proportion to the length; and whatever direction the zone may take, and whatever shape it may assume, — that of a straight line, an angle, or a curve, — it is said to constitute a chain. The term is not meant to signify an unbroken series of projections, answering to the appearance of a street in which the buildings, though diversified, are attached, but a series of parts, in many cases distinct, yet lying in the same general direction. Many chains consist of one grand central range, accompanied by two subordinate ranges of inferior elevation, one on each side, at a diverging distance from the main body, and sometimes closing up with it. Smaller chains frequently branch off from the main ridge in an angular direction, as the Apennines from the Alps, and minor branches shoot out from these, which are called spurs when their course is short. The highest points of a great chain are usually about the middle, as Chimborazo in the Andes, and Mont Blanc in the Alps; and the most elevated parts of a branch from the main ridge are at the points of junction with the parent stem. The first class chains have almost uniformly an abrupt descent on one side, and a gentler declivity on the other. This is the case with the Andes, the Alps, the Pyrenees, the mountains of Scandinavia, and the Ghauts of India. It was held by Berghaus that the western side of chains extending north and south is most abrupt, while it is the southern side that is so in the case of those running east and west. But the exceptions to this are numerous, and no general rule upon the point can be advanced, beyond one which applies to chains near the coast, which have their steepest sides fronting the ocean. Taurus, Atlas, and Lebanon present their most precipitous and craggy faces to the Mediterranean, and the Andes likewise to the Pacific. The great chains in general follow the direction in which the land of the continents where they are situated has its greatest extent. Thus the ranges which, with only a few breaks, stretch from the south-west coast of Europe to the north-east coast of Asia, traverse the old world in the line of its maximum longitude; and the Andes of South America, continued by the Stony Mountains of the north, travel through the new world in the direction of its greatest length. The course of subordinate chains, also, as of the Apennines in Italy, the Dofrafeld in Norway and Sweden, and the Ghauts in Hindùstan, corresponds with the general direction of these peninsulas.

The insulated mountains, or those which are apart from any group or chain, are not numerous. They are generally, though not always, either active or extinct volcanoes. The rock of Gibraltar, which rises up to the height of fifteen hundred feet from the level beach of the Mediterranean, the Peak of Teneriffe, and Mount Egmont in New Zealand, are fine specimens of this class. The latter is an extinct volcano, and may be seen from a vast distance, ascending above the line of perpetual snow. The mountain is in shape a perfect cone, situated on a projecting headland, about twenty miles from the coast. The neighborhood is one of the most fertile districts of New Zealand, and has been selected as the site of the settlement of New Plymouth, from whence the symmetrical form and white brow of Pouke-e-aupapa, the ancient name of Mount Egmont, forms a striking object.

The contour of mountains exhibits almost every variety of form, and their aspect changes as an observer extends his distance from them, lesser irregularities being lost in the general outline, and different colors becoming merged in a uniform shade. The appearance of solitary individual objects is generally conical; but others are circular, elliptical, or saddle-backed. The Table Mountain at the Cape of Good Hope has the shape of a gigantic altar. In the case of a number of contiguous mountains, their summits are often needle-shaped, or like the domes of Roman architecture. In many instances the entire mass resembles a vast wall, with battlements and towers, after the manner of an ancient fortress, and sometimes mountains appear piled upon each other, forming a succession of gigantic terraces. One of the most extraordinary mountains in its configuration is in the Mauritius, a volcanic region, and bears the name of Peter Botte. The name is derived from an unfortunate adventurer, who, according to tradition, after reaching the summit, perished in the descent. An enormous mass, of a globular shape, forms the head of the mountain. It rests upon a pedestal of rock, of a conical form, upwards of three hundred feet high, and overhangs it by several feet. At the bottom of the pedestal, a narrow strip of land runs out, about six feet broad and twenty yards long, on two sides of which a precipice goes down direct fifteen hundred feet to the plain, the other side being a very steep wooded gorge. The view from the narrow ledge, as may be imagined, is tremendous in the extreme, and the still ascending conical rock, with its overhanging head, seems secure enough from the intrusion of man. The Peter Botte has been usually considered inaccessible. Many endeavors to reach the top have been made without success; but the enterprise was at length effected in the year 1832, by the skill and daring of a party of British officers, who, after surmounting the uppermost block, spent the night immediately under it.

The internal structure of elevations, as well as their external shape, displays great diversities. In fact, their outward character has been determined in a great degree by the substances of which they are composed. The granite mountains are the loftiest upon the surface of the globe, and present the most rugged and broken aspect, with very precipitous sides. Those of gneiss and mica slate are not so wild and irregular, nor are their declivities so steep; and those composed of secondary formations — sandstone, limestone, and graywacke — are of inferior elevation compared with the former, and the declivities are more gentle. Humboldt has pointed out a striking difference between the great mountains of the eastern and western continents. Mont Blanc, and others of the higher Alps, lift their granite heads far above the clouds, and, with the Himalaya, form the loftiest points of the old world; but in America the newest flœtztrap or whinstone, which in Europe appears only in low mountains, or at the foot of those of great magnitude, covers the mightiest heights of the Andes. Chimborazo and Antisana are crowned by vast walls of porphyry, rising to the height of six or seven thousand feet; while basalt, which in the eastern continent has never been observed higher than four thousand feet, is, on the pinnacle of Pichincha, seen rearing aloft its crested steeps, like towers amidst the sky. Other secondary formations, as limestone, with its accompaniment of petrified shells and coal, are also found at greater heights in the new than in the old world, though the disproportion is not so remarkable.

The most elevated European sites are found in the Alps, many of which have been reached by the foot of man, but not without great difficulty and peril, and in the attempt fatal accidents have repeatedly occurred. Mont Blanc, the centre and highest summit of the great Alpine range, an enormous mass of primitive rock, rises to the height of fifteen thousand seven hundred and fifty feet above the sea level, and is visible at Dijon, a distance of one hundred and forty miles. The form of the mountain is pyramidal as seen from the north and south, but from the valley of Chamouni it resembles the back of a dromedary, on account of which *Bosse de Dromedaire* is one of its local titles. The extreme summit, a ridge nearly two hundred feet in length, was reached for the first time in August, 1785, by Dr. Paccard and James Balma; and the year following Saussure succeeded in the same enterprise, remaining five hours upon the top, making scientific experiments. In the autumn of 1834, Dr. Barry ascended, passing by "chasms of unfathomable depth, towers of ice, caverns of almost crystal walls, splendid stalactites guarding the entrance." His principal guide had been up eight times before, the survivor of four swept away by an avalanche in Dr. Hamel's attempt in 1820. In the year 1804 the Archduke John offered a reward to whosoever reached the summit of the Ortler Spitz, the highest of the Rhætian Alps. A native of the Passayer, accompanied by two peasants, accomplished the enterprise, before considered impracticable, starting with the full moon at midnight. Travellers, naturalists, and the daring peasants of the country have scaled many of the other lofty Alpine peaks; and now the Jungfrau or Virgin Mountain, so called from its supposed inaccessibility, has had the foot of the Swiss hunter upon her brow. The highest parts of Africa, as at present known, are in Abyssinia, but fall below those of Europe, though very nearly equal to them. Some of the summits of the Atlas range are supposed to reach twelve thousand feet, and the high lands of Ethiopia approximate to the loftiest of the Alps. Asia possesses in the Caucasus and eastern Taurus some very elevated positions. The culminating point of the latter, the Peak of Demavend, about forty miles from Teheran, in Persia, was ascended by Mr. Taylor Thomson in the year 1837, who found its height, by barometric measurement, to be fourteen thousand three hundred feet above the level of the ocean. The snow-crowned head of the towering Kasibeck, situated towards the European extremity of the pass of the Caucasus from Russia into Georgia, is estimated by Professor Parrot at twenty-four hundred fathoms, or fourteen thousand feet, above the level of the Black Sea; but this is exceeded by Elbûrz, which attains the height of sixteen thousand seven hundred feet, and the two peaks of the celebrated Ararat are still loftier. "These inaccessible summits," says Sir Robert Ker Porter, "have never been trodden by the foot of man since the days of Noah." Tourneforte was obliged to abandon the enterprise in the year 1700, after having endured great fatigue. At a more recent period, the Pacha of Bayazeed fitted out an expedition, and built huts supplied with provisions at different stations; but his people suffered severely amid the snows and masses of ice, and returned without accomplishing their purpose. The statement of Porter, true in 1820, ceased to be so nine years afterwards. Professor Parrot in 1829 effected the ascent of Ararat, and in 1834 the mountain was again scaled by M. Autonomoff, in order to vindicate the reputation of the Prussian traveller, whose veracity had been called in question. Its height is given at seventeen thousand two hundred and sixty feet, which exceeds by fifteen hundred and twenty-eight feet the highest elevation of Europe; but the table land of Armenia, from which it rises, is stated by Ritter to be seven thousand feet above the level of the sea. There is a far greater elevation attained by some of the Himalaya Mountains, which separate the valleys of Cashmere from Thibet, and present the loftiest projections to be found upon the terrestrial surface. On the west, Javaher rises to the height of twenty-five thousand seven hundred and forty-six feet, and on the east, Dhwalagiri to twenty-eight thousand feet above the sea. The highest summit on the new continent was once supposed to be Chimborazo, in the Andean chain, and likewise the greatest altitude on the surface of the globe; but it is now deprived of the distinction. Though twenty-one thousand four hundred and forty feet above the level of the ocean, and one of the grandest objects in the great American range, it is lower by nearly the whole height of Vesuvius than the Nevada di Sorata, in the eastern cordillera of Peru. The mean height of the Andes, apart from projecting cones, is estimated at six thousand feet in Patagonia, eight thousand in Chili, and fifteen thousand in Peru.

A remarkable instance of close approximation in calculating the height of Etna occurred between independent observers, pursuing different methods, at distinct times, unknown to each other. The Sicilians, vain of their mountain, attributed to it an elevation of thirteen thousand feet, which Captain Smyth, when surveying in the Mediterranean, reduced by more than two thousand — an abridgment which raised no little anger and contention. The result was subsequently verified by Sir John Herschel. "The height," observes the latter, "of the higher of the two summits of Etna, which I measured barometrically in 1824, came out to be ten thousand eight hundred seventy-two and a half English feet above the level of the Sea of Catania. Captain Smyth's result, with which I was not acquainted till long after the calculation of my own, gave ten thousand eight hundred and seventy-four. I have also, somewhere or other, though I cannot lay my hands on it, a memorandum of a zenith distance, observed by Cacciatore, of the summit of Etna, from Palermo; the result of which, calculated by a terrestrial refraction index, concluded by Cacciatore and myself, from observations by him and myself, on Monte Cuccio, gave a total altitude of Etna agreeing within a very few feet indeed of the same; so that I have no doubt the above is very good, unless that summit have since been blown up or blown down." It has been imagined that most of these chains are mutually connected, and form one grand consecutive scheme of high lands stretching through the extent of both continents, in the form of a vast irregular arch. Could a spectator command a view of the globe, supposing him to stand in New Holland facing the north, he would see on his right hand a continuous system of high mountains extending along the entire coast of America, linked with Asia by the Aleutian Isles. He would see also a chain on his left hand running along the coast of Africa, passing through Arabia into Persia, mingling there with the range that traverses Europe from the Atlantic, and merging in the mountains of Central Asia, which are continued north-easterly to Behring's Straits, and form the spine of the old world. Thus, while these chains of mountains, when viewed in detail, appear isolated and utterly unsystematic, yet when the globe is contemplated upon a grand scale, they seem to constitute one immense range in the form of an irregular curve, with outshoots from it, bounding the bed of the Pacific, on the north, east, and west.

Contemplating the projections of the surface with reference

to their absolute elevation above the level of the sea, some of them appear protuberances of enormous bulk; and we are apt to imagine that they must detract largely from the regularity of the earth's spherical form. But they become insignificant when compared with the volume of the globe itself, the highest eminence, that of between five and six miles, being only about $\frac{1}{800}$ of the semidiameter of the sphere. They bear, therefore, much the same proportion to the terrestrial spheroid as the little risings on the coat of an orange to the fruit. Books of travels abound with conflicting statements respecting the distance from which particular mountains may be seen. The length of the line of visibility is not only influenced by conditions of the atmosphere, but by the character of projections, apart from their height. The Peak of Teneriffe is not so frequently visible at the same distance as those tops of the Andes which are of corresponding elevation, not being, like them, invested with perpetual snow. Humboldt remarks, that the cone of the former no doubt reflects a great degree of light on account of the white color of the pumice with which it is covered; but its height does not form a twenty-second part of the total elevation, and the sides of the mountain are coated with blocks of dark-colored lava, or with luxuriant vegetation, the masses of which reflect little light, the leaves of the trees being separated by shadows of greater extent than the illuminated parts. He refers, therefore, the Peak to that class of mountains which are seen at a great distance only in a negative manner, or because they intercept the light transmitted from the extreme limits of the atmosphere. Still, it has been observed at the distance of one hundred and twenty-four, one hundred and thirty-one, and even one hundred and thirty-eight miles; and the summit of Mauna-Loa, in the Sandwich Islands, has been seen, at a period when it was destitute of snow, skirting the horizon from the distance of one hundred and eighty-three miles. This is the most remarkable example yet known of the visibility of high land; and as Mauna-Loa was negatively seen, both cases refute the theory of Bouguer, that mountains seen negatively cannot be perceived at distances exceeding one hundred and twenty-one miles.

A slight survey of the features of the external world is sufficient to show that the tendency of their general arrangement is to minister to the happiness of man, to give him pleasure in the act of contemplation, as well as to contribute to his convenience. Its surface, so finely diversified, is eminently calculated for the gratification of its occupiers, and expands around them in every clime an array of beauty and grandeur, sometimes apart from each other, but often blended in wild yet tasteful and imposing combinations. Wherever the traveller penetrates, he finds the terrestrial configuration so arranged in ever-varying outline as to spread before him an inviting picture of natural scenery, which captivates, or soothes, or elevates, or excites the mind, and furnishes such pleasurable emotions as dull uniformity would not have yielded. Especially do the elevations which mark the face of the earth, whether rising to the stately proportion of mountains, or forming only the rounded, green-clad hill, give interest, grace, or sublimity to the landscape. But the mountains perform a more important office than that of giving imposing effect and picturesque beauty to the scenery of the earth. Occupying a portion of its surface nearly equal to that which the sandy desert claims, they stand associated with political and other results of the highest importance to mankind. Where the ocean does not extend its waters to divide the families, kindreds, and tongues of the human race, the granite snow crowned rampart is frequently the line of demarcation. Nations have thus been kept apart from each other by natural boundaries; and the difficulties connected with aggressive wars between communities thus separated have contributed to promote peace and maintain independence. The mountains also give their aid to the clouds of heaven, attracting them to their summits, and storing up their precipitated waters in interior reservoirs, from whence they issue by a thousand springs; and in the dens and caves that perforate their declivities liberty and religion have often found a secure asylum, when assailed by persecuting power and grasping ambition. "The precious things of the lasting hills" — the phrase of the dying Hebrew patriarch — is not without its appropriate significancy. Inglis, wandering in the Tyrol, recognized its truth, when, as he remarks, he emerged from the mountains after a day's ramble, with pleasant recollections of lights and shadows yet lingering on the vision — of solitude and stillness, and the small mountain sounds that are more akin to silence than noise — and of all the thousand deep-felt but inexpressible emotions that are born among the eternal hills, when evening fills their valleys, creeps over their declivities, and throws its mantle on their summits.

Wherever in the torrid zone a mountain mass rises to such a height that its top is always covered with snow, a traveller may, in ascending its acclivities, pass in a short time through all the climates he would encounter in travelling from the equator to the moss-covered mountains of Lapland. At and near the base of the mountain his way lies through plantations of palms and plantains, through fields of sugar cane, cotton, and other tropical productions, and through groves of the most delicious fruits. By degrees the scene changes, and when he has mounted about eight thousand feet above the sea level, he finds himself surrounded by forests of oak, beech, and other trees of the temperate zone, which are frequently interrupted by fields of wheat, barley, and other productions of our country, interspersed here and there by groves of apple, peach, apricot, fig, and orange trees. The trees with deciduous leaves are soon displaced by conifera, such as the pine, fir, larch, &c.; the fields present only barley and potatoes, and the fruit trees have given way to bushes, such as raspberry and others. When the traveller leaves this region and approaches the snow line to within a thousand feet and more, the bushes and fields disappear entirely, and the stones of the mountains are only clad with herbage, among which, here and there, single flowers are observable. But near the snow line itself the whole mountain mass, where its acclivities are not too steep to admit of vegetation, is overgrown with mosses.

The mountains which are always capped with snow, not producing any thing useful to man or beast, would seem to be useless in the economy of nature as far as regards the maintenance of the animated creation. But such is not the case. They diffuse fertility through extensive countries, by giving rise to rivers, and by keeping them well supplied with water, which may be applied by the inhabitants, and at many places is applied, to irrigate the fields and to obtain from them richer crops than could be got by any other mode of management. This is especially the case in warm countries, where rains are periodical, and where for several months not a drop of rain falls. During these rainless seasons the soil is dried and parched by a continual evaporation, and all minor vegetation would die away were the waste of moisture not supplied by irrigation with water drawn from the rivers. It is true that mountains which do not rise to the snow line keep up the water in the streams all the year round; but their supply is but scanty when compared with those rivers whose sources are found under eternal masses of snow. Though on the banks of the first class of rivers a considerable population may subsist on the produce of the fields, it is not commonly half as large as that which owes the supply of its wants to the bounty dispersed over their fields by the snow-born streams. In countries which are blessed with an annual fall of snow and with abundant showers of rain during all seasons of the year, the advantage which hot countries derive from such rivers can hardly be understood in all their extent, and consequently has not been duly appreciated. But what immense tracts of the surface of the globe would be nothing but mere wastes were their rivers deprived of that continual supply of water which is derived from the gradual but never-ceasing melting of the snow with which the summits of their mountains are crowned!

The snow mountains are rarely visited by travellers, except

along those foot paths which lie across mountain passes, and serve as the shortest lines of communication between places situated on different declivities at some distance below the snow line. Such persons are hasty pedestrians, and commonly do not pay much attention to the operations of nature. A few scientific persons have, however, ascended the highest summits, as far as possible. They have not been diverted from their purpose or terrified at the dangers which surrounded them among these enormous masses of snow and ice, on the edge of perpendicular precipices, and on the brink of yawning chasms many hundred feet in depth; nor have they hastily withdrawn themselves from those unpleasant sensations to which they were subjected by the exceedingly rarefied air which they respired at such a great elevation. These sensations are not experienced in the vicinity of the snow line, but only when the elevation of the mountain is considerably above it. The most remarkable is the feeling of exhaustion. When Lieutenant Wood was on the Roof of the World in Pamir, he wished to ascertain the depth of the Lake Sir-i-kol, and for that purpose tried to make an opening in the ice. He found that the slightest muscular exertion was attended with exhaustion. Half a dozen strokes with an axe brought the workman to the ground; and though a few minutes' respite sufficed to restore the breath, any thing like continued exertion was impossible. A run of fifty yards at full speed made the runner gasp for breath. Indeed, this exercise produced a pain in the lungs and a general prostration of strength, which was not got rid of for many hours. The human voice was sensibly affected; conversation, especially if in a loud tone, could not be kept up without exhaustion, and the pulse throbbed at a frightful rate. Saussure, when on Mont Blanc, experienced the same effects; and, besides, he and his party complained of dizziness and headache; they lost their appetites, but suffered extremely from thirst, which could only be allayed momentarily by cold water. A complete indifference respecting all worldly objects pervaded their minds. When

Humboldt attempted to ascend Chimborazo, and had nearly attained its summit, he desisted on finding that drops of blood issued from under his nails and from his eyelids.

The greatest number of snow mountains, as far as is known, is found in the Himalaya Mountains, or those mountain masses which lie along the north-eastern border of Hindustan, and separate the British dominions from the Chinese empire. Along this line, for a distance of several hundred miles, masses of rocks occur from thirty to forty miles in width, which rise to from eighteen thousand to twenty-five thousand or twenty-six thousand feet above the sea level, and from six thousand to fourteen thousand feet above the snow line. The depressions by which those masses are divided from each other hardly at any place sink to fifteen thousand feet above the sea level, or to three thousand feet above the snow line. Through these depressions lie the mountain passes, by which the communication between the two countries extending on their sides is carried on. These passes are only practicable during two or three months of the year; and even then the cold experienced is so great that horses, mules, and other animals of burden cannot endure it. Sheep alone are by nature so well protected against the effects of frost that they are not materially affected by the intense cold of this region, and for that reason these weak animals have been converted into beasts of burden. Rice and a few other articles are conveyed on their backs from the plains of the Ganges to the table land of Thibet.

The best known snow mountains in Europe are those of the Alps. The number of the rocky masses rising above the snow line amounts to some hundreds. At a few places they are so closely connected as to constitute a snow mass covering a great extent of country. In the Alps of Berne, between the upper courses of the Rivers Rhone and Aar, an extent of country of about six hundred square miles is one sheet of snow, with the exception of three or four narrow valleys, which run into the mass, and are so depressed as to be free from snow for several months of the year. The valleys in these mountains communicate with one another by foot paths, which run for several miles over the snow, but are only practicable for a few weeks in the year, and then only for pedestrians. The snow fields of the Alps hardly ever present level spaces on their tops of any great extent, as the snow is there lodged on declivities, which are frequently broken by short but steep ascents and descents. This imparts to their scenery a certain variety, which is greatly enhanced, and converted into a most majestic and impressive view, by the great number of rocky masses with which, in the forms of needles, steeples, ruined castles, and narrow ridges, their surface is overspread. As these rocks in most cases rise perpendicularly, or nearly so, their sides are too steep to permit snow to lodge on them, and their black color contrasts in a most striking manner with the whiteness of the snow. Thus these snow fields constitute one of the most attractive beauties in the scenery of the Alps.

But all snow mountains do not present such scenery. There are in other countries extensive plains of nearly a level surface, which are raised above the snow line, and consequently always buried under snow. Such plains are found in Norway. Though these snow plains are destitute of that majestic beauty which imparts to the snow mountains such a degree of attraction, they are still interesting, as they show us the true nature of snow mountains, without the association of those impressions which are the effect of accidental circumstances. The best known of the snow plains of Norway is that of Folge Fonden. It is not quite destitute of occasional beauties, but those are only found along its edges, which are surrounded on three sides by firths, or deep and narrow inlets of the sea, affording a great variety of views on the steep acclivity of the mountain mass, over whose upper surface the snow plain extends. Folge Fonden is a peninsula, which in its greatest length, from south by west to north by east, extends more than thirty miles, and in its width varies between twenty and eight miles. On the south-east it is connected with the main land. The rocky masses of which this tract is composed rise on all sides with a steep acclivity to an elevation of more than five thousand feet, and their upper surface is a level plain covered with snow. When seen from below, it appears that the snow mass is about twelve yards deep. That which lies uppermost, and which is the produce of the snow falls of the last winter, is quite white, and forms a well-marked, thin stratum, whilst the remainder appears to constitute one compact mass, whose white color is slightly tinged with blue. Near the edges of the snow its surface is gently inclined, rising gradually towards the centre; and only at a few places, where the edge is broken by ravines, is the declivity more rapid. The inclination of the surface decreases in proportion as we advance towards the interior, and near the centre it frequently presents a dead level, across which a few low eminences extend in the form of large waves with a very gentle ascent. The snow itself appears as a conglomerate of small transparent grains of ice, resembling in form and size very minute shot, which probably at some distance under the surface are united into one mass of ice by the pressure of the superincumbent snow masses. The surface of the snow is quite smooth, and when visited in summer, after the sun's rays have made a faint impression by dissolving the outside of the grains to a small degree, it is covered by a very thin layer of ice, as if it had been glazed, whilst on the inclined portion some slight furrows are observed, which have been formed by the small quantity of water produced by slight thaws. When a stick is pushed into the snow, the resistance which is experienced continues to increase, so that at a small depth it becomes impossible to force the stick farther down.

The snow fields of the Alps are the produce of enormous snow masses, which have accumulated on steep and irregular slopes. The continuity of their surfaces is broken at numerous places, and there the snow masses, resembling ice in texture, rise like walls, crowned here and there by boldly ascending pyramids, or by groups resembling broken-down buildings of ancient date. This majestic confusion receives a peculiar charm from the bluish color with which the ruptures of the icy masses are tinged. At many places the masses are furrowed by clefts several feet wide, which descend to a depth of a hundred feet and more. These clefts are numerous, where the snow masses, in descending over a very steep slope, or into a deep ravine, have been fractured by their own weight; and they are still more numerous where an unwieldy mass, hemmed in between two mountains, in protruding downward to form a glacier, has not found a space large enough to preserve its width, and thus has been broken along its edges by the resistance offered by the rocks on its sides, or by the rapid declivity of the valley into which it descends.

The snow of these high regions consists, as already stated, of small round balls, resembling small shot. This at once shows that this snow is very different from that of the lower countries, where the snow falls in flakes. This difference is also proved by the fact, that it is impossible to press it together so as to make a snowball. The German peasants in Switzerland have well observed this difference, and express it in their language, calling the mountain snow *firn*, in contradistinction to *snow*. As no snowball can be made of this kind of snow, it is evident that none of the snow avalanches can originate on the snow fields, though that opinion has been entertained up to very recent times. At and near the surface of the snow fields the snow particles are disunited, and do not adhere to one another; but at some depth it is found that they change in some degree their form, becoming more flattened. In this form they approach closer to one another, and being pressed by the superincumbent stratum, they by degrees unite into one mass, which has a resemblance to the ice of which the glaciers are composed. When the mountain mass on which the snow rests is not much raised above the snow line, this change in its form begins to take place at a depth of a few feet below the surface; but where the mountains rise to twelve thousand feet, or four thousand feet above that line, the snow preserves its granular form to a great depth, so that only the lower stratum assumes the appearance of ice.

The difference between the snow of the lower countries and that of these elevated regions shows that they must be formed under different circumstances. It is easy to comprehend that only a small mass of aqueous vapor can ascend into the rarefied air which rises above the summits of the snow mountains. Rain of course does not fall, as all vapors rising to that elevation are converted into snow. The summits of the mountains are, besides, above the region in which rain is generated. Heavy rain clouds are only seen to hover over those declivities of the mountains which are overgrown with large trees. The region of the forests extends in the Alps from three thousand to six thousand feet above the sea level, and in this region rain in summer and snow in winter are very abundant. Where the trees disappear, and are replaced by bushes, the quantity of rain decreases gradually, and goes on decreasing in approaching the snow line. Above this line only snow falls, not in the form of flakes, but in that of very minute globules. The quantity of snow which falls in spring and autumn is not great; in winter it is still smaller, and in summer snow does not fall at all. It appears, therefore, that the whole annual quantity of snow in that elevated region is but small, which is a wise arrangement of Providence, as otherwise the snow would accumulate to an immense extent, and to such a height, that it would be impossible to pass the mountains. For these masses do not experience any diminution, except by evaporation, and it is evident that in such a rarefied air, and in such a cold climate, evaporation cannot but be very small.

CHAPTER VII.

GLACIERS. — PECULIAR FORM OF THE CRYSTALS OF ICE OF WHICH THEY ARE COMPOSED. — THEIR DEEP AND DANGEROUS CHASMS. — THE VARIETY AND BEAUTY OF THEIR COLORS. — ROCKS OF VAST SIZE TRANSPORTED BY THEM. — FORMATION OF GLACIERS. — CAUSE OF THEIR PROGRESSIVE MOVEMENT.

THE term "glacier" is frequently considered as being synonymous with that of "snow mountain," and both terms are sometimes used without discrimination; but they indicate very different objects, as the reader will convince himself by comparing the following account of the glaciers with the preceding one of the snow mountains.

Glaciers are appendages to snow mountains. There is no glacier, and there can be none, without a snow mountain. They are offsets of the snow mountains. They may be compared with the branches of a tree, which extend to a considerable distance from the trunk. The snow line itself constitutes the point where the snow mountain terminates and the glacier begins. An extensive snow mountain may send off a great number of glaciers. The number of glaciers which emanate from the snow fields covering Mont Blanc amounts to seventeen or eighteen, and the number is still greater of those which originate in the immense snow masses which divide the upper course of the River Rhone from that of the Aar.

If we suppose that a mountain, whose summit is crowned by an extensive and deep mass of snow, descends on all sides with a gentle slope, we should find that the outer edge of the snow was girded by a broad band of ice all round. The cold emanating from the snow would chill the adjacent air to a certain distance from the edges of the mass, and so far the ice would extend. As this border lies below the snow

Termination of the Nygaard Glacier, in Norway.

line, the alternation of cold and warmth to which it is exposed would convert the snow into ice of such a description as is found in the glaciers. We might, therefore, expect to find that all the edges of snow mountains are surrounded by glaciers; and so they are in reality, but the greater number of them are so small as not to excite observation. The extent of a glacier depends almost entirely on the conformation of the declivities of the mountain on which the snowy mass rests. When such a mountain descends with a perpendicular or very steep declivity to a considerable depth below the snow line, its edges terminate so abruptly as to leave no space for the formation of a glacier, except, perhaps, a very narrow border, which can hardly be distinguished from the snow which lies higher up. An instance of this kind is seen in the Folge Fonden, in Norway. Along its northern and western edges only a few depressions occur, in which glaciers of several hundred yards in extent are to be met with, and at the termination of which the mountain mass descends with great steepness. On all its other sides no traces of glaciers are found. Such a formation of the mountain masses, though frequent in many countries, rarely occurs in the Alps. The snow-covered portion of this mountain system is on all sides surrounded by other ridges, which are connected with it at different angles, and between which valleys of various extent are found. The smallest glaciers occur on the sides of the snow mountains themselves. Wherever there is a ravine which begins under or on the very edge of the snow, and thence descends, a glacier is formed. But, as these ravines have a very rapid descent, the glacier terminates at a short distance from the snow mass, where the slope of the ravine becomes too great to afford a permanent lodgment for the snow, which is borne down by its own weight. At other places the ravines terminate at their lower extremity in a level tract covered with grass, on which the descending snow is soon melted away. There are also a few instances where the declivity along the sides of the mountain for a considerable extent is so regular, moderate, and uniform, that the snow for some distance from the edge of the perpetual snow finds support on the slightly inclined plane, and where, therefore, a glacier of several hundred feet in width borders the snow masses from which it has descended. The small extent of all the glaciers of these kinds, and their remoteness from inhabited places, would hardly have excited attention, and given rise to an investigation of their peculiar nature. But there are glaciers of great extent. They are sometimes thirty miles long, and descend so far below the snow line that their termination is surrounded by full-grown trees, cultivated fields, and orchards. According to the late Professor Forbes, the very huts of the peasantry are sometimes invaded by this moving ice; and many persons now living have seen the full ears of corn touching the glacier, or gathered ripe cherries from the trees with one foot standing on the ice. These glaciers are only to be met with in valleys which descend with a gentle slope to a great distance from the snow mountain, and are enclosed on either side by a secondary ridge of considerable elevation, which is connected with the snow mountain at the beginning of the glacier.

The extent of a large glacier depends partly on the size and formation of the valley, and partly on the extent of the snow mountain of which it is a branch. The peasants in Switzerland say, A lean snow mountain cannot produce a fat glacier. A snow field must be indeed very large to be able to supply annually a quantity of snow sufficient to feed a glacier which descends several hundred feet below the snow line, and is there exposed to a great waste from evaporation and melting. On this account alone a great difference in the extent of glaciers may be expected. The glacier in Switzerland which descends to the lowest level is the famous one of the Lower Grindelwald, which is annually visited by crowds of travellers, because it descends so far, and is consequently more accessible than others. The lower extremity of this glacier is only three thousand four hundred and nine feet above the sea level, though the lower edge of the snow mountain from which it emanates is eight thousand one hundred and seventeen feet above that line. Its neighbor, the glacier of the Upper Grindelwald, terminates at an elevation of four thousand two hundred and sixty feet; and the Great Aletsh glacier, which opens into Valais, at four thousand four hundred and thirteen feet above the sea. The other glaciers which are found in the Alps do not extend so far down; but in other countries some are found which approach much nearer the level of the sea. On the western coast of Norway, near latitude sixty-six degrees, is Cape Kunnen. It is partly formed by a glacier which descends quite to the water's edge, except towards the end of the summer, when it recedes a few feet. Henderson, in his travels through Iceland, makes mention of the Bridemarker Yökul, a glacier in the eastern districts of the island, which had advanced so near the sea that there was hardly space enough left for a road, and it was feared that the glacier would extend itself to the water's edge, and close up the communication between the eastern and western parts of the island. The eastern shores of Greenland are so lined with glaciers that a great portion of the cliffs which front the sea are entirely composed of ice, and rise some hundred feet above the sea. Similar cliffs of ice occur in some of the inlets with which the western coast of Patagonia is indented. It is evident that in all these countries enormous masses of snow must cover the higher parts of the mountains, when we find that these offsets extend even to the shores of the sea.

The Alps of Switzerland are celebrated for the number and extent of their glaciers. M. Ebel estimates that there may be at least four hundred of the larger sized glaciers, or varying from three to thirty miles in length. The aggregate superficial extent of all those of the Tyrol, Switzerland, Piedmont, and Savoy is calculated by some authorities to amount to not less than fourteen hundred square miles. The greatest breadth of an individual specimen is seldom more than two miles,

The thickness varies from a hundred to six hundred feet. The declivities of all those parts which sustain large masses of ice are, as it were, striated by comparatively narrow masses of ice, which descend to the valleys between the secondary ridges, like rivers between their banks. In arriving at the lower extremity of a glacier, it is found that the icy mass rises with a broken and steep ascent to a considerable elevation. The masses which lie behind this projecting promontory are also much broken, traversed in every direction by deep chasms, and overtopped by numerous isolated pieces of ice, which exhibit the most fantastic shapes. In advancing farther, the glacier resembles a gently sloping icy stream, from half a mile to three miles wide, presenting a surface more or less undulating; and this undulating surface is more or less broken by chasms which, at their upper opening, differ in width from a few inches to many feet. These chasms sometimes extend nearly from one side of the glacier to the other. The ice of the lower part of the glacier is, in general, tinged with an exquisite blue color, which, however, in many parts passes into a green. Near the snow mountain the blue color becomes fainter, until it disappears entirely. In those parts where the glacier approaches the snow masses, its surface is again more broken than in its middle portion.

In examining more closely the phenomena of the glaciers, the ice of which they are composed first claims our attention. It differs as much from that which is formed in our rivers and lakes as the snow of the snow mountains differs from that which falls in lower regions. Whoever has paid attention to the formation of ice in a pond, or along the banks of a river, must have observed that at first crystals having the form of long and thin needles make their appearance; but after they have united into a sheet of ice, no marks of crystallization are apparent. The ice of the glaciers is composed of crystals, but their form differs greatly from those which are observed at the first formation of ice, in water. They are polyhedrons of the most irregular shapes, but more oblong than entire.

Their size varies from less than an inch to three inches in length. They have commonly on one side, rarely on both, a small protuberance, which, however, has no determinate shape, and varies greatly in form. The surfaces of the crystals are rough, warty, and slightly furrowed. The manner in which these crystals are united into one mass is very remarkable. By the pressure they have undergone they are wedged together, and by means of the protuberances are so fixed into each other, that when exposed to a temperature capable of dissolving the whole mass, the single crystals become movable to a certain extent, but they do not fall asunder even if the interstices have already loosened. When in this state it is still found a somewhat difficult matter to take out a single crystal; and for that purpose a force must be employed by which the crystal is generally broken. As soon, however, as one crystal is removed, the others may easily be detached, and the whole mass taken to pieces. Sometimes, even by the removal of a few crystals, the whole mass will directly fall asunder. It happens sometimes that large pieces of ice detach themselves from the lower extremity of a glacier, or from its outer border. These masses do not melt like common ice exposed to a high temperature, by diminishing continually. The mass keeps its size and form until the whole has been completely moistened, and the single crystals have become loosened, and then the whole mass at once falls to pieces. This singular composition gives to the whole icy mass a cellular texture, which may be distinctly observed on the surfaces of the vaults which invariably occur at the lower termination of the glacier. Neither in the interior of the mass nor on its upper surface does this cellular texture show itself; at least not distinctly, when the temperature is low, or after a cold night. But it becomes apparent if colored acids or spirits are diffused on the mass. These fluids penetrate deeply into the ice by means of the interstices, and both the crystals and interstices may be distinctly traced. It is further remarkable that these crystals attain their greatest size at the lower extremity of the glacier, and that their size is in proportion to the mass. The larger the mass, the larger the crystals. At the lower extremity of the glacier the crystals are of equal size, or nearly so, throughout; but on examining them farther upwards, and nearer the snow mountain, they are found to be smaller on the surface of the glacier than in the interior, and to increase in size in proportion to the depth. On the summit of the snow mountain itself, when the upper stratum, which consists of snow, is removed, it is found that the mass below it presents the cellular texture of the glacier, but the single crystals are of smaller size.

The surface of the ice itself is extremely uneven and rough, bearing no resemblance to the ice of our ponds and lakes, which admits of skating. This roughness is to be ascribed to the different degrees of hardness of the ice itself, and to its peculiar structure. The whole mass is composed of two kinds of ice, different in hardness and in color. They are disposed in bands or parallel veins. Thin plates of compact transparent ice alternate with others which are less hard and semi-opaque. The former are smooth, and contain nothing but ice; but the semi-opaque plates are full of air bubbles of various forms, which are disseminated through the pure ice, and always arranged in more or less abundance in parallel planes. This imparts to them a frothy and semi-opaque appearance. The color of the compact ice is blue, but that of the opaque a greenish white. The harder ice is less easily thawed than the opaque ice, and therefore the surface of the latter is more depressed under the general level than that of the former, which thus forms projecting ridges, separated from each other by grooves; and where this disposition of the ice continues for many fathoms, the grooves resemble the cart ruts of a bad road.

The upper surface of the ice is distinguished by its great dryness. This has been considered as a proof that the diminution of the mass on its surface is produced by evaporation, and not by thawing. It is indeed stated that the sun's rays, even in hot weather, hardly affect the ice of the glaciers; and in proof of this supposition, the fact is adduced that but rarely even small collections of water are met with. Wherever there appear small rills of running water, their origin may be traced to the sudden melting of recently fallen snow. But this phenomenon may be accounted for in a more satisfactory way. The interstices between the single crystals have a great capacity of absorbing water, and the slow effects of the sun's rays leave them time sufficient to abstract all the water thus generated on the surface of the glacier.

But whilst the upper surface is distinguished by great dryness, the lower, which rests on the rocky bottom of the valley, is extremely wet. It is here apparently that the greatest portion of the ice is destroyed by melting. This process is the effect of the natural warmth of the earth, and does not cease even in winter. Every body must be convinced of it who examines with attention the lower extremity of a glacier. It consists of large caverns or vaults sustained by massive columns of ice. These grottos are sometimes a hundred feet high, and from fifty to eighty feet wide, but their dimensions and shapes vary greatly. Their sides, acted on by the thawing, are smooth, so that on them the reticular texture of the glacier ice can be seen with the greatest distinctness. Through these apertures all the water is discharged which is collected by the melting of the lower surface of the glacier. In winter the stream issuing from them is but small, but in summer it gushes out in a plenteous torrent. These streams of the glaciers are remarkable for the whitish-blue color of their waters, which they preserve for a distance of several miles. This color is ascribed to the numerous particles of rocky matter which the torrents bring down in a state of the greatest comminution effected by attrition.

The surface of the glacier is not continuous and level, but more or less broken. The most level part is that in the middle, where, as we have already observed, the surface appears as a gently sloping plain, traversed by a smaller or greater number of chasms, according to the season of the year. Near the termination of the glacier, as also at its commencement, the whole mass appears to have been fractured. This is easily to be accounted for, as in these parts the bottom of the valley, in which the glacier lies, usually forms a rapid slope, and is at the same time uneven and rugged. Where the icy masses descend a steep declivity, or are propelled over very broken ground, their surfaces present nothing but a continual succession of irregular and frequently deep chasms, and cliffs of ice rising from twenty to a hundred feet. Where the slope of the valley exceeds thirty or forty degrees, the beds of ice break into fragments, which get displaced, upheaved, and piled together in every fantastic variety of form. Masses of ice resembling steeples or towers, and others having the form of walls, rise with sharp points or edges to a hundred feet, representing an immense ruin converted into ice. But these icy masses are subject to continual changes. "Every moment in summer," says a modern traveller, "such steeples, walls, or columns break down partly or entirely; and when these icy masses are standing on the edge of a perpendicular or precipitous rock, they tumble down with a loud but peculiar noise, and in falling are broken up into many thousand pieces, which, when viewed from afar, resemble the cataract of a torrent. This is one of the grandest and most extraordinary views the traveller can enjoy in the Alps."

Chasms have been frequently mentioned. There are two kinds of them, which probably owe their origin to different causes, and are distinguished by the names of "day chasms" and "night chasms" — because the first are stated to be formed only in the daytime, and the last only in the night. The day chasms may be best observed in the middle and more level portion of the glacier. They frequently stretch nearly across the whole width of the glacier, from one side to the other. In width they vary from a few inches to many feet at the upper opening: there they are widest, as in descending farther downward their sides contract, until they meet at the bottom in the form of a wedge. Some of the wider ones descend to the very base of the glacier. An eye-witness and attentive observer gives the following account of the formation of a chasm: "When I was once walking," says Hugi, "on the glacier of the Lower Aar, at three o'clock in the afternoon, and the weather being very hot, I heard a peculiar noise. Advancing directly towards the spot whence it proceeded, I had hardly walked thirty or forty paces before I felt that the whole icy mass trembled under my feet. The trembling soon ceased, and then began again, continuing by starts. I quickly discovered the cause. The ice was splitting and forming a chasm. Before my eyes it split suddenly over a space of twenty or thirty feet in length, so rapidly that I could not keep up with it. Then it appeared to cease, or rather the rent proceeded more slowly, until the trembling returned, and the splitting proceeded at an accelerated rate. Several times I advanced to the end of the new-formed rent, and laid myself down on the ice. The chasm opened under my very nose, and I experienced a considerable shock. In this way I followed the splitting of the ice for nearly a quarter of an hour, until it terminated on arriving at a *moraine*. When the chasm was forming, its opening was about an inch and a half wide. Afterwards it contracted somewhat, so that at no place was it wider than an inch. The depth I estimated at about four or five feet. I observed, at the same time, that the splitting downward still continued, but very slowly. After some days I again visited the place. I found that the opening had increased to the breadth of six inches, but did not succeed in ascertaining the depth. At a distance of about twelve feet another rent had been formed, which extended exactly parallel to the first, and was about six feet deep." These rents are only formed during hot weather, especially when the wind blows from the south-west, and rain is going to fall. With the progress of the warm season their number increases; and at its termination the face of the glacier is so changed, that it cannot be recognized by those who had seen it a few weeks before. The greatest changes occur in September. It is said that during the night the openings contract and grow narrower; and it is further stated, as a well-ascertained fact, that in winter these chasms close entirely, which is ascribed to the expansion and increase of the crystals of ice composing the mass, by the intense cold to which these regions are subject. These chasms are supposed to owe their origin to the changes of temperature produced by the succession of day and night, and of summer and winter.

We are even less acquainted with the nature of the night chasms. These do not frequently occur in the middle portion of the glacier, but are mostly found on its upper extremity, and on the adjacent part of the snow mountain itself. Their form is the reverse of that of the day chasms. They have the wider opening directed towards the base of the glacier, and terminating at its upper face, under the layer of snow which there covers the icy mass. This layer of snow falls sometimes into the chasm, but more frequently it is carried away by strong gusts of wind, which come up from the interior, and bring up an exceedingly cold air. The interior of the chasm then becomes visible, and it is found that these spacious caverns of wide dimensions are filled with piles of detached ice blocks, tossed in chaotic heaps, whilst watery stalactitic icicles of ten or twenty feet in length hang from the roof, and give to these singular vaults all the grotesque varieties of outline which are so much admired in calcareous caverns, but which here show to a far greater advantage, in consequence of their exquisite transparency and lustre, and from being illuminated, not by a few candles, but by the magical light of a tender green, which issues from the walls of the crystal chambers. The herdsmen of the Alps, who in summer frequent the tracts adjacent to the snow mountains, frequently hear at night an indistinct noise of a peculiar description, which appears to proceed from beneath the glacier. It is thought that this noise accompanies the formation of a night chasm. Chasms of this description must be much more dangerous than day chasms, as their upper opening is frequently covered with snow, and hardly ever perceptible. Many hunters of the chamois have been precipitated to their bottom. No explanation of the origin of these night chasms has been offered.

A phenomenon which has much attracted the attention of scientific travellers are the moraines, which term may be translated by "glacier walls;" they are walls of ice extending along the lateral margins of the glaciers, and usually surrounding also their lower terminations. Thus they surround the glacier on all sides, except where it is connected with the snowy masses from which it branches off. On the top of these walls are fragments of rock of different dimensions, and stony rubbish, which have there accumulated so as to cover the upper part entirely, and to form long dikes. In some of the larger glaciers such a glacier wall is found in the middle of the icy mass, where it runs parallel to the walls lying along its borders. It is remarkable that near the upper extremity of the glacier these walls are hardly raised above its general surface, but that in proceeding farther down they rise higher and higher; some of them attain an elevation of sixty or eighty feet above their base. In approaching, however, the lower extremity of the glacier, they sink gradually down, so that at the termination they are nearly on a level with the surface. At some places are found the "glacier tables;" they consist of columns of ice, rising at times to eighty feet and more, and supporting on their tops a large piece of rock, which projects on all sides over the icy column.

It is not difficult to account for the rocky masses with which these walls and tables are covered. On the snow fields from which the glaciers emanate, are numerous masses of rock, which, in many places, are quite bare of snow, in consequence of the rapidity of their slope. These masses are subject to disintegration by the alternate action of wet and frost, heat and cold. It is, therefore, easy to comprehend that, by this disintegration, large fragments of rock are frequently detached, and fall on the ice field, where they sink into the snow until they meet the compact ice. There they remain buried until they are protruded downward to the glacier, when they appear above the surface as soon as the snow melts in the lower temperature. These rocky masses are still increased by the debris which falls from the lateral mountain ridges, by which the glacier is enclosed on both sides. These facts account well for the formation of the lateral moraines, but do not apply to those which occur in the middle of the glacier. It has, however, been observed lately that the medial moraines are only found in places where two smaller glaciers have united, in the same manner as two tributary rivers form a larger river. At the place of their union the glacier walls, which skirted the two banks of the glacier which were nearest to one another before their confluence, unite into one moraine, which continues to descend in the middle of the larger glacier formed by their union. That these medial glacier walls continue to extend in the middle of the larger glacier to a great distance below the point of union, may be adduced as one of the most convincing proofs that the whole mass of the glacier is continually advancing downward.

It is, however, not so easy to assign a reason why these rocks and debris rest on a wall of ice, which, as observed before, is raised at many places sixty or eighty feet above the level of the glacier. Many scientific travellers have exercised their ingenuity in giving an explanation of this phenomenon. They have considered it, with reason, a matter of surprise that a dead insect or a fallen leaf, soon after it has fallen on the glacier, is buried under the ice, whilst large and heavy rocks, even when warmed by the sun's heat, do not sink under its surface — on the contrary are raised above it, and to such a considerable elevation. The most probable explication is the following: The upper surface of the glacier loses, partly by thawing and partly by evaporation, a considerable portion of its ice, and sinks continually to a lower level. Where, however, the access of air and light is excluded from its surface by inorganic and compact bodies, the mass cannot be affected by the above-mentioned causes. In this manner the ice on which the fragments of rock are lodged remains undiminished, whilst the adjacent parts sink lower and lower. The correctness of this explanation is supported by the peculiar form of the glacier tables, where the rocky mass on the top projects on all sides to a considerable distance, and the column of ice which supports it grows thinner and thinner the higher the table rises above the glacier, until the column is broken down by the weight of the superincumbent rock, and precipitates it on to the surface of the ice, where, however, it is soon raised again by the effects of thawing and evaporation. The circumstance that organic bodies sink into the ice and disappear in a short time, is accounted for by the well-known quality of such bodies absorbing oxygen. They thus abstract from the ice one of those elements which are essential to its existence, and the other, the hydrogen, is dispersed by evaporation.

Almost all travellers who have been in the Alps and have visited the glaciers, speak with rapture of their color. When, however, single crystals, or even small portions of the mass are broken off and viewed separately, they show nothing of this color. They are commonly white and transparent like ice, or frothy and semi-opaque. The color appears only in the entire mass. The blue color begins to appear gradually, and passes through all the shades from the slightest tinge to the darkest hue of the lapis lazuli. In some glaciers the blue has a mixture of green, which doubtless is to be ascribed to the prevalence of the frothy semi-opaque layers. In the lower parts of the chasms and clefts, where the ice of the glacier is in a state of dissolution by thawing, the blue color is of a purity and beauty which can be admired, but not described nor imitated. Where the glacier approaches the snow mountain, the color gets fainter, and at last passes into that of the ice of the snow mountain, which, as above observed, is white, with a tinge of blue which is hardly perceptible.

A natural phenomenon of such a peculiar character and such a magnitude as the glacier, has powerfully attracted the attention of scientific men, and several theories have been formed to explain their origin. When the phenomena attending them had been observed, but not closely investigated, an apparently simple method was adopted to explain their origin. It was thought to be due to the quantity of snow which falls in the higher and colder regions of the mountains, and is only partially thawed by the heat of summer. When the slopes of these elevated mountain masses are rapid, the snow, being unable to rest upon it, slides down into the adjacent valleys in the form of avalanches, and to this being added what in winter time falls directly into the valleys, an enormous quantity of snow is accumulated, which becomes compressed by its own weight. This snow is converted into ice by the rains which occasionally fall, and by the water, which results from the partial melting of the snow percolating through the whole mass, moistening it throughout; and while in this state the cold of the succeeding winter consolidates it into a glacier. This explanation, simple as it is, cannot be admitted as founded in truth, when it is considered that but little snow falls on the snow mountains, that no avalanches originate in these higher regions, and that few of the steeper slopes are so situated as to discharge their snowy coverings into the valleys, the greater number of them being near the crest of the whole mountain mass. This theory, besides, does not agree with the peculiar nature of the ice, as above described, which cannot have been produced by such a process, nor with the progress which the icy mass is continually making downward.

Saussure, a native of Geneva, the first to investigate closely the glaciers and the phenomena attending them, and to apply to them the known laws of nature, was aware of this progress, and was convinced that the ice of the glaciers originated on the snow mountain itself, from which it descended slowly to its termination. Though the fact of this movement was for a long time considered as certain, no attempts were made at any place to ascertain its rate, until Professor Forbes turned his attention to the subject.* By him and his friends the movement of the ice of the littoral part of the Mer de Glace at Montlavert, near Chamouni, was attentively observed for nearly a year, and it was found that it amounted

From June 29 to September 28, to . .	132 feet.
" October 10 to December 12, . .	70
" December 12 to February 17, . .	76
" February 17 to April 4, ...	66
" April 4 to June 8, ...	88
	432 feet.
To this Mr. Forbes adds for the time in which no observations were taken,	51
	481 feet.

On this progress of the ice Saussure rested his theory of the origin of the glaciers. He maintained, that when by the natural warmth of the earth the connection between the lower surface of the glacier and the bottom of the valley had been removed, and the ice had become slippery by the moisture collected, the whole mass was borne down by its own weight, and that thus the progress of the glacier ice was effected by a mechanical operation. To this theory it is with reason objected, that by far the larger part of the glacier rests on a slope which is not rapid enough to allow us to suppose that such heavy and enormous masses of ice could be so carried down. Besides, the glaciers do not lie in a straight line, but follow the bends of the valleys. They frequently pass through gorges, or round projecting masses. At all such places, the ice, descending of course in a straight line, would be stopped, broken, and accumulate to an immense extent,

* The author appears to be mistaken, when he says that Prof. Forbes was the first who measured the motion of glaciers. Prof. Agassiz had already obtained the results of one year's motion upon the glacier of the Aar before Prof. Forbes visited the Mer de Glace, where he made his observations.

which is not the case. On these accounts the theory of Saussure has been rejected.

In later times Charpentier and others have broached another theory. They conceive that the progress of the glacier may be considered as the effect of the freezing of the water which collects in the chasms, clefts, and smaller rents. According to their opinion, a glacier is composed of a spongy ice, which continually absorbs the water derived from the atmosphere and from the melting of the ice itself. This water penetrates into the numerous narrow rents which traverse the icy body to its lowest depth, but especially those parts of it which are contiguous to its upper surface. When this water freezes, it presses with great force on all the parts which surround it, and propels those which lie on that side where the resistance is smallest, namely, down the slope of the valley. The weight of the mass assists greatly this movement. In winter, when the whole mass is frozen throughout, the glacier ice does not move. This theory is more ingenious than solid. It appears to be quite impossible, according to all experiments and observations, that the comparatively small quantity of water collected in the rents and lower portions of the chasms, when converted into ice, should act with such a force on its sides as to be able to put in motion masses of such a magnitude as those of the glaciers. Besides, it is not true that the ice of the glacier does not move in winter. According to the measurement taken by Professor Forbes, noticed above, it is evident that it moves nearly as fast in winter as in summer.

Professor Forbes conceived a new theory. He considered a glacier as not consisting of a mass of solid ice, but as a compound of ice and water, more or less yielding according to its state of wetness or infiltration. It is an imperfect fluid, or a viscous body, which is urged down the slopes of a certain inclination by the mutual pressure of its parts; and he compared it to a thick mortar, or the contents of a tar barrel poured into a sloping channel. Whoever has looked at the manner in which such a fluid moves, will have observed that the middle part of the moving body advances more rapidly than those portions which form its outer edges, which must overcome the friction caused by contact with the channel, and which therefore are retarded, and cannot proceed with equal velocity. Evident signs of this kind of movement were discovered in the glaciers by Professor Forbes. They consist of curves, which lie across the surface ice of the glacier, and extend from one side to the other. The convexity of these curves is directed towards the lower end of the slope. In the more elevated part of the glaciers the curvature is but gentle; but it increases in proceeding farther down, and towards the lower termination it presents a very elongated form. Such curves can only be formed when an imperfectly fluid body runs down a gentle slope. The nature of the ice of which the glaciers consist is certainly in favor of this theory. The interstices between the single crystals are possessed of a great capacity of absorbing water, and conducting it to a considerable distance. When these interstices, and also the air bubbles which abound in the semi-opaque layers, are completely saturated, it is very probable that the whole mass contains as much water as solid ice, and in that state it may be considered as an imperfect fluid, and moves slowly forward. But according to our knowledge of the laws of nature, we can only conceive the ice of the glacier to be found in such a state during the warm season. The progress of the glacier could, therefore, only take place during that part of the year. From the statement of Professor Forbes himself, however, we must infer that the process of the ice is hardly retarded in winter. In less than four months, from the 12th of December to the 4th of April, it advanced one hundred and forty-two feet. If in four months complete it had advanced one hundred and sixty feet, the progress in winter would have been as rapid as in summer. In this extraordinary fact the great difficulty appears to lie, which must be removed before the theory of Professor Forbes can be considered as firmly established.

Among the inhabitants of the Alps the opinion prevails that the glaciers are continually on the increase, not in elevation, but in extent. They assert that the lower extremities of these icy masses advance farther and farther into the valleys, and on the declivities of the mountains; and they cannot overcome the apprehension that in time the ice will spread over some of their richest alpine pastures, and perhaps cover them entirely. It cannot be denied that there are many instances transmitted by tradition, and even a few recorded by history, which appear to prove that this fear is not quite without foundation, some mountain passes and elevated valleys, which formerly were free of ice, being at present filled up. Captain Hall instances the remarkable case of the glacier of Brenva falling into the lower part of the Allée Blanche, fairly crossing from one side of the valley to the other, and being so irresistibly pressed forward by the weight of snow on its shoulders, high up the sides of Mont Blanc, that on reaching the opposite side of the valley, it actually travels for a considerable distance up the bank. "The guides," he remarks, "pointed out the corners of green fields, peeping out from the sides of the glacier in the middle of the valley, and showed us traces of walls and fences which had belonged to large villages, now entirely obliterated by the moving mass. I took notice of one circumstance, which told the fatal story very well. We had walked along a well-worn footpath till our course was abruptly stopped by the edge of the glacier; but on crossing over it, we rediscovered our footpath, which had been quite hidden by the intervening mass." Scientific men who have paid close attention to this subject, who have collected all the certain information regarding this supposed increase, and investigated the matter in all its bearings, account for the isolated instances of the increase of the glaciers by observing that, in some winters, the quantity of snow which falls is larger than usual, and that when such a winter is succeeded by a summer in which the temperature does not rise to its usual height, the whole quantity of snow which has fallen in the colder regions cannot be dissolved. This may sometimes continue for several years in succession. In such a case it is very probable that the whole mass of the glacier increases to a certain extent, and advances farther into the valley than it did before. It may even happen that, under such circumstances, new glaciers of small extent are formed; but, on the other hand, it is also certain that, after some years, the reverse takes place. A smaller quantity of snow falls in winter, the mean temperature is higher, the winters are less cold, and then the new glaciers disappear, and the old ones recede within their ancient limits.

In Norway the Nygaard and several other glaciers have for many years been diminishing in extent. "The former boundary of the Nygaard," says Professor Forbes, "is as distinct, indeed much more so, than the limit of spring tides usually is on the sea shore.* It is marked upon the rocks far above and beyond the present limit of the ice by the clean and fresh-dressed surfaces they exhibit, of a shade, too, far lighter than the lichen-grown and weathered slopes of the mountain sides. Where the glacier quits the contact of rock on either side, its ancient limit is marked by the mound of fresh colored debris which it has driven before it to the utmost boundary of its overflow, and which remains there, a monument to future ages of its past extent, like the index of a register thermometer pushed on by the fluid which cannot recall it a hair's breadth. All the semilunar space included between this moraine and the existing ice is emphatically *waste.* It is almost level, and absolutely covered with rolled stones of every size, from that of an egg to blocks of several cubic yards, loose and free from any cohering soil. Within the whole limits just described there is almost no vegetation. A few blades of grass, or a weed, may here and there spring up, but they are imperceptible at any distance, whilst immediately beyond the moraine vegetation is abundant, and young birch trees are every where making their appearance. This gives quite a different tone of color to the glacial soil, and renders

* See engraving opposite page 138.

the limits as conspicuous as we have described them to be. The interval between the present and former limit of the ice is stated by Bohr, a Norwegian author, at seventeen hundred and twenty-six feet, and by Naumann and Durocher at two thousand feet."

There are, perhaps, no objects in nature which recompense the traveller more amply for the trouble of visiting than the glaciers, by their numerous and various beauties. These beauties are partly derived from their peculiar nature, and partly from the contrast they exhibit with the countries contiguous to their lower extremities. The immense extent of the huge icy masses, traversed in every direction by numerous yawning chasms descending to an unknown depth, and surrounded by turrets and perpendicular walls and cliffs of ice of the most fantastic forms, having in the background black rocks of an immense elevation, which rise in the shape of peaks out of a sea of extremely white snow, would fill the mind of the looker on with horror, were it not converted into astonishment and admiration by the peculiar bluish color which spreads over the whole region up to the very borders of the snow mountains, and attains in the chasms the deepest hue and greatest beauty. When the traveller turns his back, he finds the icy masses on which he is standing surrounded by forests, fields, pastures, and orchards. To his left is a meadow of the most verdant turf, on which flocks of sheep are feeding, attended by a shepherd who tunes his flute or sings his pastoral lay. To the right is a gentle slope entirely covered with ripe barley, in which the reapers are busy collecting the bounteous gifts of Providence; whilst before him, on the banks of a river pouring down its whitish-green waters, stands a village of neatly-constructed houses, the abodes of happiness and content, surrounded by orchards in which cherries are found in abundance. At no great distance are a few groves of high forest trees, mostly of the pine kind, which by their sombre aspect do not fail to impress a degree of earnestness on the cheerful landscape. At many places the scenery receives an additional zest by a small lake enclosed by meadows, from whose smooth surface the surrounding mountains are reflected, with their glaciers, snow fields, and dark peaks. At another spot a cataract precipitates its silvery waters down the perpendicular declivities of a black rocky mass, the falling stream being frequently deflected from its straight line by a gust of wind.

Coleridge strikingly alludes to these formations in his Hymn before Sunrise in the Vale of Chamouni; and Science will not quarrel with him for the line which expresses the optical appearance, rather than the philosophical truth.

"Ye ice falls! ye that from the mountain's brow
Adown enormous ravines slope amain —
Torrents, methinks, that heard a mighty voice,
And stopped at once amid their maddest plunge! —
Motionless torrents! Silent cataracts!
Who made you glorious as the gates of heaven
Beneath the keen full moon? Who bade the sun
Clothe you with rainbows? Who, with living flowers
Of loveliest blue, spread garlands at your feet?
God! let the torrents, like a shout of nations,
Answer; and let the ice plains echo, God!
God! sing ye meadow streams, with gladsome voice!
Ye pine groves, with your soft and soul-like sounds!
And they, too, have a voice, yon piles of snow,
And in their perilous fall shall thunder, God!"

None of the numerous glaciers of the Alps are better known than those of Grindelwald. They are annually visited by many thousand travellers, partly because they are more accessible than the others, and partly because they may be considered as fair specimens of the glaciers. They are two in number, and situated in the valley of Grindelwald, which lies in the high mountain masses extending between the cantons of Berne and Valais. This valley extends from north-west to south-east, and on both sides the higher part of the mountains rises above the snow line. In the north-eastern chain is Mount Faulhorn, which rises to eight thousand five hundred and forty-seven feet above the sea level. The south-western chain is much more elevated, being overtopped by Mount Wetterhorn, twelve thousand one hundred and seventy-seven feet high; Mount Eigher, nearly thirteen thousand feet high; and the summits of Schreckhorn and Wisherhorn, which are still more elevated. The valley is at the village only thirty-three hundred and fifty-seven feet above the sea, and therefore well inhabited. In and near it are numerous orchards of cherry trees, well cultivated fields, and large pasture grounds. The two glaciers are situated at its upper end. The lower is smaller, and lies between Mount Eigher and the Mettenberg; the larger between the last-named mountain and the Wetterhorn. They lie parallel to each other. The lower one is the more beautiful, as it descends over a much more broken surface, and consequently presents a much greater variety in the icy masses with which its surface is studded. To the south and east of the valley of Grindelwald is a mountainous country, at least three hundred square miles in diameter, which may be considered as one large glacier, (for the numerous glaciers which occur in this tract are separated from one another only by ridges of snow-capped mountains,) on whose back are placed a great number of high peaks, among which Mount Finsteraarhorn is the highest. It rises to fourteen thousand one hundred feet above the sea. Nearly as numerous are the glaciers which descend from the western base of Mont Blanc, south-east of Geneva. They lie so close together that they appear to constitute one immense mass of ice, to which the name of Mer de Glace, or Sea of Ice, is not improperly applied.

CHAPTER VIII.

AVALANCHES. — VILLAGE OF BUERAS, IN SWITZERLAND, BURIED BY AN AVALANCHE. — A FOREST TRANSPORTED ACROSS A VALLEY BY AN AVALANCHE. — VILLAGE OF RANDA DESTROYED BY THE AGITATION OF THE AIR, PRODUCED BY AN AVALANCHE. — DESTRUCTIVE FLOOD, CAUSED BY THE TEMPORARY OBSTRUCTION OF THE RIVER DRANSE BY AN AVALANCHE.

AVALANCHES are masses of snow or ice which fall from the upper declivities of high mountains into the valleys at their base, often occasioning damage, and destroying life and property. They are very frequent in the Alps, and occur also in the Pyrenees, Norway, and in all countries in which mountains rise to a great elevation. Some of them originate in those parts of the acclivities which are contiguous to the snow line, but others at a much less elevation. When the accumulation of snow on the declivities becomes so great that the inclined plane on which the mass rests cannot any longer support it, it is carried down the slope by its own weight, and precipitated into the subjacent valley, destroying forests and villages, burying men and cattle, and sometimes filling up the rivers and stopping their courses. Besides what is actually covered by these falling masses, persons are often killed, and houses overthrown by the sudden compression of the air caused by the incredible velocity with which some of the avalanches descend.

If we examine the manner in which these dangerous and terrible phenomena originate, we may distinguish four kinds of avalanches — drift avalanches, sliding avalanches, creeping avalanches, and ice or glacier avalanches.

The drift avalanches are composed of loose snow; they can only originate when the quantity of snow is very large, and has been lodged on a steep declivity, whence it is dislodged for want of support. The mass in falling loses its coherence, on account of the imperfect manner in which its particles have been united, or by striking violently against projecting rocks. These avalanches commonly take place in winter, when a very heavy fall of snow has occurred in the higher regions during a calm. Great masses are then lodged on declivities, which are sufficient to afford a support to them during calm weather, but not when the atmosphere is agitated by strong gusts of wind. Such winds, which are not rare at that season, detach the uppermost mass from the declivity of the mountain, and bring it down on other masses which lie lower, which in their turn are forced off, and thus an enormous volume of snow is collected before it reaches the valley. For a long time it was the prevailing opinion that they owed their origin to small balls of snow, which were formed near the upper edge of the most elevated snow mass, and which, in rolling down the declivities, were increased to such an enormous size as to produce, by the violence of their fall, the most extraordinary effects. This opinion arose from the erroneous, but generally diffused idea, that a loud sound, or the tinkling of a bell, was able to bring down the enormous masses of snow which cover the upper regions of the mountains. As these avalanches always descend quite unexpectedly, and without any apparent cause, — the gust of wind not being perceived in the deep valleys, — people were unable to assign any sufficient reason for their formation. This opinion of the origin of these avalanches prevails not only in the Alps, but also in the Himalaya Mountains, and in the Hindu-coosh. On a closer examination, however, it has been found that strong gusts of wind originally impart the first impulse to these masses of snow, and that they acquire their size by uniting with other masses lying lower down. The incredible velocity with which they descend, and the immense force with which they strike, prove that the drift avalanches must originate at a great elevation. They are very much dreaded, not so much on account of the damage caused by the snow itself, as from the effects of the compression of the air, with which they are always attended. The air compressed by these masses rushes off on all sides with the greatest velocity, and with a force able to break off huge pieces of rock, to uproot the largest trees, and to scatter houses like chaff. It is very fortunate that the drift avalanches are of rare occurrence, and that they rarely descend to those valleys which are thickly peopled and well wooded.

The sliding avalanches, though less destructive in their effects than the drift avalanches, cause greater damage than the others, on account of their frequency. They take place when the snow covering of the declivities, by having been slightly thawed and again frozen, has acquired a considerable degree of consistency on its surface, and has been cemented to some extent into one mass. When under such circumstances, by the natural heat of the earth, the bond has been loosened which unites the mass to its base, and the ground on which it rests has been rendered slippery, the whole mass begins to slide downwards in one sheet, and precipitates itself over every obstacle into the valleys. These avalanches originate in the middle regions of the mountains, on declivities which have not a very rapid slope, and in spring time. They are less dangerous because they are not attended by a compression of the air, but they cause great damages by the enormous masses of snow which they bring down. These masses are sometimes so great as to cover large extents of meadow and forest with such a thick layer, that several summers must pass before they are entirely melted; this affects the climate of the valley in a very disadvantageous way. But they also frequently cause considerable loss of life and property. In the year 1749 the whole village of Bueras, in the valley of Tawich, in the canton of the Grisons, was buried under, and at the same time removed from its site by, an avalanche of this description. But this change, which happened in the night time, was effected without the least noise, so that the inhabitants were not aware of it, and on awakening in the morning could not conceive why it did not grow day. One hundred persons were dug out of the snow, sixty of whom were still alive, the hollows within the snow containing sufficient air to support life. In 1806 an avalanche descended into Val Calanca, likewise in the canton of the Grisons, transported a forest from one side of the valley to the other, and planted a fir tree on the roof of the parsonage house. Several villages have been destroyed by these avalanches, and a large number of persons and cattle have been killed. But in general they do not come on unexpectedly. The places where they frequently occur are known, as also what kind of weather commonly precedes their descent. The Austrian government, some years ago, wishing to connect the province of Sondrio with Tyrol, by a mountain road which was not to pass over any portion of Switzerland, but to lie entirely within their own dominions, caused a road to be made over Mount Stelvio through a region frequently exposed to sliding avalanches. Notwithstanding the extreme care with which the galleries were constructed, which were to protect the road and the passengers against them, the snow descended in such enormous masses as to break down all the galleries, and compelled the Austrian government to give up the plan. This is the only kind of avalanche which occurs in Norway, the shape of the mountain masses in that country not being favorable to the formation of the other kinds. But as nearly all the mountain masses have along their borders gentle declivities of considerable width, they are frequent and destructive in that country. A few years ago a number of reindeer, exceeding fifty, were found dead in a narrow and uninhabited valley, within a narrow space, which, according to all appearances, had been buried by an avalanche.

The creeping avalanches are called, in Switzerland, "suoggi," (pronounced *suggy*,) from a verb *suogger*, which signifies to advance slowly, to creep. They originate in the same manner as the sliding avalanches, but on declivities which have a much more gentle slope. The snowy covering, when loosened from its rocky base, begins to move slowly down the slippery declivity, and to carry before it every thing which is too weak to withstand its pressure. When an object does not directly give way to its mass, it is either borne down by the snow accumulating behind it, or the whole mass divides, and proceeds in its course on each side of it. These avalanches are very frequent, but rarely cause any considerable damage, from the comparatively small volume of snow they bring down, and their slow advance. They occur mostly in spring, and on the lower acclivities of the mountains.

The glacier or ice avalanches are nothing but large fragments of glaciers, and their origin is especially due to the fracturing of the icy masses, when they are protruded downwards. They are frequently broken into small pieces by other masses of ice, or by rocks which they meet in their progress. When in such a state, and seen from a distance, they resemble the cataracts of a powerful stream. In summer, which appears to be the only season in which they occur, they may every day be seen on almost all the glaciers of Switzerland; and at the base of Mount Jungfrau, in the valley of Lauterbrun, in the canton of Berne, the thunder which accompanies their fall is almost continually heard. They are not in general destructive, because they descend upon places which are not inhabited. Yet occasionally their fall is attended with terrible effects. This is especially the case when a glacier terminates on the very edge of a high mountain mass, which descends with a perpendicular declivity into an inhabited valley. A very dreadful catastrophe of this kind occurred in 1819 in the valley of Visp, in Valais, where the village of Randa was destroyed by a glacier avalanche. This village was built not far from the base of a mountain mass, which rises nearly perpendicularly to an elevation of more than nine thousand feet above its base, and forms part of the snow mountain called Weisshorn, (white horn,) which is every where surrounded with huge masses of glaciers. One of these glaciers had advanced to the very edge of the precipice, and was overhanging it, when at once an enormous piece of it was detached, and with a terrible crash precipitated down into the valley, where it covered with ice, rubbish, and fragments of rock an area of two thousand four hundred feet in length, and a thousand feet in width, to a depth of more than a hundred and fifty feet. This mass fell on an uninhabited tract; but in its vicinity was the above-named village, which was destroyed by the compression of the air produced by the fall of that enormous mass. The force of the gust caused by this compression was so great that it raised millstones from the ground, and lodged them on a slope which was several yards above the place where they had been deposited. It conveyed the beams of several houses to a distance of nearly a mile into a forest, and broke down the steeple of the church, which was a massive building of stone.

The year previous to this event a catastrophe of a different description was produced by glacier avalanches in another valley of Valais, the vale of Bagnes.

The valley, or rocky glen, extends from thirty to forty miles, and presents steep and rugged mountain walls, the summits ascending above the limit of perpetual snow, and exhibiting glaciers on their slopes. At the top of the valley the River Dranse has its origin in the two glaciers of Chermontane and Mont Durand, and flows along its course to its termination at Martigny, where it joins the Rhone, of which it is one of the chief affluents. Not far from the upper end of the Val de Bagnes, it is formed into a narrow gorge by the approximating flanks of Mont Pleureur on one side, and Mont Mauvoisin on the other, between which is the glacier of Getroz. From this glacier large masses of ice are continually detached, which, falling into the ravine, tend to fill up the contracted channel, and arrest the progress of the Dranse. For several years previous to the time referred to, the river had been much obstructed by blocks of ice and snow, which at length accumulated so as to resist the heats of summer, and ultimately form a conical projection of the glacier itself

An ice avalanche in Switzerland. See page 165.

completely across its bed to the height of about a hundred feet. In the month of April, 1818, the Dranse was dammed up, and a lake began to form, which soon attained a considerable magnitude. It was obviously in the highest degree probable that the icy barrier would not be able to hold out long against the increasing pressure of the waters, and the sudden efflux of such a mighty volume as was collected would as certainly desolate the Val de Bagnes. To avoid this calamity, which every day became more impending, an engineer started the bold scheme of tunnelling the rampart of ice, and was employed by the government of the canton for that purpose. "This scheme," says the memoir of M. Escher upon it, "was begun on the 10th of May, and finished on the 13th of June, under the direction of M. Venetz. The gallery was sixty-eight feet long, and during its formation the workmen were exposed to the constant risk of being crushed to pieces by the falling blocks of ice, or buried under the glacier itself." The lake at this time contained at least eight hundred millions of cubic feet of water, which in three days was reduced to five hundred and thirty millions, by the discharge from the gallery. The sequel may best be related in the words of the memoir: —

"As soon as the water flowed from the lower end of the gallery, the velocity of the cascade melted the ice, and thus wore away the gallery at its mouth. The water which had penetrated the crevices of the glacier caused enormous fragments of ice to fall from the lower sides of it; so that, owing to these causes, the body of the glacier, which formed the retaining wall of the lake, was so much diminished in thickness that the floor of the gallery was reduced from its original length of six hundred to eight feet. As soon as the cascade had cut through the cone of ice, it attacked the debris of the base of Mauvoisin, upon which the cone rested; that is to say, the torrent undermined the glacier by washing away the loose materials forming the bed of the stream, on which the mass of ice had been piled up; and, having carried it off by degrees, it became able to push the soft soil from the foot of Mont Mauvoisin, and excavate for itself a passage between the glacier and the rocky beds which compose the mountain. As soon as this happened, the water rushed out, the ice gave way with a tremendous crash, the lake was emptied in half an hour, and the sea of water which it contained precipitated itself into the valley, with a rapidity and violence which it is impossible to describe. The fury of this raging flood was first stayed by the narrow gorge below the glacier formed between Mont Pleureur and a projecting breast of Mont Mauvoisin; here it was ingulfed with such force that it carried away the bridge of Mauvoisin, ninety feet above the Dranse, and even rose several fathoms above the advanced mass of the mountains. From this narrow gorge the flood spread itself over a wider part of the valley, which again contracted into another gorge; and in this way, passing from one basin to another, it acquired new violence, and carried along with it forests, rocks, houses, barns, and cultivated land. When it reached Le Chable, one of the principal villages of the valley, the flood, which seemed to contain more debris than water, was pent up between the piers of a solid bridge, nearly fifty feet above the Dranse, and began to attack the inclined plane upon which the church and the chief part of the village is built. An additional rise of a few feet would have instantly undermined the village; but at this critical moment the bridge gave way, and carried off with it the houses at its two extremities. The flood now spread itself over the wide part of the valley between Le Chable and St. Branchier, undermining, destroying, and hurrying away the houses, the roads, the richest crops, and the finest trees, loaded with fruit. Instead of being encumbered with these spoils, the moving chaos received from them new force; and when it entered the narrow valley extending from St. Branchier to Martigny, it continued its work of destruction till its fury became weakened by expanding itself over the great plain formed by the valley of the Rhone. After ravaging Le Burg and the village of Martigny, it fell with comparative tranquillity into the Rhone, leaving behind it the wreck of houses and of furniture, thousands of trees torn up by the roots, and the bodies of men and of animals whom it had swept away."

About fifty persons lost their lives by this inundation, and the amount of property destroyed was estimated at forty thousand pounds.

It was calculated by the writer of the memoir, that the flood for the first four miles swept along at the rate of twenty miles an hour, — nearly the speed of a locomotive, — and furnished about three hundred thousand cubic feet of water every second — an efflux five times greater than that of the Rhine at Basle. In six hours and a half it arrived at the Lake of Geneva, having passed into the Rhone, a distance of forty-five miles. Among the physical alterations effected by this debacle, there was the deposition of a stratum of alluvial matter over the whole of the lower part of the Val de Bagnes. This was several feet in thickness, and was so distributed that roads were obliged to be cut through it in some places, as when the snows have blocked up our thoroughfares. There was the transportation of an immense number of isolated masses of rock to a considerable distance, some of which must have been many tons in weight. One of these, fairly projected out of the gorge of the valley into the plain, measured twenty-seven paces round, twelve feet in height, and twelve feet across in one direction; and even larger masses bore indubitable marks of having been in motion. For some time the course of the Dranse fluctuated, and when at last it settled down into a channel, it was one widely different from that which had before been followed. Captain Hall visited Martigny a few weeks after this visitation, and found every landmark obliterated under one uniform mass of detritus, which had levelled all distinctions in a "sweeping and democratic confusion."

CHAPTER IX.

LANDSLIPS. — THE FALL OF A PART OF MOUNT CARNANS, IN SWITZERLAND. — FALL OF PART OF MOUNT RUFFI, BURYING FIVE VILLAGES AND THEIR INHABITANTS. — FALL OF PART OF MOUNT CONTO, BURYING TWENTY-FOUR HUNDRED AND THIRTY PERSONS. — FALL OF ONE OF THE MOUNTAINS CALLED "THE DEVIL'S HORNS." — FALL OF A PART OF MOUNT GRENIER, BURYING FIVE PARISHES, AND STREWING ITS FRAGMENTS OVER NINE SQUARE MILES. — LANDSLIP IN THE WHITE MOUNTAINS. — MOUNTAIN TORRENTS.

IN mountainous regions the detachment of fragments of rock and earth from abrupt and precipitous elevations is the gradual yet sure effect of the wear and tear of the atmosphere, accelerated by the occurrence of severe storms, heavy rains, and intense frost. Mam Tor, a hill on the Peak of Derbyshire, England, has become celebrated on account of the waste of its mass; and hence it is popularly called, in the neighborhood, the "shivering mountain." The summit of the hill rises about eight hundred feet above the level of the valley, and commands an extensive prospect of the high eminences of the district and its beautiful dales, retreats secluded from the bustle of the world, to which the imagination is ready to assign the attributes under which the Happy Valley of Rasselas is described. According to vulgar rumor, the shivering of the hill has been going on for ages, without occasioning any diminution of its bulk; but apart from fable, Mam Tor is a mass consisting of alternate layers of shale and gritstone, and the former readily decomposes under the influence of the weather, falling into the valley below, bringing with it detached fragments of the grit. In the winter season, after unusual rains, or in severe frost, the decomposition is the most rapid, the Tor discharging from its side immense pieces

Vale of Goldau, Switzerland. Twenty square miles of this valley are covered with huge masses of rock, which, in 1806, fell from Mount Ruffi.

of its material, the noise of which in their descent may be heard in the adjacent villages, and is described as singularly impressive in the night. In all Alpine regions, subject to great seasonal vicissitudes, frost is a powerful agent in the destruction of rocks. When the water that has entered their pores and fissures becomes frozen, it acts by its expansion with irresistible force, and detaches enormous masses, which fall from their parent bed thundering to a lower level. In the upper parts of North America, even in latitude fifty-one degrees, in some places, where the winter climate is so severe that brandy congeals and the lakes freeze eight feet thick, the rocks split with a noise resembling the explosion of artillery, and the shattered fragments fly to a considerable distance.

The action of water, in another way, operates to dislodge from their situation the higher parts of mountains, and sometimes to reduce their whole mass to ruins, producing land or mountain slips. This is by a slow process of erosion and undermining, which having proceeded to a sufficient extent, brings on in a moment the catastrophe of a slide or fall. The occurrence cannot take place in the case of unstratified rocks, which are only subject to the gradual abrading of their entire mass, and the detachment of small fragments; but with reference to the stratified mountains, where layers of different kinds of rock overlay one another, it is easy to conceive of such slides transpiring. Water percolating by rents and fissures through an upper stratum, and reaching another which readily yields to its solvent power, the lower stratum may be so far carried away in the course of ages as to be unable to support the upper, which, in consequence, falls down. But little harm would ensue, if the different strata were of uniform breadth and horizontally disposed, like a number of equal volumes piled upon each other, instead of displaying varying thickness and all manner of inclination. It is this last condition chiefly—the differently inclined plane upon which the upper stratum descends—that causes its precipitation upon the country at the base, covering it with its ruins, and occasionally overwhelming its inhabitants. Other circumstances concur to the production of land and mountain slips; but the principal agent is water, operating by a process of undermining, which, however slow and subtile, is grand and terrible in the crisis that ensues. Such events are by no means uncommon; but they generally occur in secluded and uninhabited sites, so as not to attract any wide notice, unless they happen upon a grand scale. On the night of the 29th of January, 1840, in the district of Jura, a mountain called the Carnans came down in mass on the surrounding plain, and a portion of the royal road from Dijon to Portalier sunk with this *eboulement* to a depth of more than fifty metres. That portion known as the Rampe de Carnans—the ladder or staircase of Carnans—was rendered impassable, and all communication between the places on each side was entirely suspended. A fresh mass of rock and earth, during the following day, was detached, and was distinctly seen from a great distance as it slid down. It was supposed that a fountain, which ceased to play upwards of a quarter of a century before, had then taken a new subterranean direction, and mined out a portion of the mountain. Switzerland has repeatedly exhibited these extensive falls from her giant mountains, which may form a subject of interesting reference.

It has sometimes happened that the waters of an elevated lake have insinuated themselves between the strata composing the mass of a mountain, gradually loosening and removing a quantity of material, by which the superior body of rock or earth, being deprived of its support, has fallen. In this way the catastrophe of the Rosenberg, otherwise called Mont Ruffi, is conceived to have been occasioned in the year 1806. Nearly in the centre of Switzerland, in the canton of Zug, is the lake of that name, a lovely sheet of water, and a smaller lake, that of Lowerz. Between these lakes, extending from the banks of the one to the other a distance of about six miles, is the vale of Goldau, a scene of inviting natural beauty. On one side of the valley, Mont Righi rises to the height of forty-six hundred and forty-four feet, and on the other side Mont Ruffi reaches thirty-seven hundred and forty-seven feet above the level of the Lake of Zug. These are stratified mountains, composed of conglomerate, cemented by a kind of sandstone, or a fine-grained marl, the strata varying considerably in thickness. In the year mentioned, on the morning of the 2d of September, noises were heard proceeding from Mont Ruffi, which startled the inhabitants of the valley, who little dreamed of the disaster that was impending. In the afternoon of the day the noises were repeated, becoming more frequent, and some pieces of rock were observed to fall down the declivities of the mountain. Larger masses descended towards five o'clock in the evening, and now the apprehensions of the people were thoroughly awakened; but they had little time either to fear or fly, for a few minutes afterwards a large part of the upper mass of the mountain was seen to give way, and to be coming down upon the valley. Its motion was at first slow; but in a few seconds it acquired a frightful velocity, and with a tremendous crash, the disjoined portion, with its forests and buildings was precipitated upon the lower levels, darkening the air with clouds of dust, so as to obscure for a time all further perception of the catastrophe. Some of the spectators of this event were in a house at the base of Mont Righi on the opposite side, at an elevation of three hundred feet above the bottom of the valley; but such was the tremendous impetus given to the rocks in their descent, that large blocks were forced up the acclivity, and nearly reached their situation. The movement was so sudden, that nine out of thirteen travellers, who happened to be passing, were overwhelmed; and the mass that fell was so prodigious, that it formed a ridge in the valley one hundred feet in height, and a league and a half in length and breadth. In little more than five minutes, the greater part of the whole vale of Goldau was transformed from a happy and cultivated retreat into a mass of ruins. The villages of Goldau, Busingan, Lowerz, Ober, and Unter Rother were either entirely or in part buried; four hundred and eighty-four of the inhabitants lost their lives; a great number of cattle and sheep perished; and property was destroyed, according to an estimate made by the government of the canton, to the amount of nearly one hundred thousand pounds. A portion of the mountain, dashing into the Lake of Lowerz, raised a succession of vast waves, one of which swept over the small Island of Schwanan, though sixty feet above the ordinary level of the water. The cause of this tremendous occurrence was not doubtful. About half a century before the year 1806, some considerable rents, of great depth, had been formed in Mont Ruffi, by which the water of the rains and melted snows, as well as some from the adjacent lakes, was freely admitted into the interior of the mountain. The marl and clay which united the strata of conglomerate exposed to its action were gradually washed away, depriving the upper masses of the foundation on which from immemorial time they had securely rested, which were precipitated forward upon being displaced. On the site once occupied by the village of Goldau there is now a small chapel, where the pious Switzers pray for preservation from a similar calamity, holding a service for the purpose annually on the 2d of September. The road through the valley passes over the debris which extends from the top of Ruffi far up Righi on the opposite side of the valley, and winds through enormous blocks of stone. A remarkable instance of this kind is exhibited in our engraving, where the road is seen passing between and under huge masses of rock. See eng. at p. 170.

A disruption, equally sudden, but far more fatal in its effects, took place in the year 1618 with reference to Mont Conto, which formerly overlooked a pleasant and well-built town and adjacent village in the Val Bregaglia, in the Lombardo-Venetian kingdom. Of the particulars we have less information than in the former case, as it happened in the night. While the air was calm, the sky cloudless, and most of the people of the valley were wrapped in sleep, the summit of the mountain came down, completely burying the town with its ruins, upon which a forest of chestnuts now flourishes. Only one house escaped destruction, and three inhabitants, who were absent on business, two thousand four hundred and thirty persons perishing. There had been beforehand intimations of danger sufficient to have induced observant and reflecting persons, aware of the dreadful incidents to which such localities are subject, to have removed to a safer spot. For ten years previous, large chasms had been formed in the mountains, into which the rains descended, and ultimately wrought the mischiefs that occurred. On the afternoon before the fatal night some fragments of rock had fallen; but in the spirit of confident and happy security, the inhabitants of the Val Bregaglia retired to rest among their native and much loved mountains, and saw them no more. It has been correctly enough observed, that "until the fatal moment of destruction arrives, or, at all events, till the hour of danger approaches, mankind, all the world over, are pretty nearly equally indifferent, and go on dancing and singing, marrying and giving in marriage, under the very jaws of death, with as much unconcern as if they were living in perfect safety. The inhabitants of Portici and Resina, for instance, living at the base of Vesuvius, or those of Catania, at the foot of Mount Etna, where torrent upon torrent of lava has flowed in endless succession, never dream of an eruption till the parched volcano drinks up their wells, and, in the language of Scripture, 'fire runs along the ground.'" In like manner, the writer remarks, "I have observed the gay voluptuaries of Lima scarcely disturbed in their reckless enjoyment of life by the shock of an earthquake, which interrupted only for a transient moment of fear and impatient prayer their darling 'Tertullas,' while the ceilings and walls of their houses cracked in their ears, and church steeples toppled round them." It is clear that in the two preceding cases of mountain falls, which involved a large sacrifice of human life, much of it might have been avoided by heeding the warnings given. But thus it happens, that men are slow to believe themselves endangered, and when the disaster comes, the survivors of friends, relatives, and property are apt to dwell only upon the physical evils of their condition, forgetful of their own imprudence, and of the millions of terrestrial sites secure from the catastrophe.

An elevated piece of table land between the cantons of Valais and Berne, which rises nearly to the snow line, was the scene of the same phenomenon in the year 1714 and 1749. Three sharp peaks ascend from it to the height of ten thousand six hundred and twenty feet above the level of the sea, called *Les Diablerets*, or the devil's horns. Originally there were four; but one was demolished at the two periods named, covering the plain with its fragments. The shattered blocks and heaps of rubbish upon it are indeed so extensive as to lead to the conclusion that the group of the Diablerets has lost other members in bygone ages; but of any occurrence of this nature prior to 1714 no account exists. The event of that year has been related in the following words: "Before the first catastrophe a subterraneous noise was heard, and some of the herdsmen, who had brought their herds to the pastures in the vicinity, took this hint, and returned home; others, however, were buried under the rocks. When the mount precipitated itself down, the whole country in its vicinity trembled, and a thick smoke rose to a considerable height in the air. It was only dust, which was detached from the rocks when they broke to pieces. The compression of the air was so great that some of the trees which were near the places along which the rocks descended were bent to the ground or broken. Many of the summer huts of the Alpine herdsmen were destroyed, fourteen persons lost their lives, and a large number of cattle and sheep were killed. One of the herdsmen belonging to the village of Aven, in Valais, was among those who had not returned home, and was considered as having lost his life. His children were declared orphans by the court. Three months afterwards, on Christmas eve, he suddenly appeared in his village — pale, thin, covered with rags, resembling a spectre. All the inhabitants of the village were frightened. The doors of his own house were shut to him. Some people ran to the priest, requesting him to exorcise the supposed spectre. After some delay, the man succeeded in convincing the people that he was alive, and then he told them that the moment on which the mountain slip took place, he had been on his knees praying to the Preserver of life, when an enormous fragment of rock, in descending, struck the ground before his hut, and resting, leaned over against the rocky wall, at the base of which his hut was built. It was immediately followed by a terrible crash, and by an immense quantity of stones and rubbish, entirely covering the piece of rock which protected his hut. 'When all became quiet,' he continued, 'I was no longer in fear; I did not lose my courage; and directly I set myself to work to open an issue. A few pieces of cheese which I had were my food, and a rill of water, which descended among the ruins, quenched my thirst. After many days, which I was unable to count in the long darkness of my subterraneous prison, I discovered, by creeping about among the rocks, an opening. I saw again the sun's light, but my eyes were for some time unable to bear it. The Almighty, in whom I always confided, and who always kept alive my hope of preserving life, has sent me back to my family, to be a witness and a proof of his power and bounty.'" The second slip of the Diablerets, in 1749, took place without injury to the peasantry, who obeyed a warning given by the mountain to escape in time; but five Bernese citizens, travelling in the neighborhood, refused to fly, believing the fears of the people to be unfounded, and the house in which they remained is thought to be five hundred feet below the present surface.

A part of Mont Grenier, about five miles south of Chamberry, in Savoy, gave way in the year 1248, and exhibits marks of the disruption in its present appearance, which has been sketched by Mr. Bakewell, to whose Travels in the Tarentaise we are indebted for most of the particulars concerning the event. The ruins of the mountain entirely buried five parishes, with the town and church of St. André, spreading over an extent of about nine square miles. These ruins are now called *les Abymes des Myans;* and, notwithstanding the lapse of many centuries, and the presence of numerous vineyards which have since been planted, they present in many places a singular and impressive scene of desolation. A favorable view of the fall, at a safe distance, was afforded by the locality, for Mont Grenier is almost isolated, advancing into a broad plain, which extends to the valley of the Isere. It is several miles in length, but very narrow, and attains the height of four thousand feet above the plain, being an abutment of the mountains of the Grand Chartreux. The summit is capped with an immense mass of limestone strata, not less than six hundred feet in thickness, presenting on every side the appearance of a wall. The strata dip gently to the side which fell into the plain. This mass of limestone rests on a foundation of molasse, a term applied by the Genevese to the softer beds of sandstone, and underneath this, strata of limestone alternate with it. There can be little doubt that the disruption was occasioned by the gradual erosion of the soft strata, which undermined the mass of limestone above, and projected it into the plain. The part that fell had probably been for some time nearly detached from the mountain by a shrinking of the southern side, where there is at present a large rent upwards of two thousand feet deep, which seems to have cut off a section that

"Hangs in doubtful ruins o'er its base,"

and threatens a renewal of the event of 1248. The projected portions forming the Abymes des Myans exhibit a series of small conical hills, varying in height from twenty to thirty feet, composed of fragments of calcareous strata, precipitated to the distance of two or three miles from the mountain. Falling from the upper bed of limestone with which Mont Grenier is capped, the velocity they would acquire by descending from so great a height, making due allowance for the resistance of the atmosphere, Mr. Bakewell estimates at not less than three hundred feet a second. The projectile force gained by striking against the base of the mountain, or against each other, has spread them over the plain, where, in the course of years, the rains and currents of water from dissolving snows have washed away the loose earth, and furrowed channels, giving to the masses of stone the aspect they now present,—that of detached conical hills. The chronicles which have preserved a record of this occurrence do not state whether the fall of the mountain was preceded by any forewarnings that allowed to the inhabitants the opportunity to escape. Certain it is that the town of St. André, then a place of some importance, being the ancient seat of the deanery of Savoy, and other parishes, were so entirely overwhelmed, and to such a vast depth, that nothing has ever been discovered belonging to them except a small bronze statue. It has been calculated that the quantity of matter that fell would be more than four hundred millions of tons in weight, occasioning a shock inconceivably awful, being precipitated from the height of three quarters of a mile into the plain. The dislodged material stopped a little short of the church at Myans, dedicated to the Virgin, and called Notre Dame des Myans. Hence the church acquired celebrity, and pilgrimages are made to its shrine by the Savoyards, to whom it would be heresy to intimate that the elevation of the ground assisted the efforts of the Virgin in arresting the calamity.

A sudden and extensive landslip occurred, in the year 1826, in the White Mountains, New Hampshire. Here there is a pass, or *notch*, about six miles in length. The mountains on each side rise from eighteen hundred to two thousand feet, at an angle of about forty-five degrees, and form a valley less than half a mile in width, along which a roaring streamlet, the Saco, takes its course. At the period in question, a farmer, of the name of Willey, with his wife, five children, and two laborers, occupied a small farm at the upper end of the valley, hospitably entertaining the benighted travellers who sought the shelter of their roof. It was the only house in the notch, and their nearest neighbors were six miles distant. At that time the hills were mantled with large forest trees and shrubs, so that no disturbance of their site could have happened for ages, nor had any thing occurred to render the family doubtful as to the perfect safety of their position. But in the month of June a small slide of earth took place from the top of the surrounding hills, which so alarmed the dwellers below by the devastation it made, as to induce them to retreat half a mile down the Saco, erecting a temporary camp upon an apparently safer spot. After two unusually dry seasons, in the beginning of July, the clouds collected about the summits of the mountains, and commenced the discharge of a deluge of rain, while the wind blew a hurricane, which continued with unabated violence for several days. On the night of the 26th the tempest raged with tremendous fury, accompanied with loud thunder and vivid lightning. The valley was inaccessible, owing to the great swelling of the Saco; but when a man entered it by swimming his horse across an eddy, the terrible spectacle presented itself of the entire face of the hills having descended in one confused mass into the valley. The Willey house appeared upon its old site uninjured in the midst of the vast chaos. But the home was desolate. The lifeless bodies of its former inmates, after some days' search, were found buried beneath a mass of wood and rubbish, not far from their own door. It seems that, after retiring to rest, they had been alarmed by the noise of the descending materials, and flying out of their dwelling, they had been swept away by the torrent of earth, stones, trees, and water that came rushing down the hills with the impetuosity which an abrupt declivity of eighteen hundred feet would give it. What was most remarkable, the torrent, after coming within four feet of the house, had divided into two branches, sweeping round it, and forming a junction within a few yards of the front, so that a flock of sheep under the lee of the house were saved, while the family leaving it perished. Every other part of the valley was covered with the dislodged matter of the hills to the depth of several feet, and a person from the rear of the house might step upon its roof with ease. The sides and summits of the mountains presented immense scars and seams, from which masses of earth and rock, with the vegetation upon them, had slid down. Some days afterwards, a small mass, bearing a thick pine forest, was seen to be in motion, and proceeding slowly from its place, it began to totter, and then fell headlong into the valley. In accounting for this fearful incident, which answered to what fancy pictures of the wreck of nature, it may be supposed that the previous hot seasons had so dried and cracked the ground, that the subsequent rains found easy admission to a considerable depth below the surface, their violence rapidly undermining the substratum, and the action of the wind upon the trees contributing to put the whole in motion.

The removal of loose materials, the tearing up of fragments of rock, and their transportation to a distant site, transpire under the action of those temporary torrents which are produced by heavy rains in mountainous districts. The pen of Captain Hall has sketched in a lively manner a specimen of their vigor as exhibited in the high lands behind the town of Funchal, in the Island of Madeira. The whole of the upper part of the mountain is split into crevices, in some instances deep enough to be called ravines, or in the larger cases even valleys, which have been cut by the rapid rush of the descending currents. Many of these crevices run into one another, so that when the rain falls in any quantity, the whole series are set in operation at once, like so many gigantic sluices, to conduct the water into the main channels which convey it into the sea. In less precipitous countries, the minor streams take some time to collect their waters; but at Madeira, where the hills are steep, the whole is done almost at a blow, and with an impetuosity that seems formidable to eyes unaccustomed to it. A few hours after a heavy rain has commenced, the torrents are all at work. Behind Funchal, the side of the mountain is indented by a valley of considerable dimensions, into which a number of ravines run, and bring down the discharges of rain from the highest ridges of the island. This is frequently the bed of a torrent, filled to the depth of twenty feet, partly with water and partly with stones, many of them of great dimensions, and moving together with a noise like continuous loud thunder. The angle which the bed makes with the horizon is sufficient to cover the surface of the stream with waves more tumultuous than those of the Canadian rapids, bearing along rocks with the utmost velocity, which the St. Lawrence would not cause to budge an inch. Sometimes huge blocks are jerked half out of the stream by the violence with which they are dashed against one another, or against some opposing angle of the channel, the bottom and sides of which, every time the torrent is in action, undergo an amount of wear and tear which effects great changes in the course of years. The writer before referred to describes this torrent, when in full play, as the grandest thing possible, requiring an effort of considerable resolution to advance to its brink, and far surpassing the surfs, breakers, and rapids, in any part of the world, in the impression of irresistible power it makes upon the senses. The roar is such that hardly any elevation of the voice can make two persons audible to one another, though standing side by side, while the ground trembles in a manner indicating the enormous weight passing over the surface. Soon after the rain ceases, this immense watercourse becomes dry, and exhibits a pavement covered with blocks of stone, variously distributed, which the current has conveyed from the upland regions, to be transported farther when its flow is renewed.

Earthquake at Lisbon, in 1755, which destroyed the City and 60,000 of its inhabitants.

CHAPTER X.

EARTHQUAKES.—DIFFERENT KINDS OF CONCUSSIONS.—EARTHQUAKE OF 1755, WHICH DESTROYED LISBON AND SIXTY THOUSAND OF ITS INHABITANTS.—EARTHQUAKE OF 1812, WHICH DESTROYED CARACCAS, AND EFFECTED GREAT CHANGES IN THE MISSISSIPPI VALLEY.—EARTHQUAKE OF 1783, WHICH LAID CALABRIA IN RUINS.—EARTHQUAKE OF 1815, IN SUMBAWA, WHICH DESTROYED A POPULATION OF TWELVE THOUSAND, WITH THE EXCEPTION OF ONLY TWENTY-SIX PERSONS.—EARTHQUAKE OF 1835, WHICH DESTROYED THE CITIES OF CONCEPTION AND TALCAHUANO.—VARIOUS REMARKABLE EFFECTS PRODUCED BY EARTHQUAKES.—FORMATION BY EARTHQUAKES OF DEEP CHASMS, OF LAKES, AND OF MOUNTAINS.—VOLCANIC FIRES IN THE OCEAN.—THEORY OF EARTHQUAKES.

EARTHQUAKES are undoubtedly the most fearful, and at the same time the most destructive, phenomena of nature. They are motions produced on the earth's solid surface by a force originating in the interior of the globe, and thence acting upward. This force, which is not palpable to our senses, appears to be subject to great variations in its intensity. In most cases the commotions occasioned by it on the earth's surface are exceedingly slight. The motion is scarcely felt, and passes away in the same moment. The larger number of earthquakes consist of a slight trembling of the ground, which can only be perceived by attentive observation, and then only under very favorable circumstances. When they have passed away, it is impossible to discover the slightest traces of their transitory activity. But at other times they are attended with effects so terrible and destructive, that no other calamity can be compared with them. When the subterraneous force to which they owe their origin acts with a violent degree of energy, it produces such convulsions on the earth's surface, that not only are the works destroyed that men have raised to render their lives comfortable, and the buildings levelled to the ground that they have erected to protect them against the inclemency of the seasons, but in some cases the face of the country is changed that has been subjected to their operation. It is happily the case that earthquakes attended with such fearful effects are not of frequent occurrence; they would otherwise render the countries visited by them uninhabitable for man and beast.

In countries frequently subject to earthquakes, only those convulsions which are attended by destructive consequences are remembered by the inhabitants for any long time after. The slight ones are hardly noticed, or are only recorded by some more curious observer. It appears, therefore, to persons living at a great distance from such places, and receiving information of them only when producing some great calamity, that earthquakes are not frequent, and occur only at periods remote from each other. This, however, is an error. Earthquakes are very frequent. By an exact observer not less than fifty-seven earthquakes have been noticed within the space of forty years in the town of Palermo, in Sicily, which were attended by such smart shocks that it was possible to determine their direction. There occurred, consequently, three earthquakes in every two years in Palermo. At other places they are still more frequent. In the town of Copiapo, in the northern province of Chile, one or more shocks are felt almost every day; and though they commonly pass off without causing any damage, the town has suffered by them so frequently, and so many lives have been lost by the downfall of buildings, that the inhabitants rush out of their houses as soon as the least commotion of the earth is perceived. "If it was possible," says Humboldt, "to obtain daily information respecting the state of the whole surface of our globe, we probably should convince ourselves that this surface is nearly always shaken at some point or other, and that it is subject to an uninterrupted reaction between the interior and the exterior."

Some parts of the globe's surface are much more subject to

Volcano bursting from the ocean near the Azores.

earthquakes than others; but it is hardly possible to point out any country that can be considered as entirely exempt from their visitations. They are as frequent in mountain regions as in plains, and are experienced in both the high table lands of the Andes and the low coasts of Belgium and the Netherlands. Where mountains and level plains are contiguous to each other, it has been observed at some places that the mountain region, and at others that the plains, were most violently convulsed. In the great earthquake of Caraccas, in 1812, the valley in which this town is built experienced the most violent shocks, whilst in the plains surrounding the Lake of Valencia, near Caraccas, hardly any commotion was perceived. The reverse took place in Calabria, in 1783, where it was the plain whose face was entirely changed in a few minutes by the violence of the concussions.

It does not appear either that the geological constitution of the country has any influence upon them. Large and high rocky masses of primitive formation, mountains consisting of successive layers and low alluvial plains, are equally subject to earthquakes. Thus the low alluvial plains surrounding the mouth of the Scheldt experienced many smart shocks in 1822, whilst the extensive plains drained by the Mississippi were visited by very violent concussions ten years before.

Many persons are apt to suppose that those countries which are situated in the vicinity of active volcanoes are more frequently subject to violent concussions than those which lie at greater distances from them. This opinion is not correct; but it is true that earthquakes are common in the neighborhood of volcanoes. Every eruption of the mountain, and even every new flow of lava, or every ejection of ashes, is accompanied by a shock, which, however, is so slight, that it can only be perceived by persons who are near the crater, or on the declivities of the volcano. These slight shocks can hardly be considered as earthquakes, as they are not felt in the plain at its base. But many eruptions are preceded by real earthquakes. When the inhabitants of a country surrounding an active volcano observe that the mountain has ceased to emit smoke from its crater, they consider it as a sign of an approaching earthquake, and in many cases their fear has not proved unfounded. It may be true that earthquakes are most frequent in countries lying in the vicinity of a volcano; but few of the more disastrous convulsions of this description have occurred in such localities. The greater number have happened at considerable distances from any active volcano, and even from places which by the nature of the rocks show that they have once been the seat of volcanic activity. It is also observed that earthquakes occurring at no great distance from volcanoes are of comparatively short duration, whilst the convulsions visiting countries lying far from them are repeated almost daily for months together, and frequently several times in one day. Of such a description were the earthquakes which were experienced during more than a whole year (1812) in the plains of the Mississippi, and those which shook, in 1808, the Alpine valleys of Fenestrelles and Pinerolo, lying at the base of Mount Cenis. The numerous earthquakes which have occurred in the countries situated between the eastern part of the Mediterranean and the banks of the Euphrates have almost always been distinguished by the violence of their shocks, and their frequent repetition for several months. Copiapo, which, as we have observed before, is perhaps more frequently subject to earthquakes than any other spot on the globe, is more than two hundred and fifty miles distant from any active volcano. Of those earthquakes which have proved most disastrous in their effect, only those of Calabria, in 1783, of Riobamba, in the Andes, in 1797, and of Molise, in 1805, in the kingdom of Naples, have occurred within a distance of less than a hundred miles from an active volcano.

By far the greater number of earthquakes have been experienced in countries lying near to, or at no great distance from, the sea shore. But it is not every part of the globe thus situated that is equally subject to them. The extensive coast line of Africa, with the exception of the countries bordering on the Mediterranean, is rarely visited by earthquakes; and many other coasts appear also nearly free. The countries which have most frequently experienced their destructive effect are the countries surrounding the Mediterranean in the old continent, and in America those which enclose the Gulf of Mexico and Caribbean Sea, and those which lie between the Andes and the Pacific, inclusive of the mountain region itself. On the islands of the Indian Archipelago, and as far north as Japan, earthquakes appear also to be very frequent, and to be attended by dreadful effects.

Earthquakes are certainly much less frequent in countries forming the central portions of continents, and lying at great distances from the ocean; but even there very severe ones are sometimes experienced. They appear to be quite frequent at Irkutsk, in Eastern Siberia, which is at least a thousand miles from the Pacific and Arctic Seas. That part of the plain of the Mississippi River, which, in 1812, experienced a great number of strong concussions, and those repeated for several months together, extends between New Madrid, on the Mississippi, to the Little Prairie, north of Cincinnati. The principal seat of the earthquake was consequently nearly equi-distant from the Gulf of Mexico and from the Atlantic Ocean.

The following particulars respecting this earthquake are from Sir Charles Lyell: "Flint, the geographer, who visited the country seven years after the event, informs us that a tract of many miles in extent, near the Little Prairie, became covered with water three or four feet deep; and when the water disappeared a stratum of sand was left in its place. Large lakes, of twenty miles in extent, were formed in the course of an hour, and others were drained. The graveyard at New Madrid was precipitated into the bed of the Mississippi; and it is stated that the ground whereon the town is built, and the river bank for fifteen miles above, sank eight feet below their former level. The neighboring forest presented for some years afterwards a singular scene of confusion; the trees standing inclined in every direction, and many having their trunks and branches broken.

"The inhabitants relate that the earth rose in great undulations; and when these reached a certain fearful height, the soil burst, and vast volumes of water, sand, and pit coal were discharged as high as the tops of the trees. Flint saw hundreds of these deep chasms remaining in an alluvial soil, seven years after. The people in the country, although inexperienced in such convulsions, had remarked that the chasms in the earth were in a direction from S. W. to N. E.; and they accordingly felled the tallest trees, and laying them at right angles to the chasms, stationed themselves upon them. By this invention, when chasms opened more than once under these trees, several persons were prevented from being swallowed up. At one period during this earthquake, the ground not far below New Madrid swelled up so as to arrest the Mississippi in its course, and to cause a temporary reflux of its waves. The motion of some of the shocks is described as having been horizontal, and of others perpendicular; and the vertical movement is said to have been much less desolating than the horizontal.

"Having in March, 1846, had an opportunity myself of visiting the disturbed region of the Mississippi, and conversing with many eye witnesses of the catastrophe, I am able to add some remarks on the present face and features of the country. I skirted part of the territory immediately west of New Madrid, called "the sunk country," which was for the first time permanently submerged during the earthquake of 1811–12. It is said to extend along the course of the White Water and its tributaries for a distance of between seventy and eighty miles north and south, and thirty miles east and west. I saw on its borders many full-grown trees still standing, leafless, the bottoms of their trunks several feet under water, and a still greater number lying prostrate. An active vegetation of aquatic plants is already beginning to fill up some of the shallows, and the sediment washed in by occasional floods, when the Mississippi rises to an extraordinary height, contributes to convert the sunk region into marsh and forest land. Even on the dry ground along the confines of the submerged area, I observed in some places that all the trees of prior date to 1811 were dead and leafless, though standing erect and entire. They are supposed to have been killed by the loosening of their roots during the repeated undulations which passed through the ground for three months in succession.

"Mr. Bringier, an experienced engineer of New Orleans, who was on horseback near New Madrid when some of the severest shocks were experienced, related to me, in 1846, that 'as the waves advanced the trees bent down, and the instant afterwards, while recovering their position, they often met those of other trees similarly inclined, so that, their branches becoming interlocked, they were prevented from righting themselves again. The transit of the wave through the woods was marked by the crashing noise of countless boughs, first heard on one side and then on the other. At the same time powerful jets of water, mixed with sand, mud, and fragments of coaly matter, were cast up, endangering the lives of both horse and rider.'

"I was curious to ascertain whether any vestiges still remained of these fountains of mud and water, and carefully examined between New Madrid and the Little Prairie several 'sink holes,' as they are termed. They consist of cavities from ten to thirty yards in width, and twenty feet or more in depth, and are very conspicuous, interrupting the level surface of a flat alluvial plain. I saw abundance of sand which some of the present inhabitants saw spouting from these deep holes, also fragments of decayed wood and black bituminous shale, probably drifted down at some former period in the main channel of the Mississippi, from the coal fields farther north. I also found numerous rents in the soil left by the earthquake, some of them still several feet wide, and a yard or two in depth, although the action of rains, frost, and occasional inundations, and especially the leaves of trees blown into them in countless numbers every autumn, have done much to fill them up. I measured the direction of some of the fissures, which usually varied from ten to forty-five degrees west of north, and were often parallel to each other; I found, however, a considerable diversity in their direction. Many of them are traceable for half a mile and upwards; but they might easily be mistaken for artificial trenches, if resident settlers were not there to assure us that within their recollection they were 'as deep as wells.' Fragments of coaly shale were strewed along the edges of some of these open fissures, together with white sand, in the same manner as round the 'sink holes.'

"Among other monuments of the changes wrought in 1811–12, I explored the bed of a lake called Eulalie, near New Madrid, three hundred yards long by one hundred yards in width, which was suddenly drained during the earthquake. The parallel fissures by which the waters escaped are not yet entirely closed, and all the trees growing on its bottom were at the time of my visit less than thirty-four years old. They consisted of cottonwood, willows, the honey locust, and other species, differing from those clothing the surrounding higher grounds, which are more elevated by twelve or fifteen feet. On them the hickory, the black and white oak, the gum, and other trees, many of them of ancient date, were flourishing."

When the motion of the earth's surface caused by the earthquakes is more closely examined, it is found that it is not always of the same character; and it appears that the damage produced is less in proportion to the violence of the shock than to the manner in which the ground is put into motion. Four kinds of movement have been noticed, and they are distinguished by the epithets *tremulous*, *undulating*, *upheaving*, and *rotatory*.

The tremulous shocks are called in South America *tremblores*, and are the least destructive. The surface of the earth is put into a trembling motion by them, not dissimilar to that felt in a steam vessel running under high pressure. The walls of houses which do not rest on a solid foundation are observed to incline slightly inward or outward, and objects which are not well supported are occasionally thrown down; but it is rarely any material damage is caused by these motions. These *tremblores* appear to be the most common kind of earthquake, especially in those countries of South America which lie along the Pacific, where they are felt very frequently, at least in certain seasons. Commonly they pass away in a moment, but sometimes they continue for several days. The town of Sciacca, in Sicily, was, in 1816, shaken by such a tremor for several days consecutively.

The undulating shocks are much more destructive. By their agency the surface of the earth assumes horizontal oscillations, by which the ground is alternately raised and let down again, somewhat in the manner in which the surface of the sea is agitated by a moderate breeze. They proceed in a simple and determinate direction; and Alexander von Humboldt, who paid great attention to these phenomena, and has himself experienced a great number of them, thinks that their progress may be estimated at from twenty to thirty miles per minute. They produce that motion of the ground which is called a *smart shock*, and are sometimes attended by disastrous effects. Those of a more powerful description throw down pieces of furniture, and rend asunder walls of houses not substantially built.

The upheaving shocks are far more dreaded. They are accompanied by violent perpendicular upliftings of the ground, as if repeated explosions were exerting their force upon the roof of a hollow cavern, threatening to burst open the ground and blow into the air every thing placed on it. They may also be compared to the bursting of a mine, which explodes with great force and removes the earth which it meets within its passage. When the surface of the earth is split by them, it is hardly to be conceived what terrible destruction must be produced in a few minutes by such convulsions following each other in quick succession. There are numerous instances on record which prove the immense force with which these shocks act on the surface and on every thing on it; some of them, indeed, appear almost incredible. In the great earthquake of Calabria, on the 28th of March, 1783, the most elevated portion of the granite mountain mass of the Aspromonte was seen to move up and down rapidly; persons were raised from the ground and thrown to a distance from the place where they were; houses were removed from their site and carried to places higher than those on which they had been built. The famous French naturalist Dolomieu, who examined the country attentively a short time after that frightful catastrophe, states that the foundation of many buildings had been removed from beneath the ground with such violence, that the stones had been broken to pieces and scattered about, and the hard cement which united them had been crushed into dust. After the great earthquake of Riobamba, in 1797, on the table land of Quito, the corpses of several of the inhabitants of the town were found on the top of a hill, separated from the place by a river, and several hundred feet higher than the site of the town. These persons had been hurled to the top of the hill by the violent upheavings of the ground.

It would seem that the upheaving shock is almost always accompanied by an undulating motion. Humboldt, at least, states that in his opinion these two kinds of motion were combined in all the stronger earthquakes he has experienced. Dolomieu makes the same observation respecting the earthquake of Calabria. In all the accounts he collected respecting the first great shock (5th of February) the inhabitants concurred in stating that the motions had been horizontal and perpendicular at the same time, and he thinks that a pretty just idea of their united efforts may be formed by making small cubes of damp clay mixed with sand, and by placing them near each other on a table, and in that situation putting them into motion by a violent concussion from below, whilst at the same time the table is moved horizontally from one side to the other.

The rotatory shocks are certainly the most destructive, but are those also which occur most rarely. They have only been observed in the most calamitous earthquakes, and not in all of them. The whirling motion with which they affect the surface appears to be the result of a combination of the undulating and upheaving motions, or perhaps of two or three undulating motions crossing one another at right angles or obliquely. The surface of the earth is put into a movement by them resembling that of the sea when agitated by irregular waves crossing and repulsing each other in different directions. Many naturalists have expressed a doubt of the occurrence of this kind of shock; but there are many well-established facts on record which do not admit of an explanation but by admitting that the changes of position observed in walls and other objects have been effected by shocks of such a description. In the earthquake of Catania, in Sicily, in 1818, the general motion was clearly directed from south-east to north-west; but many statues had been turned round, and a large piece of rock had its former position from south to north changed to that of east to west. Several instances of this kind were observed after the great earthquake of Valparaiso, in Chile, in 1822, when that town was levelled to the ground. The large church La Merced presented the most remarkable ruin. The tower was built of bricks and mortar, and its walls up to the belfry were six feet thick. They were shivered into blocks, and thrown to the ground. On each side of the church were a number of square buttresses of good solid brick work, six feet square. Those on the western side were all thrown down, as were all but two on the eastern side; these two were twisted from the wall in a north-easterly direction, each presenting an angle to the wall. The twisting to the north-east was noticed in several other places. In a village thirty miles north of Valparaiso, the largest and heaviest pieces of furniture were turned in the same direction. In the last great earthquake of Conception, in Chile, in 1835, rotatory shocks must also have occurred, as it was found that an angular stone pinnacle had been turned half round, without being thrown down or leaving its base. Humboldt mentions that rows of trees, running in a straight line, were, after an earthquake, found to present a very perceptible curve in their line.

There are recorded some other well-ascertained changes produced by earthquakes, which cannot be satisfactorily explained but by supposing that the motion produced by the shock must have been of a still more complicated nature. In some instances it has been found that large pieces of ground had exchanged their respective situations. This was the case at several places in Calabria, after the first great shock had passed by. A plantation of mulberry trees had been carried into the middle of a cornfield, and left standing there; and a piece of ground sown with lupines had been forced into a vineyard. For several years after the earthquake, lawsuits were brought in the courts of Naples to decide the claims which had originated in the confusion of territorial possessions by the effects of that terrible catastrophe. Facts of such a description are not recorded as having resulted from other earthquakes, except from that of Riobamba, in 1797, where also several lawsuits were brought in the courts respecting the possession of pieces of ground, which in a similar manner had exchanged their positions. It is difficult to conceive by what kind of motion the earthquakes acquire this translatory power. But Humboldt has recorded a still more extraordinary fact. When he was surveying the ruins of the destroyed town of Riobamba for the purpose of making a map, he was shown the place where the whole furniture of one house was found buried beneath the ruins of another. The upper layer of the soil, formed of matter not possessing a great degree of coherency, had moved like water in running streams; and we are compelled to suppose that these streams flowed first downwards, then proceeded horizontally, and at last rose upwards. The motion in the shocks which were experienced in Jamaica on the 7th of July, 1692, must have been not less complicated. According to the account of an eye witness, the whole surface of the ground had assumed the appearance of running water. The sea and the land appeared to rush on one another, and to mingle in the wildest confusion. Some persons, who, at the beginning of the calamity, had escaped into the streets, and to the squares of the town, to avoid the danger of being crushed under the ruins of the falling houses, were so violently tossed from one side to the other, that many of them received severe contusions, and some were maimed. Others were lifted up, hurled through the air, and thrown down at a distance from the place where they had been standing. A few who were in the town were carried away to the harbor, which was rather distant, and there thrown into the sea, by which accident, however, their lives were saved.

Dr. Kreil, director of the Observatory of Vienna, invented an instrument, in 1855, by means of which he can discover the intensity and direction of shocks of earthquakes. It is composed of a pendulum oscillating towards any point, and at the lower extremity of which is fixed a vertical cylinder, containing a watch movement, which causes it to turn on its axis once in twenty-four hours. Close to this cylinder is placed an upright piece of wood, to which is fixed an elastic arm, carrying a pencil coming in contact with the cylinder, on which, as long as the pendulum is still, is described an uninterrupted line; but as soon as the earth moves, and the pendulum consequently makes some oscillations, the pencil traces on the cylinder marks, the length and variety of which show the strength and direction of the shocks.

Having given an idea of the nature of the motions attending earthquakes, a description of the effects they produce on the works and life of man should be added. This, perhaps, cannot be done more completely than by giving an account of two of those earthquakes which were distinguished by their destructive effects, and of which a pretty complete picture may be formed by collecting the facts recorded by eye witnesses in the reports published by them. These are the earthquakes of Lisbon, in Portugal, and that of Caraccas, in Venezuela.

The earthquake of Lisbon happened on the 1st of November, 1755. The day broke with a serene sky and a fine breeze from the east. About nine o'clock in the morning the sun began to grow dim, and about half an hour later a rumbling noise was heard, which proceeded from under ground, and resembled that made by heavy carts passing over a distant ground covered with pebbles. This subterraneous noise increased gradually, but quickly, so that after a few seconds it resembled the firing of cannons of heavy calibre. In this moment the first shock was felt. Before its violent concussions the foundations of many large buildings, especially the palace of the Inquisition and several churches, gave way, and the whole of these edifices were levelled to the ground. After a short pause, perhaps of not more than a minute's duration, three other shocks followed in quick succession, by which nearly all the other larger buildings, palaces, churches, convents, public offices, and houses were thrown down. All these shocks occurred in a space of less than five minutes. At the time the first shock was felt in the city, some persons were in a boat on the Tagus River, about three miles distant from the capital. They were astonished at hearing the boat making a noise, as if it were running aground, as they knew it was in deep water. In the same moment they observed on both banks of the river that the buildings were tumbling down. About four minutes later a similar noise was heard under the boats, and other buildings were seen falling to the ground. During this time a strange commotion was observed in the water of the river. It appears that at some places the bottom of the river was raised to the level of the water. Many vessels were lying in the harbor opposite the town. Some of them were torn from their anchors and dashed against each other with great violence; in others the sailors did not know whether their vessels were afloat or aground.

The minds of the inhabitants had not yet had time to recover from the terror caused by this terrible and quite unexpected catastrophe, when they were again plunged into dismay by a phenomenon of a different description, but hardly less terrible and destructive. About half an hour after the most severe shocks had ceased, the sea suddenly rushed with incredible velocity into the river. Although the water had been ebbing for two hours, and the wind blew fresh from the east, the sea at the mouth of the Tagus rose instantaneously about forty feet above high water mark, according to the statement of some eye witnesses, who observed it at Colares and other places between the Bay of Lisbon and the sea. It would certainly have laid more than half the town under water, and completed the work of destruction, had not the large bay, which the river forms opposite the capital of Portugal, permitted this enormous volume of water to spread itself over a surface of many square miles. But even this favorable circumstance did not entirely exempt the city from the effects of an inundation. The sea entered the lower streets, and a large stone-built quay, which had been probably detached from its foundations by the earthquake, and on which about three thousand people had taken refuge, was suddenly hurled bottom upward, and every soul was lost. As quickly as the water had filled the river, so quickly did it retreat to the sea. The high wave, however, returned three or four times before the water attained its usual level, but every time with a diminished force and a less volume of water.

It is stated that, by the effects of the earthquake and of the inundation, not less than sixty thousand persons perished. The larger number, it appears, were crushed by the ruins of the falling churches. For as it was a holiday, a great number of persons were at their devotions in the churches and convents, which, being very substantial edifices built of stone, suffered much more than the houses of private persons, and were reduced to heaps of ruins by the first shock. Towards evening a smart shock was felt; it was strong enough to split the walls of several houses which had still kept their position. The rents caused by this shock in the walls of these houses were more than half a foot wide; but as soon as the shock had passed away, they closed again, and so firmly that it was impossible to find a trace of them.

In addition to the horrors occasioned by the shocks of the earthquake and the inroads of the sea, the devoted inhabitants were exposed to the ravages of fire. Mr. Davy, an English merchant residing in Lisbon, who escaped, and published an account of the calamity, says, "As soon as it grew dark another scene presented itself, little less shocking than those already described—the whole city appeared in a blaze, which was so bright that I could easily see to read by it. It may be said without exaggeration, it was on fire at least in a hundred different places at once, and thus continued burning for six days together, without intermission, or the least attempt being made to stop its progress.

"It went on consuming every thing the earthquake had spared, and the people were so dejected and terrified, that few or none had courage enough to venture down to save any part of their substance; every one had his eyes turned towards the flames, and stood looking on with silent grief, which was only interrupted by the cries and shrieks of women and children calling on the saints and angels for succor, whenever the earth began to tremble, which was so often this night, and indeed I may say ever since, that the tremors, more or less, did not cease for a quarter of an hour together. I could never learn that this terrible fire was owing to any subterraneous eruption, as some reported.

"The 1st of November being All Saints Day, a high festival among the Portuguese, every altar in every church and chapel (some of which have more than twenty) was illuminated with a number of wax tapers and lamps, as customary; these setting fire to the curtains and timber work that fell with the shock, the conflagration soon spread to the neighboring houses, and being there joined with the fires in the kitchen chimneys, increased to such a degree that it might easily have destroyed the whole city, though no other cause had concurred, especially as it met with no interruption."

He also gives a vivid picture of the destruction occasioned, and of its effects on the population.

"The nobility, gentry, and clergy, who were assisting at divine service when the earthquake began, fled away with the utmost precipitation, every one where his fears carried him, leaving the splendid apparatus of the numerous altars to the mercy of the first comer; but this did not so much affect me as the distress of the poor animals, who seemed sensible of their hard fate; some few were killed, others wounded, but the greater part, which had received no hurt, were left there to starve.

"From the square the way led to my friend's lodgings, through a long, steep, and narrow street; the new scenes of horror I met with here exceed all description; nothing could be heard but sighs and groans. I did not meet with a soul in the passage who was not bewailing the death of his nearest relations and dearest friends, or the loss of all his substance; I could hardly take a single step without treading on the dead or the dying; in some places lay coaches, with their masters, horses, and riders, almost crushed in pieces; here mothers with their infants in their arms; there ladies richly dressed, priests, friars, gentlemen, merchants, either in the same condition or just expiring; some had their backs or thighs broken, others vast stones on their breasts; some lay almost buried in the rubbish, and crying out in vain to the passengers for succor, were left to perish with the rest."

All the country lying round Lisbon suffered more or less from the effects of this earthquake. Many of the large mountains were shaken to their very foundation, and some had their summits rent. Large pieces of rock were detached from them, and precipitated into the valleys, where they caused considerable damage to the plantations and vineyards. At Colares, it was observed that a very thick smoke issued from a rock not very distant from the place. The quantity of smoke which arose was always in proportion to the loudness of the subterraneous rumblings. The smoke continued to issue for some time after the earthquake had subsided. When the place was afterwards closely inspected, no traces of any rent were discovered in the rock.

Though the destructive effects of these shocks were most severely felt at Lisbon, which appears to have been the centre of the earthquake, the whole coast of Portugal was afflicted by them. At Oporto the shocks were nearly as violent as at Lisbon. At about forty minutes past nine a frightful hollow noise was heard, similar to distant thunder. By some it was compared to a number of carts running over an uneven stone pavement. In the same moment the first shock was felt, which lasted about five minutes, and shook the whole town to its very foundation. The damage, however, was comparatively small. Only a few houses suffered material injury, but the walls of several churches were split. In many places it was observed that the ground of the streets alternately rose and subsided. The waters of the river were in great commotion. They rose and fell five or six feet within each two minutes; and this movement continued for about four hours. At several places the surface of the water appeared to divide, to give vent to large volumes of gas or of steam, and at the same time the sea at the mouth of the river appeared to be in a state of agitation resembling that of vehement ebullition. It was supposed that in this part, too, gas must have escaped from the bottom of the sea.

South of Lisbon the destruction was much greater. The harbor of Setubal was changed considerably by the shocks of the earthquake, and almost entirely destroyed by the inundation of the sea. The town of Ayamonte, near the mouth of the River Guadiana, suffered still more. The shocks continued for fourteen or fifteen minutes, and injured nearly all the houses. At the same time the surface of the earth opened at several places, and large volumes of water rushed out from those chasms. The sea rose three times, and all the streets were inundated.

Cadiz, too, had its share of the effects of this earthquake. The rock on which the town is built, and which is joined to the continent by a narrow and low isthmus, was shaken nearly at the same time that Lisbon experienced the first shock. The oscillations of the ground continued for about three minutes and a half, and put the population into great terror; but it was afterwards found that the damage done by these convulsions was but trifling. Hardly had the first impression of fear passed away, when, about ten minutes past eleven o'clock, another phenomenon, of more terrific appearance, was seen approaching, and threatening the whole town with destruction. At a distance of about ten miles west of the place, the sea was suddenly rising to a height of about sixty feet above its common level, and thus a watery wall was formed, which advanced with great velocity towards the town. At this sight the whole population was thrown into the utmost consternation. The sentinels placed on the fortifications erected towards the open sea, observing the advance of the huge wave, abandoned their posts, and the people, informed of the impending danger, rushed towards the gate which leads to the above-mentioned isthmus. It was a very happy circumstance that the governor of the place was a man of sense and resolution. He directly ordered the gates of the place to be closed, so that but few succeeded in getting on the isthmus. Meanwhile the wave had reached the shore, and dashed against the rocks with a terrible crash. But its force was greatly broken by the cliffs which lie in front of the rock on which the town is built. It was, however, still strong enough to demolish the walls and fortifications on that side, and to remove some heavy pieces of artillery to a distance of more than a hundred feet. When the wave, however, reached the town, its force had so abated, that it inundated only the lower streets, and caused very little damage. Still, the loss of life was considerable; for, having passed the town, it rushed with great force over the low isthmus lying at the back of it, and all those who had retreated to it, hoping thus to provide for their safety, were drowned. The sea retreated with as much velocity as it had advanced, and carried off a large volume of the waters filling the Bay of Cadiz; for it was observed that, for a few minutes, the shallower parts of the bay were laid dry. Then the large wave returned. This alternate advancing and retiring of the sea took place four or five times, but at every repetition the volume of water was less.

At Gibraltar the earthquake lasted for about two minutes. The oscillations of the surface were quick and strongly undulating, so that some of the cannons standing on the walls of the place were raised at one place, whilst others were sinking lower. Many of the inhabitants felt their heads turning; others were attacked by sickness; some fell to the ground; whilst others were stunned. Many who were walking or riding on horseback did not feel any motion, but they were affected by a feeling of illness. At every quarter of an hour the sea swelled about six feet, and then retired, so as to leave aground all the boats and smaller vessels which were at anchor near the shore. Those tracts left dry by the sea were strewed with dead fish. The alternate changes of high and low water continued till six o'clock the following morning; but after two o'clock in the afternoon they began to diminish in height, and went on gradually decreasing until they ceased.

The earthquake of Caraccas, the capital of Venezuela, in South America, occurred on the 26th of March, 1812. This city is built in a valley about five miles wide, on uneven ground. Its principal square is two thousand eight hundred and eighty feet above the sea level. On the southern side of the place runs a river of moderate size called Guayra. Between the town and the sea, from which it is about twenty miles distant, are mountain masses, which occupy nearly the whole space, and rise to upwards of five thousand feet above the sea. One of the summits, called the Silla of Caraccas, rises more than eight thousand feet.

The 26th of March was a remarkably hot day. The air was calm and the sky cloudless. It was Holy Thursday, and a great part of the population was assembled in the churches. There was nothing observed which presaged the calamities that were impending. At seven minutes after four in the afternoon the first shock was felt. It was sufficiently powerful to ring the bells of the churches, and lasted about five or six seconds. During its action the ground was in a continued undulating motion, and seemed to heave up like a boiling liquid. It was thought the danger had passed, when a tremendous subterraneous noise was heard, resembling the rolling of thunder, but louder and of longer duration than even that which is heard between the tropics in the season of storms. This noise was immediately followed by a perpendicular shock, which lasted three or four seconds, closely succeeded by an undulating movement somewhat longer. The motion of these undulating shocks was complicated, some running north and south, and others east and west. Nothing was able to resist the movement of the shocks raising the ground upward from the bottom, and of the undulations which crossed one another. In a few instants the town was almost levelled to the ground. A large portion of the population, between nine and ten thousand according to the most credible statements, was buried under the ruins of the houses and churches. The procession, which is usually made on that day in all Catholic countries, had not yet set out; but the crowds assembled in the churches were so numerous, that between three and four thousand persons are said to have been crushed by the downfall of their vaulted roofs. The explosion was strongest along the northern skirts of the town, the quarter which is situated nearest the mountains of Avila, and the Silla. The churches of La Trinidad, and of Alta Gracia, which were more than a hundred and fifty feet high, and the naves of which were supported by pillars of twelve or fifteen feet diameter, left a mass of ruins scarcely exceeding five or six feet in elevation. It was evident that the site of these buildings had sunk; and this sinking had been so considerable, that hardly any vestiges of the pillars or columns could afterwards be discovered. The large barracks, very substantial buildings, which were situated to the north of La Trinidad, disappeared almost entirely. A regiment of troops of the line, that was assembled there under arms, to be ready to join the procession, was, with the exception of a few men, buried under the ruins of that great edifice. Nine tenths of the town were levelled to the ground. The walls of the houses which were not thrown down were cracked in such a manner that nobody was inclined to run the risk of inhabiting them. The effects of the shocks were somewhat less destructive in the western and southern quarters of the city, where the cathedral, supported by enormous buttresses, remained standing. The duration of the earthquake, that is to say, the time in which both the undulating and upheaving shocks were perceptible, was by some estimated at one minute and twelve seconds, by others at only fifty seconds.

The night following Holy Thursday presented a most afflicting scene of desolation and sorrow. The thick cloud of dust which, rising from the ruins during the day, had hovered above the ruined city and darkened the sky, now settled on the ground. No shock was felt, and never was a night more calm and more serene. The moon, nearly full, illumined the rounded domes of the Silla, and the aspect of the sky formed a terrific contrast to that of the earth, covered with corpses and heaped with ruins. The mind of the looker-on was afflicted by the most heart-rending scenes. Mothers were seen carrying in their arms the children whom they hoped to recall to life. Distressed families were climbing over the ruins to find out a brother, a husband, or a friend, of whose fate they were ignorant, and whom they believed to be lost in the crowd. The people, oppressed by the weight of the calamity, passed silently along the street, which could only be traced by the long lines of ruins. Those who were buried under the ruins, and were unable to extricate themselves, implored the assistance of the passengers by their cries, and a number amounting to nearly two thousand were afterwards dug out. Never was pity displayed in a more affecting manner, never had it been seen more ingenious in its activity, than in the strenuous attempts made for the purpose of saving the miserable victims whose groans reached the ear. Implements for digging and clearing away the stones and rubbish were not at hand: they had been buried under the ruins. The people, therefore, were compelled to use their bare hands to disinter the living. The wounded, as well as the sick who had escaped from the hospitals, were carried to the borders of the River Guayra, but the only shelter they found was the foliage of the trees. Beds, linen to dress the wounds, instruments of surgery, medicines, objects of the most urgent necessity, were many feet deep under the ruins. Every thing, even the coarsest provision, was wanting during the first few days. Water, also, became scarce in the interior of the city. The repeated concussions had rent the pipes of the fountains; the falling in of the earth had choked up the springs that supplied them, and to get water people were compelled to go to the river, which, happily, was considerably swollen. But it was impossible to convey the water to any distance, as vessels for that purpose were wanting.

People applied themselves to the exercise of those religious duties, which, in their opinion, were most fitted to appease the wrath of Heaven. Many assembled, and passed through the streets in processions singing funeral hymns; others, thrown into a state of distraction by these calamities, confessed their sins aloud in the streets; numerous marriages were contracted between persons who for many years had neglected to sanction their union by the sacerdotal benediction; children found parents by whom they had not been acknowledged up to that time; restitutions were promised by persons who had never been accused of fraud or theft; families, which for many years had been estranged from one another by enmity and hatred, were drawn together by the tie of common suffering. Though these feelings, by which the passions of some were soothed, and the hearts of others were opened to pity and humanity, were prevalent, there were not wanting other persons whose indurated minds were rendered more inhuman and cruel.

The night passed in quietness. For fifteen or eighteen hours after the great catastrophe the ground remained tranquil; but on the 27th of March the commotions recommenced. They were attended by a very loud and long-continued subterraneous noise. The inhabitants of the town abandoned the place, and dispersed themselves over the surrounding country; but finding that all the villages and hamlets in the valley had suffered as much as the city, and could not supply them with the first necessaries of life, they repaired to the valley of Aragna, more than thirty miles distant from the capital. Meanwhile the shocks continued to shake the city — no less than fifteen oscillations being felt in one day. On the 5th of April there was a shock almost as violent as that by which the capital had been overthrown. During several hours the ground was in a state of perpetual undulation. Large masses of earth were shaken off from the declivities of the mountains, and enormous rocks were detached from the Silla of Caraccas. The commotions ceased only on the 30th of April.

The mountainous country lying to the west of Caraccas also experienced the dreadful and destructive effects of the earthquake. It appears that the motion proceeded in a line running east-north-east and west-south-west from the harbor of La Guayra and Caraccas, to the lofty mountains of Nequitao and Merida. Along this track it acted with great violence, and many towns were entirely destroyed, especially La Guayra and San Felipe. But in the valley of Aragna, which lies between Caraccas and San Felipe, the convulsions were very weak, and did not cause any material damage. Many places along the coast, as far as the Lake of Maracaibo, suffered greatly; but at Coro no commotion was felt, though the town is situate upon the coast, and between other towns which suffered from the earthquake. The waves of the agitated ground extended westward as far as the valley of the Rio de la Magdalena, and smart shocks occurred at St. Marta, Bogotá, and Honda.

There is no event which makes so deep and lasting an impression on the mind as an earthquake, nor does any other phenomenon of nature affect it to an equal degree; hence those who have not experienced an earthquake are unable to judge of the state of mind into which people are thrown by it. Confusion, distraction, and horror, carried to the highest pitch, do not convey an adequate idea of what is passing in their breasts. The principal cause of this extraordinary state of mind is doubtless founded on the circumstance that an earthquake unsettles our whole system of thinking and reasoning, by withdrawing the foundation on which it rests. From our earliest years we have been accustomed to consider the soil under our feet as firm and immovable. We have unconsciously connected this idea with all our conceptions, feelings, and actions; and it thus becomes the base of all our plans, intentions, and wishes. Our whole life, with all its events and operations, rest on this idea as on an immutable foundation. An earthquake, by turning it into a delusion, overthrows our whole system of thinking and acting. We are no longer able to collect our thoughts so as to form an idea; we cannot conceive any plan, nor take any resolution. The faculty of thinking is, as it were, paralyzed, and our mind thrown into the utmost confusion. The difference between a strong and a weak mind disappears. We are no longer guided by principles or reason; we follow only the involuntary impulses of instinct; or, in the most favorable circumstances, we are influenced by some feelings arising from some previous ideas, which, fortunately, have been indelibly impressed on our mind.

A gentleman of Copiapo expressed himself on this point, to

Captain B. Hall, as follows: "Although I am not a man to cry out and play the fool on such occasions, yet I do fairly own that these earthquakes are very awful, and indeed must be felt to be understood in their true extent. Before we hear the sound, or, at least, are fully conscious of hearing it, we are made sensible, I do not know how, that something uncommon is going to happen; every thing seems to change color; our thoughts are chained immovably down; the whole world appears to be in disorder; all nature looks differently from what it was wont to do; and we feel quite subdued and overwhelmed by some invisible power beyond human control or comprehension. Then comes the terrible sound distinctly heard; and immediately the solid earth is all in motion, waving to and fro like the surface of the sea. Depend upon it, a severe earthquake is enough to shake the firmest mind. Custom enables us to restrain the expression of alarm, but no custom can teach any one to witness such earthquakes without the deepest emotion of terror."

The utter confusion and uncertainty of the mind, which must arise from the complete overthrow of our common system of thinking and acting, are converted into terror by those circumstances which always attend earthquakes, and which powerfully affect our senses. All the attempts at keeping one's footing, whilst the earth is continually and violently heaving up and down with a quickness of which no one can form an idea but those who have witnessed it, prove useless and embarrassing in the highest degree. The tottering buildings, the crashing of the timbers of the roofs, and the falling of the tiles, together with the loud rumbling noise immediately under the spot on which we are standing, completely distract the senses. Men would abandon themselves entirely to the overwhelming operations of nature, if they had not strongly impressed on their minds the sad experience that most persons have perished in earthquakes by having been crushed under the ruins of the buildings. This impression acts like an instinct on them. They rush out of the houses, but, too frequently, not to find safety out of doors. They soon find that they cannot keep their footing without support; they cling to one another, to trees, or to posts. Some throw themselves to the ground; but the motion of the earth is so violent that they are compelled to stretch out their arms to prevent themselves from being tossed over. Here and there the earth opens, and deep chasms present themselves to their eyes. There are no means of escaping from these threatening dangers. Persons may retire in safety out of the reach of the eruption of a volcano, they may easily avoid the current of burning lava advancing towards them, and even when suddenly overtaken by an inundation, they soon perceive in what direction they have to fly to avoid being overwhelmed by the rushing volume of water; but during an earthquake every one is impressed with the conviction that wherever he goes he places himself over the focus of destruction.

It may easily be conceived that all those who have experienced a severe earthquake are terrified at any uncommon appearance. The slightest undulation of the ground, or any unusual noise, rouses their attention, and they immediately rush out of their houses. But habit influences the mind in this case too. When for a number of years a place has only been visited by moderate shocks, not attended by destructive effects, the inhabitants, by degrees, get rid of every kind of fear. "In Lima," says Humboldt, "this habit, united to the generally prevailing opinion that destructive earthquakes do not occur more than two or three times in a century, has rendered the inhabitants so indifferent to slight shocks that they do not pay more attention to them than we do to a hail storm."

When, after a very severe earthquake, the sufferers' minds become sufficiently collected to contemplate the effects produced, they are astonished at the extent of destruction, and they feel another kind of terror when they consider in what a short time it has been brought about. The most destructive shocks are of very short duration, and seem quite out of proportion to the effects they have produced. In some cases it even appears that the amount of destruction and the time of duration are to each other in an inverse proportion — the shorter the shock, the greater the devastation. The most destructive shocks, by which thousands of persons lost their lives, flourishing towns were converted into heaps of ruins, and whole provinces convulsed, lasted, in many cases, as it were, only an instant. Thus, as we observed in giving an account of the earthquake of Caraccas, that place was entirely levelled to the ground by three shocks, each of which did not continue for more than three or four seconds, and all of them occurred within a space of less than a minute. The shock which, on the 5th of February, 1783, converted a large portion of Cala bria into one general ruin, did not, according to the statement of the inhabitants, exceed two minutes in duration; and in 1692 the face of the Island of Jamaica was in three minutes so changed, that hardly a tract could be found which had preserved the appearance it had borne previous to the earthquake. We may even suppose that the time of duration in the two last-mentioned cases has been probably overrated. For, as there were no signs indicating the approach of the earthquake, the precise moment of its beginning cannot easily be determined exactly; and we may assume that people, placed suddenly in such a state of terror, and longing for the moment of its cessation, have estimated the time of duration much longer than it really was. When this is considered, we may well agree with Humboldt when he says that there is no force known to exist, — not even the murderous inventions of our own race contrived for each other's extirpation, — by which, in the short period of a few seconds or minutes, such a number of persons can be killed, as by an earthquake. In Sicily, in 1692, not less than sixty thousand perished; in Riobamba and its neighborhood, in 1797, from thirty to forty thousand; in Calabria, in 1783, perhaps one hundred thousand; and in Asia Minor and in Syria, in the time of Tiberius and Justinian, perhaps not less than two hundred and fifty thousand.

It happens sometimes, though not frequently, that an earthquake which is attended by smart shocks affects only a comparatively small tract of country. Thus a portion of the mountains of Madonia, in Sicily, not extending over a great number of square miles, experienced, in 1832, during several months, a considerable number of smart shocks, whilst all the surrounding places, though frequently subject to earthquakes, did not evince the least commotion of the ground. In general, however, countries of considerable extent are affected by them. In many cases it appears that the shock is felt at the same moment in places distant from each other. The shocks which destroyed Lisbon occurred at ten minutes to ten o'clock in the forenoon, and the town of Madrid suffered much damage by shocks which occurred at seventeen minutes past ten, which is the same moment of time when the geographical longitude of the two places is computed. In most cases, however, it is found that the shocks are felt somewhat earlier in one place than in those which are distant from it, and that the interval between the time in which they are affected is in proportion to the distance. It is remarkable that, as far as our observations go, the shocks are always most severe and most destructive at the place where they are first felt. Such a place is, therefore, reasonably considered as the centre of the earthquake. From this centre the earthquake proceeds either in a determinate direction towards certain points of the compass, or it spreads round the centre over all the adjacent countries. In the first case it is called a linear earthquake, and in the second a central one.

The linear direction of earthquakes is most common in those countries which are traversed by mountain ranges. It is usually found that in such countries the tracts shaken by the commotion form a band parallel to the ranges, and at no great distance from their bases. This linear direction has been distinctly observed in the countries lying between the Andes and the Pacific, more especially in the earthquakes of Lima, in 1746, of Copiapo, in 1819, of Valparaiso, in 1822, and of Conception, in 1835. The earthquakes proceeded from the centre to the south, and to the north, and the shocks were felt sooner or later, according to the distance of the places from the centre. Humboldt thinks that in general the earthquake progresses from twenty to thirty miles in each minute. According to the statement of this scientific traveller, there occur in these countries certain tracts of land or places which do not experience the shocks, though the countries contiguous to them on the north and south are convulsed to a considerable degree; and it is remarkable that none of the numerous earthquakes have ever visited such places. To describe this curious exemption from earthquakes, the creoles of the country say that *they form a bridge* — expressing by this phrase their opinion that the shocks pass under these places at too great a depth to affect them, whilst beneath the adjacent tracts they approach nearer the surface of the earth.

In the central earthquakes the shocks are not propagated in a certain determinate direction, but spread on all sides like rays issuing from a common centre. The progress of these shocks may be compared to the ring-like waves produced on the surface of still water by a pebble being thrown into it; such waves grow wider and fainter in proportion to the distance from the spot on which the stone fell. For it is generally observed that the farther the wave of the earthquake — if such a term may be used — advances from the centre, the less the shock is felt. The earthquake of Lisbon was a central one, and its waves extended over a very large section of the globe. The centre was unhappily under or near that capital; for it is stated by persons who were at Colares, near the mouth of the Tagus River, that the severe shocks which were experienced at that place were felt as if coming from the side on which Lisbon lies, though at that moment nothing was known of the calamity which had overtaken the capital. At the Island of Madeira the earthquake was felt somewhat later, and the shocks appeared to proceed from the north. People inhabiting the Antilles and the coasts of the Columbian Sea were of opinion that they came from the north-east. When the wave, originating at Lisbon, reached England, it had already greatly expended its force. Smart shocks, however, were still felt along the southern coast, and at Cork, in Ireland; but in proceeding farther north, its force gradually died away.

In the earthquake which occurred in Belgium, in February, 1828, it was also evident that the shocks had spread over the country like rays round a centre. The first and smartest shock was felt in a tract of land having the form of an ellipsoid, extending from east to west. It comprehended that part of the country which lies between Brussels, Waterloo, Liege, and Maestricht. From this centre the waves advanced to the places lying higher up on the banks of the Meuse and of the Rhine. On the east they were perceptible as far as Soest, in Westphalia, and on the west they reached the towns of Flushing and Middelburg, on the Island of Walcheren.

In by far the greater number of earthquakes of which we have accounts to be relied on, the centre of the catastrophe was at a fixed point; but in earthquakes which are protracted over several weeks or months, it appears that the centre sometimes changes its place. This appears to have been the case with the earthquakes which, in December, 1811, were first felt on the banks of the Lower Mississippi, and afterwards proceeded slowly farther north, increasing at the same time in force until, in February, 1812, they reached the country between the Lower Ohio and the middle course of the Mississippi, where their rather severe shocks continued for many months. In the earthquakes which, in February and March, 1783, afflicted the province of Calabria, three centres have been distinctly pointed out; and it appears that the shocks at one time proceeded in a linear direction, and at another spread round the centre. These earthquakes affected, indeed, only a comparatively small part of the country; but if the intensity of the shocks and the amount of damage are considered, they were much more severe than most of those of which a detailed account has been recorded. The earthquake which, in 1692 convulsed the Island of Jamaica, appears to have been the only one attended with nearly the same destruction. Considering the great changes the earthquakes of Calabria produced on the face of the country, and the peculiar phenomena above mentioned, it appears not to be out of place to give a detailed account of them. No eye witness has given a description of what he observed or experienced; but as shortly after the cessation of the motions several scientific men of great reputation visited the country, and were at great pains to collect every kind of information concerning these horrible phenomena, and as, on the whole, their statements agree with one another, we may rely on the information contained in their publications.

The destructive effects of the earthquakes of Calabria were severely felt in the most southern portion of the Italian peninsula, and in the north-eastern part of Sicily. That portion of the peninsula which suffered most is known by the name of Calabria Ultra. It is a tongue of land extending south-south-west and north-north-east, about sixty miles in length, with a mean breadth of somewhat more than twenty miles. The Straits of Messina separate it from the Island of Sicily. With the broader portion of the peninsula of Italy it is connected by an isthmus, which, on the west, is washed by the Gulf of St. Euphemia, and on the east by that of Squillace. The surface of this isthmus rises only to a moderate elevation above the sea level, so that the mountain masses lying north and south of it are not connected, but constitute separate systems. The tongue of land lying south of this isthmus exhibits some singularities in the formation of its surface. At each of its extremities are mountain masses, which extend over the whole width of the country, from sea to sea. The northern mass rises in the middle to about four thousand feet above the sea level, and sends off several offsets, which on the east terminate on the sea with Cape Stilo, and on the west fill up with hills the projecting tract of land between Cape Zambrone and Cape Vaticano. The southern mountain, known by the name of Mont Aspromonte, rises to more than five thousand feet above the sea, and constitutes a more compact mass, its sides being only furrowed by short and narrow valleys, separated from each other by high ridges. These two masses are connected by a ridge of little width, which runs nearly in the middle of the tongue of land, but somewhat nearer the eastern than the western shores. Low offsets from this ridge render the country east of it hilly; but that which lies on the west of the ridge is a plain, whose surface is covered with a very thick layer of clay mixed with sand, and full of marine shells. In this plain the numerous small rivers which originate in the ridge have scooped out their beds many feet below the general surface. The face of this plain was almost entirely changed by the first two earthquakes, whilst it was little affected by the third. The first two earthquakes occurred on the 5th and 7th of February. The centre of the first and most destructive shock was at Oppido, near the southern extremity of the plain, and that of the second at Soriano, near the northern extremity. These two places are about twenty miles distant from each other. The shocks began with strong undulations, which were soon changed into rotatory motions. The concussions were so violent that the heads of the largest trees are stated to have almost touched the ground from side to side. No kind of building was able to resist the effects of these violent motions; they were all thrown into heaps of ruins. The surface of the country was rent by deep chasms running in different directions, many of which remained open for a long time afterwards. Some, when visited three months after the earthquake, were found to be still more than a foot in width; but they had been much wider during the earthquake. Others closed as soon as the shocks had passed away; in one of them an ox and a hundred goats were swallowed up. By these rents such pieces of ground as were contiguous to the deep ravines in which the rivers flow, were detached, and precipitated down; and in this way the ravines were partly filled up, and the courses of the rivers stopped or altered. Many springs of water appeared in places which had been dry before, and others totally disappeared. Pieces of ground of several acres in extent, with the plantations of olive trees or mulberry trees on them, were carried to a distance of a quarter of a mile and upwards from their original site; other pieces of similar extent, with timber trees or crops of corn, had sunk eight or ten feet, and others had been raised as many. In two or three places it was found that fields planted with different kinds of trees, or sown with different kinds of corn, had exchanged their situations. Where the soil contained a considerable portion of sand, numerous holes were found, which were some feet in depth, and had the form of an inverted cone; during the shocks hot water had issued from them. The ruin of the towns and villages was as complete as the wildest imagination could fancy. The complicated shocks had thrown the houses upon each other, so that they formed heaps of ruins, in which it was impossible to distinguish streets or buildings.

From the centres above mentioned the waves of the earthquake extended all around. On the east they passed through the ridge which lies on that side of the plain; but it appears that the mountain masses had broken their force, as the damage done by these shocks along the eastern coast of Calabria was not considerable. In a northern direction the shocks were felt on the isthmus between the Gulfs of St. Euphemia and of Squillace, but caused no great injury. On the west the oscillations extended to the Lipari Islands, whose inhabitants assured Dolomieu that there was no doubt that the shocks on the 5th of February had proceeded from the side on which the town of Oppido is situated. Severe shocks were also felt in Reggio and Messina, two towns built on the Straits of Messina. Reggio suffered severely, but much less than Messina, probably because the mountain masses of the Aspromonte had broken the violence of the concussions; a great part of Messina was destroyed. The inhabitants of this rich mercantile town stated that the earthquake had proceeded along the coast of Calabria to the north-eastern point of Sicily, Cape Peloro, and thence along the shores of the island to the town of Messina. When the rumbling noise which usually attends earthquakes was heard at this place, the opposite coast of Calabria was seen enveloped in dust, and the houses built there were tumbling down one after the other, until the oscillations of the ground reached the Pallazzata, a lofty series of buildings enclosing the port of Messina in the shape of a crescent, and converting them into a heap of ruins, partly precipitated them into the sea.

The third great earthquake in Calabria occurred on the 28th of February, seven weeks after the last great shock in the plain. The centre of this earthquake was removed much farther to the north. It was near the town of Grifalco, situated more than twenty miles distant from Soriano, and on the very isthmus between the Gulfs of St. Euphemia and Squillace. It is very remarkable that the plain which had been so violently convulsed on the 5th and 7th of February was very little affected by this last earthquake, whilst the town of Messina experienced a very severe shock, which considerably increased the injury occasioned by that of the 5th of February. It would appear, therefore, that this earthquake followed a linear direction, keeping close to the ridge which unites the Aspromonte to the northern mountain tract. The scientific travellers, who visited Calabria a short time after the earthquake had occurred, mention several circumstances which prove that the mountains had also been convulsed by the shocks. According to the information they collected from the inhabitants and eye witnesses, it appears that huge mountain masses had been split asunder, and a portion of them removed to a considerable distance; that the summits of some of the granitic mountains had been seen moving up and down in quick succession; and that the layers of earth which covered the bases and lower declivities of these masses of rocks had been shaken from their situation, and chasms formed between them and the bare rocks of several feet in width and many miles in length.

The manner in which the shocks of an earthquake are propagated has been compared with the ring-like waves produced by a stone thrown into a lake. Such waves decrease in height in proportion as they increase in circumference. So it is also with the central earthquakes. In places which are near the centre the shocks are severe; in those which are farther removed from it they are smart, but gradually they decrease in violence, and at a certain distance they lose the power of putting in motion the solid surface of the earth. Beyond this limit the effects of earthquakes are only felt on those parts of the surface of the globe which are covered with water. The sea and lakes are still strongly affected, which is proved by their levels rising above the common water mark. Springs cease to flow for a time, or rush out with increased vehemence. These facts must be borne in mind when we wish to form an exact idea of the extent of the countries which are affected by an earthquake.

The earthquakes which convulsed Calabria did not extend to a great distance from their centre; but it was quite otherwise with that of Lisbon. Its effects have been traced over a space which, according to a rough calculation, comprehended about fifteen millions of square miles, or nearly equal to one twelfth of the area of the globe. Besides the greater part of Europe, that portion of Africa was affected by it which lies between the Mediterranean and Mount Atlas. The shocks passed the Atlantic, and we find that not only several parts of North America felt them, but also that the sea surrounding the Lesser Antilles was put in motion by these shocks.

In many parts of Spain very severe shocks were felt, as in Madrid, Malaga, and other places. France was much less affected, and the motions of the earth do not appear to have extended beyond the Pyrenees. But the northern part of Italy experienced very violent shocks, especially Milan, which was shaken so strongly that the inhabitants feared the whole city would be levelled to the ground. The Lake of Como exhibited extraordinary commotions, and the mountain region between it and the Lake of Geneva suffered very much, especially the town of Brieg, in the Valais, where several houses were thrown down, and the walls of a number of others were split. Nearly all the Alpine lakes of Switzerland had their water set in motion; that of Neufchâtel rose over its banks, and flooded the adjacent country. The Lake of Murten, on the other side, is said to have lowered its level by six feet, and to have retained this level. Slight shocks were felt even to the north of the Alps, in Bavaria, especially at Augsburg. Farther north no shock was experienced, and the effects of the earthquake were limited to the waters of some lakes, which were put in motion, and to some springs. Thus the hot springs at Töplitz, in Bohemia, ceased for a minute to flow, and then burst forth with increased force. The commotion of the waters was even observed in some lakes of Sweden, among which Lake Wenner is particularly mentioned.

Near Ashford, in Derbyshire, England, the miners engaged in a mine felt so strong a commotion that they were alarmed, and thought the pit was falling in. In its vicinity a rent was formed in the ground which was nearly one hundred and fifty yards long, about a foot deep, and six inches in width. On the coast of Cornwall the sea rose eight or ten feet above its common level, and many vessels were torn from their anchors and wrecked. The commotion was rather stronger at Cork, but much less at Liverpool and in the harbors of Scotland. In Essex some ponds overflowed their banks, and several of the lakes in Scotland, as Loch Lomond, Loch Ness, and Loch Ketturin rose several times from two to three feet above their usual level.

The waves of the earthquake which proceeded to the south from Lisbon appear to have acted with much greater force. We have already mentioned their effects on Cadiz, Ayamonte, and Gibraltar. The empire of Morocco was affected by them even more violently. All the larger towns, as Tangier, Tetuan, Fez, Mequinez, and Morocco, were greatly damaged in their buildings. Not far from Morocco a large village was entirely ruined, and the whole population perished. In the harbor of Funchal, in Madeira, the sea rose fifteen feet above its common level, and great damage was caused in the town by this inundation.

The Lesser Antilles also experienced an extraordinary rising of the sea. Around Barbadoes, where the tide commonly rises only from twenty-four to twenty-eight inches, the sea rose on the 1st of November, at some places, twenty feet, and round Martinique and Antigua fifteen feet. Around Barbadoes the water was as black as ink. Humboldt is of opinion that this color of the sea water was derived from the petroleum, with which the bottom of the sea is covered between the Islands of Barbadoes and Trinidad, and which had been stirred up by the violence of the shocks. In the United States smart shocks were felt at several places in Massachusetts and Pennsylvania. The country surrounding Lake Ontario and the adjacent parts of Canada experienced also slight shocks. It is remarkable that at the last-mentioned places the commotions of the earth preceded the earthquake of Lisbon, as they were felt during the last days of October.

An earthquake, which extended over the whole of the Indian Archipelago, occurred in 1815, and was noticed by Sir Thomas Raffles, then governor of Java. Its centre was in the Island of Sumbawa, where the shocks continued almost without interruption from April to June, and did not cease until after an eruption of the volcano of that island.

The sound of the explosions was heard in Sumatra, at the distance of nine hundred and seventy geographical miles in a direct line; and at Ternate, in an opposite direction, at the distance of seven hundred and twenty miles. Out of a population of twelve thousand, in the province of Tomboro, only twenty-six individuals survived. Violent whirlwinds carried up men, horses, cattle, and whatever else came within their influence, into the air, tore up the largest trees by the roots, and covered the whole sea with floating timber.

Along the sea coast of Sumbawa and the adjacent isles, the sea rose suddenly to the height of from two to twelve feet, a great wave rushing up the estuaries, and then suddenly subsiding. Although the wind at Bima was still during the whole time, the sea rolled in upon the shore, and filled the lower parts of the houses with water a foot deep. Every prow and boat was forced from the anchorage, and driven on shore.

The town called Tomboro, on the west side of Sumbawa, was overflowed by the sea, which encroached upon the shore so that the water remained permanently eighteen feet deep in places where there was land before. Here we may observe, that the amount of subsidence of land was apparent, in spite of the ashes, which would naturally have caused the limits of the coast to be extended.

Great tracts of land were covered by lava, several streams of which, issuing from the crater of the Tomboro mountain, reached the sea. So heavy was the fall of ashes, that they broke into the resident's house at Bima, forty miles east of the volcano, and rendered it, as well as many other dwellings in the town, unhabitable. On the side of Java the ashes were carried to the distance of three hundred miles, and two hundred and seventeen towards Celebes in sufficient quantity to darken the air. The floating cinders to the westward of Sumatra formed, on the 12th of April, a mass two feet thick, and several miles in extent, through which ships with difficulty forced their way.

The darkness occasioned in the daytime by the ashes in Java was so profound, that nothing equal to it was ever witnessed in the darkest night. Although this volcanic dust, when it fell was an impalpable powder, it was of considerable weight when compressed, a pint of it weighing twelve ounces and three quarters. "Some of the finest particles," says Mr. Crawfurd, "were transported to the Islands of Amboyna and

Banda, which last is about eight hundred miles east from the site of the volcano, although the south-east monsoon was then at its height." They must have been projected, therefore, into the upper regions of the atmosphere, where a counter current prevailed.

Having described the nature of the motion, the direction in which the shocks spread over a country, the great extent of country which is sometimes affected by them, and the common effects produced by severe earthquakes, it remains yet to notice some of the phenomena commonly attending earthquakes; namely, the subterraneous noises, the chasms, the different kinds of matter issuing from these chasms, and the rising of the sea.

A subterraneous noise usually accompanies severe earthquakes, but not always. No noise was heard during the shocks which in 1797 levelled the town of Riobamba to the ground, and killed from thirty to forty thousand persons, and which is called by Humboldt one of the most frightful phenomena recorded in the physical history of our globe. A very loud noise issuing from under the ground on which the towns of Quito and Ibarra stand, alarmed the inhabitants of these places; but it occurred eighteen or twenty minutes after the catastrophe had taken place by which Riobamba was destroyed; and even then no noise was heard at Tacunga and Hambato, two places situated near the centre of the earthquake. The same absence of noise was noticed in Peru, in 1746, when Lima and Callao were destroyed by an earthquake, whilst a quarter of an hour later a loud, subterraneous noise, similar to a clap of thunder, was heard at Truxillo, which is more than three hundred miles farther north; but at this place no commotion of the ground was perceived. In the earthquake at New Granada, in 1827, the shocks passed away without noise; but some time afterwards, subterraneous detonations were heard, which followed one another at regular intervals of about thirty minutes, but were not attended with any convulsion. In most cases the noise is heard when the earthquake begins; but in some it precedes the first shock by a few minutes or seconds.

The sound of this noise is not in all places of the same description. In most cases it is compared to a rumbling sound produced by a continuous series of small explosions, not dissimilar to the rolling of thunder, or, when less intense, to the rattling of a number of carts passing at a distance over an uneven stone pavement. In Quito the sound frequently resembles abrupt broken peals of thunder. Sometimes it is like the sound produced by iron chains, when they are violently shaken; and sometimes it is more shrill, as if obsidian and other masses of vitreous matter were broken to pieces with violence in subterraneous caverns.

This subterraneous noise is sometimes heard, and apparently at the same moment, over an immense extent of country—a circumstance which has excited, with reason, the astonishment of the natural philosophers. The best ascertained fact of this description occurred in the northern countries of South America, in 1812, on the 30th of April, shortly before an eruption of the volcano in the Island of St. Vincent. This noise, as Humboldt states, was heard in all the countries lying contiguous to the southern shores of the Caribbean Sea, and as far inland as the Llanos or Cattle Plains. At Calabozo, and on the banks of the River Apure, which falls into the Orinoco, it was apparently as loud as on the shores of the sea. Humboldt calculates that the countries in which this noise was heard nearly at the same time and with the same degree of intensity, and without being attended with the least motion of the ground, had an area of about fifty thousand square miles. The two well-ascertained circumstances, that the noise was heard at the same time and with the same degree of intensity, are certainly very remarkable. We must infer from them that the sound cannot have been propagated by the air, as it is well known that claps of thunder are only heard at distant places after a proportioned lapse of time. Solid bodies are indeed much better conductors of sound than air. Thus burned earth propagates the sound quicker than air, in the proportion of ten or twelve to one. But all the ascertained facts respecting the propagation of sound, by repeated experiments, are not sufficient to explain the two above mentioned. It would seem that the noise originated in the interior of the earth, at a spot equally distant, or nearly so, from the surface of the globe at all the places where it was heard. A similar fact is mentioned as attending the great eruption of the volcano of Cotopaxi, in Ecuador, in 1744. At the moment of eruption, or shortly before, a subterraneous thunder was heard at Honda, in the valley of the Rio de la Magdalena. These two points are five hundred miles distant from each other, and between them are heaped up the colossal and immense mountain masses of Quito, Pasto, and Papayan, with their numberless valleys and ravines. Besides, the summit of the volcano is elevated eighteen thousand feet above the site of the town of Honda.

It is also remarkable, that sometimes, though rarely, a subterraneous noise is heard which is not connected either with an earthquake or with the eruption of a volcano. These subterranean thunders have been mentioned by ancient writers; but in modern times they have not been frequently observed. The most remarkable fact of this description occurred at the town of Guanaxuato, in Mexico, in 1784. At midnight, on the 9th of January, it was heard for the first time. It continued to increase by degrees from that day to the 13th, when it attained its greatest intensity. It seemed then as if heavy thunder clouds had gathered under the town, whence issued a slowly rolling thunder, frequently interrupted by short and extremely loud claps. From the 16th of January the noise began to decrease; but it did not cease before the 12th of February. No interruption took place during the whole time of its duration; no commotion of the ground was observed in the vicinity of the town of Guanaxuato, nor on any other part of the table land of Anahuac; nor did it appear that any of the volcanoes of this table land were in activity. What renders this phenomenon still more remarkable is, that it was limited to a comparatively small extent of country, as people living at a distance of only twenty miles from the town did not hear the least noise. But it was as loud in the numerous mines which are found in the vicinity of the town, and of which some are of the depth of sixteen hundred feet, as in Guanaxuato itself. The inhabitants of the place, as may easily be imagined, were put into the greatest consternation. They abandoned the town with precipitation, in which great masses of silver, drawn from the neighboring mines, had been accumulated, and which were thus left without protection. Some robbers, taking advantage of this circumstance, got into the town, and took possession of the treasures; but a number of the less timid of the inhabitants had meanwhile become habituated to the noise, and had in some degree got rid of their fright. They reentered the place, and regained possession of the treasures. A similar subterraneous noise had never been heard in the country before, nor has recurred since.

Much less intense, but of much longer duration, was the subterraneous noise which alarmed the inhabitants of Melida, a small island in the Adriatic Sea, not far from Ragusa in Dalmatia. It was heard for the first time in March, 1822, and resembled the sound of a remote cannonade. It did not continue uninterruptedly, but ceased sometimes for weeks, and even months together, and then commenced again. Some of the detonations were attended by very slight shocks of earthquake. This noise did not entirely cease before 1826.

Hardly any account exists of a severe earthquake in which the formation of chasms, rents, and cracks is not mentioned. These openings are commonly of a very considerable extent, but of moderate width. The number of such rents which were found in the plain of Calabria, after the earthquake had ceased, was very great; in the vicinity of Polistena, especially, they were so numerous that the roads were rendered impassable. During the earthquake which in 1805 happened in the province of Molise, in the kingdom of Naples, numerous chasms of considerable width and great extent had been formed, which, for a length of time afterwards, were still open. In 1818 the chasms opened by the earthquake in Catania split the walls of the houses standing over them so widely that the moon could be seen through the rents thus produced; but immediately afterwards they closed so firmly that it was hardly possible to perceive any trace of them in the walls. The last-mentioned event, strange as it may appear, is mentioned in many accounts of earthquakes.

It is easily to be conceived in what way these chasms are formed. The crust of the earth, consisting of solid matter, cannot yield like a fluid. When, therefore, it is raised up ward, and at the same time affected by the undulatory shocks, its surface must crack and open. It may also be explained why some of these chasms remain open after the earthquake has passed away, whilst others close as soon as the motion ceases. The chasms of the first description are caused by the undulatory motion on a level tract, whose outer edge is formed by a steep and abrupt descent to a lower level. When such a tract has cracked and opened, the chasms are always found to run parallel to the outer edge; and in most cases the perpendicular layer constituting the outer edge, which has no support on the side towards which it is propelled, is thrown down on the lower ground. This process has been the cause of much destruction. According to the account of Hamilton, the greatest part of the Pallazzata of Messina was precipitated into the sea, because the spot on which it was erected separated by a crack from the contiguous ground, and as it had no support on the side next the sea, it fell into the Straits of Messina. It is very probable that the stone quay of Lisbon was in a similar state before it gave way to the inundation. Hamilton is also of opinion that most of the translocations of the pieces of ground, which on the borders of the deep ravines of Calabria had sometimes sunk twenty feet to the bottom of the watercourses, were effected in this way. By the downfall of the perpendicular layer forming the outer edge the body is withdrawn, by the reaction of which the other chasms which traverse the level ground parallel to the outer edge could be closed, and therefore these chasms remain open until they are filled up by the effects produced on the earth's surface by rain, watercourses, &c. Houses and other buildings, which are erected on such level ground, of course have their walls split by the change of level on which their foundations are laid, and many are so ruined that they do not retain the least trace of their former shape.

But when a tract of country is so constituted that none of its edges can give way, — a place, we will suppose, enclosed on all sides by mountains, — the effects of the shocks on its surface must be different. The shocks, by raising the ground, make the surface crack and open; but as soon as the force to which the earthquake owes its origin ceases to act, the surface sinks to its former position, and the chasms are closed. Thus we may explain how it happens that during an earthquake rents are occasionally formed in buildings half a foot, or even a foot, wide, which, however, on the cessation of the motion, close so firmly that it is impossible to discover the traces.

Another description of openings, owing their origin to earthquakes, are those which have the form of inverted cones; they are sometimes several feet deep, and occur only in a soil which contains a considerable proportion of sand. It is stated that, during an earthquake, hot water mixed with sand issues from these openings. The sand has a ferruginous appearance, and at first a smell of sulphur. Such openings were numerous at several places in Calabria, and also on the banks of the Mississippi after the earthquake of 1812.

We find that different kinds of gas, smoke, fire, water, and in some cases more solid matters, are frequently brought from the interior of the earth to its surface by earthquakes. It is remarkable that no chasms have been found at the places where these matters were ejected. During the earthquake of Lisbon a thick smoke was seen rising from the declivity of a rocky mountain, which continued for some time after the commotion of the earth had ceased; but when the place was afterwards inspected, no trace of a chasm could be discovered. Humboldt mentions that during the earthquake of Cumana, in 1797, flames issued at some places on the banks of the Rio Manzanares; but he does not mention that they had been emitted by cracks. Water, however, and earthy matter cannot be brought from the interior of the earth to its surface without the formation of chasms; and we find that in several accounts this is expressly stated. As these chasms, however, closed with the cessation of the earthquake, and have never been examined with attention, we have not the means of forming an idea of the manner in which they were made. It is probable that they reached to a much greater depth than the chasms we have noticed before.

In some cases water is stated to have rushed out of a chasm, and risen several feet in height like a fountain. The surface of the Island of Jamaica, during the great earthquake of 1692, was deeply rent at several places, and these rents swallowed up several persons, but, quickly reopening, ejected them again by means of jets of water, which rushed out of the ground with great violence, and rose to a considerable elevation. At the same time thick clouds of vapor issued from the chasms, diffusing an insupportable stench, and for a short time obscuring the atmosphere to such a degree, that the air, which up to that moment had been perfectly serene, suddenly assumed the appearance of a burning furnace. In the beginning of the last century (1702 and 1703) the provinces of the Abruzzi, in the kingdom of Naples, were visited by a very severe earthquake. The town of Aquila, among other places, was levelled to the ground. During this earthquake several chasms were opened in the fields surrounding that place, from which volumes of gas or steam rushed out, carrying with them such volumes of water, and such quantities of stones and earthy matter, as were sufficient to cover the fields in the neighborhood, and to render them unfit for agricultural purposes for a number of years. The water ascended like a fountain, and rose so high that its summit overtopped the highest trees in the vicinity; flames and thick clouds of smoke were seen escaping from the neighboring mountains, and these clouds continued for three days, almost without intermission.

The ejection of mud appears to be of less frequent occurrence. Humboldt, however, mentions a very remarkable instance, which is connected with the great earthquake of Riobamba, in 1797. At a time when none of the neighboring volcanoes ejected any kind of matter, a chasm opened, from which issued a very strange mass of mud, consisting of a mixture of charcoal, crystals of augite, and scales of infusoria. This mass, called *moya* by the natives, covered several fields, which were rendered sterile by this thick coat, and which formed besides a series of small eminences. A similar effect was produced by the earthquake of Valparaiso, in 1822. In the valley of the Quillota River, numerous hillocks, consisting of sand and mud, were forced through the crevices caused by the shocks. They appeared like mud volcanoes in miniature; and some of them sunk again, leaving in their places muddy pools.

As gas is not visible, it is not frequently mentioned as issuing from the earth during earthquakes. But a learned Frenchman, who has given an account of the earthquake which occurred in 1827 in the valley of the Rio Magdalena, states that large quantities of carbonic acid gas escaped from some crevices; and that a great number of snakes, rats, and other small animals living in holes in the earth, were killed by it. In several instances it has been observed that during an earthquake the surface of the sea, or even of a river, as, for instance, that of the Douro at the earthquake of Lisbon, was in a state of agitation not dissimilar to that of water in a high state of ebullition. This phenomenon was also observed in the Straits of Messina during the earthquake of Calabria, and not far from the mouth of the Douro in the sea during that of Lisbon. It is supposed that air or gas has escaped from the sea at such places.

That gas, occasionally, really escapes from the bottom of the sea and reaches its surface during an earthquake, was proved by an event which took place in the harbor of Callao, in 1828. A British vessel of war, the Volage, was anchored in that harbor with several other vessels. The morning of the 30th of March was clear, and a light breeze came from the southward. At half past seven o'clock a thin black cloud passed over the ship, with very heavy distant thunder. At the same moment the shock of a severe earthquake was felt. Persons on board the vessel thought that it continued seventy or eighty seconds. The ship trembled violently. The commotion was compared to that which would have been felt had the ship been placed on trucks and driven with rapidity over coarse paved ground. The ship was moored with two chain cables, and, on raising the anchor a few days after, it was found that fifty-six links of the best bower cable were much injured; the iron had the appearance of being melted, and nearly one sixth of each link was destroyed. The part of the chain so affected was thirty fathoms from the anchor, and twenty fathoms from the ship. The bottom was soft mud, in which the cable was buried. During the earthquake the water alongside the vessel was full of bubbles, and emitted a hissing sound. The city of Lima suffered considerably at the same moment, and a number of lives were lost. Such is the account of this remarkable fact. The damaged state in which a part of the chain cable was found compels us to adopt the supposition that an expansive fluid or gas had escaped from the bottom of the sea with a development of an uncommon degree of heat. It remains doubtful whether the gas escaped from a crevice or any opening in the bottom of the sea; but the small number of links which were affected by it appears to be rather in favor of the supposition.

One of the most destructive of the phenomena accompanying earthquakes is the alternate rising and retiring of the sea.

It does not appear that all great earthquakes are attended by this phenomenon. In the accounts published of the earthquakes of Cumana in 1797, of Caraccas in 1812, and of Valparaiso, no rise of the sea, either during the earthquake or immediately after it, is mentioned. Some state that this phenomenon occurred during the earthquakes of Calabria; but that is very doubtful, as Hamilton makes no mention of it, though he expressly observes that the inundation, by which a small portion of low land was covered, was caused by the fall of a rocky mass detached from the mountains lying on the other side of the Straits of Messina, and the consequent high wave produced by its being precipitated into the sea. This author, who visited Calabria immediately after the earthquakes had ceased, could certainly not have overlooked this circumstance; as by rising twenty or thirty feet above its usual level the sea would have rushed with great violence into the deep ravines by which the plain of Calabria is furrowed, and all of which are open to it. The rising of the sea, however, proved very destructive in the earthquakes of Lisbon in 1755, and those of Callao in 1585 and 1746. In Lisbon it caused the downfall of the stone quay, by which accident three thousand persons were drowned, as mentioned before. When the earthquake of Lima had ceased to agitate the ground, the sea rose in the following night about eighty feet above its common level in the harbor of Callao. It rushed with such violence over the place that every thing was destroyed and washed away, and nothing remained standing except a few ruins of the fortifications. The population, consisting of about five thousand individuals, was drowned, with the exception of about two hundred. When the wave rushed into the harbor twenty-three vessels were at anchor there; four of them were carried by the flood over the walls of the fortress, and put down on the continent at a distance of about two miles from the shore; the other ships were broken to pieces.

Immediately after the shock of an earthquake in Japan on the 23d of December, 1854, the sea commenced bubbling up along the shore, and then receded with great rapidity, and as soon returned with such increased volume as to flood the entire town of Simoda to the depth of six or seven feet — sweeping away houses, bridges, and temples, and piling them up in a mass of ruin.

Five times during the day the sea advanced and receded in this manner, spreading desolation far and wide. The largest junks in the harbor were driven from one to two miles above high-water mark, where they were seen lying high and dry. About two hundred of the inhabitants lost their lives by the overflow — the remainder saving themselves by fleeing to the mountains with which the town is surrounded.

The Russian frigate Diana, having Vice Admiral Pontiatine on board, was lying in the harbor at the time, engaged in finishing up the treaty they had made with the Japanese. Immediately after the shock was felt, the water in the harbor became convulsed to such a degree in eddies and whirlpools, that in the space of thirty minutes she swung entirely round forty-three times, twisting her chains up into knots. So rapid was the motion that the people on board could not keep their feet, and all were made giddy. When the sea receded, it left the frigate in eight feet of water on her side, when her usual draught was over twenty-one feet. On its return, it is stated, the water rose five fathoms above its ordinary level.

On its again receding, four feet only of water remained. The heaving of the bottom of the bay was then so violent that the frigate — although requiring seventeen feet more of water to float her — was moved bodily past her anchor. The officers momentarily expected that the bay would become the outlet of the subterranean fires, and that they would be ingulfed in it. When the frigate again floated, they saw her keel and rudder, which had been wrenched off, floating alongside, and the ship filling with water. By getting sails upon her, they managed to keep her afloat; and the next day, things having got quiet once more, they hauled her off into deeper water. The earthquake was felt over the whole Island of Niphon.

On the 24th of December, at six P. M., thirty-four hours after the destruction of Simoda, the sea rushed over the beautiful and wealthy city of Osaka, said to be the most beautiful in the empire, and totally destroyed it. The shocks were but slight; and the first intimation that the inhabitants had of great danger was the fearful influx of the sea. In Yedo Bay, at Yedo, and the numerous adjacent populous towns, more or less damage and loss of life occurred. Occasional shocks of earthquake continued to be felt; but none were attended with serious consequences.

Instances of earthquakes at sea are frequently recorded in the journals of navigators. In most cases the motion felt on board the vessel is compared with that experienced when a ship strikes on a rock under water. During the earthquake of Lisbon, an English vessel, sailing at a distance of about fifty miles from the coast of Portugal, experienced a shock of such violence that a part of the deck was damaged. The captain, greatly surprised, thought that a great mistake must have crept into his dead reckoning, and that his vessel had got on a rock. He gave orders to put out the long boat to save the crew; but he was soon convinced that there was no danger. Shaw, in his Travels in Barbary, states that he experienced, in 1724, at a place where the sea was thirty fathoms deep, three severe shocks. It appeared to him as if great masses of stone, of from twenty to thirty tons in weight, had been thrown on the ballast. The Dutch navigator Schouten, when navigating among the Moluccas, experienced frequent shocks, when his vessel was out of soundings; and every time it appeared to him as if he had run aground. Le Gentil mentions that he once felt so powerful a shock that the guns of the vessel were put into a skipping motion, and part of the rigging was torn to pieces.

All the phenomena attending earthquakes hitherto noticed occurred in the last great earthquake of South America, that of Conception and Talcahuano, of which Captain Fitz Roy has given the following graphic description, which is the more valuable as it shows in what manner the shipping in the harbor of Talcahuano was affected by the alternate rising and retiring of the sea: —

"At ten in the morning of the 20th of February, very large flights of sea fowl were noticed passing over the city of Conception from the sea coast towards the interior. In the minds of old inhabitants, well acquainted with the climate of Conception, some surprise was excited by so unusual and simultaneous a change in the habits of those birds, as no signs of an approaching storm were visible, nor any expected at that season. About eleven the southerly or sea breeze freshened up as usual; the sky was clear and almost cloudless. At forty minutes after eleven a shock of an earthquake was felt — slightly at first, but increasing rapidly. During the first half minute many persons remained in their houses; but then the convulsive movements became so strong that the alarm was general, and all rushed into the open spaces for safety. The horrid motion increased; people could hardly stand; buildings waved and tottered. Suddenly an awful shock caused universal destruction. In less than six seconds the city was in ruins. The stunning noise of the falling houses; the horrible cracking of the earth, which opened and shut rapidly and repeatedly at numerous places; the stifling heat; the desperate, heart-rending outcries of the people; the blinding, smothering clouds of dust; the utter helplessness and confusion, and the extreme horror and alarm, can neither be described nor fully imagined.

"This fatal convulsion took place about a minute and a half or two minutes after the first shock. During this time no one could stand unsupported. People clung to each other, to trees, or to posts. Some threw themselves on the ground; but there the motion was so violent that they were obliged to stretch out their arms on each side to prevent being tossed over and over. Horses and other animals were greatly frightened, standing with their legs spread out, and their heads down, trembling violently. Birds flew about wildly.

"After the violent shock had ceased, the clouds of dust which had been raised by the falling buildings began to disperse. People breathed more freely, and began to look around them. Ghastly and sepulchral was their appearance; had the graves opened and given up their dead, the sight would have been scarcely more shocking. Pale and trembling, covered with dust and perspiration, they ran from place to place, calling for their relations and friends. Many seemed to be quite bereft of reason.

"Considerable shocks continued at short intervals, harassing and alarming. The earth was never long quiet during that and the next day, nor indeed the three days following the great shock. For many hours after the ruin the earth was tremulous, and the shocks were very frequent, though not severe. Many shocks, but not all, were preceded by a rumbling subterraneous noise, like distant thunder; some compared the sound to the distant discharge of many pieces of artillery. These sounds came from the south-west quarter, and preceded the shock by one or two seconds. Sometimes, but not often, the sound was heard unaccompanied by any shock.

"Roofs fell in every where. Houses built of unbaked bricks fell into a confused heap. The cathedral, whose walls were four feet in thickness, built of good brick and mortar, and supported by large buttresses, suffered more than other buildings. Adhering to the remains of the walls were the lower parts of some buttresses, the upper parts of others, while in one place a buttress stood on its own foundation, separated entirely from the wall.

"The city of Conception stands on a plain, having an alluvial and loose soil, and at the back of it are rocky, irregular hills. From the foot of these hills the earth was every where parted by the great convulsion, great cracks being left from an inch to a foot in width. It seemed as if the low land had been separated from the hills, having been more disturbed by the shock. Besides a waving or undulatory movement, vertical, horizontal, and circular or twisting motions were felt. An angular stone pinnacle was particularly noticed, which had been turned half round without being thrown down or leaving its base.

"Persons riding at the time of the great shock were stopped short: some, with their horses, were thrown to the ground; others dismounted, but could not stand. So little was the ground at rest after the great ruin, that between the 20th of February and the 4th of March more than three hundred shocks were counted.

"At Talcahuano the great earthquake was felt as severely as in the city of Conception. It took place at the same time, and in a precisely similar manner. Three houses only, upon a rocky foundation, escaped the fate of all those standing upon the loose sandy soil which lies between the sea beach and the hills. Nearly all the inhabitants escaped uninjured; but they had scarcely recovered from the sensations of the ruinous shocks when alarm was given that the sea was retiring. As in former times a place in the Bay of Talcahuano had been destroyed, with its whole population, by an overwhelming wave, preceded by a retiring of the sea, all became apprehensive of a similar fate, and hurried to the hills as fast as possible.

"About half an hour after the shock — when the greater part of the population had reached the heights, and the sea had retired so much that all the vessels at anchor, even those which had been lying in seven fathoms of water, were aground, and all the rocks and shoals in the bay were visible — an enormous wave was seen forcing its way through the western passage which separates Quiriquina Island from the main land. This immense wave passed rapidly along the western side of the Bay of Conception, sweeping the steep shores of every thing movable within thirty feet vertically from the high-water mark. It broke over, dashed along, and whirled about the shipping as if they had been light boats; overflowed the greater part of the town, and then rushed back with such a torrent that almost every movable, which the earthquake had not buried under heaps of ruins, was carried out to sea. In a few minutes the vessels were again aground, and a second great wave was seen approaching, with more noise and impetuosity than the first. Though this wave was more powerful, its effects were not so considerable, simply because there was less to destroy. Again the sea fell, dragging away quantities of woodwork, and the lighter materials of houses, and leaving the shipping aground.

"After some minutes of awful suspense, a third enormous swell was seen, between Quiriquina and the main land, apparently larger than either of the former waves. Roaring as it dashed against every obstacle with irresistible force, it rushed along the shore, destroying and overwhelming. Quickly retiring, as if spurned by the foot of the hills, the retreating wave dragged away such quantities of household effects, fences, furniture, and other movables, that, after the tumultuous rush was over, the sea appeared covered with wreck. Exhaustion appeared to follow these efforts. Earth and water trembled. Numbers of the inhabitants now hastened to the ruins, anxious to ascertain the extent of their losses, and to save some money or a few valuable articles, which, having escaped the sweep of the sea, were exposed to depredators.

"During the remainder of the day and the following night, the earth was not quiet many minutes at a time. Frequent, almost incessant, tremors, occasional shocks more or less severe, and distant subterraneous noises, kept every one in anxious suspense. Some thought the crisis had not arrived, and would not descend from the hills into the ruined town. Those who were searching among the ruins started at every shock, however slight, and almost doubted that the sea was not actually rushing in again to overwhelm them. Nearly all the inhabitants, excepting a few who went on board vessels in the harbor, passed the night upon the hills, without shelter; and next day they began to raise sheds and huts upon the high ground, still dreading the sea. It was said, and generally considered certain, that every dog at Talcahuano had left the town before the shock which ruined the buildings was felt.

"In the harbor were three large whale ships, a bark, two brigs, and a schooner, in from four to seven fathoms; they were lying at single anchor, with a good scope of cable. With the southerly breeze, which was rather fresh at the time of the earthquake, these vessels lay to seaward of their anchors, having their sterns towards the sea. At the appearance of the first great wave all hands took to the rigging for safety. The wave came in an unbroken swell to the stern of one of the whale ships, broke over and lifted her along without doing any material harm, more than sweeping her decks, as the hatches were battened down and deadlights shipped. The slack chain, dragging over the mud, checked her gradually, as the first impetus of the wave diminished. Whirling her round, the water rushed out to seaward again, leaving the vessel stranded nearly in her former position. From two fathoms, when aground, the depth alongside increased to ten, when the water rose highest during the last swell. The two latter waves approached the shipping; some of the vessels were thrown violently against others, and whirled around as if they had been in the vortex of a whirlpool. Previous to the rush of waters, two merchantmen were lying a full cable's length apart, and after it had passed they were side by side, with three round turns in their cables. Each vessel had, therefore, gone round the other with each wave; the bow of one was stove in; to the other little damage was done. A small vessel was on the stocks, almost ready for launching; she was carried by the sea two hundred yards in shore, and left there unhurt. A little schooner, at anchor before the town, slipped her cables, and ran out in the offing as the water fell. She met the wave unbroken, and rose on it as an ordinary swell. Many boats put off from the shore before the sea retired; some met the advancing waves before they broke, and rose safely over them; others, half swamped, struggled through the breakers.

"For several days the sea was strewed with wreck, not only in the bay, but outside in the offing. The shores of Quiriquina Island were covered with broken furniture and woodwork of all kinds, so much so that for weeks afterwards parties were constantly at work collecting and bringing back property. During three days succeeding that of the ruin, the sea ebbed and flowed irregularly and very frequently, rising and falling for some hours after the shock, two or three times in an hour.

"Two explosions or eruptions were witnessed whilst the waves were coming in. One, in the offing, beyond the Island of Quiriquina, appeared like a dark column of smoke in the shape of a tower. Another arose in the bay of San Vincent like the blowing of an immense whale; its disappearance was followed by a whirlpool which lasted some minutes. It was hollow, and tended to a point in the middle, as if the sea was pouring into a cavity of the earth. At the time of the ruin, and until after the great waves, the water in the bay appeared to be every where boiling; bubbles of air or gas were rapidly escaping; the water also became black, and exhaled a most disagreeable sulphureous smell. Dead fish were afterwards thrown ashore in quantities; they seemed to have been poisoned or suffocated; and for days together the shores of the bay were covered with fine corvinos and numerous small fish. Black fetid water burst up from the earth in several places, and at one the ground swelled like a large bubble, and then bursting, poured forth black, fetid, sulphureous water.

"It was ascertained that in Talcahuano the body of water reached twenty-five feet above the usual level of high water. It penetrated into the first-floor rooms, and left seaweed hanging to the remains of roofs or to the tops of broken walls. Those who watched the waves coming in considered them, while beyond the shipping, about as high as the upper part of the hull of a frigate, or from sixteen to twenty feet above the level of the rest of the water in the bay. Only those parts of the wave which encountered opposition broke until within half a mile of the beach, when the roar became appalling. At the time of the great shock the water swelled up to high-water mark on the sea beach, without having previously retired. It then began to retire, and continued falling about half an hour before a great wave was seen approaching. For some days after the devastation the sea did not rise to its usual mark by four or five feet vertically. But this difference gradually diminished, till, in the middle of April, it amounted only to two feet between the existing and former high-water marks. It was considered as a proof that the land had been elevated.

"Wherever the invading waves found low land, the destruction was great, from those lands being in general well cultivated, and the site of many houses. The low grounds lying at the bottom of Conception Bay were overflowed and injured irreparably; quantities of cattle, horses, and sheep were lost. Similar effects, in an equal or less degree, were felt on the coast between the River Itata and Cape Rumena. Large masses of earth and stone, many thousand tons in weight, were detached from the cliffs and precipitous sides of the hills. It was dangerous to go near the edge of a cliff; for numerous chasms and cracks in every direction showed how doubtful was the support. When walking on the shore, even at high water, beds of dead muscles, numerous chitons and limpets, and withered seaweed, still adhering, though lifeless, to the rocks on which they had lived, every where met the eye, as proofs of the upheaval of the land."

In countries where earthquakes occur frequently, it is commonly supposed that such unusual and powerful phenomena, which appear to shake the whole earth to its centre, cannot take place without being preceded by some signs. In most parts it is thought that an unusual state of the atmosphere must precede each earthquake. In Italy the opinion prevails, that long calms, an oppressive heat, and a foggy sky are indices of the approach of an earthquake. But besides that such a state of the atmosphere often occurs without being followed by one of those terrible events, it has been found by long-continued and exact observation, and by comparing the phenomena of the air preceding earthquakes, in the numerous accounts of the most severe of them which have been published in the last and present century, that no connection exists between the state of the weather and the earthquakes. Severe shocks have occurred in calms, and when gales were blowing; whilst the atmosphere was obscured with fogs, and when the sky was cloudless and a fresh breeze was agitating the air; whilst heavy rains poured down, and during storms of thunder. It is true that several of the severe earthquakes were preceded by a fog of a reddish appearance; but this phenomenon has not been observed previous to a much larger number which have occurred when not the least cloud could be observed on the whole vault of heaven.

It cannot be maintained either that earthquakes occur only at certain seasons of the year. During the last fifty or sixty years the naturalists have paid particular attention to the seasons when these phenomena occurred; and by comparing the lists thus collected, it was found that in the higher latitudes they occur at all times, but more frequently during the cold weather, especially about the equinoxes, either shortly before or shortly after them: the smaller number have occurred between the vernal and autumnal equinoxes. In the intertropical countries a large majority have happened when the rainy season was about to begin or cease. They are especially severe when the dry season has been so long protracted as to have injured the crops and the vegetation in general. In South America it frequently happens, when an earthquake follows a season of long drought and dearth, that rain is much more abundant after it than usual. In these countries the native population, whose huts, built of reeds, are rarely damaged by earthquakes, and who have no fear of being crushed by the downfall of their habitations, preserve the remembrance of great earthquakes as joyful events, keeping festivals on their anniversaries; while the descendants of Europeans form processions and perform religious ceremonies to avert the repetition of such disastrous calamities. In the Indian Archipelago the smartest shocks are felt when the monsoons change.

It has been observed in many cases that the weather becomes considerably colder after an earthquake. It is doubtful if the climate of a place can be changed by the occurrence of an earthquake, though Humboldt mentions a very remarkable instance of the kind. In giving a description of the town of Quito, in Ecuador, he says, "It is a fine place, but the sky is unpleasant and foggy; the mountains surrounding the town are clothed with a very scanty vegetation, and it is extremely cold. The severe earthquake which, on the 4th of February, 1797, convulsed the whole country, and killed between thirty-five and forty thousand persons, has proved disastrous in this respect also; for it has greatly changed the temperature of the air. At present the thermometer commonly ranges between four and ten degrees of the scale of Réaumur, (forty-one and fifty-four and a half of Fahrenheit,) and rarely rises to sixteen and seventeen degrees, whilst at the time of Bouguer (between 1730 and 1740) it usually ranged between fourteen and fifteen degrees, (sixty-three and a half and sixty-five and three quarters degrees.")

Many persons suppose that, before the beginning of an earthquake, noxious exhalations of an invisible description are emitted from the surface of the earth. This supposition rests on the well-established fact, that several kinds of animals evince an uncommon degree of restlessness when an earthquake is approaching. This is especially the case with the smaller animals which inhabit caverns and holes in the ground, as rats, mice, lizards, moles, and snakes. They leave their holes and run about with trepidation. Some even of the larger domestic animals participate in this restlessness, especially those which are gifted with a very acute organ of smell, as goats, hogs, and dogs. The dogs, as before stated, abandoned the town of Talcahuano before the first shock was felt. Hogs in many places are considered as having a quicker presentiment of the approach of an earthquake than other domestic animals, so that timid persons, when they think that they have reason to anticipate an earthquake, pay particular attention to all the motions of these animals. Horses and cattle also appear to be affected, but in a less degree.

It appears also, in some cases, that persons have been attacked by a kind of indisposition before the beginning of an earthquake. The most common symptoms are sickness, giddiness, attacks of headache, and depression of spirits. It is asserted that an hour before the great earthquake of Lisbon reached the towns of Cadiz and Gibraltar, several of their inhabitants were attacked by fits of sickness.

An Italian writer, after having given a detailed account of the earthquake which was experienced in the city of Naples, and more severely in the province of Molise, in 1805, adds, "I must not omit in this place to mention those prognostics which were derived from animals. They were observed in every place where the shocks were such as to be generally perceptible. Some minutes before they were felt, the oxen and cows began to bellow; the sheep and goats bleated, and rushing in confusion one on the other, tried to break the wickerwork of the folds; the dogs howled terribly; the geese and fowls were alarmed, and made much noise. The horses, where fastened in their stalls, were greatly agitated, leaped up, and tried to break the halter with which they were attached to the mangers; those which were proceeding on the roads suddenly stopped and snorted in a very strange way. The cats were frightened, and tried to conceal themselves, or their hair bristled up wildly. Rabbits and moles were seen to leave their holes; birds rose, as if scared, from the places on which they had alighted; and fish left the bottom of the sea, and approached the shores, where, at some places, great numbers of them were taken. Even ants and reptiles abandoned, in clear daylight, their subterraneous holes in great disorder, many hours before the shocks were felt. Large flights of locusts were seen creeping through the streets of

Naples towards the sea the night before the earthquake. Winged ants took refuge during the darkness in the rooms of the houses. Some dogs, a few minutes before the first shock took place, awoke their sleeping masters by barking, and pulling them, as if they wished to warn them of the impending danger; and several persons were thus enabled to save themselves."

By far the greater number of earthquakes pass away without leaving any traces of their activity. This may be said of all those which manifest themselves by slight, or even by smart shocks. Severe earthquakes usually destroy only houses and other buildings, and produce very slight changes on the surface of those tracts of land beneath which their force is directed. These changes owe their origin chiefly to the chasms which are formed in the manner already described. A few, however, among those which have acted with an uncommon degree of energy, have left more lasting testimonials of their occurrence, either by depressing a large tract of land below its former level, or by raising it considerably.

In the year 1772, Papandayang, formerly one of the loftiest volcanoes in the Island of Java, was in eruption. Before all the inhabitants on the declivities of the mountain could save themselves by flight, the ground began to give way, and a great part of the volcano fell in and disappeared. It is estimated that an extent of ground of the mountain itself and its immediate environs, fifteen miles long and full six broad, was by this commotion swallowed up in the bowels of the earth. Forty villages were destroyed, some being ingulfed, and some covered by the substances thrown out on this occasion, and two thousand nine hundred and fifty-seven of the inhabitants perished. A proportionate number of cattle were also killed, and most of the plantations of cotton, indigo, and coffee in the adjacent districts were buried under the volcanic matter. This catastrophe appears to have resembled, although on a grander scale, that of the ancient Vesuvius in the year

79. The cone was reduced in height from nine thousand to about five thousand feet; and, as vapors still escape from the crater on its summit, a new cone may one day rise out of the ruins of the ancient mountain, as the modern Vesuvius has risen from the remains of Somma.

During a tremendous earthquake, which destroyed a great part of St. Domingo, innumerable fissures were caused throughout the island, from which mephitic vapors emanated, and produced an epidemic. Hot springs burst forth in many places where there had been no water before; but after a time they ceased to flow.

In a previous earthquake, in November, 1751, a violent shock destroyed the capital, Port au Prince, and part of the coast, twenty leagues in length, sank down, and has ever since formed a bay of the sea.

The town of Chittagong, in Bengal, was violently shaken by an earthquake on the 2d of April, 1762, the earth opening in many places, and throwing up water and mud of a sulphureous smell. At a place called Bardavan a large river was dried up; and at Bar Charra, near the sea, a tract of ground sank down, and two hundred people, with all their cattle, were lost. It is said that sixty square miles of the Chittagong coast suddenly and permanently subsided during this earthquake, and that Ces-lung-Toom, one of the Mug Mountains, entirely disappeared, and another sank so low that its summit only remained visible. Four hills are also described as having been variously rent asunder, leaving open chasms from thirty to sixty feet in width. Towns which subsided several cubits, were overflowed with water; among others, Deep Gong, which was submerged to the depth of seven cubits. Two volcanoes are said to have opened in the Secta Cunda Hills. The shock was also felt at Calcutta. While the Chittagong coast was sinking, a corresponding rise of the ground took place at the Island of Ramree and at Cheduba.

The mountain of Galongoon, or Galung Gung, was, in 1822, covered by a dense forest, and situated in a fruitful and thickly-peopled part of Java. There was a circular hol low at its summit, but no tradition existed of any former eruption. In July, 1822, the waters of the River Kunir, one of those which flowed from its flanks, became for a time hot and turbid. On the 8th of October following, a loud explosion was heard, the earth shook, and immense columns of hot water and boiling mud, mixed with burning brimstone, ashes, and lapilli, of the size of nuts, were projected from the mountain like a waterspout, with such prodigious violence that large quantities fell beyond the River Tandoi, which is forty miles distant. Every valley within the range of this eruption became filled with a burning torrent, and the rivers, swollen with hot water and mud, overflowed their banks, and carried away great numbers of the people, who were endeavoring to escape, and the bodies of cattle, wild beasts, and birds. A space of twenty-four miles between the mountain and the River Tandoi was covered to such a depth with bluish mud that people were buried in their houses, and not a trace of the numerous villages and plantations throughout that extent was visible. Within this space the bodies of those who perished were buried in mud and concealed; but near the limits of the volcanic action they were exposed, and strewed over the ground in great numbers, partly boiled and partly burnt.

It was remarked that the boiling mud and cinders were projected with such violence from the mountain, that, while many remote villages were utterly destroyed and buried, others much nearer the volcano, were scarcely injured.

The first eruption lasted nearly five hours, and on the following days the rain fell in torrents, and the rivers, densely charged with mud, deluged the country far and wide. At the end of four days (October 12) a second eruption occurred, more violent than the first, in which hot water and mud were again vomited, and great blocks of basalt were thrown to the distance of seven miles from the volcano. There was at the same time a violent earthquake, and in one account it is stated that the face of the mountain was utterly changed, its summits broken down, and one side, which had been covered with trees, became an enormous gulf in the form of a semicircle. This cavity was about midway between the summit and the plain, and surrounded by steep rocks, said to be newly heaped up during the eruption. New hills and valleys are said to have been formed, and the Rivers Banjarang and Wulan changed their course; and in one night (October 12) two thousand persons were killed.

The first intimation which the inhabitants of Bandong received of this calamity, on the 8th of October, was the news that the River Wulna was bearing down into the sea the dead bodies of men, and the carcasses of stags, rhinoceroses, tigers, and other animals. The Dutch painter Payen determined to travel from thence to the volcano; and he found that the quantity of the ashes diminished as he approached the base of the mountain. He alludes to the altered form of the mountain after the 12th, but does not describe the new semicircular gulf on its side. The official accounts state that one hundred and fourteen villages were destroyed, and above four thousand persons killed.

It is probable that a similar event, or a series of subsidences, produced the Val del Bove, on the eastern side of Etna. A narrow ravine, about a mile long, twenty feet wide, and from twenty to thirty-six in depth, has been formed, within the historical era, on the flanks of the volcano, near the town of Mascalucia; and a small circular tract, called the Cisterna, near the summit, sank down, in the year 1792, to the depth of about forty feet, and left on all sides of the chasm a vertical section of the beds exactly resembling those which are seen in the precipices of the Val del Bove. At some remote periods, therefore, we might suppose more extensive portions of the mountain to have fallen in during great earthquakes.

The Val del Bove is a vast amphitheatre, four or five miles in diameter, surrounded by nearly vertical precipices, varying from one thousand to above three thousand feet in height, the loftiest being at the upper end, and the height gradually diminishing on both sides. The feature which first strikes the geologist as distinguishing the boundary cliffs of this valley is the prodigious multitude of vertical dikes, which are seen in all directions traversing the volcanic beds.

If the reader has beheld that most picturesque scene in the chain of the Pyrenees, the celebrated "Cirque of Gavarnie," he may form some conception of the magnificent circle of precipitous rocks which enclose, on three sides, the great plain of the Val del Bove. This plain has been deluged by repeated streams of lava; and, although it appears almost level, when viewed from a distance, it is, in fact, more uneven than the surface of the most tempestuous sea. Besides the minor irregularities of the lava, the valley is in one part interrupted by a ridge of rocks, two of which, Musara and Capra, are very prominent. It can hardly be said that they

> "like giants stand
> To sentinel enchanted land;"

for although, like the Trosachs, in the Highlands of Scotland, they are of gigantic dimensions, and appear almost isolated, as seen from many points, yet the stern and severe grandeur of the scenery which they adorn is not such as would be selected by a poet for a vale of enchantment. The character of the scene would accord far better with Milton's picture of the infernal world; and if we imagine ourselves to behold in motion, in the darkness of the night, one of those fiery currents which have so often traversed the great valley, we may well recall

> "yon dreary plain forlorn, and wild,
> The seat of desolation, void of light,
> Save what the glimmering of these livid flames
> Casts pale and dreadful."

The face of the precipices already mentioned is broken in the most picturesque manner by the vertical walls of the lava which traverse them. These masses usually stand out in relief, are exceedingly diversified in form, and of immense altitude. In the autumn their black outline may often be seen relieved by clouds of fleecy vapor, which settle behind them, and do not disperse until midday, continuing to fill the valley while the sun is shining on every other part of Sicily, and on the higher regions of Etna.

The elevation of the ground has attracted the attention of naturalists more than its depression, because it exhibits more strikingly the immense force with which the cause operates which produces earthquakes. We have reason to believe that the solid crust of our globe is several miles in thickness. How immense must be the force which tears it asunder and raises one part of it to a permanently higher level than it before possessed! Well-ascertained instances of such elevations are not wanted; several such were observed after the earthquake of Calabria. In the small town of Terranuova, not far from Oppido, some houses had been raised above their former level, whilst others had sunk under it. But an old tower in this town was particularly noticed, which had been split from its summit to its foundation, and of which one half had been raised about fifteen feet above the other half, though both pieces had remained closely contiguous. Near the village of Cossoleto, a farm house, together with its out-buildings and adjacent fields, was found raised some hundred feet above its former site; and a water mill was lifted many feet above the rivulet which formerly had moved its wheels.

In Calabria, however, only small portions of the surface of the country were raised above their former levels. But by the earthquake of Valparaiso, which in 1822 convulsed the western shores of South America from Valdivia on the south to Copiapo on the north, an extent of coast line not less than fifty miles long was raised nearly three feet above its level; at some places the rocks on the shore were found to be four feet higher than they had been before. It is reported that some places on which the fishermen, before the earthquake, had gathered a kind of shell fish adhering to the rocks, were, subsequent to it, projected above the sea level even at high water. In the vicinity of a small harbor called Quintero people were accustomed to dig shells for lime-burning from a stratum four or five feet thick, which was found in the recesses of the rocks at a height of about fifteen feet above the sea. This stratum, which evidently at some remote period had been submerged, as is proved by the layers of shells, but afterwards raised above it by one of the great convulsions to which this coast is frequently subject, was, by the earthquake of 1822, again raised at least three feet. The harbor of Quintero had from about two fathoms and a half to three fathoms of water before the earthquake, but after it the bottom of the bay was found to be raised full four feet.

In Captain Fitz Roy's account of the earthquake of Conception, he states that the coast near the harbor of Talcahuano was raised about two feet, and gives the facts which induced him to come to that conclusion. He states further that the Island of Santa Maria, which is not far off the coast, was upheaved nine feet. He adduces many circumstances to prove this fact; among others, that the soundings had diminished a fathom and a half round the island.

Since it has been known that earthquakes are powerful enough to raise the solid surface of the earth to a higher level, naturalists have paid much attention to this point, and the searching eye of the modern geologist has discovered many places where the formation and composition of the rocks show clearly that at some remote time they have been under water, and have been raised above it by some agency acting from the interior of the globe towards its surface.

Perhaps the most remarkable instance of upheaval of land by internal forces hitherto discovered is that exhibited in the great mountain chains of South America. The following extracts from the writings of Mr. Darwin will convey some idea of the magnitude of these phenomena as exhibited in the Andes and Uspellata ranges. "I was much pleased at Chiloe by finding *a thick bed of recent oyster shells capping the tertiary plain*, out of which grew large forest trees. I can prove that both sides of the Andes have risen, in this recent period, to a considerable height. Here the shells were three hundred and fifty feet above the sea. On the bare sides of the Cordilleras complicated dikes and wedges of variously colored rocks are seen traversing, in every possible form and shape, the same formation; and thus proving, by their intersections, a succession of violences. The stratification in all the mountains is beautifully distinct, and, owing to a variety of coloring, can be seen at great distances. Porphyritic conglomerates, resting on granite, form the principal masses. I cannot imagine any part of the world presenting a more extraordinary scene of the breaking up of the crust of the globe than these central peaks of the Andes. The strata, in the highest pinnacles, are almost universally inclined at an angle of from seventy to eighty degrees. The Uspellata range is, geologically, although only six or seven thousand feet high, a continuation of the grand eastern chain. It consists of various kinds of submarine lava, alternating with volcanic sandstones and other remarkable sedimentary deposits, the whole having a very close resemblance to some of the tertiary beds on the shores of the Pacific. From this resemblance I expected to find silicified wood, which is generally characteristic of these formations. I was gratified in a very extraordinary manner. In the central part of the range, at an elevation of about seven thousand feet, I observed on a bare slope some snow-white projecting columns. These were petrified trees, eleven being silicified, and from thirty to forty converted into coarsely crystallized white calcareous spar. They were abruptly broken off, the upright stumps projecting a few feet above the ground. The trunks measured from three to five feet each in circumference. They stood a little way apart from each other, but the whole formed one group. Mr. Robert Brown has been kind enough to examine the wood: he says it belongs to the fir tribe, partaking of the character of the araucarian family, but with some curious points of affinity with the yew. The volcanic sandstone, in which the trees were embedded, and from the lower part of which they must have sprung, had accumulated in successive thin layers around their trunks, and the stone yet retained the impression of the bark.

"It required but little geological practice to interpret the marvellous story which this scene at once unfolded, though I confess I was at first so much astonished that I could scarcely believe the plainest evidence. I saw the spot where a cluster of fine trees once waved their branches on the shores of the Atlantic, when that ocean (now driven back seven hundred miles) came to the foot of the Andes. I saw that they had sprung from a volcanic soil which had been raised above the level of the sea, and that subsequently this dry land, with its upright trees, had been let down into the depths of the ocean. In these depths the formerly dry land was covered by sedimentary beds, and these again by enormous streams of submarine lava, — one such mass attaining the thickness of a thousand feet, — and deluges of molten stone and aqueous deposits five times alternately had been spread out. The ocean which received such thick masses must have been profoundly deep; but again the subterranean forces exerted themselves, and I now beheld the bed of that ocean forming a chain of mountains more than seven thousand feet in height. Nor had those antagonist forces been dormant which are always at work wearing down the surface of the land. Now all is utterly irreclaimable and desert — even the lichen cannot adhere to the stony casts of former trees."

The greatest change recorded in history as produced on the surface of the globe by an earthquake occurred in our own times in Hindustan. By an earthquake which happened in 1819 a large tract of country, not far from the eastern mouth of the Indus River, was submerged and converted into a lake, whilst an adjacent tract, still larger in extent, was raised considerably above its former level. In the beginning of the present century, and for many years previous to that time, the eastern mouth of the Indus, called the Koree, no longer received the waters of that arm of the river which is called the Phurraun, as had formerly been the case. Partly by some changes which had occurred in its course, and partly by artificial means, all the waters of this branch were absorbed before it reached the twenty-fourth parallel of northern latitude. The Koree had thus been converted into an arm of the sea, between which and that part of the Phurraun which still preserved a flow of water, a sandy waste spread out about fifty miles in width. On this waste, at a place called Sindree, was a custom-house station for the goods which passed from Scinde to Cutch, or *vice versa*, and for the protection of the merchandise a fort had been erected about one hundred and fifty feet square. On the 15th of June, 1819, the district of Cutch was convulsed by a frightful earthquake, by which many hundred persons lost their lives, and almost all the solid buildings of the country were converted into heaps of ruins. On this day great changes were effected on the sandy waste. Towards evening the fortress of Sindree was inundated by a rush of waters, which advanced from the sea on the occurrence of a severe shock, and a few hours afterwards the whole country surrounding it, to a distance of sixteen miles, was converted into a lake. At the same time it was observed that on the north of the new lake a kind of dike had been formed, which extended about fifty miles east and west, and which now constituted the barrier between the bed of the Phurraun branch of the Indus and the lake. This dike was called by the natives Ullah Bund, or God's dike, to distinguish it from other dikes erected by artificial means on the banks of the Indus for the purposes of irrigation. These events passed almost unnoticed at that time; but eight years later, information was brought to Bombay that the Phurraun branch of the Indus had, in 1826, returned to its ancient bed, breaking through the Ullah Bund, and had reached the Runn, so that its waters again entered the sea by the Koree mouth. This news induced Captain Burnes to examine the country and the changes it had undergone with great attention. He sailed over the lake, and found that the site of the ancient fortress was occupied by pools, except at one place, which was dry, because the stones of the ruined building had fallen so as to form a large heap. The water of the Lake of Sindree was sweet. The Ullah Bund rose about ten feet above its base, and consisted of soft clay and sand intermixed with shells. The channel which the Indus River had scooped out across this dike was about thirty-five yards wide and three fathoms deep, and a large volume of water passed through it to the Koree. Captain Burnes was astonished at finding that this so called dike did not in the least resemble those dikes made by the natives to divert a portion of the water of the river to their fields. The Ullah Bund was not an embankment a few yards in width, but a table land about fifty miles in length, according to the statement of the natives, and nearly sixteen miles in width, extending northward to the Roama Bazar, a commercial place in the vicinity of the Phurraun River. Its soil was impregnated with saline particles. In this part of Hindustan, therefore, a tract of country occupying probably not less than seven hundred and fifty square miles, has been raised, in our own times, about ten feet above its former level; whilst south of it another tract of perhaps six hundred square miles — for this is about the area of the Lake of Sindree — has been submerged by the same earthquake.

We may here, also, appropriately notice one of the most interesting monuments of antiquity, which, on its face, bears undeniable signs of having been submerged under the sea, and having remained in that state for a considerable time, though now again above the sea level. This monument is the ruins of the Temple of Serapis, in the vicinity of the town of Puzzuoli, on the northern shores of the Gulf of Naples. Up to the middle of the last century the study of antiquity had been confined to the reading of the classical authors; but it then began to be directed to remains of ancient buildings, temples, palaces, and other ruins. The zeal developed by this change was at first directed to the discovery of such remains as still existed. It was then noticed that in the vicinity of Puzzuoli, hardly more than a hundred yards from the sea, three massive columns projected several feet above the ground. The dimension of the portions above ground showed that the greater part of them was hidden. An excavation was commenced, and when the earth had been removed the extensive ruins of a magnificent temple were revealed. They consisted of the three columns above mentioned, still standing, and a number of others, mostly of smaller size, lying on the ground; portions of a wall of solid masonry which enclosed the temple were also in good preservation. The antiquary, the sculptor, the architect, all found something to admire. Ancient authors and the older records of history were searched for the purpose of finding out the facts relating to the erection of this magnificent edifice, but in vain; nothing was discovered. Those, however, who had studied the history of architecture, and made themselves acquainted with the changes in the style of that noble art from the earliest times, came to the conclusion, after a minute examination of the ruins, that the Temple of Serapis had been erected probably in the time of the Emperor Augustus or his successor, and certainly not later than that of Hadrian. This point was, therefore, pretty well settled. The question next arose, At what time and in what manner had the temple been buried under such a mass of earth as was found in excavating it? That it was not rubbish produced from the ruins was evident at first sight; but the records of history were equally silent respecting this event. In the ruins themselves an inscription of the third century after Christ was discovered, which proved that up to that period it had not been covered with earth.

As soon as the ruins were inspected by naturalists a very extraordinary fact was discovered. It was found that all the columns of marble, the larger as well as the smaller, those which were standing no less than those which were lying prostrate, were perforated by a shell fish, the *pholades*, at an elevation of about fifteen feet above their bases, and that the holes made by these mollusks in the columns constituted a band about three feet in width. This was in exact conformity with the habits of the pholades, which live a few feet only below the surface of the sea, making their cells in calcareous rocks, forming generally a narrow stripe on the face of the cliffs. It was, therefore, concluded, and there remained no doubt respecting the certainty of this fact, that the sea level at this spot must have been at some period at least eighteen feet higher than it is at present, and must have remained so for a considerable period to have afforded the pholades sufficient time to establish themselves in the columns of marble.

How was this extraordinary fact to be explained? The temple could not have been built at the bottom of the sea; and naturalists were, therefore, compelled to assume that this part of the coast had undergone two changes since the third century, A. D. It must have been submerged, and have remained so for a considerable time; and at a later period it must have been raised again above the sea level. Such changes were not recorded in any documents. It was, therefore, impossible to know historically in what way they had occurred; and it was, therefore, left to the fancy and sagacity of natural philosophers to explain the facts in a satisfactory way.

The first authors who touched on this subject thought that the matter could be explained by assuming that the level of the sea had first been raised, and afterwards subsided. They fancied they had discovered a proof of these changes in the traditional accounts of the irruption of the Black Sea into the Mediterranean, when the Straits of Constantinople and those of the Dardanelles were opened by some unknown cause. This change must, of course, have considerably elevated the level of the Mediterranean; and this time, according to their opinion, the temple was immerged in the sea. At a much later period, according to tradition, the Mediterranean was united to the Atlantic by the disruption of the rocky masses which closed the Straits of Gibraltar; it then sank again to its former level, and the temple reappeared. This explanation was considered as satisfactory for a much longer time than it deserved; for it was utterly impossible to bring it in accordance with historical facts, or with the laws of nature. For if the traditional accounts respecting the formation of the Straits of Constantinople, of the Dardanelles, and of Gibraltar were really true, they must have occurred more than a thousand years before the time when the Temple of Serapis was erected. So far for history. Next, according to the well-known laws of hydrostatics, no part of a sea, or of any sheet of water, can be permanently raised above its former level, unless the whole of it be equally elevated. If it could be imagined, even, that such a change had only affected the level of the Mediterranean, the effects of it must have been perceived on all its coasts. The numerous towns built on its shores must have been inundated and destroyed — a fact which would certainly have been observed and recorded by the early historians; in whose writings, however, not the slightest allusion to such a change has been discovered.

When this theory was exploded, the matter might have been settled in a satisfactory manner if it had been assumed that the part of the coast on which the temple was built had been first depressed, and afterwards raised. But up to that time the effects of earthquakes in raising or depressing a part of the solid surface of the earth had been overlooked by naturalists. Some instances of the kind were certainly known; but they had only affected very small tracts, and philosophers did not think themselves authorized by them to conclude that earthquakes could produce such extensive changes as were required to explain what had evidently happened to the temple. Another hypothesis was broached. It was suggested that when the temple fell into ruins the rubbish had accumulated around the building so as to form a small basin. It was next assumed that the basin thus formed had been filled with sea water by some extraordinary phenomenon, — as, for instance, an exceed ingly heavy gale, — and that it had thus been converted into a lagoon filled with salt water. A third step in the theory brought by accident some pholades into the lagoon, which established themselves in the columns of marble; and then, as a conclusion to the series of assumptions, the lagoon, after subsisting for some centuries, was filled up with earth detached from the adjacent hills, and which covered the temple to the height already stated.

This hypothesis, though it rests on four suppositions, none of which can be considered as very probable, was prevalent up to a recent period, and was supported by some authors of great celebrity, but has now lost its credibility by the close examination to which some geologists have subjected the site of the temple and the adjacent country. These investigators found no trace of a lagoon ever having existed there. On the contrary, they found that the adjacent shores, to the extent of more than a mile, bore evident signs of having been covered by the sea for a considerable time. The coast there is formed by a narrow strip of low ground, backed by a more elevated tract, which rises from it with a steep acclivity. The lower tract is composed of layers of earthy matter, loosely united, and uniform in its composition. These layers contain numerous remains of ancient buildings — as pieces of brick, marble, granite, and porphyry; also fragments of vessels of earthenware. On the top of these earthy layers lies a stratum of fine sand, resembling in every particular that which is found at the bottom of the Mediterranean. With this sand are mixed up numbers of well-preserved shells and muscles, all of them of species of frequent occurrence in that sea at the present day. The lower layers of this tract show that they were once inhabited and built on, while the upper have evidently been formed at a long subsequent time. That this layer was deposited at the same time when the columns were perforated by the pholades is evident from the circumstance that it is found nearly at the same elevation above the sea level with the upper border of the band which contains the holes made by the pholades.

The discovery of these facts led to the opinion which at present prevails, that part of the coast of the Bay of Baiæ,— for so this portion of the Gulf of Naples is called,—on which the Temple of Serapis stands, was submerged by an earthquake, and after having rested below the level of the sea for centuries, was again raised above its level by another earthquake. The changes which have been produced on the surface of the earth by such phenomena, especially those on the coast of Chile already mentioned, render such a supposition very probable. It is true that such a subsidence is not recorded in the historical documents; but as hardly any trustworthy accounts have been transmitted to us of what passed in these countries in the tenth and part of the eleventh centuries after Christ, when these coasts were frequently laid waste by the incursions of the Saracens, we can hardly be surprised at the total want of historical notice respecting these changes. This want, however, may be considered as fully supplied by a number of other facts, which prove, beyond all doubt, that the whole coast of the Bay of Baiæ has undergone great alterations since the time when it contained the most frequented watering-places of the Romans; that by these changes considerable tracts of land, which were formerly embellished with country houses, extensive baths, and other sumptuous buildings, have been immerged in the sea by some catastrophe of which history has left no record. This fact is proved by the existence of a great number of ruins at the bottom of the sea, about fifteen or twenty feet below its level. When the sea is calm, they may be clearly distinguished. They consist of pedestals of whole rows of columns; of staircases of stone descending into the depths; of arches; of gates, doors, and windows. Two Roman roads are also discerned—one leading from Baiæ to Misenum, the other from Puzzuoli to the Lake of Lucrino. It can, therefore, be scarcely doubted that a subsidence of a large tract of country has taken place on these shores at a comparatively modern period.

The subsidence of the Temple of Serapis must have happened during the obscurity of the middle ages, when our historical information of Southern Italy is extremely scanty; but as the rise of the country must have evidently taken place at a much later period, that has probably happened in times of different character. Still there is no mention made of it by the latter historical writers. It is, therefore, supposed to have happened when the attention and thoughts of the inhabitants of this part of Italy were absorbed by some event of uncommon interest. Such an event was the formation of the Monte Nuovo, which, after a long continuance of frequent earthquakes, was thrown up, in 1538, at a place but a very few miles distant from the site of the temple. This event, which spread terror among the population of the country, probably made persons overlook the small tract in the vicinity of the newly-created mountain which had been raised from the sea. It is stated that some documents have been lately discovered referring to that period, by which a tract of land along the coast, *which had been abandoned by the sea*, was ceded by the government to some ecclesiastical corporation.

In this hypothesis, it is supposed that the subsidence of the Temple of Serapis was effected by an earthquake, and suddenly; but it is possible that the piece of ground on which it stands had subsided slowly, gradually, and without any convulsion of nature. Such an event would certainly be in accordance with the changes which the site of the building is undergoing at present. It is beyond all doubt that the foundation of the temple is now subsiding, and has been for many years past. Mr. W. Wittich visited the temple in 1813 and in 1819. At his first visit the area included by the walls surrounding the temple was every where quite dry, and did not appear to have been under water for a long time before. At his second visit he was astonished at finding nearly the whole of the area inundated, and in some parts the water more than two inches deep. The sea had got access to it, and government about this time found itself obliged to take some measures to keep the water out, but which were not attended with the desired effect. As it now became evident that either the sea was rising, as it was supposed by some, or that the ground was subsiding, as others thought, an hydrometer was erected within the precincts of the temple in 1822, to enable those interested in the matter to mark the progress of this extraordinary phenomenon. In 1839 a paper was published at Naples, in which a detailed account of the rise of the sea within the temple is given, the result of which is, that in sixteen years,—i. e., from 1822 to 1838,—the level of the water has risen one hundred eleven and two thirds millimetres, or nearly four inches and a half. Such are the facts which prove that along this coast of the Mediterranean a small tract of ground is really subsiding gradually and continually, as a number of other observations published in our times have a tendency to convince us that the northern part of Scandinavia is actually rising also, gradually and continually, but much more slowly. The force by which such changes are effected cannot be reasonably considered as proceeding from any other source than the interior of the globe, where is also seated that power which produces earthquakes and all the frightful phenomena accompanying them.

The source whence earthquakes spring, the power by which the ground under our feet is convulsed, is withdrawn from our investigation. The eye of the most inquisitive naturalist cannot reach it. He must content himself with contemplating and examining the phenomena which are exhibited by that unknown force on the earth's surface, and with attempting to trace them backward to their origin. That which strikes him first and instantaneously, is the immense energy with which this subterraneous power acts. It is beyond all comparison greater than all the forces of which he has acquired any knowledge by experience. If he investigates the phenomena still further, and especially the substances which are brought by earthquakes from the interior of the earth and deposited on its surface, it must strike him that all of them bear evident signs of having endured the action of fire, and that some of them cannot have attained the state in which they appear without having been exposed to an intense heat. Such observations intruded themselves, as it were involuntarily, on the notice of the ancient philosophers; and we find, therefore, that the Greek and Roman writers frequently express the opinion that earthquakes were brought about by a force originating in a mass of fire, which fire they imagined to compose the nucleus of our globe.

This opinion, ascribing the origin of earthquakes to a central fire in the interior of the earth, prevailed from the most ancient times to the middle of the last century, when the study of electricity was pursued with great zeal, and this department of science was enriched by numerous discoveries. The theory was then started that the origin of earthquakes must be looked for in electricity. According to this hypothesis, electric matter accumulated by degrees on the surface of the earth to such an extent, that the difference between the electric state of the globe and that of the surrounding atmosphere became extreme; and then the equilibrium between these two contiguous bodies could not be reëstablished without a violent explosion and concussion, and this was an earthquake. The whole phenomenon was, therefore, compared to a thunder storm, and the shocks to powerful lightning. This hypothesis had certainly a great degree of probability to recommend it. For it cannot be denied that there exist many analogies between the phenomena accompanying thunder storms and those of earthquakes; such as the extraordinary quickness with which either of them is propagated over immense tracts of country; the concussions of the air and of the earth's surface; the thunder accompanying the lightning, and that which is commonly heard when a severe shock is felt; the smell of sulphur which has sometimes been observed to attend both phenomena; the sultry weather which precedes, and the coolness of the air which commonly follows them. It may even be assumed that the restlessness which manifests itself in several kinds of animals shortly before an earthquake takes place, is produced by the different states of electric matter in the two bodies, the air and the earth. It may easily be imagined that a theory by which such a number of phenomena could be explained, and which, besides, was founded on a branch of science which for a length of time constituted the favorite study of philosophers, soon gained ground, and in a short time became generally considered as perfectly satisfactory. But when this theory was more closely applied and examined, great difficulties were met with. It was found impossible to explain the manner in which such large masses of electric matter could be accumulated on the earth's surface without being conducted away, enfeebled, and dispersed, by the numerous caverns and chasms in the earth, whose sides always contain a great deal of moisture. It was found equally incomprehensible why the shocks, by which the equilibrium of the electric fluid in the air and in the earth was reëstablished, should extend over such immense distances, and in general follow certain directions. But the most decisive objection against the electric theory of earthquakes is, the frequent repetition of the shocks, and their long continuance, they having at some places lasted for years together.

Modern philosophers have, therefore, returned to the central fire of the ancients. The existence of this fire was merely imaginary with the ancients; but our naturalists have ascertained some facts, which, indeed, cannot prove its existence, but which give some foundation to the hypothesis. The most important of these facts is the increase of the temperature of the earth in proportion as we descend and get farther from its surface. This fact has been constantly observed in those mines which descend to a great depth below the surface of the earth. It is also confirmed by the water brought up by artesian wells from different depths. The deeper the stratum lies from which the water is obtained, the warmer it is. The numerous facts of this description which have been collected, have suggested the idea that we shall find the temperature of the earth continually increasing the farther we succeed in getting below its surface, and that at last we shall arrive at a point where we shall be compelled to stop, as the heat will be greater than the human frame can bear. If we could approach nearer to the centre of the earth, we should probably at some distance farther arrive at a depth where the solid matter of the earth gradually passes into a fluid, consisting of a mixture of all kinds of matter melted by the excessive heat proceeding from the centre. At what distance from the surface of the earth this heated fluid exists, we have no means of determining. We are not able to estimate the thickness of the earth's crust, as the solid portion of it may be called. The heated fluid enclosed by this crust, however, is considered as the part where that power originates which produces earthquakes. If the earth's crust was every where of equal thickness, it is probable that all parts of its surface would be equally affected by these phenomena. This, however, is not the case. It has been before stated that some countries are visited frequently by these frightful phenomena, and apparently convulsed to their very foundation, whilst others suffer rarely, and experience only slight shocks. The earth's crust must, therefore, be of different thicknesses. As it is also found that most of the severer earthquakes are propagated in a linear direction, and at each occurrence always take the same direction, it is supposed that below such countries as are frequently convulsed by them, the earth's crust is split by wide chasms, whose wider opening is directed towards the heated central fluid, and whose narrower opening pierces the earth's crust to within a short distance from its surface. Into these chasms the elastic vapor, which is supposed to be developed from the surface of the heated fluid, escapes, and in the progress of time is there accumulated and compressed. When this accumulation of the elastic vapors (air, gas, or steam) has continued to go on until the chasm is overcharged, or when their expansive force is suddenly increased, they will seek to escape, and will act on the sides of the chasms with a force of which we can have no conception.

The lateral sides of the chasm, being composed of very solid matter, will powerfully and effectually resist this pressure; but the layer of solid matter which lies between the upper termination of the chasm and the surface of the earth will be less able to resist. It will be convulsed by the elastic fluids, whilst they are forcing a passage to the atmosphere. Thus earthquakes originate. As, however, only a small portion of the enclosed elastic vapor can escape at each shock, these shocks are commonly repeated, and sometimes follow each other very quickly, and for a length of time. They probably do not cease until the quantity of the elastic vapor compressed in the chasm is so reduced that it can freely circulate within its boundaries.

Some of these chasms, and probably those of the largest dimensions, are united with the atmosphere by one or more openings, by which elastic vapors find a ready way to escape. Such are the volcanoes. They may be considered as safety valves for the countries in which they lie. For as long as the compressed elastic vapor can escape, the countries in the vicinity are free from earthquakes. But it sometimes happens that these safety valves get out of order, their openings being blocked up by the accumulation of earthy matter or otherwise. Then the countries in their vicinity are convulsed by earthquakes until the aperture or chimney has been reopened by an eruption.

The theory just expounded brings volcanoes into a close connection with earthquakes. The facts which in modern times have been collected to prove this connection are so numerous and so comprehensive that hardly any doubt remains respecting this point, which may be considered as having been nearly established. It is true that all severe earthquakes are not followed by an eruption. This may be ascribed to the circumstance that there are many large chasms in the earth's crust which are not provided with a safety valve; and Humboldt sagaciously observes, that those earthquakes which last with little interruption for several weeks and months occur only in countries which are far distant from active volcanoes. In such earthquakes the elastic vapors are supposed to escape by some of the rents formed during the continuance of the convulsion; and as such rents do not appear to have a great capacity, the accumulated quantity of elastic matter can only escape by repeatedly convulsing the surface. But though all earthquakes are not succeeded by an eruption, eruptions are commonly preceded by earthquakes. It is true that many eruptions of volcanoes have occurred which were not preceded by those phenomena to any extent; but that is only the case when the eruptions of a volcano follow each other at such short intervals that the canal between the elastic vapors under the earth's crust and the atmosphere has remained open, and time has not been allowed for choking it up. Whenever this canal has been closed, which is indicated by smoke no longer issuing from the crater of the volcano, earthquakes may be expected; and it has been observed that the shocks of these earthquakes are the more severe, and extend over a larger tract of country, and the more energetic is the volcanic paroxysm which follows, the longer the cessation has endured. Earthquakes continue to occur, and their shocks increase in number and intensity, up to the very moment that the canal of the volcano has been reopened, and the volcanic matter begins to flow from the crater, or the elastic vapors have again forced a free passage to the atmosphere. When that has taken place the earthquakes cease, and are no longer felt in the countries surrounding the volcano. Persons, however, who wish to have a near sight of the eruption, and who for that purpose ascend the volcano whilst it is in activity, feel that every new eruption of matter is preceded by a slight shock, whose intensity is proportioned to the time which passes between the shock and the flow of the volcanic matter.

These facts are universally known in all those countries in which active volcanoes are found. In the towns of Naples, Messina, and Catania, it is an opinion generally diffused among the population, that there is not the least fear of an earthquake as long as the smoke freely escapes from the craters of Mount Vesuvius and of Mount Etna. The same opinion prevails in Ecuador. The inhabitants of the elevated valleys of Quito and Hambato, residing round the bases of the volcanoes Tunguragua and Cotopaxi, dread the visitation of an earthquake when for any length of time no smoke has been seen rising from their craters; and they are firmly convinced that the earthquakes, which have so frequently proved destructive to their country, will entirely cease as soon as the porphyritic cupolas of Mount Chimborazo shall have been removed, and thus a free exit been formed for the escape of volcanic matter or vapor.

In all the cases just noticed the connection between earthquakes and volcanoes is so evident that it hardly admits of any doubt. But a number of facts have been collected which evidently show that there must exist a subterraneous connection between these phenomena, even when they occur at great distances from each other. Some of these facts are very interesting and curious. Stromboli, a small volcano situated on one of the Lipari Islands, which is in continual activity, and never ceases to eject volcanic matter and smoke, fell suddenly into a state of inactivity, when, in 1783, the plain of Calabria was visited by the great earthquake. The distance between the volcano and the centre of the earthquake does not much exceed fifty miles. Humboldt mentions that for many months the volcano of Pasto had uninterruptedly continued to emit a column of thick smoke, which suddenly disappeared on the 4th of February, 1797, just at the moment when the valley of Hambato was convulsed by the earthquake which levelled the town of Riobamba to the ground. In this case the distance was two hundred and twenty miles. On the 1st of November, 1755, a whirling column of smoke ascended from the crater of Mount Vesuvius, which is commonly a sign that the volcano is in a state of disturbance; but all at once the flow of smoke was stopped, and that which had issued reëntered the crater. The distance between Lisbon and Mount Vesuvius exceeds one thousand two hundred miles. As it is a well-established fact that the strong oscillation of the earth during the great earthquake of Lisbon extended to the centre of England, Lombardy, and the Alps, and even to Massachusetts and Pennsylvania, it can hardly be considered a bold assumption, when it is supposed that this change in the crater of Mount Vesuvius was effected by that earthquake.

These events, though they occurred at great distances from each other, were simultaneous; and it was this last circumstance which first suggested the idea of there being a natural connection between them. When the supposition of this connection was considered as founded on a well-established base, naturalists began to think it probable that such a connection might exist between these two phenomena, even when they occurred at still greater distances than those mentioned, and not quite at the same time. In such cases, however, the earthquakes must precede the eruptions of the volcano. It was thought probable that earthquakes might often continue to convulse extensive countries, until the earth was relieved by the eruption of a volcano, though this volcano might be situated at a considerable distance from the places most severely affected by the convulsions. Against this hypothesis it was objected, that the greater number of earthquakes had occurred in countries and places far removed from the vicinity of any active volcano, and near which not even the traces of an extinguished crater have been discovered. Such places and countries are Lisbon, Syria, Caraccas, and the valley of the Mississippi River. Humboldt even acknowledges that he does not know of any severe earthquake which has continued to convulse the surface of an extensive country almost daily for many months in continuation, except such as have taken place at great distances from any active volcano. He observes that there was no neighboring volcano to the earthquakes which, in 1808, visited the country lying on the eastern declivity of the Alps, at the base of Mount Cenis, round Fenestrelles, nor to Pinerolo; and that which convulsed the central part of the valley of the Mississippi between New Madrid and the Little Prairie, near Cincinnati, in the first months of 1812. A similar occurrence of a number of severe shocks happened in 1822, in the pachalic of Aleppo. These facts at first sight appear to militate against the opinion of a subterraneous connection between earthquakes and volcanoes, when the first occur at great distances from the site of the volcanoes; but, on maturer consideration, it is found that they are in fact favorable to that hypothesis. For if it be true, as is now almost universally supposed, that earthquakes are only produced by the efforts made by the accumulated elastic vapors to escape from the interior of the earth, we can easily comprehend that such efforts must be most violent, or be continued for thc greatest length of time, at such places as are distant from those openings in the surface of the earth (the volcanoes) where the discharge of the elastic vapors may be readily effected. The greater the distance between the volcano and the place of the earthquake, the severer must be the shocks, and the longer the convulsions must last; the later also will the confined elastic vapors reach the place where they can escape into the atmosphere.

As these facts prove the above-mentioned subterraneous connection between earthquakes and the eruptions of volcanoes at least probable, even though at great distances from each other, philosophers have tried to ascertain the supposed connection which existed between two real events of this description, by comparing the times in which they took place. Humboldt even thinks that when two places, lying at great distances from each other, experience severe earthquakes at two periods not separated from each other by many months, and when this event takes place repeatedly, we may suppose that there exists a connection between them. To elucidate his opinion, he notices the earthquakes by which the towns of Guatemala, in Central America, thirteen degrees twenty-eight minutes north latitude, and of Lima, in Peru, twelve degrees two minutes south latitude, have been damaged.

At Guatemala.	At Lima.
November 30, 1577.	June 17, 1578.
March 4, 1679.	June 17, 1678.
February 12, 1689.	October 10, 1688.
September 17, 1717.	February 8, 1716.

These earthquakes, as it is evident, take place at long intervals of time from each other. When we compare the periods at which they occurred at the two places, which are nearly two thousand miles distant from each other, it would seem that each couple of them were produced by the same force, which proceeded slowly along the mountain ranges which lie between the two places, sometimes from north to south, and at others from south to north.

Less doubtful than in this case appears to be the connection between some events which occurred in South America and the adjacent islands in 1797. In the beginning of that year the elevated table land in Ecuador was visited by that frightful earthquake which levelled to the ground the town of Riobamba, and destroyed a great number of villages. The number of persons who perished by it is stated to have amounted to forty thousand. Most of them were buried under their houses; but many also were swallowed up by the wide chasms occasioned by the earthquake, while others were drowned in the lakes, which filled up such tracts as had subsided below their former levels. This event took place on the 7th of February. Hardly had these concussions ceased, when the inhabitants of the Lesser Antilles were frightened by severe shocks, which kept them in a continual state of uneasiness for eight months, and did not cease until the volcano of Guadaloupe, which had been inactive so long that it was considered as extinct, forced its crater open, and ejected lava and other volcanic matter on the 17th of September. But it appears that even by this eruption the subterraneous pressure was not entirely removed, as shortly afterwards several severe shocks were experienced in the northern countries of South America, which at last terminated on the 14th of December, with the destruction of the town of Cumana.

A more extensive series of earthquakes and volcanic eruptions, apparently connected with each other, took place in 1811 and 1812, in the countries surrounding the Columbian Sea. The subterraneous force first tried to open a vent by means of a submarine eruption in the Atlantic. Smart shocks of earthquakes were for several days felt on the Island of St. Michael, one of the Azores; and on the 30th of January, 1811, large volumes of smoke, with which flames were observed to mingle, were seen issuing from the surface of the sea, at a distance of a few miles from the western coast of the island. They threw up mud, stones, and other matter, which in a short time accumulated so as to form a small island, called Sabrina, but which, after the lapse of a few months, disappeared in the sea. Not long after this event the Lesser Antilles, which are twenty-four hundred miles distant from the Azores, experienced very severe shocks; these were extremely frequent on the Island of St. Vincent, more than two hundred having been counted in the space of one year — from May, 1811, to April, 1812. In December, 1811, whilst the Antilles were still convulsed by repeated earthquakes, the first shocks were felt in the countries along the lower course of the Mississippi, whence they gradually extended northward, so that in February, 1812, the countries between New Madrid and the Little Prairie experienced, more or less, smart shocks every day, and at some places almost every hour. About the same time (in December, 1811) when the first earthquakes were felt on the banks of the Mississippi, the town of Caraccas experienced the first shock. It was not attended by destructive effects; but three months later the town was levelled to the ground by that frightful earthquake of which we have given an account. Other shocks followed until the 5th of April. At the end of the same month the volcano of

St. Vincent, from which there had been no eruption since 1718, was opened with a tremendous explosion; after which the earthquakes in South America and the Antilles ceased, and those in North America gradually decreased, until they also ceased entirely in the beginning of 1813.

These facts, and still more the circumstance of eruptions of volcanoes being commonly ushered in by earthquakes, attest the close connection existing between these two phenomena. It must appear the more remarkable, therefore, that the substances which are brought from the interior by earthquakes are different from those which are ejected by volcanoes. Those which issue from the chasms made by earthquakes, as we have mentioned, are water, sand, mud, and stones; whilst those derived from volcanic eruptions are lava, pumice stone, cinders, ashes, and sand. Though sand is mentioned as being thrown up by both phenomena, it is essentially different; that ejected by volcanoes consisting mostly of particles of lava in the minutest degree of comminution. Lava never appears to have flowed from any fissure originating in an earthquake. It is indeed mentioned in Strabo, that after the Island of Eubœa had been visited by a long continuation of earthquakes, a wide chasm was formed in the plain of Lelantus, not far from Chalcis, from which a stream of heated mud ran out. This, by some writers, has been interpreted as lava; but as no such fact has been noticed in modern times, the fact remains doubtful, and it is not improbable that it was much similar to the moya in the plain of Hambato, which we have before mentioned.

The quantity of matter is not generally large which issues from the fissures of the ground during earthquakes; though, if the nature of the ejected matter is to be taken as a criterion between volcanic eruptions and earthquakes, we are compelled to ascribe to the last-mentioned phenomenon the formation of hills of considerable elevation, such as the Monte Nuovo, on the shore of the Gulf of Naples, not far from Puzzuoli. According to the accounts which have been transmitted by several eye witnesses, the countries situated on the shores of this gulf had been convulsed for two years by severe earthquakes, when it was observed that in the vicinity of Lake Averno the ground had a peculiar motion; it split in many directions, and from the fissures issued water and flames; the sea receded from the shores, and a considerable tract along them was left dry. This happened on the 28th of September, 1538. On the following day solid matter, accompanied by smoke and flames, began to issue, and in such quantity that, in the space of two days, the hill attained nearly its present size and elevation. In these accounts no lava or any other volcanic matter is noticed. This omission cannot be ascribed to a want of knowledge, as every inhabitant of Naples is well acquainted with lava, pumice stone, scoria, &c. The correctness of these accounts is only confirmed by the actual state of the hill; for it is composed of earth and fragments of conglomerate, without any mixture of lava or other volcanic production. We must, therefore, consider this hill as having been formed by the matter issuing from a wide fissure made by an earthquake, without the intervention of volcanic action, though it resembles a volcano so far as to have in the centre a wide depression, similar to a crater; but the resemblance between the Monte Nuovo and a volcano is limited to this particular alone. Its most elevated part is about four hundred and forty feet above the sea level; but the depression in the middle sinks so deep that its bottom is little more than sixty feet above the sea. The circuit of this crater is somewhat more than sixteen hundred feet, while the base of the hill has a circumference of more than eighty-five hundred feet.

Nearly in the same manner, and by a process very similar to that which threw up the Monte Nuovo, three hills were formed during an earthquake on the Island of Lanzarote, one of the Canaries, in 1828. In the middle of the month of July some slight shocks of an earthquake were felt in the country about Tao, Tiagua, and Teguire, nearly in the centre of the island, and north of the crater formed in 1730, which is called Fire Mountain (Montaña del Fuego.) On the 31st of July, when it grew light, some severe shocks were experienced, more particularly in the vicinity of Tao. It was soon discovered that the surface of the country, which is nearly a level, had been split at several places. At the same moment a dull subterraneous noise was heard, and it was found that all the water contained in the reservoirs of Tiagua had disappeared. A few hours later a column of thick smoke was seen rising from the plain, whilst the shocks were increasing in number and intensity to such a degree that the inhabitants were thrown into the utmost consternation. The crevices in the ground were gradually widening so as to form spacious abysses, out of which smoke and fire were continually issuing. Stones of considerable size were hurled out of them. They were thrown in every direction, and produced a peculiar whizzing sound in the air, which, with the clattering occasioned by their striking one another, and the continual subterraneous thunder, excited an intense feeling of terror. In the following night twenty-five columns of fire of different color were seen issuing from as many abysses. By degrees they joined each other, and formed three craters, of which the middle one is the largest. After about eighteen hours the eruption ceased, and nothing was seen except columns of smoke rising from the craters, particularly from the larger. In this state the convulsed tract remained up to the 22d of August, when a large quantity of matter, mostly consisting of pieces of conglomerate and rounded stones, was thrown out from several openings in the ground. Together with these, large volumes of water ran out of the craters, but did not rise to any height above their edges. This water was turbid and brackish, though less bitter than sea water, and had a very disagreeable smell of sulphur. These eruptions continued for three or four days. The smoke, however, and the dull subterraneous noise, lasted for some time longer, and both decreased gradually until they ceased. The matter brought from the interior of the earth by this eruption formed three moderate hills of irregular form. The sand and ashes which arose, mingled with the smoke, were carried by a gale to a considerable distance. It must, however, be observed, that this eruption was, after a lapse of more than a month, followed by another of a truly volcanic character, by which lava and other volcanic matter were ejected; but this last-mentioned eruption occurred at a distance of several miles from the place where the first appeared.

When a country is convulsed by severe shocks of earthquake for any length of time, the inhabitants commonly begin to fear that an eruption will take place, and that a volcano will be formed in some place in their vicinity. This fear, however, is ill founded, for there is only one well-ascertained fact on record of earthquakes having terminated in the formation of a volcano. This event happened in 1759, in Michoacan, one of the states of Mexico, where a volcano, called Jorullo, which rises five thousand one hundred and nineteen feet above the sea level, and one thousand six hundred and eighty-three feet above the plain on which it stands, issued from the interior of the earth. The plain on which the volcano rose was, up to 1759, chiefly covered with sugar and indigo plantations, which were irrigated by the waters derived from two small rivers; the plain itself, however, is surrounded by basaltic rocks, the structure of which appears to indicate that this part of the country, at some remote period, had experienced more than once the effects of volcanic agency. In the month of June, 1759, a subterraneous noise was heard, which continued for fifty or sixty days, and was attended with frequent earthquakes. At the beginning of September all was quiet; but in the night between the 28th and 29th of September a terrible subterraneous crash filled the inhabitants with such terror that they abandoned their houses, and sought refuge on some mountains bordering the plain. A portion of the plain, covering an area of from twenty-two to thirty square miles, was then seen rising in the form of a bladder; and is at present called El Mal Paes — a name which frequently occurs in Mexico, and is given to such tracts as are rendered sterile by the effect of volcanic action. The border of this raised tract is still distinctly marked by the fractured rocks which constitute it. Near this border the raised ground is not quite forty feet above the plain, but, in advancing to the centre and the base of the volcano, it rises gradually to more than five hundred and twenty feet. Over the surface of the raised ground some thousands of small conical eminences are dispersed. Their summits are only from seven to ten feet above their bases, and have openings on their most elevated points, from which smoke constantly issues, rising into the air from forty to sixty feet: in several of them a subterraneous noise is heard, which seems to indicate that there is a hot fluid not far below the surface. Though the heat of the air produced by these vapors had, according to the statement of the natives, much diminished during the last fifteen years preceding the visit of Humboldt, that traveller found that the thermometer rose to one hundred and eighty-three degrees when placed over the fissures which discharged the watery vapor. In a line traversing the raised ground from north-north-east to south-south-west stand six large hills, rising from fifteen hundred to sixteen hundred and eighty-three feet above the ancient level of the plain. The most elevated of these hills is the volcano of Jorullo. It is still active, and has thrown out on its northern side an immense quantity of scorified and basaltic lava, which contains small fragments of primitive rocks. Up to the month of February, 1760, the eruptions of this volcano were very violent and frequent; but since that time they have become less powerful and more rare. During the first eruption the roofs of the houses in Queretaro, though the distance between the two places is one hundred and thirty-five miles, were covered with ashes. Humboldt descended into the crater to the depth of one hundred and eighty feet below the outer edge, but he could not go lower on account of the dense hot vapors which ascended from its bottom. According to his estimate this bottom is nearly one hundred and eighty feet below the point which he reached in his descent.

Others who had observed the progress of this volcanic formation from some mountains not far distant, state that they saw flames issuing from the earth over a surface of more than four square miles; that fragments of red-hot rock were thrown up to great heights; and that through a thick cloud of ashes, which was illuminated by the volcanic fire, it appeared as if the softened crust of the earth was swelling, and resembled a sea in violent motion. The two rivers which watered this part of the plain rushed into the fiery vents, and the decomposition of their waters contributed to increase the flames, which rose to such a height that they were visible in a town which stands on a large plain three thousand seven hundred and sixty feet above that on which the volcano rests. The two rivers above mentioned are at present lost under the lava; but on the western side of the Mal Paes there are now found some hot springs, in which the thermometer rises to one hundred and five degrees.

The most remarkable phenomenon produced by the concurrence of earthquakes and volcanic agency is the emerging of new islands from the sea. They rise suddenly, and their appearance is attended with nearly all the phenomena accompanying eruptions; they exist for some time, and then they commonly disappear gradually. It is a circumstance worthy to be noticed, that such islands make their appearance repeatedly on the same spot, and that such spots may be pointed out in each of the volcanic systems of Europe.

In the volcanic system of the Azores the spot where the volcanic islands appear is about a mile west of the western extremity of the Island St. Michael. An island has risen there above the sea at three different periods — in 1628, in 1720, and 1811. It has been considered as a remarkable fact, that about ninety-one or ninety-two years have passed between the reappearances of the island. Respecting the phenomena which attended the first appearance of the island nothing is known; but the second (1720) was preceded and attended by a very high column of smoke, and the ejection of ashes and pumice stone. Its declivities were very steep, as at a short distance from its shores no ground was found with twenty fathoms. Its elevation was estimated at about three hundred and fifty feet above the sea level. After having preserved its size for about two years, it disappeared by degrees.

In 1811 the formation of the island was preceded by severe and numerous shocks on the north-western side of St. Michael. Before these shocks ceased, on the 13th of June, a column of smoke rose out of the sea, within which, from time to time, large masses of black cinders, sand, and ashes were observed rising, accompanied by frequent flashes of lightning and a noise like thunder, which was compared to a continual firing of guns and muskets. In a short time a black body was perceived to form the base of the column, and was soon recognized as the upper border of a crater-formed rock, rising from the sea, which, on the fourth day after the beginning of the phenomenon, formed a coherent mass. This mass increased, by the addition of new matter, to the 4th of July, when it had attained its largest dimensions. The eruptions of matter then ceased, and a landing could be effected on the shores of the island. The island had nearly the form of a circle, and was about a mile in circuit. Its greatest elevation above the sea level was estimated at about three hundred feet. In the middle was a circular crater, which, by an opening across the solid mass, communicated with the sea, from which water, in a high state of ebullition, was continually and rapidly flowing. The declivities of the island towards the sea were very steep, and the sea round it deep; for at a distance of twelve or fifteen yards it was more than fifteen fathoms deep. Captain Tillard, who had witnessed its formation from the adjacent shores, called this island Sabrina, after the name of the vessel under his command; and the accompanying engraving is from a sketch made at the time. In the following month of October the island began to diminish in size. Some months later only a reef was observed, which at high water was covered by the sea. In February following a column of smoke of very little density was seen rising from the same spot for a short time. In 1823 it was found that the sea at that spot was sixty fathoms deep — twice as deep as it had been before the appearance of the island.

In the Icelandic volcanic system the spot at which an island has risen from the sea is opposite Cape Reikianaes, at a distance of about five or six miles from the promontory. Only one appearance of this island is on record. It took place in 1783, shortly before a great eruption of the Skaptaar Yökul. No detailed account has been published of this event.

Up to a recent period it was unknown that such a spot existed, also, in the volcanic system of Southern Italy; as in none of the numerous records of history which we possess of the events that have taken place in the countries surrounding the Mediterranean, during more than two thousand years, is any mention made of such an occurrence. The greater was the surprise of all persons who take an interest in such extraordinary facts, when, in the summer of 1831, an island rose out of the sea between the town of Sciacca, in Sicily, and the volcanic Island of Pantellaria, in thirty-seven degrees eleven minutes north latitude, and twelve degrees forty-four minutes east longitude. As the phenomena which attended the appearance of this island were observed by some naturalists, and several scientific men, we possess a much more detailed account of them than of those of any other of these strange products of the bottom of the sea; and as they certainly are of a very extraordinary description, a short enumeration of them will probably be acceptable to the reader.

We shall premise that, among the inhabitants of Malta, a tradition is current that a volcano existed on the same spot about the commencement of the last century; and that in an old chart of the Mediterranean a shoal is laid down on nearly the same place with only four fathoms of water on it. Before the period of the eruption, however, it is stated that the sea at this place was from one hundred to one hundred and twenty fathoms deep.

Before any appearance of a change was observed in the sea, the inhabitants of the town of Sciacca were alarmed by a number of very smart shocks, of which two might be called severe. They occurred between the 28th of June and the 2d of July. An Italian vessel, passing on the 8th of July near the place where afterwards the island rose out of the sea, observed a great disturbance of the waters at that spot. According to the account of the captain, a considerable space of the surface of the sea was seen rising to an elevation of from eighty to ninety feet above its level; the water appeared to bubble, as if boiling; and the phenomenon was attended by a noise resembling thunder. After this agitation had lasted about ten minutes, the watery mass sank to the sea level, but after some time rose again. These risings of the water were repeated at irregular intervals of ten, fifteen, and twenty minutes. A thick cloud of smoke, which enveloped the whole horizon, issued from the raised mass of water. The surface of the sea surrounding the raised mass was also considerably agitated, and a number of dead fish were floating about. For several days the atmosphere surrounding the town of Sciacca was dim and foggy, so that it was impossible to observe what was going on at sea. On the 12th of July, in the morning, people were surprised at finding on the surface of the sea in front of the town a great quantity of small porous scoriæ, which had been carried there by a fresh breeze from the south-west. On the beach the accumulated scoriæ formed a layer several inches thick; and the fishermen found, at some distance from the shore, the surface of the sea so covered with scoriæ that they were compelled to push them out of the way with their oars. At the same time a very unpleasant smell of sulphuric hydrogen gas incommoded the inhabitants of the town and the country near it. Dead fish, recently killed, were floating in all directions.

On the following day the sky cleared up, and at Sciacca a tall column of smoke was observed issuing from the surface of the sea. This smoke continued to rise without interruption, and in a straight column; from time to time a noise was heard similar to distant thunder; and when it became dark, frequent flashes of fire appeared to issue from the column resembling sheet lightning, in warm summer nights. On the following days it was observed that a dark mass formed, as it were, the base to the column of smoke.

On the 18th of July, Captain Swinburne, of his majesty's ship Rapid, on his passage from Marsala to Malta, had a nearer view of what was passing. He approached the spot towards night, stopped to examine it, and gives the following account: "A high irregular column of white smoke rose from the sea. I saw flashes of brilliant lightning mingled with the smoke, which was still distinctly visible by the light of the moon. In a few minutes the column became darker and larger; almost immediately afterwards several successive eruptions of lurid fire rose up amongst the smoke; they subsided, and the column became gradually white again. During the night the changes from white to black, with flashes, and the eruptions of fire, continued at irregular intervals, varying from half an hour to an hour. At five o'clock in the morning, when the smoke had for a moment cleared away at the base, I saw a small hillock of a dark color a few feet above the sea. This was soon hidden again, and was only visible through the smoke at the intervals between the more violent eruptions.

"The volcano was in a constant state of activity, and appeared to be discharging dust and stones, with vast columns of steam. At half past seven the rushing noise of the eruption was heard. At nine o'clock, being distant from it about two miles, I hove to, and went in a boat to sound round and examine it. We rowed towards it, keeping on the weather side, and sounding, but got no bottom till within twenty yards, on the western side, where I had eighteen fathoms, soft bottom. This was the only sounding obtained, except from the brig, one mile true north from the centre of the island, where the depth was one hundred and thirty fathoms, soft dark-brown mud. The crater (for it was evident such was its form) seemed to be composed of fine cinders and mud of a dark-brown color. Within it was to be seen, in the intervals between the eruptions, a mixture of muddy water, steam, and cinders dashing up and down, and occasionally running into the sea over the edge of the crater, which I found on rowing round to be broken down to the level of the sea on the west-south-west side, for the space of ten or twelve yards. Here I obtained a better view of the interior, which appeared to be filled with muddy water, violently agitated, from which showers of hot stones or cinders were constantly shooting up a few yards, and falling into it again; but the great quantity of steam that constantly rose from it prevented my seeing the whole crater.

"A considerable stream of muddy water flowed outward through the opening, and, mingling with that of the sea, caused a discoloration which had been observed before in various places. I could not approach near enough to observe its temperature, but that of the sea within ten or twelve yards of it was only one degree higher than the average, and to the leeward of the island in the direction of the current (which ran to the eastward) no difference could be perceived, even where the water was most discolored; however, as a mirage played above its source, it was probably hot there. The dark objects on the surface of the sea proved to be patches of small floating cinders. The island, or crater, appeared to be seventy or eighty yards in its external diameter, and the lip as thin as it could be consistently with its height, which might be twenty feet above the sea in the highest, and six in the lowest part, leaving the rest for the diameter of the arch within. These details could only be observed in the intervals between the great eruptions, some of which I witnessed from the boat. No words can describe their sublime grandeur. Their progress was generally as follows: After the volcano had emitted for some time its usual quantities of white steam, suddenly the whole aperture was filled with an enormous mass of hot cinders and dust rushing upward to the height of some hundred feet, with a loud, roaring noise, then falling into the sea on all sides with a still louder noise, arising in part perhaps from the formation of prodigious quantities of steam, which instantly took place. This steam was at first of a brown color, having imbodied a great deal of the dust: as it rose, it gradually recovered its pure white color, depositing the dust in the shape of a shower of muddy rain. While this was being accomplished, renewed eruptions of hot cinders and dust were quickly succeeding each other; while forked lightning, accompanied by rattling thunder, darted about in all directions within the column, now darkened with dust and greatly increased in volume, and distorted by sudden gusts and whirlwinds. The latter were most frequent on the lee side, where they often made imperfect waterspouts of curious shapes. On one occasion some steam reached the boat; it smelt a little of sulphur, and the mud it left became a gritty, sparkling, dark-brown powder when dry. None of the stones or cinders thrown out appeared to be more than half a foot in diameter, and most of them much smaller."

Another of his majesty's ships, the Philomel, Captain Smith, was there on the 22d of July. He found the north-west part the highest, being about eighty feet above the level of the sea, and becoming lower towards the southern extremity. The south-east side was broken down even with the water, which kept rushing into the crater with great noise; whence rose in turn an immense volume of white vapor, curling and spreading to an extraordinary height, intermixed in rapid succession with magnificent eruptions of cinders and lava thrown to the height of from four and five hundred to a thousand feet, forking and branching out as they ascended, and then pouring down with a noise like thunder, making the water a sheet of foam to a considerable distance around it. During the night the eruptions were not remarkable for a very great quantity of fire, though a constant shooting of small columns was visible, with occasional flashes of sheet lightning; when near to it to leeward, the sulphur nearly suffocated the crews of the boats. The island appeared to be composed almost entirely of cinders, with a sprinkling of lava, of an oblong shape, about three quarters of a mile in circumference, and, as was ascertained from the soundings, it had a very small base.

The next eye witness was a German naturalist, Hoffmann, who was on the spot two days later. He estimated the diameter of the crater at about six hundred feet, and states that the ring of matter which enclosed it was continually increasing in height and width by the addition of what was thrown out from the crater. He also distinguished two different states of action; one of comparative repose, and the other of increased energy. During the first, the crater emitted continually, and with great velocity, immense volumes of vapor, white as snow; no kind of noise attended them. Rushing across each other and whirling upwards in large convolutions, these masses of vapor formed a column, which, according to his estimate, rose to about two thousand feet above its base, and afforded a most splendid and magnificent sight when shone upon by the sun. From time to time eruptions of cinders, distinguished by their black color, were seen shooting across this column, and disturbing the large convolutions of vapors in their regular ascent. The state of increased activity was indicated by a black column, of awful aspect, rising immediately below and at the side of the white one, to an elevation of about six hundred feet, or even more; at its upper extremity it expanded so as to take the shape of a wheat sheaf. Within this black column large masses of sand, ashes, and stones were seen moving up and down. Numbers of these masses were thrown out of the column, and fell down. Every stone, which by the impulse it had received rose higher than the great masses, left behind it in the air a train of black sand. In this way ray-formed groups were formed, similar to the twigs of a cypress tree, or the tufts of a rocket flower, of dark color; they afforded an extremely beautiful appearance. During the whole time of this paroxysm the sea was hissing, doubtless from the great number of masses of sand and stone which were falling into it, evidently heated to a great degree, while clouds of steam then rose from the surface of the water, and enveloped the island, so that it could not be seen any longer. Meanwhile a rattling and crashing was heard, occasioned by the stony masses meeting and clashing against one another; and also a continual rustling like that of a hail storm, or a very heavy shower of rain. No flames were observed to issue from the crater, nor was any light perceived; but at the periods of the most intense energy a great number of lurid flashes of lightning were seen shooting in every direction through the dark column, and each of them was followed by a loud and protracted thunder, which, when heard at a distance, appeared as one uniform and rumbling noise. These awful eruptions continued sometimes only for eight or ten minutes, but sometimes they were prolonged for the space of almost an hour. When they ceased they were followed by a state of repose, in which the above-mentioned column of white vapor only continued to issue from the crater.

Captain Senhouse effected a landing on the island on the 3d of August, took possession of it, and called it Graham Island. He found the form of the crater to approach that of a perfect circle, and to be complete along its whole circumference, excepting for about two hundred and fifty yards on the south-east side, which was broken and low, not apparently above three feet high. The height of the highest part he found, by a rough computation, to have been about one hundred and eighty feet. The outer diameter he estimated to be almost six hundred and forty yards, and the inner about four hundred. The whole circuit of the island he conceived to be from a mile and a quarter to a mile and one third. He collected a quantity of the materials of which the island is composed. They were all very hot when gathered. They were compact and heavy, and the whole surface of the island dense and perfectly hard under foot. No variety of stones was found, nor any lava; nor did he observe any jets or streams of lava.

In the beginning of the month of August, the eruptions began to be less active, and then they decreased gradually, until they ceased on the 12th of August. Persons who visited it after that date, estimated the height of the island at about two hundred feet; but soon afterwards the waves of the sea began to reacquire their ancient dominion: they tore off by degrees one piece after the other, and in the month of December the whole island had disappeared. Afterwards it was ascertained that not even a trace of a shoal had remained behind.

In all the instances hitherto adduced, the islands which had risen from the bottom of the sea vanished after a short existence. But there is one instance on record in which an island thus formed has existed for a great length of time, and probably continues to exist, as no information has reached us of its disappearance. This island made its appearance in 1796, in that chain of volcanic islands which connects the ancient continent with the new world, extending in a curved line from the peninsula of Kamtschatka to that of Aliaska, and which is called the Aleutes. The new volcanic island lies near a larger one called Umnak. A violent gale had been raging for several days, when, on the 8th of May, after the weather had cleared up, a large column of smoke was seen rising from the surface of the sea, and on the same day the island was observed. In the following night flames and stones were seen to issue from the new formation, and some of the stones were flung so far that they reached the Island of Umnak. At the same time the last-mentioned island was convulsed by a severe shock of an earthquake. All these phenomena, with the exception of the earthquake, continued for a long time, and increased the volcanic island to a considerable size. By degrees, however, the flames decreased, and at last ceased entirely; but smoke was seen continually rising from the newly-formed masses. In 1804 the eruption had ceased so far that some persons ventured to land. The sea near the shores was still very hot, and the soil of the island at many places so heated that it was impossible to walk. The island continued to increase even after that period, at least up to 1806. In that year it was visited by some scientific men, whom it took six hours to sail round the island, and five hours were required to walk from the beach to its summit, which shows its great extent, and the great elevation of its summit. The northern side was still in a state of convulsion, and here a stream of lava was found to extend from the summit to the sea. This evidently shows that this island is different from those which rose from the sea near the Island of St. Michael, and in the vicinity of Sicily, where it is stated no lava was thrown up. The island near Umnak is, therefore, to be considered rather as a true volcano of new formation, like Jorullo, in Mexico.

Though we have no certain record that an island which has risen from the bottom of the sea in the above-described manner has preserved its existence, we can hardly doubt the fact, when we find that, in nearly every group of islands of volcanic origin, one or more small ones are found which in form exactly resemble the islands which have risen from the sea. These islands have always the shape of a horseshoe, or of a half moon, and in most cases enclose basins, forming excellent harbors for small vessels, within which they can lie protected against all winds; but the enclosed area is rarely deep enough to afford anchorage for larger vessels. The ring-like ridge of high land which surrounds the basin rises from its shores with a very steep, almost perpendicular acclivity, so that hardly any path can be found by which the crest of the ridge may be attained from the bay. The declivity towards the open sea is also rather steep, but less so than that directed towards the basin; and on this side the summit may be ascended, though always with difficulty. The sea surrounding such islands, in most cases, if not in all, is of considerable depth. As these islands occur only in those groups which are of volcanic origin, and always have the form of a crater, except that at one place the circular ridge of land surrounding the basin is broken down so as to constitute a strait, by which the basin communicates with the sea, it is evident that they owe their origin to a process similar to that of a volcanic eruption. It is, however, commonly found that lava is one of the components of the ridge, which has not been observed in those islands which have only had a temporary existence.

One of the islands of this description has attracted the especial attention of philosophers on account of the islands which have been raised from the bottom within its basin, and have not again disappeared, like those already described. This is the Island of Santorin, one of the Greek islands called the Cyclades. This island has the shape of a horseshoe, and encloses nearly two thirds of an almost circular basin. In the opening which constitutes the remainder of the circle are situated two other islands, called Therasia and Aspronesi, which by three narrow straits are separated from each other and from Santorin. The three islands together form a complete ring, only broken at three places, and these openings are, as observed before, of small extent. At the bottom of the basin thus included, volcanic force has been active at several times within the period of which we have historical records. In the year 184, or, according to some, in 197, before our era, a new island appeared within the basin, which was called Hiera by the ancients. This island still exists, and is sometimes called Hiera Nisos, but is better known under the name of Palaia Kameni. Another island arose in the year 18 after Christ's birth, very near to Hiera. This island, which was called Thia, is not to be found at present, but it is doubtful whether it has returned to the bottom or has been joined by other eruptions to Hiera; for, according to some accounts, Hiera has received considerable addition to its size by some eruptions which took place in 726 and 1427.

Another island arose nearly in the middle of the basin in 1573. It is called Mikra Kameni, and forms, according to the most recent accounts, a perfect cone, about a hundred feet high, with a crater on its summit. Much larger was the island formed there in 1707, and which bears the name of Nea Kameni. Its appearance was immediately preceded by a severe earthquake. From a place where no ground was found with eighty or a hundred fathoms a rock suddenly emerged, which soon increased in size by accumulation. This happened on the 23d of May, and on the 15th of June the island was nearly two miles in circumference, and from twenty to thirty feet high. On the 16th of July eighteen rocks are stated to have emerged from the surface of the sea, near the new island, whilst a very loud subterraneous noise was heard. Two days later a column of smoke issued at these places, to which, the day after, flames were added; and these phenomena of the process were continually increasing in intensity. During the night the island resembled a number of furnaces, from which fire was shooting out. All the rocks, which for some time were isolated, were at last connected by the quantity of new matter brought up from the bottom of the sea, and formed at length a conical mountain more than three hundred feet in elevation, from the crater of which vapors and stones for a considerable time were thrown out, and streams of lava descended. As late as 1712 this island was still acquiring large additions to its size in this way.

CHAPTER XI.

VOLCANOES. — CRATER OF AN EXTINCT VOLCANO IN JAVA, CONTAINING A LAKE OF SULPHURIC ACID. — GUEVO UPAS, OR POISON VALLEY. — VOLCANOES OF BOILING MUD. — PHENOMENA ATTENDING VOLCANIC ERUPTIONS. — ERUPTION OF VESUVIUS WHICH BURIED POMPEII AND HERCULANEUM. — THE VOLCANIC MATTER WHICH BURIED POMPEII COMPOSED IN GREAT PART OF THE FOSSIL REMAINS OF MINUTE LIVING BEINGS. — LARGE VOLUMES OF WATER CONTAINING FISH EJECTED BY VOLCANOES. — VOLCANIC ROCKS. — MOUNT STROMBOLI AND ITS ERUPTIONS. — MOUNT KRAABLA AND ITS ERUPTIONS. — ERUPTION OF MAUNA LOA. — ERUPTION OF MOUNT SKAPTAAR, IN ICELAND. — THEORY OF THE ORIGIN OF VOLCANIC AGENCY.

BY earthquakes the earth is relieved from the pressure produced by the elastic fluids confined in its interior. This pressure may be the effect of an increase of their mass, or of their elastic forces becoming more active. The solid and liquid matter which is occasionally ejected appears rather to have been collected during the passage of the elastic fluids through the earth's crust, than to proceed from the central regions of the globe. Besides, those chasms which are opened by earthquakes, and from which elastic vapors escape and solid matter is sometimes thrown up, are only temporary, and of very short duration. In most cases it is hardly possible to convince one's self that such chasms have really existed as soon as the earthquake has ceased.

But there exists a much more permanent and more complete communication between the interior of the globe and its surface, by which not only immense volumes of elastic vapors find their way to our atmosphere, but solid matter of a peculiar character is brought to the surface, which has evidently originated below the solid crust of the earth. This communication is formed by volcanoes, which are openings in the earth's surface, and from them the elastic vapors and melted matter in the highest state of ignition escape from the interior of the globe. We may, therefore, safely assume that volcanoes are the orifices of long conduits or pipes, which traverse the earth's crust through all its thickness, and are, with reason, compared to chimneys. We are totally unacquainted with the structure of these volcanic chimneys; and all we know of this great process of Nature is confined to our knowledge of the openings of the chimneys, and of the manner in which the subterraneous force acts and the subterraneous matter is ejected.

The number of volcanoes is very great, but not in all of them is the communication between the interior of the earth and its surface equally complete. In this respect we must distinguish four classes of volcanoes. A great number of them are completely extinct, or, in other words, their communication with the interior has ceased to exist long ago. Many others are semi-extinct. In these volcanoes the communication between the interior of the globe and its surface is not entirely interrupted, but is limited to the discharge of vapors and gases which escape through narrow rents. No actual solid matter is brought up by them; but various solid bodies, soluble in vapors and gases, are deposited by these elastic fluids, when, by their contact with the atmosphere and their condensation by cold, they form chemical combinations different from those in which they previously existed. The solid matter brought to the earth's surface in this manner is, however, but small. The third class is formed by the intermittingly active volcanoes. When in a state of repose these volcanoes resemble in their operations the semi-extinct volcanoes in every respect; but at intervals of shorter or longer duration they acquire for a short time an increased activity, by which they are enabled to eject great masses of melted matter, which overflow the countries contiguous to them. Such paroxysms of volcanic agency are called *eruptions*. The fourth class of volcanoes comprise those which are permanently active, discharging from their orifices melted matter without intermission.

It happens, however, sometimes, though not frequently, that at some particular spot the surface of the earth opens, and discharges large quantities of volcanic matter without forming a volcano. Such chasms, after having remained open for some time, are blocked up, and do not open again. Such may be called *irregular volcanic eruptions.*

To whichever of the four classes above mentioned a volcano may belong, the orifice of the volcanic chimney is always surrounded by a deposit of matter, which takes the form of a hill, or even of a mountain. These volcanic mounds are distinguished from other hills and mountains by a peculiar shape. The upper part of them is always a regular cone, and on its summit, or near it, a depression occurs which terminates at the orifice of the volcanic chimney. The conical hill by which the volcano is crowned is not accidental, but is the effect of its own operations. A quantity of the matter which is ejected by the subterraneous forces from the depression in the middle of the summit, is lodged on all sides round about the opening, and there it is accumulated by degrees, so as to form, in the lapse of time, a smaller or larger hill, according to the quantity of matter which has issued from the opening.

Volcanoes are found in different situations. Many occur in plains but little elevated above the level of the sea, and at considerable distances from other mountains, so as to stand quite isolated. It is supposed, when so situated, that the volcanic mountain has risen from the bottom of the sea by the effects of the volcanic agency, and that the plain which surrounds it has been raised above the sea level by the gradual accumulation of the matter ejected from the orifice of the mountain. This supposition is, in most cases, supported by the fact that the upper layer of the soil of such plains is almost entirely composed of materials derived from the decomposition of volcanic matter, and that it rests on a thick stratum of such matter.

Many volcanoes are situated in the midst of mountain ranges, or contiguous to them. In either situation they are placed in a line, but at distances from each other varying greatly in extent. Such lines extend parallel to the longitudinal direction of the mountain masses. An exception to this arrangement, however, occurs on the table land of Mexico. On this table land, which is supported by mountain masses rising to between six thousand and seven thousand feet above the sea level, the volcanoes are disposed in a line which runs transverse to the elevated plain.

In looking at the exterior shape of an isolated volcano, it is at first sight evident that it consists of two different parts, the base and the cone.

When a volcano is situated in a plain, its base forms, in most cases, a circular elevation, which is frequently tolerably regular, but in some instances assumes a lengthened form. Its surface is very uneven, but not much broken, and its general slope mostly rather gentle, so that it may be ascended without fatigue. Its soil is a firm mass, and when examined is found to be composed of volcanic substances. Its upper layer consists of cinders, ashes, and rapilli, which, by themselves, would form a loose mass; but as a portion of these materials have been decomposed by the effect of the atmosphere and its moisture, and thus have been converted into a mouldy earth, the whole has been cemented together by this new product, and acquires a considerable degree of firmness. Such a soil is of great fertility. At some places streaks of lava are found, left there by the streams which at former times have run down the declivity to the base. A few of these layers of lava are destitute of vegetation. This is the case when the lava has but recently left the mountain, or is of so hard a texture that its surface has not been decomposed by the atmospheric moisture, though exposed to it for a century or longer. These tracts of lava, where they can be brought into cultivation, are very fruitful; and, as every kind of fruit especially thrives well, they are covered with extensive orchards and vineyards. Even when such a layer of lava has not yet been decomposed on its surface, the industrious husbandman tries to turn it to account, provided its thickness be not too great, that is, if it does not exceed twelve or fifteen feet. Holes are made in it of a depth sufficient to reach at the lower end the earthy soil over which it has flowed. These holes, which vary from one to two feet in diameter, are filled up with earthy matter and mould, and then vines or orange trees are planted in them. The best vineyards on the base of Mount Vesuvius are planted in this way, and the same is done on the Island of St. Michael with the orange plantations. It is easy to be conceived that such an operation must be very expensive, on account of the labor required to pierce so hard a mass to such a depth; but the produce of such plantations is so superior to others in abundance, and the flavor of the fruits and grapes so excellent, that in a few years the expenses are covered, and the labor compensated. To the superior fertility of the soil at the base of the volcanoes, and over the adjacent country, it is owing that these spots are cultivated in preference to all others. This is especially the case in Central America and some other parts of the new continent, where almost all the populous towns are built near volcanoes, in despite of the danger to which they are exposed when an eruption takes place. When the ascent of the base is too steep to admit of cultivation, as the upper portion of the base of Mount Etna, in Sicily, it is overgrown with fine large forest trees. In sinking wells on the base of a volcano it is found to be composed of a large number of layers of lava, sometimes as many as twenty and more. They are separated from each other by comparatively thin layers of earth, which evidently proves that a considerable time has elapsed between the eruptions which have produced the streams of lava, as the surface of the older lava has undergone decomposition before the issue of the more recent one. In penetrating still deeper into the interior of the mass it is ascertained that below the lavas that kind of rock is found which is called *trachyte*, and which our modern naturalists are inclined to consider likewise as a volcanic production.

The cone, which has obtained its name from its shape, is nearly always of a regular form, which is owing to the materials of which it is composed. Its whole surface is covered by a deep layer formed by the accumulation of rather small pieces of volcanic matter — of scoriæ, ashes, and sand; and as in this aggregate no kind of matter enters which could cement them into a solid and firm mass, they lie loosely upon each other, and give way even to a moderate pressure. Persons ascending the cone of a volcano are soon aware that the soil under foot slides down, and that they lose frequently by one step what they have gained by many. Under such circumstances it would in most cases be impossible to attain the summit of the cone of a volcano, especially as it commonly rises with an acclivity of from thirty-six to forty-two degrees, if it were not that at a few places this movable soil is covered with a narrow strip of lava, which has run down the cone, and affords a firm footing. It is supposed that this loose volcanic matter forms a layer of many feet in depth; but it is certain that the whole mass of the cone is not composed of similar materials, and that the loose matter rests on the same kind of rock (trachyte) which constitutes the principal body of the base; for when, by an eruption of the volcano, the loose volcanic matter filling the crater has been carried away so as to lay bare the rocks which constitute the body of the volcano, it is found that it is trachyte. It is hardly necessary to add that the surface of the whole cone is entirely destitute of vegetation, and by its black color affords a contrast with the well-cultivated and wooded base which forcibly strikes the mind of the observer.

The proportion between the height of the base and that of the cone is not the same in all volcanoes, but differs materially. The least difference appears to be that observed in Mount Vesuvius, whose cone constitutes nearly one third of the elevation of the mountain. In the Peak of Teneriffe the elevation of the cone falls short of one twenty-second part of the whole height of the volcano. This difference is not accidental; it is the effect of the difference of the part whence the eruptions of the volcano occur. When the eruptions are commonly or uniformly effected from the crater enclosed by the cone, the loose volcanic substances ejected from the crater are shed over the cone, and thus its height is gradually increased. This is the case with Mount Vesuvius. But when, on the other hand, the eruptions do not break out from the crater at the summit, but from an opening at the side of the volcano, as appears to be always the case with the Peak of Teneriffe, the volcanic matter is dispersed over the base, and the cone is not increased by accumulation.

The cone encloses the crater on all sides; for the crater is the deep depression which is found on the summit of the cone, and sometimes descends a thousand feet below the highest part of its rim. In most cases a full view of the crater is obtained as soon as the summit of the cone is reached, as there is no level ground between the outer and inner declivity of the cone. Where the upper edge of the outer declivity terminates, the descent into the crater begins. In few volcanoes, however, a remarkable difference in the structure of this part of the mountain has been observed. Humboldt found that the summit of the cone of Mount Cotopaxi, in the Andes, terminated in a nearly perpendicular wall of rocks, from twenty to thirty feet in height, which runs round the crater, and prevents any descent into it. On this account the crater of that volcano has never been visited. The same traveller found a similar mural enclosure, but of much less elevation, surrounding the crater of the Peak of Teneriffe; but as this wall is broken down at one place, travellers obtain an easy access by this opening to the bottom of the crater.

The crater itself has the form of a funnel. It consists of regularly-descending sides, which terminate in a plain at their lower end, where they approach each other. The descent to this bottom is as rapid as the ascent of the cone; which is easily accounted for, as the same loose matter covers the interior declivity of the cone which lies on its outer surface. The bottom in which these declivities terminate is commonly of a circular shape, but in some volcanoes it has an elliptical form. This is, for instance, the case with the bottom of the crater of the Peak of Teneriffe, which, in its greatest length, measures about three hundred feet, and in its width only about two hundred. This bottom does not undergo any change in the extinct, nor in the semi-extinct volcanoes, but it is subject to great and frequent changes in the intermittingly-active and in the permanently-active volcanoes. These changes are greatest in the intermittent volcanoes, as this bottom is the place at which the temporary opening is effected, by which the interior of the globe is brought into immediate communication with our atmosphere, and from which frequently the melted matter issues, ejected by the elastic forces. But it is not only during the eruptions that the bottom of the crater is changed; even in the intervals between two eruptions, when the volcanic forces are considered as being inactive, the bottom undergoes various changes, as will be noticed hereafter.

The extinct volcanoes are very numerous. Numbers of them are met with even in countries where at present no traces are observed which could lead us to suppose the existence of any volcanic power — as in the south of France, and in some countries near the banks of the Rhine. They are not, however, easily recognized at first view, as the features which distinguish them from other hills do not present themselves in a striking manner when they are overgrown with woods or bushes, or covered with crops; but on a closer inspection their conical shape, and a depression on the summit, betrays their origin. In many cases it is found that the bottom of the crater is partly occupied by one or two small lakes, and in some it forms one large lake. When this is not the case, the bottom, as well as the acclivities which surround it, is almost always overgrown with bushes and woods, which are much resorted to by wild animals. In most cases some streams of old and decomposed lava are discovered in their vicinity; and by digging to a small depth volcanic matter is found in such abundance as to leave no doubt respecting their origin. In a few of these volcanoes a very feeble index occurs of their not being entirely extinct: at some place in the bottom of the crater an irrespirable gas, commonly carbonic acid, is emitted.

In some volcanic countries, also, there are found a great number of extinct volcanoes, as in the vicinity of the town of Naples, where two remarkable ones are situated close to each other, so that they may be seen and examined at the same time. The larger one has its bottom filled up by a lake of considerable extent, the Lake of Agnano; and on its eastern bank is the Grotto del Cane, from the bottom of which carbonic acid is emitted. On the other side of the lake is a very beautiful extinct volcano of smaller dimensions, which bears the name of Gli Astruni. Though it is known that for more than two thousand years the volcanic power has not been active in its crater, this volcano still preserves its conical shape, and every other sign of volcanic origin, in its greatest perfection. The rim of the crater may be about six miles in circumference, and in the small plain which constitutes the bottom are two small lakes. Its sides are almost entirely overgrown with bushes, interspersed here and there with large walnut and chestnut trees. As this crater has been converted into a royal deer park, it is surrounded by a wall.

The crater of Taschem, at the eastern extremity of Java, contains a lake strongly impregnated with sulphuric acid, a quarter of a mile long, from which a river of acid water issues, which supports no living creature, nor can fish live in the sea near its confluence. There is an extinct crater near Batur, called Guevo Upas, or the valley of poison, about half a mile in circumference, which is justly an object of terror to the inhabitants of the country. Every living being which penetrates into this valley falls down dead; and the soil is covered with the carcasses of tigers, deer, birds, and even the bones of men, all killed by the abundant emanations of carbonic acid gas, by which the bottom of the valley is filled.

In another crater in this land of wonders, near the volcano of Talaga Bodas, we learn from Mr. Reinwardt that the sulphureous exhalations have killed tigers, birds, and innumerable insects; and the soft parts of these animals, such as the fibres, muscles, nails, hair, and skin, are very well preserved, while the bones are corroded and entirely destroyed.

It is frequently asked whether or not it is possible or probable that volcanoes, which at present are in such a state, can again be reanimated by volcanic agency, and reassume their former activity. Though there is no great probability that such an event will take place, its possibility cannot be denied, when it is considered that Mount Vesuvius, during the period of which records are preserved, has been twice considered as an extinct volcano. Before the first known eruption of this mountain, which occurred in 79, several ancient authors noticed the state in which it then existed. They all agree in stating that it must have been active at a very remote period, but no eruption was then recorded or known. Strabo gives a description of it, which characterizes it as an extinct volcano. Again, between 1500 and 1631 it presented a similar aspect. A scientific Italian, who visited the volcano a few years before its eruption of 1631, gives the following description of its then state: "The crater was five miles in circumference; its sides were overgrown with brushwood, and at the bottom was a plain on which cattle grazed. In the woods boars frequently harbored. In the midst of the plain within the crater was a narrow passage, through which, by a winding path, you could descend about a mile among rocks and stones, until you came to another more spacious plain, covered with ashes, in which were three little pools."

Extinct volcanoes commonly offer little or nothing that can strike the imagination of the observer; but it is quite otherwise with the *semi-extinct* volcanoes. These are called by the inhabitants of Italy *solfataras*, which term has also been adopted by scientific writers. In the West Indies, where several of them occur, they go by the name of *soufrières*. Both these terms indicate that such places are natural deposits of sulphur.

On obtaining sight of the crater of a semi-extinct volcano for the first time, the observer is astonished at the total change of nature. Every thing is different from what he has been accustomed to see. The white color which is spread over the whole space before him makes the strongest impression. It greatly resembles chalk; but it fills the mind directly with the idea of desolation, as nowhere can the least sign of vegetation be perceived. On account of this extraordinary white color, the solfatara near Puzzuoli, in the Bay of Naples, was called by the ancient writers *campi leucogæi.* When the first impression which this uncommon aspect produces has somewhat abated, the observer perceives that from several places in the bottom, as well as from the sides of the crater, thin streams of smoke escape, which in many cases unite so as to constitute a considerable column. In advancing towards the bottom of the crater, the traveller is rather alarmed by the hollow sound which is heard when he stamps the ground with his feet, or throws down a stone. It appears to him as if he was walking over an arched vault; and the natural inference is, that there must exist a cavern at no great distance under ground. In approaching the places where smoke is seen issuing from the ground he finds that this is effected by means of numerous cracks, whose edges are covered with white, yellow, orange, and brown incrustations, which, by the numerous shades their colors assume, please the eye and agreeably engage the imagination. Sometimes these incrustations cover large tracts in the most striking manner, and the effect is heightened by the white or gray smoke which rises between them. The pieces of rock with which the surface is strewed have usually a very rough surface, and they sometimes assume very fantastic shapes; some of them are split, and others are covered with protuberances not unlike large teeth. When the traveller passes through the streams of vapor escaping from the cracks, he soon finds that they are of different qualities. Through many he may pass without feeling his respiration in the least affected, whilst others produce violent coughing, and sometimes seem to threaten him with suffocation. These vapors are called in Italy *fumarole.*

Of such a character are the phenomena presented by the semi-extinct volcanoes. Natural philosophers have attempted to account for them, and, assisted by the progress of modern chemistry, they have succeeded in doing so in most cases in a satisfactory way.

It has been ascertained that what at first sight appears to be smoke, is, in most cases, nothing but steam or aqueous vapor. This fact had already been inferred from the circumstance that persons, in passing through a column of such smoke, do not feel their respiration affected, nor do they perceive any peculiar kind of taste or smell; and it is confirmed when a knife, or any cold body, is exposed to the vapor; for the vapors, in touching such a body, are instantaneously condensed, and form drops on its surface consisting of pure water devoid of any peculiar taste. The water obtained from such vapors may be used for drinking, and is used so at some places, — as on the Island of Pantellaria, which lies in the Mediterranean, north-west of Malta. This island is of volcanic origin, and no springs are found there; it would be uninhabitable on that account were it not for some large streams of vapor, which ascend without interruption from the most elevated portion of the highest hill of the island. These vapors are condensed by the inhabitants, who place bushes over the spots whence the vapors rise. Thus they obtain a sufficient supply of sweet water for their own use and their herds of goats. Such hot aqueous vapors, when passing over colored bodies, have the power of whitening them; and they thus act on the lava of which the bottom and the sides of the solfataras are composed. Hence the white color is derived which is spread over the whole surface of the crater, and strikes the observer so forcibly. Several facts have been observed which support this explanation. Sometimes white spots are observed in streams of lava which have elsewhere preserved their natural black color. When the places where such white spots occur are more closely examined, it is always discovered that hot vapors protrude through the layer of lava. Again, when large blocks of lava which have been bleached by the vapors are broken to pieces, it is found that at some distance from the surface the lava is less bleached, and in the middle it is quite black.

All the semi-extinct volcanoes do not exhibit an equal degree of activity. Where the volcanic activity is still powerful, the crater is almost entirely filled up with fetid vapors and noisome smoke, its sides and bottom being covered with incrustations of sulphur and other deposits of different colors. When to this we add that no traces of vegetation are any where perceptible, and that no animal of any description is to be met with in its precincts, it is easy to comprehend that the impression which the sight of such a spot makes on the beholder must be dismal in the extreme. The ancients were so struck at the sight of the solfatara of Puzzuoli that they considered themselves as having arrived at the gates of the infernal regions, and thence called that semi-extinct volcano *Forum Volcani.* It is at present, however, considered as a very insignificant one when compared with others with which we have become acquainted, especially with that on the Island of Volcano. The crater of this solfatara is nearly fourteen hundred feet in diameter, and its bottom about four hundred feet below its rim. This immense cavity is always filled with volumes of thick smoke, which escapes with a loud noise from the fissures, and in the lower portion of the crater is so dense that those who attempt to descend to the bottom expose themselves to the danger of being suffocated.

The largest of the semi-extinct volcanoes to be met with on the surface of the globe appear to be those which occur in the central countries of Asia, on the northern declivity of the Thian-shan Mountains. The Chinese geographers mention two of large dimensions there, both situated in the vicinity of the town of Urum-tsi. One of them is stated to have a circumference of a hundred li, equal to thirty-five statute miles; and the circuit of the other amounts to ninety li, or thirty English miles.

Many of the streams of vapor issuing from the craters of semi-extinct volcanoes contain a smaller or larger proportion of hydro-sulphuric acid. The presence of this gas manifests itself instantaneously by the manner in which the organs of respiration are affected. When the hydro-sulphuric gas constitutes a considerable proportion of the vapor, it affects the lungs so forcibly that persons are compelled to remove promptly for fear of being suffocated. Hydro-sulphuric gas is decomposed in the atmosphere into its bases, hydrogen and sulphur, at a very low temperature. This takes place with that gas which rises mixed with vapor from the crater of the semi-extinct volcanoes. The hydrogen combines with the oxygen of the atmosphere and forms water. The sulphur, of course, is dropped, and either crystallizes alone, or forms salts by combining with other bases. By the crystallization of the sulphur the yellow incrustations are formed with which the rents of the crater are invested, and which assume different shades according to the lesser or greater state of purity of the mineral. It happens sometimes that large masses of beautifully crystallized sulphur are met with. In this way the semi-extinct and also the intermittent volcanoes produce large quantities of sulphur, which is also occasionally turned to account by collecting and purifying the mineral; it is even supposed that when sulphur occurs in places where no vol canoes exist, it nevertheless owes its origin to a similar process.

When sulphur combines with other bases it yields different products. Combining with lava containing a large proportion of clay, it forms alum. The largest portion of this valuable mineral which is brought to market is extracted from the craters of extinct or semi-extinct volcanoes. When the sulphur combines with lime, which also constitutes an ingredient of many volcanic productions, gypsum is formed. In many semi-extinct volcanoes sulphur is found combined with arsenic.

These combinations mostly occur in the proportions which constitute those two sulphurets of arsenic which are known by the names of *realgar*, or red sulphuret of arsenic, and *orpiment*, or yellow sulphuret of arsenic.

There is hardly a semi-extinct volcano in which sulphur is not found in a liquid state, as sulphuric acid. It sometimes covers large tracts of lava; and to the corrosive quality of this matter the rough surface of many of the rocks, and their peculiarly fantastic shapes, are to be ascribed.

Hydro-chloric acid is also found frequently, though not in all volcanoes, combined with aqueous vapors. When such is the case, the vapors form small convolutions, in rising from the cracks, of a snow-white color. When a person enters such a current, his organs of respiration are so excited as to produce a violent coughing. Several substances are formed by combination with this acid. The most remarkable is sal ammoniac, which is found in nearly all volcanoes, and in some of them in such quantities as to afford an article of trade. This substance appears nowhere to be so abundant as in the volcanoes of Chinese Turkistan, where a whole province pays the taxes imposed by government by a supply of this valuable article. Another combination formed by the chlorine in volcanoes is chloride of sodium, or common salt. Large layers of it occur in some extinct volcanoes; and it is also sometimes thrown up in large lumps by intermittent volcanoes during their eruptions. This was done by Mount Vesuvius in 1822 and in 1832, and has also occurred during an eruption of Mount Hecla, in Iceland. Several observers have occasionally found rents of volcanoes covered with a crust of common salt to a thickness of three inches. Chloride of iron is also frequently met with in volcanoes; and as this matter liquefies in the air, the internal sides of the crater are sometimes wonderfully adorned by the numerous shades of yellowish brown and red brown which this chloride imparts. Chloride of copper appears also to occur sometimes among the products of the semi-extinct and intermittent volcanoes.

It is supposed that the beautiful green color which is assumed by several salts adhering to the cracks of the volcanoes, is imparted to them by the chloride of copper. Salts of this color are much sought for by travellers on account of their beauty, and specimens of it are found in nearly all mineralogical collections.

Besides the minerals just now enumerated, there are also found in semi-extinct volcanoes boracic acid and selenium. These substances are frequent, particularly in the crater of the Island of Volcano, one of the Lipari Islands. The boracic acid there covers large tracts of rocks with small, scaly, brilliant crystals, white as snow; and the selenium is there found combined with sulphur, to which substance it imparts a deep orange color, which greatly increases the beauty of such incrustations.

Mr. R. Bunsen, in his account of the pseudo-volcanic phenomena of Iceland, describes many valleys where sulphurous and aqueous vapors burst forth with a hissing sound from the hot soil formed of volcanic tuff. In such spots a pool of boiling water is seen, in which a bluish-black argillaceous paste rises in huge bubbles. These bubbles, on bursting, throw the boiling mud to a height of fifteen feet and upwards, accumulating it in ledges round the crater or basin of the spring.

The formation of a new mud volcano was witnessed on the 27th of November, 1827, at Tokmali, on the peninsula of Abscheron, east of Baku. Flames blazed up to an extraordinary height for a space of three hours, and continued for twenty hours to rise about three feet above a crater, from which mud was ejected. At another point in the same district where flames issued, fragments of rock of large size were hurled up into the air, and scattered around.

At a place called Macaluba, near Girgenti, in Sicily, are several conical mounds from ten to thirty feet in height, with small craters at their summits, from which cold water, mixed with mud and bitumen, is cast out. Bubbles of carbonic acid and carburetted hydrogen gas are also disengaged from these springs, and at certain periods with such violence as to throw the mud to the height of two hundred feet. These "air volcanoes," as they are sometimes termed, are known to have been in the same state of activity for the last fifteen centuries; and Dr. Daubeny imagines that the gases which escape may be generated by the slow combustion of beds of sulphur, which is actually in progress in the blue clay, out of which the springs rise. But as the gases are similar to those disengaged in volcanic eruptions, and as they have continued to stream out for so long a period, they may perhaps be derived from a more deep-seated source.

In the district of Luss, or Lus, south of Beila, about one hundred and twenty miles north-west of Cutch and the mouths of the Indus, numerous mud volcanoes are scattered over an area of probably not less than one thousand square miles. Some of these have been well described by Captain Hart, and subsequently by Captain Robertson, who has paid a visit to that region, and made sketches of them. These conical hills occur to the westward of the Hara Mountains and the River Hubb. One of the cones is four hundred feet high, composed of light-colored earth, and having at its summit a crater thirty yards in diameter. The liquid mud which fills the crater is continually disturbed by air bubbles, and here and there is cast up in small jets.

The intermittent volcanoes, during their state of repose, frequently so much resemble the solfataras, that the difference between them can only be perceived by very attentive observation. According to the statements of Humboldt, the bottom of the intermittent volcanoes during their repose is covered with layers of scoriæ, which are very rough, sonorous, and shining; and small eminences occur, and swellings of the ground, raised, without doubt, by the operations of the elastic fluids; there are also small cones of very diminutive cinders and scoriæ, under which narrow openings are concealed. In the semi-extinct volcanoes, on the other hand, the bottom of the crater is strewed with large blocks of stony lava, which, in the lapse of time and by the action of the hot vapors, have been detached from its sides, and which have assumed a white color. In intermittent volcanoes the white color is not general, and occurs only at a few places of small extent.

The crater of the intermittent volcano sometimes remains in such a state for a length of time, until the volcanic powers acquire a more intense degree of activity. The changes the crater then undergoes by the operation are great and numerous, and continue to occur until an eruption takes place.

The eruptions are commonly preceded by certain phenomena. The most striking of them are the earthquakes, which are usually felt in the countries contiguous to the base of the volcano, when a great eruption is in course of preparation. They are sometimes very severe, at other times but slight; and eruptions also occur which are not attended by earthquakes. In some cases it has been observed that the earthquakes occur many months, or even years, before the eruption takes place. The most striking instances of this kind are the earthquakes which preceded the eruption of Mount Vesuvius in 79. For many centuries previous the volcano had been considered as extinct, as no eruption had been recorded, though during that period the country near it was inhabited by persons who paid considerable attention to the passing events, and recorded them with some degree of exactness. It appears that the subterraneous force, long before the eruption took place, made some efforts to reopen the vent which had been shut up for so long a time. Fifteen years previous, very destructive earthquakes had been experienced in the country surrounding the base of the volcano. The towns of Pompeii and Herculaneum were levelled to the ground, and Naples and Nocera, which lie at a greater distance from the volcano, suffered considerably; more distant places less. Thus it was evident that the centre of the earthquake was within or under Mount Vesuvius. Considering this earthquake as being connected with the eruption which took place at a much later period, it would appear that the subterraneous forces, when they began to assume a greater degree of activity in the mountain, had first to remove an immense obstacle before they could open the channel by which they were enabled to give vent to the elastic vapors penned up in the interior, and to eject the accumulated matter. But at the time of the earthquake the inhabitants of these regions had not the least suspicion that this phenomenon was in any way connected with the mountain. Therefore the inhabitants of Pompeii busied themselves with the rebuilding of their destroyed palaces and houses; and they had not completed their work when the town was buried under the volcanic matter thrown out by the first eruption of the volcano; for many of the disinterred buildings of Pompeii are still found in such a state as to make it evident that they were in the course of being built or repaired when they were covered with the ashes and scoriæ of the mountain. The great earthquake of 63 was followed by several others of less force; but they became more severe as the eruption drew nearer. Some days before the eruption several severe shocks occurred, and the very night preceding the 23d of August such a powerful shock was experienced, that even at Misenum, a place which is more than thirty miles distant from the volcano, every building was shaken to its very foundation. Shortly after it had passed off, the summit of Mount Vesuvius was seen enveloped in that cloud of ashes which deposited its contents on the towns of Pompeii, Herculaneum, and their vicinity, and buried them under so thick a layer that no traces of the most elevated buildings were perceptible.

Not much less severe were the earthquakes which preceded the eruption of Mount Vesuvius in 1794; but they occurred a few days only before the eruption. It was then noticed that the surface of the country contiguous to the base of the volcano moved like a fluid from east to west; and even in the town of Naples the concussions were so strong that people passed the nights in the open places for fear of being crushed by the downfall of the buildings. The night previous to the eruption a very smart shock occurred. It did not manifest itself by an undulatory motion, but by short and irregular shocks, which rent the walls of the strongest buildings, and threw every thing into the utmost confusion. Immediately afterwards the reflection of the melted matter in the crater was observed above the summit of the volcano. That these earthquakes were intimately connected with the eruption, and, as it were, only phenomena attending the process going on in the interior of the mountain, was evident from the manner in which they affected the contiguous country. The nearer a place was situated to the base of the volcano, the more severely it was shaken. The volcano was, therefore, the centre of the earthquake, from which it proceeded regularly on all sides, except where the bulky masses of the Apennines obstructed its progress. Its force decreased also in proportion to the distance from the place where it originated. This was proved by the fact that the towns of Nocera, Salerno, Capua, and Benevento suffered much less than Naples, which, however, was not so fearfully shaken as Portici and Torre del Greco.

It is very probable that the degree of severity with which earthquakes act is determined by the actual state of the crater. When the volcanic chimney is not much obstructed by thick masses of solid matter, or when these masses are so disposed as to yield easily to the subterraneous forces which strive to remove them, the shocks of the earthquakes are but slight. Several eruptions have taken place which do not appear to have been attended by such consequences as those of 1737, 1813, and 1822. When, on the other hand, the obstructions experienced in the narrow pipe are very great, they can only be removed by the confined elastic vapors after several repeated and powerful efforts. In such a case the earthquakes must prove destructive.

A less constant attendant of the eruptions is the retiring of the sea. This has only been observed to precede some of the eruptions of Mount Vesuvius, and not those of other volca noes. At the first recorded eruption (79) it must have been very remarkable, to judge from the expressions in which it is mentioned by Pliny the younger. In modern times it has been noticed twice. Sir William Hamilton observed it in 1775. The sea, according to his statement, rose as if it was agitated by a violent gale, and then retired from the shores with great rapidity. The last-mentioned circumstance appeared so striking that many persons were inclined to suppose that the water of the sea had suddenly fallen into some rents in the base of the volcano, which carried it immediately to immensely large cavities in the interior of the mountain. In these two cases the retiring of the sea occurred nearly simultaneously with the eruptions. In 1813 the sea retired many months before the mountain opened. The eruption took place late in December, and in the months of May and June it was noticed that the sea retired several times, suddenly and with great swiftness, to a distance of from fifteen to twenty paces from the beach.

It is not easy to explain this phenomenon. According to the theory which prevailed in the last century respecting the origin and activity of volcanic agency, the accession of water was required to reanimate the subterraneous conflagration. It was therefore supposed that the water of the sea found access to the interior of the volcano by means of some submarine clefts. The retiring of the sea appeared a natural consequence of this process, and was easily accounted for by such an absorption. But this idea, as an explanation of the retiring of the sea, was speedily rejected. It was observed that even if it is supposed that the whole mountain was hollow, and formed in its interior an immense cavity, the filling it up with water could not in the least affect the level of the sea in a perceptible manner; for, huge as the volcano is, its bulk is very insignificant when compared with the volume of water filling the sea. Others have compared this phenomenon with the retreating of the sea which has occurred during some of the most severe earthquakes; but as that phenomenon has not been yet accounted for in any satisfactory manner, our knowledge is not advanced by this comparison. Some think that the retreating of the sea may be effected by the rising of the bottom of the sea, in consequence of the elastic vapors under ground exerting their forces against it, and raising it above its former level. This explanation is less to be objected to than others.

The approach of an eruption is also indicated by a diminution of the water in the wells and springs at places which lie on or near the base of the volcano. In some instances the wells are stated to have dried up entirely. It has not yet been ascertained whether or not this phenomenon precedes the eruption of all volcanoes; but the inhabitants of the places near Mount Vesuvius consider it as the most infallible of all prognostics, and on that account pay great attention to it. In our times some philosophers have also adopted this belief, and have collected several facts by which the common opinion is confirmed. Twelve days before the eruption of Mount Vesuvius in 1804, the water in all the wells near its base sank considerably below their common level. More attention was paid to the wells in 1830; the decrease of their water was very regular. In the month of May they sank more than ten feet, though very heavy rains had fallen. The decrease of the waters continued during the summer months, but less rapidly, until the month of October, when a slight rise was perceptible; they then preserved their level to the month of December, when an eruption took place. The explanations which have been offered of this phenomenon are far from being satisfactory, and may on that account be omitted.

During the time which passes between two eruptions, and when the volcano is said to be in repose, its crater undergoes several changes. Immediately after an eruption it forms a deep funnel, more or less regular; but shortly before such an occurrence it is found to be filled up with volcanic matter. According to the facts collected and recorded by modern observers, it would appear that the filling up of the crater is not always affected in the same way, but by two different processes.

When the crater of a volcano is examined immediately after an eruption, it is found that its bottom is deeply depressed below its rim. In some cases the declivities leading to it are so steep that it is almost impossible to get down to the bottom. This might have been expected. The immense force with which the elastic vapors act when they escape from the interior of the earth has removed all the masses of lava and other volcanic materials which had previously accumulated in the crater. The last lava which was raised by them in the volcanic chimney—but for the ejection of which the decreased force of the vapor was insufficient—remained in the crater; but, as it was in a liquid state, it sank down to the lowest depths of the opening to the narrow orifice of the chimney, and there it hardened as it became cold. After this state of the crater has continued for some time, its bottom begins to be covered with volcanic substances and rubbish, which, in different modes, are detached from the sides of the crater and roll down; thus the narrow rents at the bottom are gradually covered with layers of scoriæ and of cinders. When in this state, which sometimes lasts for many years, the crater of the intermittent volcano greatly resembles, as we mentioned before, that of a semi-extinct one; but after some time it begins to undergo a change. It is found that the bottom is gradually raised higher and higher. This appears to be effected by the elastic vapors confined within the volcano. When, either by accumulation, or by the increase of their elasticity, their force has been considerably augmented, they press on all sides on the surrounding objects, and, consequently, also against the bottom of the volcano. The effects of such a pressure manifest themselves by the splitting of the bottom at numerous places, and by the rising of its whole mass. In this manner the subterraneous forces continue to raise the bottom of the volcano until it has risen to the level of the rim of the crater,—which event is commonly soon followed by an eruption, which, in this case, takes place without being preceded by any discharge of melted matter. By the process just described the crater of Mount Vesuvius was filled up with volcanic matter between the eruptions which took place in 1804 and 1813.

But frequently — probably in the majority of cases — the crater is filled up by a different process. It appears that the bottom of the crater is sometimes not entirely shut up by the lava which, after the eruption has terminated, falls back upon it, and there becomes a solid mass. A small opening remains, by which a free and uninterrupted communication between the interior and exterior of the globe is established. This opening emits, for some time after the eruption has ceased, only white vapors. But after a time these vapors begin to assume a deeper color; and at length, when their color has grown darker, they bring up small pieces of lava, known by the name of scoriæ, which have been apparently torn off from the melted matter below the crater. These scoriæ are raised to a considerable elevation by the elastic vapors escaping through the opening Whenever they get beyond the reach of the elastic vapors they fall to the ground. A portion falls back into the opening, but another portion is lodged round it, where this matter soon accumulates to such an extent as to form in time a small hill round the opening. Such hills formed within the precincts of the crater are called cones of eruption. They are entirely composed of scoriæ and ashes, like the cone of the volcano, but they do not move when pressed upon. This is probably owing to the thinness of their walls, and to the heat existing in the opening. By this heat the accumulated matter is partially melted, and the whole mass becomes so cemented as to acquire a considerable degree of consistency. These cones of eruption may be ascended without the least danger; and thus the opening in the midst of them may be approached nearer than can be done under other circumstances. When a cone of eruption has increased for some time, and has attained some height by the continual accession of fresh matter, the subterraneous powers raise the melted matter higher, and push it into the pipe. By this operation the sides of the cone are burst open at one or more places, and from the lowest part of the rents, which is always near the base of the cone, a greater or smaller quantity of melted matter is discharged, which overflows the lower tracts surrounding the cone, where it soon hardens. Meanwhile the ejection of scoriæ continues increasing the cone of eruption, and is from time to time attended by an effusion of lava from the base or from the top of the cone. In this manner the crater is gradually filled up by successive layers of lava, which have issued from the cone of eruption. At last this cone attains such an elevation that it projects above the rim of the crater, and becomes visible to the country surrounding the volcano. When this has taken place, the effusion of lava from the cone of eruption soon fills up the lower space which lies between it and the rim of the crater, and thus at last the bottom of the crater is raised to a level with its rim. Sometimes it is found that a part of it is even higher than the rim. When this has taken place, the lava issuing from the cone of eruption begins to run over the rim of the crater, and to descend on the declivities of the cone of the volcano and over its base. This process continues until an eruption puts a stop to it by clearing the chimney, and by removing in a few hours or days the immense quantity of volcanic matter which, in the course of many years, has accumulated in the crater. After the eruption has passed away the process just described begins its course anew.

In this manner the crater of Mount Vesuvius was filled up in the interval which elapsed between the eruptions of 1813 and 1822, as also in that which occurred between the last-mentioned year and the eruption in 1834. By the violent eruption of 1822 the crater of the volcano had been so completely cleared of all the matter which had accumulated during the nine preceding years, that it presented a deep and immense cavity. It was then measured by Mr. Babbage, who ascertained that its bottom was nine hundred and thirty-eight feet below the highest part of its rim, and four hundred and fifty-nine feet below the lowest part. In this state it appears to have remained up to 1827, when it was observed that a change was going on in the bottom of the crater. An opening was soon effected, from which showers of scoriæ were thrown up. In a short time they accumulated round the orifice so as to form a cone of eruption. In 1828 the first effusion of lava from a rent in the cone was noticed, and it was followed by a number of others during the two following years. The quantity of lava which in this manner was brought up must have been very considerable, as appears from a measurement taken in August, 1830, when the bottom was found to be only six hundred and forty feet below the highest, and one hundred and sixty feet below the lowest part of the rim of the crater. The depth of the crater had consequently decreased nearly three hundred feet in two years. We may form an idea of the quantity of lava which was required to fill up the crater, when we consider that, according to a trustworthy statement, the diameter of the crater at its upper opening exceeded nineteen hundred feet. A little more than a year later, in September, 1831, the cone of eruption in the middle of the crater had been so elevated by the continual accession of scoriæ and other volcanic materials that its summit became visible in the town of Naples, and a few months later the whole crater was completely filled up. In the beginning of 1832 the lava began to flow over its rim, and to descend in streams on the declivity of the cone which encloses the crater. Sometimes these floods of lava ceased for weeks, or even months, and then began again. In this state the volcano remained for more than two years. At last an eruption took place, in 1834, after which the crater was found to have entirely changed its aspect. The cone of eruption, which had originated on its bottom in 1828, had disappeared with a most terrible crash, and on the newly-formed bottom were only two abysses, which descended so deep that it was impossible to see their termination, and which were divided from each other by a narrow ridge.

The facts respecting the filling up of the crater between two eruptions have only been lately ascertained, and they support the assertion of the geologist Von Buch, who maintains that the approach of an eruption may be known by an examination of the state of its crater; that when the lowest part of it is but little depressed below its rim, an eruption is not distant; but that, on the other hand, such a phenomenon is not to be apprehended when the distance between the rim and the bottom of the crater is considerable.

It is very probable that the different modes in which the crater is filled up modify the phenomenon with which an eruption commences, and also the degree of energy with which it manifests itself. When the crater is filled up in the manner described in page 313, there is an opening which evidently passes through the whole crust of the earth, and terminates near the spot where the matter to be ejected is heated, and reduced to or kept in a fluid state. When the subterraneous powers do not assume a great degree of intensity, the matter is brought up by them in such quantities only as can easily be discharged by the existing chimney, as happened in Mount Vesuvius for two years before the eruption of 1834. In such a case the eruption begins with a discharge of melted matter from the top of the volcano. When in the progress of the eruption, and by the increase of the subterraneous forces, a larger quantity of melted matter is driven into the existing volcanic chimney than it is able to contain, it must be broken to pieces by the pressure of the matter. This, however, is commonly effected with such ease that the event is brought about without violently convulsing the mountain and the adjacent country. Such eruptions, therefore, are not usually preceded by earthquakes, or they are not of such a description as to cause great damage. When by the last-mentioned process the crater has been freed of the volcanic matter which encumbered it for many years, the lava in many cases finds a free exit by its mouth. But when the volume of the lava is too great to be discharged, even by the much-widened mouth of the crater, it presses against its sides, which are forced open at such places as are least able to afford resistance to the immense pressure to which they are exposed. It is therefore found that in such circumstances the eruption begins at the top of the mountain, and the lateral eruptions somewhat later.

All these circumstances vary considerably when the crater has been filled up in the manner noticed in page 312. There is occasionally no opening which can be widened by the subterraneous vapors without great effort. A much greater pressure is required to break open the contiguous and solid mass by which the crater has been filled in a manner which is still a mystery to us. The efforts which the subterraneous vapors must make to produce such a pressure are probably the cause why the eruptions happening in such circumstances are preceded by such violent earthquakes as were experienced in 1779 and in 1794. It is usually the case that the melted matter accumulates in the interior of the volcano before the upper part of the crater has been opened, and the lower parts of the crater, being unable to resist the pressure of the matter, burst open at the weakest spots. Consequently we find that in such circumstances the lateral eruptions precede the great eruption from the top of the mountain, as happened in the eruption of Mount Vesuvius in 1794.

With a violent crash, if not with an earthquake, the crater is broken open by the subterraneous vapors, and the eruption begins. Whilst it is going on a loud noise is heard from the interior of the volcano. It is a continual hollow, rumbling sound, similar to the roaring of the sea during a heavy gale, but interrupted by violent detonations, which resemble the explosions of inflammable gases. The white smoke which, previous to the eruption, issued from the cone, assumes by degrees a much darker tint as the period of the eruption approximates, and after its commencement turns quite black It also increases rapidly in intensity, and forms a column which gradually rises higher and higher above the summit of the volcano. Within this column of smoke pieces of solid matter are seen moving upwards, evidently supported and impelled by the invisible vapors issuing from the crater. They are of different dimensions. Some are pieces of rock of considerable size and weight. They are thrown up at intervals of a few minutes and with a crashing noise. In ascending above the summit of the volcano they diverge gradually, assuming the shape of a sheaf. Part of them fall back into the crater, but many descend on the declivities of the mountain, where they roll down with a tumultuous noise, or, bursting asunder, cover the immediate vicinity with a shower of splendidly shining sparks. But the greatest portion of solid matter contained in the column of smoke consists of scoria, sand, and ashes. By contemplating this column of smoke in the daytime the mind of the beholder is oppressed by forebodings, and its emotions are kept in suspense; but in the night it is filled with a sensation in which awe and admiration are mingled; for the reflection of the light issuing from the lake of burning lava in the crater illuminates the column, and imparts to it the tint of the clouds of a thunder storm when illuminated by the setting sun. The masses of glowing rocks rising and sinking within this stream of light greatly increase the grandeur of this awful though magnificent sight.

When this spectacle has continued for some time without any perceptible variation, a change is observed gradually to take place. The larger pieces of rock decrease in number and size, and at the same time the minute solid matter, especially the ashes, is astonishingly increased. In consequence of this change the column of smoke rises higher and higher, and when it has attained a great elevation, its upper extremity begins to expand on all sides, until it forms a very extensive cloud, of a circular form, which appears in its middle to be supported by a comparatively slender columnar shaft. The whole bears some resemblance to a Chinese umbrella, or a large mushroom. The Italians compare it with that kind of pine tree which bears edible fruit, frequently met with in

Italy. This tree is distinguished by its elegant shape, a slender and straight trunk, surrounded at its upper extremity by a circular crown, formed by numerous branches, diverging in nearly horizontal lines from the stem. On that account the Italians name it the pine. This beautiful phenomenon, which hardly ever fails making its appearance towards the close of the eruption, is an object of admiration even in the daytime; but in the dark night it presents one of the most impressive scenes of beauty which nature can afford. The column of smoke is converted into a magnificent column of fire by the reflection of the light from the crater, and its interior is literally dotted by numberless shining points of great splendor, which are the many millions of glowing grains of sand and ashes rising up and down in the column. In the column, but still more frequently in the cloud above it, flashes of forked lightning are seen every moment in all directions, and are accompanied by thunder. After this phenomenon has lasted for some hours, the cloud imperceptibly vanishes, and the column of ashes gradually disappears. The eruption is at an end.

Most of these phenomena appear to have attended the first eruption of Mount Vesuvius, in 79. We have an account of this event in the letters of Pliny the younger to his friend Tacitus. Though this account is not quite satisfactory, according to our present knowledge of the subject, it must always be read with great interest, as it proves that the phenomena produced by that eruption were on a much greater scale, and much more destructive, than ever has been experienced in modern times, and as it involved the death of his uncle, Pliny the elder, the famous author of the Natural History.

"My uncle," writes Pliny, "was at that time with a fleet under his command at Misenum. On the 23d of August, about one in the afternoon, my mother (his sister) desired him to observe a cloud which appeared to be of a very unusual size and shape. He went upon an eminence to view it more distinctly. It was not at that distance discernible from what mountain the cloud issued, but it was found afterwards to ascend from Mount Vesuvius. I cannot give you a more exact description of its figure than by comparing it with a pine tree; for it shot up in the form of a trunk, which extended itself at the top into a sort of branches. This form was occasioned, I imagine, by a sudden gust of air that impelled it, the force of which either decreasing as it advanced upwards, or the cloud itself being pressed back again by its own weight, expanded in this manner. It appeared sometimes bright and sometimes dark and spotted, as it was either more or less impregnated with earth and cinders. This extraordinary phenomenon excited my uncle's curiosity to take a nearer view of it. He immediately ordered a light vessel to be got ready; but as he was coming out of the house with his tablets for his observations, the mariners belonging to the galleys stationed at Resina entreated him by a messenger to come to their assistance, since, that place being situated at the foot of Mount Vesuvius, there was no way for them to escape but by sea. He therefore ordered the galleys to be put to sea, and went himself on board, with the intention of assisting not only Resina, but several other towns situated upon that beautiful coast. When hastening to the place, from which others were flying with the utmost terror, he steered directly to the point of danger, and with so much calmness and presence of mind as to be able to make and to dictate his observations upon the motion and figure of that dreadful phenomenon. He went so near to the mountain that the cinders, which grew thicker and hotter the nearer he approached, fell into the ships, together with pumice stones and pieces of burning black rock. They were also in danger not only of running aground by the sudden retreat of the sea, but also from the vast fragments which rolled down from the mountain and encumbered all the shore. Here he stopped to consider whether he should return. When the pilot advised him to that step he said, 'Fortune befriends the brave; take me to Pomponianus.' Pomponianus was then at Stabiæ, a town separated by a gulf, which the sea, after several windings, forms upon that shore. The wind being favorable, my uncle soon reached the villa of Pomponianus, whom he found in the greatest consternation; he embraced him with the greatest affection, and exhorted him to keep up his spirits; and to dissipate his fears the more, he took a bath and sat down to supper. In the mean while the eruption from Mount Vesuvius flamed out in several places with much violence, which the darkness of the night contributed to render still more visible and dreadful. My uncle, having tried to soothe the apprehensions of his friend, retired to rest, and soon fell asleep. The court which led to his apartment being in the mean time almost filled with stones and ashes, if he had continued there any longer it would have been impossible for him to have made his way out; it was therefore thought proper to awaken him. He got up and went to Pomponianus and the rest of the company, who had not ventured to go to bed. After a short consultation, it was resolved to leave the place, and retire to the fields, as the less dangerous situation. They went out, therefore, having pillows tied upon their heads with napkins, which was all their defence against the storms of stones that fell around them. Though it was now day every where else, where they were a deeper darkness prevailed than in the most obscure night, except that for moments it was dissipated by the flashes from the mountain. They thought proper to go down farther upon the shore, to observe if they might safely put to sea; but they found the waves still running extremely high and boisterous. Here my uncle, having drank a draught or two of cold water, threw himself down upon a cloth, which was spread for him, when immediately the flames, and a strong smell of sulphur, which was the forerunner of them, dispersed the rest of the company, and obliged him to arise. He raised himself with the assistance of two of his servants, and instantly fell down dead, suffocated, as I conjecture, by some gross and noxious vapors; for he had always weak lungs, and was frequently subject to a difficulty of breathing.

"Meanwhile I was at Misenum pursuing my studies. There had been for many days before some shocks of an earthquake, but they were particularly violent the night after my uncle had left us. They not only shook every thing about us, but seemed indeed to threaten total destruction. My mother awoke me, and we went into a small court belonging to the house, which separated the sea from the buildings. When it grew day the light was exceedingly faint and languid, and the buildings all around tottered. As there was no remaining there without certain and great danger, we resolved to quit the town. Having got at a convenient distance from the buildings, we stopped in the midst of a dreadful scene of danger. The carriages which we had ordered out of town, though standing on a level spot, were so violently pushed forward and backward that they could not be kept steady, even when propped by large stones. The sea also appeared to roll back upon itself, and to be driven from its shores by the strong concussions of the earth. It is certain that the beach was considerably widened, and that many of the inhabitants of the sea were left upon the strand. On the other side a black and dreadful cloud, bursting with an igneous, serpentine vapor, darted out a long train of fire, resembling flashes of lightning, but much larger. Soon afterwards, the cloud, descending, covered the whole bay, and we could no longer see the Island of Caprea and the promontory of Misenum. The ashes began to fall upon us, but in moderate quantities. I looked back. A thick, black smoke, just behind us, rolled along the ground like a torrent, and followed us. Soon afterwards we were enveloped in darkness, not like the darkness of a cloudy night, or when there is no moon, but such as is in a close room when all light is excluded. Nothing was then to be heard but the shrieks of women, the screams of children, and the cries of men; some calling for their parents, others for their children, others for their husbands, and only distinguishing each other by their voices. Some bewailed their own fate, others the fate of their relations; some wishing to die from the very fear of dying; some lifting up their hands to the gods; but the greater part imagining that the last and eternal night was come, which was to destroy both the gods and the world together. At length a glimmering light appeared. We imagined it to be rather the forerunner of an approaching burst of flames (as it really was) than the return of the day. However, the fire fell at a great distance from us, and then we were again immersed in darkness. A heavy shower of ashes rained upon us, which we were obliged now and then to shake off; otherwise we should have been crushed and buried in the heap. I supported myself with the consolation that all mankind was involved in the same calamity, and that I was perishing with the world itself. At last this dreadful darkness was dissipated by degrees, like a cloud of smoke; the daylight returned, and even the sun appeared, but with a faint light, as when an eclipse is coming on. Every object that presented itself to our eyes appeared changed, being covered with white ashes as with a deep snow."

This account of Pliny, when compared with the descriptions of more recent eruptions of Mount Vesuvius, or any other volcano, may be considered as an exaggerated statement, especially that portion where he reports what happened in the vicinity of Misenum, thirty miles from the place of eruption. But when it is remembered that, by the volcanic matter then thrown up, the towns of Pompeii, Herculaneum, and Stabiæ were so buried that the highest parts of the villas and palaces which they contained were not visible above ground, we can hardly doubt the correctness of his statements.

There is no object in nature so calculated to create extreme surprise in our mind as the force with which the subterraneous vapors act in effecting an eruption. We know that at the eruption of Mount Vesuvius, in 1834, its crater was filled with a succession of layers of lava, which formed a mass at least five hundred feet thick, consisting of very hard and compact matter. This mass was removed from the crater, to which it was apparently firmly fixed, with the greatest ease, as the operation was not even attended by an earthquake. We are totally unacquainted with the chemical nature of the elastic vapors by which such extraordinary changes are effected. From the immense force which steam acquires when confined and exposed to a degree of heat which continually increases its expansibility, it is supposed that this elastic fluid is more active than any other in bringing about the eruptions; and this supposition is strongly supported by the immense quantity of water which descends in rain from the cloud above the column of smoke, and which appears to be produced by the condensation of the vapors accumulated in that part of the volcanic column. When, by the escape of immense volumes of elastic vapor, the interior of the earth has been sufficiently relieved from the pressure, the eruption ceases, but only after having ejected large quantities of rocks, scoriæ, sand, ashes, and lava.

During the eruption, but especially in the beginning, large pieces of rock are thrown up, as already noticed. Many of them are ejected at once; the discharges, however, are not continual, but succeed one another at intervals of some seconds. It is very probable that these rocks do not proceed from the interior of the volcano, but are the fragments of the lava with which the crater was filled up previous to the eruption. After having been broken to pieces by the force of the elastic vapors, they are raised from their sites and ejected. They are carried to a considerable elevation, and in descending some of them fall on the declivities of the volcano, whilst others return into the open crater. This explains some facts which have been observed long ago. Though many of these rocks are broken to pieces, on reaching the ground, by the great momentum they have acquired in descending from an elevation of some thousand feet, a considerable number of isolated lava rocks are met with in single masses on the base of the volcano, at spots where no stream of lava is found. They are mostly of small dimensions, but sometimes pieces are found of five or even ten feet in diameter. Attentive observers state that such pieces of rock are enveloped in a thin coat of more recent lava, assuming mostly the form of scoria, and that this coat is so loosely attached to the rock that it may be separated from it by the application of a small force. When the rocks return into the crater they are deeply immerged in the fluid mass by the momentum they have acquired; but they do not seem to experience such a degree of heat as is required to convert them into a fluid, which is proved by the circumstance of pieces of more ancient lava being frequently found embedded in the streams of lava which have issued from the volcano in a fluid state.

All the solid matter which is emitted by volcanoes consists of the same substance: it is lava. As, however, it reaches the surface of the globe under different forms, these are distinguished by different names. The term *scoria* is applied to the smaller pieces of solid matter, which are thrown up and reach the ground after passing through the air. These scoriæ, in their surface, resemble the dross of our furnaces, or coke, being full of holes, and consequently very rough and uneven. Their origin is not doubtful: they are pieces of lava which have been detached from the surface of the melted mass in the interior of the volcano by the force of the elastic vapor. These detached portions of the melted matter are probably in a different state of liquidity when they are propelled into the air. When the matter is very liquid, it assumes a more or less globular shape. Numerous pieces of scoria, however, are found, which have the form of a pear, one extremity being rounded off, whilst the other is elongated: pieces of such a shape are called, in Italy, volcanic bombes, or tears. They are not usually of large dimensions. Though many have been found of the size of a large pear, the greater number do not exceed that of a nut. Sometimes, though rarely, they are so large as to weigh from fifty to sixty pounds. The smaller ones have the most regular form. They pass through the air with a hissing sound. In reaching the ground they break to pieces, when, during their fall, they have become so cold that their outer crust has attained some degree of hardness; but they are commonly in such a state of liquidity and softness that their surface easily yields to pressure, and therefore they are flattened on that side on which they touch the ground, or take the impression of the body on which they chance to fall. Some of the poor people residing near the base of Mount Vesuvius, on observing such soft pieces, press coins or other hard objects into them, which they afterwards find an opportunity of selling to curious travellers.

Many pieces of lava, however, appear to be in a semi-liquid state upon leaving the crater, but not sufficiently soft to assume the globular shape during their passage through the air. On the other hand, they have not attained such a degree of consistency as to exclude every kind of change occasioned by the resistance of the air. They are then distorted by this resistance, and at the same time puffed up by the vapors permeating their mass whilst cooling. Such pieces assume very strange and distorted forms before they reach the ground, sometimes resembling twisted cables, at others trunks of trees, icicles, or other objects. Many pieces of scoria of such forms are found on the declivities of volcanoes and in their vicinity.

By far the greatest quantity of scoria emitted by volcanoes is of a more minute size, and this kind is known in Italy by the name of *rapilli* or *lapilli*. These pieces are in size like gravel; their surface is also extremely rough and uneven. Their origin is explained in the following way: Small pieces of lava become nearly cold and hard whilst being carried through the air to an elevation of some thousand feet; when in that state they are descending towards the crater of the volcano, they meet other pieces of lava ascending under the impulse of the elastic vapors, and are again struck upward. Thus they are repeatedly impelled up and down, and by continually coming into contact with other pieces of scoria, are broken and divided into small fragments. These rapilli are found in layers several feet deep in the vicinity of volcanoes, and are extensively used in the composition of that excellent mortar which is called Roman Cement.

Nothing, however, is ejected by the subterraneous vapor in such immense quantities as volcanic sand and ashes. They appear to be two different kinds of matter, but are really the same substance. When the substance consists of heavy, black, shining particles, it is called sand. But more commonly it is composed of much more minute particles, and resembles fine dust or flour; it has then a much lighter color, being either white, or reddish, or brownish gray. As this matter greatly resembles white wood ashes, the term ashes has been applied to it. Sand and ashes, however, have been found to be properly lava, and differ only in the degree of comminution. The sand resembles the lava even in color; but when that substance is so minutely divided as to be converted into dust, it assumes a much lighter color. It is supposed that the origin of this substance is similar to that of the rapilli, both receiving their form by the continual attrition of the pieces of lava which meet one another in the air, and are brought into violent contact by the great force with which they are impelled upward and downward. But modern philosophers, taking into consideration the almost incredible quantities of ashes which are thrown out at each eruption of a volcano, do not consider this explanation as sufficient; for it sometimes happens that streams of ashes continue to issue from the crater for several days in succession, and that the quantity ejected is so great as to fill the atmosphere in the neighborhood of the volcano to such a degree as to produce a complete darkness; therefore another explanation of the origin of the ashes has been suggested: it is supposed that a mass of lava, in a state of great liquidity, is suddenly exposed to a violent rush of elastic vapor, in which event the lava must be converted into a froth, which, when ejected from the crater, is instantly divided into the most minute particles.

A most singular and unexpected discovery was made about the year 1845 by Professor Ehrenberg respecting the remote orig n of many of the layers of ashes and pumice enveloping Pompeii. They are, he says, in great part, of organic and fresh-water origin, consisting of the silicious cases of micro scopic infusoria. What is still more surprising, this fact proves to be by no means an isolated or solitary example of an intimate relation between organic life and the results of volcanic activity. On the Rhine several beds of tuff and pumiceous conglomerate, resembling the mass incumbent upon Pompeii, and closely connected with extinct volcanoes, are now ascertained to be made up, to a great extent, of the silicious cases of infusoria, (or diatomaceæ,) invisible to the naked eye, and often half fused. No less than ninety-four distinct species have already been detected in one mass of this kind, more than one hundred and fifty feet thick, at Hochsimmer, on the left bank of the Rhine, near the Laacher-see. Some of these Rhenish infusorial accumulations appear to have fallen in showers, others to have been poured out of lake craters in the form of mud, as in the Brohl valley.

In Mexico, Peru, the Isle of France, and several other volcanic regions, analogous phenomena have been observed, and every where the species of infusoria belong to fresh-water and terrestrial genera, except in the case of the Patagonian pumiceous tuffs, specimens of which, brought home by Mr. Darwin, are found to contain the remains of marine animalcules. In various kinds of pumice ejected by volcanoes the microscope has revealed to Professor Ehrenberg the silicious cases of infusoria often half obliterated by the action of heat; and the fine dust thrown out into the air during eruptions is sometimes referable to these most minute organic substances, brought up from considerable depths, and sometimes mingled with small particles of vegetable matter.

In what manner did the solid coverings of these most minute plants and animalcules, which can only originate and increase at the surface of the earth, sink down and penetrate into subterranean cavities so as to be ejected from the volcanic orifices? We have of late years become familiar with the fact, in the process of boring artesian wells, that the seeds of plants, the remains of insects, and even small fish, with other organic bodies, are carried in an uninjured state by the underground circulation of waters to the depth of many hundred feet. With still greater facility in a volcanic region we may conjecture that water and mud, full of invisible infusoria, may be sucked down, from time to time, into subterranean rents and hollows in cavernous lava which has been permeated by gases, or in rocks dislocated by earthquakes. It often happens that a lake which has endured for centuries in a volcanic crater disappears suddenly on the approach of a new eruption. Violent shocks agitate the surrounding region, and ponds, rivers, and wells are dried up. Large cavities far below may thus become filled with fen mud, chiefly composed of the more indestructible and silicious portions of infusoria, destined, perhaps, to be one day ejected in a fragmentary or half-fused state, yet without the obliteration of all traces of organic structure.

The quantity of ashes which is sometimes thrown up by volcanoes can hardly be comprehended. The town of Pompeii was entirely buried under the ashes which were ejected from the crater of Mount Vesuvius in 79. The quantity which issued from the same volcano in 1822 was also astonishing. The ashes continued falling for twelve days, and for four days they fell very thick. In places built near the base of the volcano, as in Resina, Torre del Greco, Bosco-tre-case, the atmosphere was so filled with the dust that the darkness produced by it was as intense as in the most obscure nights, and people were obliged to carry lanterns when they left their homes. It is stated that this happened even at Amalfi, a place which, in a straight line, is sixteen miles distant from Mount Vesuvius, and separated from the volcano by a mountain ridge which rises to more than four thousand feet in height. The inhabitants of that place were astonished that day did not dawn; and when they observed that sand and ashes were falling down from the atmosphere, they were seized with a panic; for they had not the least suspicion that Mount Vesuvius was in a state of eruption — and besides, none of the inhabitants had ever witnessed a similar fall of ashes. When the ashes had ceased falling, some pains were taken in ascertaining the quantity which covered the neighborhood of the volcano, and it was found that on the declivities of the mountain it formed a layer of about three feet, and on the plain surrounding the base of the mountain from sixteen to twenty inches in depth. These heavy falls of ashes are the most destructive phenomenon with which the eruptions of volcanoes are attended. They cause much more damage than the lava, for the injury resulting from the latter is limited to comparatively small tracts, which, being overflowed by the stony mass, are rendered unavailable to cultivation sometimes for centuries. But the ashes, when they fall in large quantities, occasionally crush down buildings, cover up hamlets or towns, and choke their inhabitants. Even when the quantity is not so large they are commonly attended with considerable loss of property, as they destroy large plantations of fruit trees and vineyards. The ashes on reaching the ground are not dry; they are soaked by the moisture of the vapors issuing from the volcano, and in that state they possess a great degree of adhesion; they therefore stick to the branches and leaves of the trees, which are covered by them with a thick coat. To ascertain the quantity of ashes which may thus adhere to trees and plants, a small branch of a fig tree, having only three leaves and two immature figs, was weighed when covered with the coat of ashes, and was found to have the weight of thirty-one ounces; when the ashes were removed its weight did not exceed three ounces.

But, on the other hand, there is hardly any kind of manure which imparts to the soil such a degree of fertility, and that for a great length of time, as these volcanic ashes. It is stated that every kind of seed sown in them germinates much more quickly than in any other soil, and that plants vegetate with more vigor than in the most fertile mould. To explain this fact, it is supposed that the fructifying principle consists of a small quantity of acid, which is intimately combined with the ashes. Considering the great degree of fertility the ashes impart to every kind of soil, many authors have not hesitated to express their conviction, in the most decided manner, that all the damage produced by a fall of volcanic ashes is abundantly compensated in a few years. The knowledge of this fact is sufficient to account for the circumstance, that hardly any part of the globe can be compared, in respect of fertility, with the country surrounding volcanoes. This is well known respecting the plain of Campania, surrounding Mount Vesuvius, and that of Catania, extending along the southern declivities of Mount Etna. In South America, and especially in Central America, the most populous tracts are those situated in the vicinity of volcanoes.

With what an astonishing degree of velocity the elastic vapors must rush out from the crater of a volcano may be inferred from the elevation to which even large pieces of lava are raised by them. During an eruption of Mount Etna an attentive observer ascertained that some pieces of rock took twenty-one seconds in descending from the elevation they had attained to the top of the volcano; they were consequently carried to a height of more than seven thousand feet.

But the less heavy matter — the scoriæ, rapilli, and ashes — are carried to a much higher elevation. The column of smoke, which we mentioned in noticing the phenomena attending an eruption, is almost entirely filled with these more minute solid substances. In some instances its elevation has been measured with some degree of exactness; and it was found that the cloud at its upper extremity was six or seven miles distant from the summit of the volcano. Some persons have assigned to it a much greater elevation. Incredible as such statements may appear, we are obliged to give credit to them, when the great distances are considered to which the ashes are carried by the winds before they descend to the surface of the globe. The Greek historian Procopius states that during an eruption of Mount Vesuvius in 472 its ashes were carried to the town of Constantinople. According to the statement of Sir William Hamilton, in 1794, ashes of Mount

Vesuvius descended on some parts of Calabria, and fell at a place which was not less than one hundred and forty miles distant from the volcano. There are instances on record of ashes ejected by Mount Etna being carried to Malta, though the distance between the two places exceeds one hundred and twenty miles. Still more astonishing is the fall of volcanic ashes on the Island of Java, which happened in 1815, and is mentioned by Sir Thomas Raffles. It proceeded from the volcano of Sumbawa, which is about two hundred and eighty miles distant from the eastern extremity of Java. Yet the quantity of ashes which fell on the eastern districts of this island were sufficient to form a layer eight inches deep.

One of the most remarkable falls of ashes was that which descended on the Island of Barbadoes on the 1st of May, 1812. The day previous to that date an eruption of the volcano of St. Vincent occurred, and the detonations with which the breaking up of the volcano was attended were so intense that they were heard in the Island of Barbadoes. As it was during the war, they were taken for the firing of cannon. On the morning of the 1st of May a dark cloud was observed advancing towards the island from the west. A short time afterwards it descended and enveloped the whole island in the deepest darkness, accompanied with a very heavy fall of ashes. Persons who were out of doors were unable to see the trees, under the foliage of which they had taken refuge; in the houses it was not possible to distinguish the openings of the windows. The ashes continued falling till noon, and then the quantity which had descended had so increased that the branches of the trees were bent to the ground, and the canes of the sugar plantations were crushed. This phenomenon excited a great deal of astonishment, partly on account of the distance of the two places, which exceeds a hundred miles, but still more from the circumstance that the ashes had been carried against the trade wind, which in these parts, particularly at that season of the year, is very constant, and blows with considerable force. No satisfactory explanation can be given of this strange event, unless by supposing that the elastic vapors, on being released from the earth, escaped from the crater of the volcano with such an impetus as enabled them to carry the ashes through that region of the atmosphere in which the trade winds blow, and to raise them to the elevation in which, according to the theory of the trade winds, a current of air exists in a direction diametrically opposite to that of these winds.

Coseguina, on the south side of the Gulf of Fonseca, was in eruption in January, 1835, and some of its ashes fell at Truxillo, on the shores of the Gulf of Mexico. What is still more remarkable, on the same day, at Kingston, in Jamaica, the same shower of ashes fell, having been carried by an upper counter current against the regular east wind which was then blowing. Kingston is about seven hundred miles distant from Coseguina, and these ashes must have been more than four days in the air, having travelled one hundred and seventy miles a day. Eight leagues to the southward of the crater the ashes covered the ground to the depth of three yards and a half, destroying the woods and dwellings. Thousands of cattle perished, their bodies being in many instances one mass of scorched flesh. Deer and other wild animals sought the towns for protection; many birds and quadrupeds were found suffocated in the ashes; and the neighboring streams were strewed with dead fish. Such facts throw light on geological monuments; for in the ashes thrown out at remote periods from the volcanoes of Auvergne — now extinct — we find the bones and skeletons of lost species of quadrupeds.

In enumerating the phenomena with which an eruption is attended, it was stated that towards its close the column of smoke rises to an immense elevation, and expands at its upper extremity uniformly on all sides, so as to form a circular cloud of immense diameter resting on a proportionally slender and very high column. The constant recurrence of this phenomenon has, of course, excited the attention of natural philosophers, who try to explain it in the following manner: when the ashes carried up by the elastic vapors attain a great elevation, they begin to descend towards the crater by the effect of their gravity as soon as the force of the elastic powers begins to decrease. When thus descending they meet in their way the ascending ashes. The elastic vapors which propel these ashes upward resist the impulse which has been imparted by their gravity to the descending particles, and compel them to rise again. As, however, the mass which they have to sustain is in this manner greatly increased, the elastic vapors are unable to overcome entirely the resistance opposed to their rising in a perpendicular line, and a portion of them is thus pressed out on the sides. This process going on for some time, the upper extremity of the column begins to spread, and by degrees forms in the air that hanging circular roof on the top of the column.

In this cloud phenomena are constantly observed which apparently originate in electricity. Flashes of forked lightning, frequently a dozen at once, are seen rushing through the cloud in zigzag lines in every direction, and they are attended by a rolling thunder, which may easily be distinguished from the rumbling noise proceeding from the volcano. Though all circumstances concur to impart to these phenomena an electric character, the naturalists for some time doubted whether they owed their origin to electricity. They were rather inclined to consider them only as explosions of inflammable gases. Such explosions, however, could not kill persons at a great distance from the spot where they originated; but it is recorded that during an eruption of Mount Katlugia, in Iceland, in 1755, the lightning originating in the volcanic cloud killed eleven horses and two persons, and some rocks standing in its way were perforated with cylindrical holes. This proves them to be real electric phenomena.

Their origin may be also satisfactorily explained by the well-established laws of nature. By numerous experiments it has been proved that electricity is developed when aqueous vapors are condensed and converted into water, or when water passes into steam. It can hardly be questioned that the first kind of process is continually going on in a volcanic cloud of such dimensions. We cannot doubt that the condensation of hot vapors must be very rapid along the periphery of the cloud, where the vapor comes in contact with the much colder air of the atmosphere surrounding the cloud. In this part of the cloud, therefore, the electric phenomena ought to be very frequent — almost incessant; and so they are. The most exact observers state unanimously that the strongest flashes of lightning are observed to spring from near the outer edge of the cloud, and that usually they thence pass towards its centre.

The most remarkable of the volcanic productions is the lava. It has been stated that, a long time before an eruption takes place, small quantities of lava frequently issue from the cone of eruption in the middle of the crater, and that its cavity is gradually filled up by them. It has also been noticed that when no cone of eruption is formed in the crater, the lava sometimes forces its way through the sides of the volcano before it succeeds in breaking open the centre of the crater. But by far the largest quantity of lava is emitted during the eruption.

When a cone of eruption exists in the crater, the approach of the eruption is indicated by the appearance of fire, which is observed for many days, or even weeks, on the top of the mountain. This is not an actual fire, but only the reflection of the melted and hot masses which are alternately ascending and descending in the volcanic chimney. The light issuing from them is reflected by the vapors, which are continually evolved from the burning mass, and escape through the orifice of the chimney.

The lava is for a long time ascending and descending in the volcanic chimney before it rises so high as to attain its orifice, and, running over the rim of the crater, descends on the declivities of the volcano to the lower countries. This delay is easily accounted for, when it is considered that it is by the increase of the expansive powers of the elastic vapors that the lava is expelled from the volcano. These powers are, doubtless, continually on the increase. When their intensity is considerably augmented, they press on the lava in the volcanic chimney, and raise it to some elevation, but soon find the means of escaping through the liquid matter in the form of vapors and smoke. When, however, the vapors have for a longer time been exposed to a very intense degree of heat, their expansibility is augmented to such a degree that they are enabled to raise the whole mass of lava to a great elevation, and to form a counterpoise to a column of such matter several thousand feet in height. Then the lava is pushed up to the very orifice of the chimney, and overflows the rim of the crater.

The manner in which the lava runs from the crater is so natural that it does not require to be further noticed. But when it breaks out of the sides of the volcano, this event is attended by some phenomena which deserve to be considered. It frequently happens that a lateral eruption takes place whilst the lava is running out from the crater at the top. In such a case it ceases flowing from the crater, and though the other phenomena of the eruption continue, they are commonly observed to abate perceptibly. The lateral eruptions are effected by means of rents. It would appear that whilst the lava is gradually raised higher and higher in the volcanic chimney by the increased expansion of the elastic vapors, and consequently presses with greater force on its sides, it often happens that at some spots the sides of the mountain are not strong enough to resist the pressure. They give way at such places by bursting open and forming a chasm. These chasms are sometimes of great length. During an eruption of Mount Etna a chasm was formed which began at the top of the cone, and extended for more than ten miles to a place called Nicolosi. Before Mount Vesuvius opened its crater in 1794, its western side burst with a chasm, which, at its upper extremity, was two hundred and forty feet wide and more than three thousand feet long. The bursting of these chasms is accompanied with a very loud crash. As these chasms extend far below the level which the melted matter has attained in the volcanic chimney, the lava presses into the opening; but as the pressure, of course, is greatest at the lowest extremity of the chasm on which the whole column of lava in the chimney above it presses with all its force, the lava issues from that spot in greater abundance and with great violence. Consequently, an opening of considerable dimensions is soon formed. The lava in the chimney sinks down to the level of this opening, and a portion of the elastic vapor soon finds its way through it. These outpourings bring with them scoriæ and ashes, which are lodged on the sides of the opening, and thus a cone of eruption is soon formed. But when so much of the melted matter has run out through this cone of eruption that the mass in the chimney sinks below its level, the flow of the lava, of course, ceases, and only scoriæ and ashes are thrown up, by which the cone of eruption is considerably increased in size. Now, it occasionally happens that the opening in this cone of eruption is blocked up either by an accumulation of scoriæ and ashes, or more probably by a portion of the lava getting so cold as to lose its liquidity. As soon as this vent is closed, the heat in the chimney is increased, and with it the expansion of the subterraneous vapors. This again raises the mass in the chimney, and the consequence is another pressure. In such circumstances, the old chasm opens at a lower point, and is prolonged towards the base of the volcano. At its lower extremity lava runs out, and another cone of eruption is soon formed, which lies below the first on the same line. This process is sometimes repeated several times. On the declivities of Mount Etna twelve such cones of eruption are found lying one below the other, in a straight line. It is reasonably conjectured that they have been formed by the same chasm, which must therefore have been subjected to twelve breakings up. Several of them are also met with on the sides of Mount Vesuvius. When these cones of eruption are of small dimensions, it commonly happens that they disappear after a time, the loose matter of which they consist being dispersed over the adjacent grounds. But there are still many found which are of considerable size. When, by the lapse of time and the effect of the atmospheric moisture, the volcanic matter forming their surface has been decomposed, and changed into a rich mould, these hills soon become covered with vegetation, and are generally found overgrown with bushes and trees. In such a state these conical hills impress a peculiar character of beauty on such volcanic regions.

It is a remarkable fact that the frequency of the eruptions appears to be in an inverse proportion to the height of the volcanoes. The lower the volcano, the more frequent are its eruptions. Those volcanoes which are permanently active, as Stromboli on the Lipari Islands, and Izalco in Central America, are comparatively only large hills. The first-mentioned of these two volcanoes attains an elevation of only twenty-eight hundred and seventy-eight feet above the sea level. Mount Vesuvius is but about a thousand feet higher, yet its eruptions occur only at intervals of many years. They are, however, much more frequent than those of Mount Etna, which rises to ten thousand two hundred and eighty feet. The Peak of Teneriffe, which is twelve thousand three hundred and eighty feet high, very rarely has an eruption, and the colossal volcanic cones which crown the great masses of the Ecuadorian Andes do not exhibit a decided activity more than once in a century.

Not less remarkable is the fact, that from the volcanoes of small size the lava always flows off by the crater, but in those of larger dimensions the heated matter is frequently discharged by lateral eruptions. From Mount Stromboli the lava always issues from the crater, and never by a lateral rent. In Mount Vesuvius both kinds of eruption are in most cases united. Sometimes all the volcanic matter is thrown out from the crater; but frequently one or two lateral rents are formed,

Peak of Teneriffe. Height 12,250 feet.

from the apertures of which large quantities of lava are discharged. In Mount Etna the lateral discharges of lava are much more frequent than those from the top of the volcano. Dolomieu thinks that the eruptions from the crater at the top are in proportion to those by lateral rents as one to ten. The Peak of Teneriffe, as far as our historical knowledge reaches, has never discharged lava from the crater at its top, which appears only as a solfatara of moderate activity; its lava has always been ejected by apertures in the sides of the mountain. The largest volcanoes in the world, as those of the Andes, do not appear to throw out lava; for, with the exception of Mount Antisana, at whose base Humboldt observed a small stream of lava, he could not discover that substance in their vicinity. The volcanic matter issues from them only in the form of scoriæ and volcanic ashes.

These two facts appear to be connected with each other, and to arise from the same cause. Perhaps they may be explained, by supposing that the differences mentioned depend on the state of liquidity in which the volcanic matter reaches the orifice of the chimney. In low volcanoes the melted mass is nearer the seat of heat, and consequently it enters the chimney and rushes out of it in such a state of liquidity, that it never possesses that degree of consistency which would be required to shut the chimney and crater completely. Therefore these smaller volcanoes never have their activity interrupted. In volcanoes of medium size, as in Mount Vesuvius and in Mount Hecla, the melted matter reaches the orifice of the crater in such a state of liquidity only when the heat in the interior has attained a great degree of intensity. When this heat begins to diminish, the melted matter gets cold on its surface, and consolidates, and thus the volcanic chimney is blocked up, and does not reopen until the heat in the interior has again acquired such intensity as to melt the lava, and to break its upper crust by the expansive power of the elastic vapors. The volcanoes which exceed ten thousand feet in elevation have the orifice of their volcanic chimney so far from the focus of heat, that the lava which obstructs the passage can only be melted and thrown out in extraordinary cases; and even then it more frequently breaks through the sides of the volcano than through the crater at the top. The colossal volcanoes of the Andes have their roots in an extensive mountain mass, whose elevation above the sea level varies between eight and ten thousand feet. The melted matter in their volcanic chimneys must, therefore, rise to that elevation before it can break out at the base of the volcanic cones. Ere it attains such a height, it may be supposed to have become so cold as to be hardly liquid, and therefore no lateral eruptions appear to have ever occurred, except at the base of Mount Antisana, as already observed. At a great distance below the orifice of the chimney, the surface of the melted matter has probably acquired a degree of consistency bordering on that of a solid body. The liquid matter is covered with a solid crust, like the water of our lakes, in winter, with ice. The elastic vapors, rushing up from below, break this crust into pieces, and raise it in the chimney; but its gravity prevents it from being ejected, until the pieces of the rock are broken into scoriæ, or even converted into ashes, by being tossed about for a length of time in the volcanic chimney. This theory is, perhaps, sufficient to account for the fact, that these volcanoes never emit lava, but only immense quantities of scoriæ and ashes.

The manner in which the lava is disgorged from the crater of an intermittent volcano during an eruption has not been observed, on account of the danger with which any approach to it at that time is attended; but the breaking out of the melted matter from lateral rents has frequently been seen. It would seem that the velocity with which the lava rushes from such an opening is in an inverse proportion to the elevation of the opening. The less elevated the opening, the more rapid the rush of the burning stream. When, in 1794, Mount Vesuvius made one of its most memorable eruptions, the lava issued in the night from an opening which was only sixteen hundred and fifteen feet above the sea. Many persons, who observed it from the flat roofs of the town of Naples, stated that they had seen the burning mass shot out from the opening in parabolic lines. Sir William Hamilton had, in 1767, an opportunity of observing such an eruption, and describes it in the following manner: "On a sudden I heard a violent noise, and about a quarter of a mile from the place where I stood, the mountain split, and with much noise from this new mouth a fountain of liquid fire shot up many feet high, and then like a torrent ran directly towards us. The earth shook, and at the same time a torrent of pumice stones fell thick upon us; in an instant clouds of black smoke and ashes caused an almost total darkness; the explosions from the top of the mountains were much louder than any thunder I ever heard, and the smell of sulphur was very offensive." All eye witnesses agree in stating that the lava issues from the lateral rents with a violent rush. This probably is partly the effect of the great pressure with which it is driven out, and partly of the state of extreme liquidity of the melted matter.

At a short distance from the opening the lava begins to run with a regular current, similar to the water in a river. At its upper end the stream is of narrow width, but it grows wider in proceeding farther downward. Whenever the liquid mass meets with an obstacle to its straight course, it divides into two or more branches, which, however, usually join again somewhat lower down. When the surface over which the stream runs presents a steep descent, the liquid mass shoots down in a cascade, and after having collected below it, it continues flowing, until a depression in the ground, or the diminished declivity of its surface, puts a stop to its farther progress. At the lower extremity of the stream the matter unites so as to form a pond or lake. Sometimes, however, as is frequently the case with the lava of Mount Vesuvius and Mount Etna, the stream reaches the sea, and, in pouring its contents into the water, encroaches on its dominions. In daytime, unless the observer is quite close to the stream, the lava has no appearance of fire; only a white, thick smoke is seen, which marks its course. At night it affords a most magnificent spectacle—that of a burning river descending from the declivity of a mountain.

During its course the liquid matter undergoes a succession of changes. Having been exposed to the air for a short time, the lava begins to lose a portion of its heat by radiation, and assumes on its surface a greater degree of consistency. The heat which is evolved from the mass soon diminishes so much, that the lava may be closely approached without danger at no great distance from the spot where it left the mountain. At such places experiments have been made to ascertain the degree of consistency of the matter. Large stones thrown on it with great force do not sink; they make but a slight impression, float on the surface, and are carried down the stream. Some attempts have been made to push a sharp-pointed stick into the running matter, but they were attended with very little effect; the impression was but slight, though the lava appeared to be as liquid as water. In this state the matter runs very regularly, and almost without a noise. The only sound which is heard is a kind of bubbling, produced by the evolution of the vapors from the hot matter. From time to time a crackling is audible, which arises from the lava passing with greater force at some places. These feeble sounds, and the quiet flow of the red-hot masses, contrast in a very striking and not unpleasant manner with the continual and thundering explosions on the top of the volcano, and the loud crashings proceeding from its interior.

Lower down, the surface of the lava assumes a different aspect. When the consistency of the matter has so far increased as to impart to the upper layer a considerable degree of viscidity, its surface begins to be partly covered with solid matter of a peculiar form and description. The heat is evolved from the mass in the form of bubbles of vapor. These bubbles, in passing through the viscous layer, raise a portion of it, impressing on the raised matter their own form. Many of these protuberances are solidified during the process, and the stream appears to be strewed with little eminences of a conical form, which at their highest point are perforated by one or more small openings, by which the vapors find a vent. When, however, the matter has not attained that degree of consistency completely, only the most elevated portion of the protuberances are solidified, and the lava, being still soft, gives way. Then the cone-formed eminences fall into the stream, where they preserve their shape, forming small funnel-shaped depressions, which bear some resemblance to the eddies which are observed near the pillars of bridges. Some of these depressions are several inches in diameter. Thus the surface of the burning stream is by degrees covered with alternate eminences and depressions, flowing down with the current, which imparts to the whole mass a very peculiar aspect.

Still farther down it is found that the stream of running lava is bridged over by a layer of scoria. This change is produced in the following mode: From the sides of the slowly advancing mass hot scoria falls down, which by degrees accumulates on its sides so as to form a dike, similar to those dikes by which rivers are prevented from inundating the adjacent countries. The lava now begins to run in a channel of its own construction. When the dikes on the sides have been raised, by the continual addition of new scoria, to such an elevation that they are equal in height to the upper surface of the stream, the bridging over of the mass begins from either side. The pieces of scoria which are floating on the surface of the mass are arrested by some projecting piece united to the dikes, and are soon cemented together by the heat radiating from the mass below. Other pieces of scoria are soon attached to them in the same way, and thus layers of scoria are formed on the surface of the running lava, which gradually approximate to each other until they meet in the middle and are united. The lava then begins to run beneath an arched vault. It sometimes happens that the lava, having left the vault, is not succeeded by any body of running matter. The vault preserves, of course, its form, and thus it happens that hollow cylinders or pipes of great dimensions are frequently met with. Sir William Hamilton describes several cylinders of this kind. Their outer surface presented the greatest imaginable roughness and unevenness, but in the interior he found their sides as smooth as if they had been polished, which he with reason ascribed to the hot lava having for many weeks run through them. At many places he found large pieces of indurated lava attached to the sides or upper surface of the vault, and many of the rents which occurred there were incrusted by beautiful efflorescences of salt. Some of these cylinders have been found fifty yards long and upwards. In some parts of Iceland they are very numerous.

The forming of these pipes, however, can only take place when the lava descends a declivity having a regular slope. As this is rarely the case, the hollow cylinders of lava are not of frequent occurrence. When the slope is irregular, as is commonly the case, the upper part of the vault is broken down, and separated into many pieces. These large pieces of scoria, of course, fall on the running lava, and are carried away with it. They rapidly increase in number by the accession of other pieces; so that at last the whole surface of the stream is completely covered with them. When, therefore, a stream of lava is examined near its termination, this matter, which near its source is a glowing fiery mass, appears to be nothing but a heap of black, rough pieces of scoria, huddled together in an irregular manner, but which are in continual motion. When these pieces jostle and are pressed against each other, they emit a peculiar sound, not unlike that produced by small pieces of glass tossed together. Only where a small interstice occurs between the masses of scoria can the red-hot lava be perceived flowing under the black layer. It sometimes happens that whilst the great mass is slowly continuing its course, a portion of it is detached, breaks through the dike by throwing the scoria aside, and running out with the pure, clear color of fire, alarms the looker-on who chances to have approached too near the spot.

There is probably no other liquid matter which is possessed of such a degree of cohesion as the running lava. We must come to this conclusion when we find that this matter does not spread over the inclined plane down which it runs, but forms a ridge, having exactly the shape of an embankment, or a rampart with regularly sloping sides. The ridge has commonly a considerable height. Even small streams of lava are found to rise from ten to twelve feet above the adjacent ground. Larger streams are sometimes from forty to fifty feet high. The lava which issued from the Skaptaar Yökul was at some places from ninety to a hundred feet above the ground over which it had flowed.

That portion of the lava which forms the upper surface runs more rapidly than that which flows near the solid surface of the earth. This portion of the stream has not only to overcome the pressure of the mass above it, but also the inequalities of the ground over which it passes. Its progress is therefore considerably slower. The effect of this difference is, that the upper layers are always sliding over those below them, and consequently it is found, at the lower extremity of the stream, that the lava advances by the upper layers involving the lower ones. As in the mean time quantities of scoria are falling down from the upper layer of the stream, the descending lava finds its way paved, as it were, by such pieces of volcanic matter. When, therefore, a stream of lava is examined after it has ceased flowing, it is found that not only are its surface and sides covered with scoria, but also that it rests on a stratum of such volcanic matter, which, however, is firmly attached to the lava, the scoria having been partially remelted by the hot matter which covered it.

In several accounts of volcanic eruptions, instances are mentioned in which the lava has been observed flowing up hill. This phenomenon is explained as follows: When the flowing stream of lava arrives in its progress at an eminence elevated several feet, and is therefore compelled to change the direction of its course, it cannot be effected suddenly on account of the heaviness of the matter and its cohesion. Meanwhile it is pressed forward from behind by the whole mass which descends from the place of eruption. By means of this pressure it is forced in a straight line up the eminence opposing its progress until it can escape on one or the other side. At such places, therefore, it appears to flow up hill. This is also the reason why hills of lava of considerable dimensions are met with at places where the matter has been compelled to ascend by any such cause.

Another phenomenon has still more attracted the attention and exercised the ingenuity of natural philosophers. When a running stream of lava approaches a high wall which extends exactly across its course, it does not touch it, but stops at a distance of a few inches. When that enormous mass of lava was descending from Mount Etna, in 1669, which partially destroyed the town of Catania, it advanced to the strong walls of a convent of Benedictines, but turned aside without touching them. This fact was considered as a miracle by the inhabitants. At the same time the Castle of Catania was surrounded by high masses of lava, which, after having filled up its moats containing sea water, stopped a very short distance from the walls. In 1808 an eruption took place in the Island of St. George, one of the Azores. One of the streams of lava ran to the convent of the Ursuline nuns. At its approach the nuns appeared on the walls with the image of their saint, and when the lava had approached close to the walls, it turned aside and flowed into the sea. This was, of course, also considered as a notable miracle. Philosophers, rejecting such an explanation, have accounted for the phenomenon in a different way. They say that this singular fact is to be ascribed to the resistance produced by the aqueous vapors which evolve from the slowly advancing mass. These vapors are compressed in the narrow space between the lava and the walls, from which they can only escape at the top. Their expansibility is thus increased to such a degree that they are enabled to stop the progress of the mass, and to turn it aside.

In some accounts of eruptions it is stated that flames have been seen issuing from a stream of lava; it was therefore formerly supposed that the lava contained inflammable matter. But modern writers have discovered that these flames are to be ascribed to the combustion of heterogeneous matter. When the lava reaches such parts of the country as are covered with vegetation, all the grass and plants are dried up at its approach by the heat evolved. The scoria falling down from the extremity of the advancing lava pushes this dry vegetable matter forward, so that after a time a heap of it is seen in front of the stream. Now, it must sometimes happen that these heaps of dry grass come into contact with the red-hot lava, and then they take fire in an instant, and produce the flames that have been noticed.

When a stream of lava comes into contact with a large tree, it sometimes happens that the lava touches the tree only on one side. In such a case that side of the tree which was in contact with the lava is converted into charcoal, whilst the other continues to vegetate. When the tree is surrounded by the lava, the heat radiating from the mass causes that part which is above the stream to take fire, and it is consumed with flames resembling flashes of lightning. But the lower part of the trunk, which is suddenly enclosed on all sides so that the access of air is excluded, is not consumed; its exterior parts are converted into charcoal, whilst the pith is dried up. It is therefore not a rare occurrence to find charcoal and brown, dry pieces of wood embedded in the lava. When, by the lapse of time, these embedded trunks have been decayed by moisture and other causes, the lava is found to be perforated by a number of perpendicular cylindrical holes, resembling exactly the form of the trees.

Occasionally a very loud report, similar to the firing of a cannon, attended with a flash of lightning, is heard to proceed from a stream of lava. This happens when the lava runs over a swampy ground or a very moist soil. The sudden conversion of the water into steam, and its decomposition, produce a commotion which for some moments is able to stop the progress of the stream. The steam breaks with great noise through the mass, tears asunder the crust of scoria which envelops it, and throws both the lava and the scoria into great confusion. As a portion of the steam is decomposed, the hydrogen explodes, and produces the loud report above mentioned, with the accompanying flash.

The influx of the running lava into the sea has given occasion to many elevated poetical descriptions. It is represented as an awful spectacle, as a struggle between two inimical elements. But in all these pictures the event is much exaggerated, though the facts which give rise to them are true to a certain extent. When the hot lava reaches the sea, the water with which it comes into immediate contact is suddenly raised to the boiling temperature. It is consequently converted into steam, which process is attended with a loud, hissing sound. But as by the conversion of the water into steam a great quantity of caloric is absorbed, the cold which is thus generated speedily converts the surface of the glowing mass into a thick and solid crust, by which all communication between the liquid lava and the sea is directly intercepted. Then the sea water sinks, of course, below the boiling point. The hardened lava is, however, pushed farther into the sea by the succeeding masses, and thus the sea is compelled to recede. In this progress the lava frequently splits; but in the same moment the aqueous vapors issue from the rent with such a violence that the water is prevented from penetrating into its recesses. Whilst this process is in action the water becomes turbid to some distance from the lava, and fish which chance to be in the vicinity are killed.

The masses of lava which are thus protruded into the sea are sometimes of very considerable dimensions. At the eruption of Mount Vesuvius in 1794, a stream of lava, after destroying the town of Torre del Greco, entered the sea, and drove it back to a distance of three hundred and eighty feet from its former shores. The width of this mass is, according to an exact measurement, twelve hundred and four feet. It is elevated fifteen feet above the sea, and is believed to have an equal depth under water. The lava, therefore, which entered the sea during this eruption, forms a mass of more than thirteen millions of cubic feet. The streams of lava flowing from Mount Vesuvius which have reached the sea are numerous, as may be inferred from the fact that the eastern shores of the Bay of Naples, between Portici and Torre dell' Annunziata, which two places are about ten miles distant from each other, are formed by a succession of promontories composed of lava. The same observation applies to the eastern shores of the Island of Sicily, where the coast between Taormina on the north and Catania on the south, a distance of more than thirty miles, consists of high cliffs of lava, with only a few spots between them of low tracts of moderate extent covered with a soil deposited by the sea. At some places, as for instance near Aci Reale, these lava cliffs are more than fifty feet high.

In the published accounts of eruptions we find that particular care has been taken to notice the velocity with which the stream of lava advanced. By comparing these statements it is found that the difference in this respect is very great. As an instance in which the lava ran with extraordinary rapidity, that of Mount Vesuvius in 1794 may be adduced. This stream of lava took only six hours to run from the spot of the eruption to the sea, a distance of more than four miles. Much greater still was the velocity of that stream which, in 1804, broke out from the southern declivity of Mount Vesuvius. It is said that it moved forward with the rapidity of wind. In a few minutes it had reached the vineyards; and an author asserts that in four minutes it passed over a space of three quarters of a mile in length, though the slope over which it ran was very gentle. It appears that in these two instances the lava broke out at a place not greatly elevated above the level of the sea, and that in such cases the lava is possessed of a very high degree of liquidity, which of course must greatly promote its rapid progress — perhaps more so than a greater declivity of the descent. The above-mentioned stream reached the sea five hours after it had issued from the volcano. As the melted matter had its consistency continually increased by the radiation of the heat and its exposure to the atmosphere, it is evident that the stream runs slower the farther it advances from its source. This appears, also, to be the reason why the streams of lava get wider in proportion as they advance from the spot where they left the volcano.

Numerous instances are also recorded of streams of lava which advanced very slowly. A still living observer found a stream on the declivities of Mount Etna which had continued flowing for nine months, and did not advance more than five feet in twenty-four hours. It is stated that a stream of lava broke out at the base of Mount Etna in 1614 which continued in motion for ten years, and in this time did not advance more than about two miles.

The philosophers who have made the phenomena attending eruptions an object of their most assiduous researches, have been particularly anxious to ascertain the degree of heat of the lava when it leaves the interior of the volcano. They think that by ascertaining this they would be enabled to form some idea of the degree of heat employed in the interior of the globe to melt the matter there collected. The shortest way of ascertaining this point would doubtless have been to measure by a pyrometer the heat of the lava at its efflux from the volcano. But no attempt of this kind could be made, because the heat radiating from the lava near its source is so intense that it is impossible to approach the mass within a distance of thirty or forty feet. The possibility of placing the instrument so as to make it available for the required observation is therefore quite hopeless.

The want of such direct observation has given rise to a difference of opinion among philosophers. Some are of opin-

The Val del Bove, on Mount Etna, as seen from the crater of 1819.

ion that the heat of the lava cannot be very intense. They think it probable that it does not equal the heat which we are able to produce in our furnaces. They are inclined to consider the lava as a kind of liquid pap strongly heated, and compare it to clay which has been well soaked with water, and thus has attained a degree of cohesive liquidity; but they deny that the nature of the particles of this mass is changed by the heat. Others, and among them the most conspicuous of the living philosophers, consider the degree of heat possessed by the lava as being at least equal to the most intense heat we are able to produce by artificial means. The flowing lava is, in their opinion, a substance completely melted, like molten metals or glass, which acquires its solidity only by cooling, and not as an aggregate of solid particles, which, during their state of liquidity, are gliding over each other.

To support this opinion they have collected a number of facts, and made several experiments. They first point out the state of extreme liquidity in which the lava issues from the volcano. It has, as already stated, been frequently seen spouting out like a fountain in parabolic curves; it sometimes runs down a declivity with a velocity which can only be compared to that of a torrent; it has in some cases been found to flow, in the space of an hour, over a distance of four thousand feet,—as at Mount Vesuvius in 1804. When such a heavy matter as lava runs so quickly, it must be extremely liquid, and must therefore be completely melted. But it is known that lava is one of the substances which can only be reduced to such a state by the application of a very intense degree of heat.

Several facts have been recorded, proving that the flowing lava is able to melt masses of rock and pieces of ancient lava. An Italian naturalist, who visited Mount Vesuvius during its eruption in 1779, observed in the crust of a stream of lava one of the funnel-formed openings, through the orifice of which he saw the lava in a constant state of ebullition. The sound which issued from the opening resembled that murmuring noise which is heard when a fat liquid is boiling. He threw into the opening several pieces of scoria which he picked up in the neighborhood, and observed that these scoriæ soon became hot, and shortly afterwards melted like pitch. When Spallanzani became acquainted with this fact, he tried to melt such scoria by artificial means, to effect which he was obliged to apply a degree of heat in a reverberatory kiln which was sufficient to melt iron. Nevertheless, the place where the Italian naturalist made the experiment was at a considerable distance from the opening in the mountain from which the lava had issued.

When the running lava, after reaching inhabited places, comes in contact with metallic substances, it effects such changes as could only be produced by the application of the most intense heat. This was ascertained beyond all doubt with regard to the lava which, in 1794, destroyed the town of Torre del Greco. It was found that glass had been transformed into a milk-white, transparent, stony mass; and it was then mentioned that in 1767 some vessels of glass had been melted by the lava running under the place where they stood. Iron had been expanded so as to occupy three or four times its former volume, and its internal texture was entirely changed. Other metals had undergone similar, or even greater changes. The chemists, examining all these changes with attention, and comparing them with those effected in these metallic substances when placed in furnaces, came to the conclusion that the lava which issued in 1794 from Mount Vesuvius must have possessed, when it came to Torre del Greco, a degree of heat which was at least equal to that required to melt iron. Iron can only be melted, according to the experiments of the most accredited chemists, when the scale of Reaumur has risen to six thousand and sixty degrees, or that of Fahrenheit to thirteen thousand six hundred and sixty-seven. Torre del Greco, where these metals were thus changed, is at least three miles from the place where the lava left the mountain; and in arriving at this distance the melted matter had been exposed for six hours to the effects of the atmosphere.

When all these facts and experiments are duly considered, we cannot but agree with the opinion of Sir James Hall, that the heat in the interior of the volcano must be much more intense than is required to melt the stony mass of the lava into a perfectly liquid body, and that consequently it greatly exceeds any degree of heat which we are able to produce by artificial means.

We may arrive at nearly the same conclusion by considering the length of time required for lava to become quite cold. Its surface, indeed, soon becomes so cooled as to be covered by a crust of solid matter; and it is probable that this is partly accelerated by the vapors escaping from the interior of the mass. The solid covering is composed, as already stated, of scoria. This matter is a very bad conductor of heat; the refrigeration of the mass therefore goes on very slowly. This is proved by the fact that it is possible to pass over a stream of running lava, when covered with scoria, without sustaining any injury. Sir William Hamilton, when examining the lava which had issued from Mount Vesuvius in 1779, had very closely approached to a stream, when, by the change of the wind, he found himself suddenly exposed to a very thick cloud of suffocating vapors, and a current of extremely hot air. The nature of the locality prevented him from retracing his steps, and he was aware that he was in danger. But his guide extricated him from this perilous situation by informing him that it was possible to pass over the lava. He got over without making any perceptible impression on the surface of the stream, and without experiencing any inconvenience, except a very sensible degree of heat beneath his feet. He therefore recommends this course to persons who find them selves unexpectedly enclosed by the sudden separation of a stream of lava into two arms, as sometimes happens. That a stream of running lava may be passed in this way was shown by the inhabitants of Torre del Greco in 1794, who, only twelve hours after their town had been overrun by the lava, returned to their homes, passing over the stream which was still flowing.

"A remarkable discovery," says Sir Charles Lyell, "was made on Etna, in 1828, of a great mass of ice, preserved for many years,—perhaps for centuries,—from melting, by the singular accident of a current of red-hot lava having flowed over it. The following are the facts in attestation of a phenomenon which must at first sight appear of so paradoxical a character. The extraordinary heat experienced in the south of Europe during the summer and autumn of 1828 caused the supplies of snow and ice, which had been preserved in the spring of that year for the use of Catania and the adjoining parts of Sicily and the Island of Malta, to fail entirely. Great distress was consequently felt for want of a commodity regarded in those countries as one of the necessaries of life rather than an article of luxury, and the abundance of which contributes in some of the larger cities to the salubrity of the water and the general health of the community. The magistrates of Catania applied to Signor M. Gemmellaro, in the hope that his local knowledge of Etna might enable him to point out some crevice or natural grotto on the mountain where drift snow was still preserved. Nor were they disappointed; for he had long suspected that a small mass of perennial ice at the foot of the highest cone was part of a large and continuous glacier covered by a lava current. Having procured a large body of workmen, he quarried into this ice, and proved the super-position of the lava for several hundred yards, so as completely to satisfy himself that nothing but the subsequent flowing of the lava over the ice could account for the position of the glacier. Unfortunately for the geologist, the ice was so extremely hard, and the excavation so expensive, that there is no probability of the operations being renewed.

"On the 1st of December, 1828, I visited this spot, which is on the south-east side of the cone, and not far above the Casa Inglese; but the fresh snow had already nearly filled up the new opening, so that it had only the appearance of the mouth of a grotto. I do not, however, question the accuracy of the conclusion of Signor Gemmellaro, who, being well acquainted with all the appearances of drift snow in the fissures and cavities of Etna, had recognized, even before the late excavations, the peculiarity of the position of the ice in this locality. We may suppose that, at the commencement of the eruption, a deep mass of drift snow had been covered by volcanic sand showered down upon it before the descent of the lava. A dense stratum of this fine dust mixed with scoria is well known to be an extremely bad conductor of heat; and the shepherds in the higher regions of Etna are accustomed to provide water for their flocks during summer by strewing a layer of volcanic sand a few inches thick over the snow, which effectually prevents the heat of the sun from penetrating.

"Suppose the mass of snow to have been preserved from liquefaction until the lower part of the lava had consolidated, we may then readily conceive that a glacier thus protected, at the height of ten thousand feet above the level of the sea, would endure as long as the snows of Mont Blanc, unless melted by volcanic heat from below. When I visited the great crater in the beginning of winter, (December 1, 1828,) I found the crevices in the interior incrusted with thick ice, and in some cases hot vapors were actually streaming out between masses of ice and the rugged and steep walls of the crater.

"After the discovery of Signor Gemmellaro, it would not be surprising to find in the cones of the Icelandic volcanoes, which are covered for the most part with perpetual snow, repeated alternations of lava streams and glaciers. We have, indeed, Lieutenant Kendall's authority for the fact that Deception Island, in New South Shetland, latitude sixty-two degrees fifty-five minutes south, is principally composed of alternate layers of volcanic ashes and ice."

The layer of scoria, enveloping the lava on all sides, being, as we stated before, a bad conductor of heat, is of course unable to abstract the caloric quickly from the flowing mass so as to promote its consolidation. But this circumstance alone is certainly insufficient to account for the well-established fact, that the lava preserves for a great length of time, for many months, and even years, a very high degree of heat. Spallanzani, in visiting the summit of Mount Etna in 1788, passed a stream of lava, at the base of the cone, which had ceased running eleven months before, but was still smoking. In the crust of scoria he found some rents, through which the still red-hot matter was perceptible even in the light of day; and a stick which he pushed into one of these rents caught fire immediately. Sir William Hamilton made the same experiment with the lava of Mount Vesuvius, five years after it had left the volcano; and he mentions several instances of lava having been found still smoking three, or even five years after it had issued from the mouth of the volcano. Such facts compel us to assume that the lava has been heated in the great furnace of nature to a degree of intensity of which we can form no idea, for want of any kind of experience which could serve us as a point of comparison.

When the lava, after having become solid, is examined, it is found that it is a hard, sonorous mass. Its outer surface presents nothing but a succession of irregular cavities and depressions, resembling bubbles which have burst. Where no disruption, translocation, or swelling of the interior has occurred, the mass is extremely rough, and resembles coarse porous scoria full of holes. Below this layer of scoria the lava continues to enclose bubbles; but they grow smaller in proportion as we penetrate deeper, and at the same time these bubbles occur at greater distances from each other. Towards the middle of the mass they disappear entirely; for the lava there forms a compact and uniform substance, without any trace of the peculiar form which it assumes in the scoria.

The occurrence of the bubbles in the lava is easily accounted for. They owe their origin to the escape of the vapors from the interior of the mass whilst cooling. As the process of refrigeration proceeds from the exterior to the interior, while the vapors and gases take an opposite course, they soon arrive at those parts of the mass which have already attained such a degree of consistency as not to yield to the pressure of the vapors, and consequently they are there stopped and shut up.

Though the lava is a compact and uniform mass, it is not always of the same mineralogical character, but differs according to the proportion of the various substances which have been subjected to the process of melting in the interior of the earth. It is even found that the lavas of the same volcano, which have been ejected at different periods, varied considerably, if examined in their component parts. Mineralogists distinguish a considerable number of lavas, and have arranged them under two principal heads—the stony and the glassy lavas. The first-mentioned class comprehends those which have the appearance of hard stones; their texture is sometimes granular, at others close, and others earthy. The glassy lavas resemble in every respect the vitreous matter which is produced in our furnaces by the process of melting; they possess a lively lustre, a great degree of brittleness, and in the interior a compact texture, which gives them the resemblance of jellies which have attained a great degree of solidity. The most remarkable of these vitreous lavas is known by the name of obsidian.

Among the products of volcanoes is that class of rocks denominated trappean, including greenstones, basalts, porphyries, and amygdaloids. The Palisades on the Hudson River are an example of greenstone, also the Bass Rock off the coast of Scotland, a portion of which is represented by the engraving opposite the next page. This rock is remarkable for the immense numbers of sea fowl which resort to it, and it is celebrated in Scottish history in consequence of its having for a long time served as a royal fortress and state prison.

The igneous origin of the members of the trap family is very clearly shown by a common appearance exhibited in the carboniferous system, that of the coal being reduced to a cinder, and converted into coke, in contact with the trap dikes which intersect the strata. In general, also, strata of every kind acquire a greater degree of induration in contiguity with trap rocks, loose grits passing into compact quartz, and shales into flinty slates, evidencing the action of a high temperature upon them.

One of the characteristic forms of volcanic rocks, especially of basalt, is the columnar, where large masses are divided into regular prisms, sometimes easily separable, but in other cases adhering firmly together. The columns vary in the number of angles, from three to twelve; but they have most commonly from five to seven sides. They are often divided transversely, at nearly equal distances, like the joints in a vertebral column, as in the Giants' Causeway, in Ireland. They vary exceedingly in respect to length and diameter. Dr. McCulloch mentions some, in Skye, which are about four hundred feet long; others, in Morven, not exceeding an inch. In diameter those of Ailsa measure nine feet, and those of Morven an inch or less. They are usually straight, but sometimes curved; and examples of both these occur in the Island of Staffa. In a horizontal bed or sheet of trap the columns are vertical; in a vertical dike they are horizontal. The Chimney, in St. Helena, is an interesting specimen of vertical dikes. It is a pile of hexagonal prisms, sixty-four feet high, evidently the remainder of a narrow dike, the walls of rock which the dike originally traversed having been removed by the tooth of time down to the level of the sea. The Columbia River passes through basaltic mountains, which range from four hundred to one thousand feet high, the walls consisting of successive rows of columns, superimposed upon one another, separated by a few feet of amygdaloid, conglomerate, or breccia. In India rocks of this class appear to occupy an area of two hundred thousand square miles. The Chimney Rock, in St. Helena, is represented opposite page 360, as a specimen of basalt.

In North America the columnar arrangement is very commonly assumed by greenstone. A spot on Mount Holyoke, Massachusetts, which has been called Titan's Piazza, exhibits a group of greenstone columns, which hang over the observer's

Bass Rock, a remarkable volcanic formation off the coast of Scotland.

head, the projecting ends being exfoliated in such a manner as to present a convex surface downwards. The Palisades on the banks of the Hudson are another example.

In Wales the columnar structure is developed in the porphyritic trap on the northern side of Cader Idris.

In several accounts of the eruptions of volcanoes, large volumes of water are mentioned as having been ejected. The concurrent opinion of those who live in their vicinity is certainly in favor of such statements, and it is supported by the undoubted fact, that large volumes of water descend round the base of the volcanoes during their eruption. A most conspicuous instance of this kind is stated to have occurred in 1742, during an eruption of Mount Cotopaxi, in Ecuador, when the water formed a torrent, which filled the low tracts near Quito to a height of one hundred and twenty feet, and ran four feet in a second.

Modern philosophers, being firmly convinced that this water is not derived from the interior of the earth, and is not a subterraneous production, account for this phenomenon by having recourse to the effects produced by the ascending currents of air. The air reposing over the crater, being strongly heated, rises rapidly upward, and the cool air, taking its place, is also soon compelled to take the same direction. On arriving at a great elevation, the vapor it contains is condensed into a cloud, which soon acquires large dimensions. A further condensation converts it into water, which then pours down in large streams. This water, in descending, is mixed up with the ashes with which the contiguous portion of the atmosphere is filled. This mixture falls on a country which is already covered with a layer of ashes that prevents the water from penetrating into the soil, or from running off in the usual way. In this manner swamps are formed, which, being constantly increased by matter of a similar description, suddenly burst the material forming their boundaries, and inundate large tracts of country. As this commonly happens at places where it has been thought impossible to account for the inundation in any other way, people have jumped to the conclusion that large volumes of water must have been thrown up by the volcano.

The great volumes of water by which the eruptions of the Ecuadorian Andes are attended are partly of a different origin. The summits of these colossal mountains rise above the snow line. The most elevated part of them is, therefore, covered with snow and ice, which in the long intervals between the eruptions accumulate to an astonishing depth. When the subterraneous fire begins to heat the mass of which the cone of the volcano is composed, the bond is loosened by which the snowy covering is attached to its base, and then it rushes down the steep declivities of the mountains. The adjacent country is instantaneously inundated by torrents of water, in which thick masses of ice and snow are mixed up with smoking scoriæ and hot ashes.

From the volcanoes of the Andes large volumes of water are sometimes disgorged, which are filled with fish during their eruptions. Humboldt has explained this phenomenon. He ascertained that the rocks composing the mass of the mountains enclosed on their declivities, or at their bases, caverns of very large dimensions. These caverns are, during the intervals between the eruptions, filled with water, which is derived from the snow lying on the top of the mountains, and descends to the caverns by infiltration. Thus in time large subterraneous reservoirs of water are formed in the interior of the volcanoes. The collections of water usually communicate by narrow channels with some of the small rivers and torrents of the table land. By means of these channels the fish inhabiting the rivers get into the reservoirs, where they multiply in an astonishing manner. When, under these circumstances, the volcano begins to assume a certain degree of activity, the earthquakes, which always precede the eruptions of the volcanoes of the Andes, forcibly shake the whole mass of the mountain, the subterraneous reservoirs are suddenly thrown open, and there follows an immense rush of water

The Chimney, a volcanic dike composed of horizontal prisms of basalt. St. Helena.
(See page 358.)

over the adjacent country, mixed up with fish and with a matter resembling tufa. When, in the night between the 19th and 20th of June, 1698, the summit of Mount Carguairazo was broken down by an eruption, so that only two large horns of the ancient crater remained standing, a liquid, consisting of tufa and mud, intermixed with a loam of great sterility, was poured over a surface of about forty square miles, and in those substances a great number of dead fish were found embedded.

The permanently active volcanoes resemble, in general, the intermittent ones, except that the ejection of scoria and lava is not attended by such violent phenomena. Only a few of these are found on our globe, and they are, as already stated, of a much lower elevation than the intermittent volcanoes. They can hardly be called mountains. Their permanent activity is ascribed to their moderate elevation. The chimney by which the communication between the interior and exterior of the globe is established, being much shorter than in other volcanoes, it is very probable that in this passage fewer obstacles occur to the rising of the volcanic matter. Besides, this matter, arriving sooner at the orifice of the chimney, is in a greater state of liquidity. These two circumstances must facilitate the overflowing of the lava, and this phenomenon goes on with greater ease, as is proved by the very slight commotions of the ground which accompany it, the very moderate noise, and the total absence of that awful column of smoke and ashes with which all the eruptions of intermittent volcanoes terminate.

Those philosophers who interested themselves particularly in the study of the volcanic phenomena were of course desirous of obtaining a sight of the manner in which the lava is brought up in the volcanic chimney and ejected from its orifice. The imminent danger to which they would have exposed their lives in approaching close to the orifice of the crater of an intermittent volcano, during an eruption, prevented them from making an attempt of this kind. When, however, it was known that this process was much more regular and less violent in the permanently active volcanoes, they resolved to profit by this circumstance, and to complete their knowledge of the volcanic activity, by observing the eruptions of one of them. For that purpose they chose Mount Stromboli, the only permanently active volcano which is found in Europe. The following account of this mountain, and the observations made on the manner in which the subterraneous forces operate in its crater, is taken from the German writer Hoffmann, who visited the volcano in December, 1831, and January, 1832.

Stromboli is the most northern of the Lipari Islands. It lies about seventy miles due north of Mount Etna, and somewhat more than fifty miles north of Capo Bianco, in Sicily. The island consists of a single mountain, which has a circumference of about nine miles, and whose summit rises to about two thousand nine hundred feet above the sea. This mountain is a volcano which has been constantly active for a time beyond record. Homer noticed it; and in ancient times it was called the lighthouse of the Tyrrhenian Sea, because a fire is perceived during the night hovering over its summit.

The crater of this volcano, according to Hoffmann, is rent by a chasm which runs across the whole island from south-west to north-east. One half of the cone enclosing the crater has collapsed, and the other half forms a semicircular enclosure. The sides of this semicircular ridge are very steep, especially towards the crater, where they are apparently only composed of accumulated volcanic matter. This circumstance enables the observer to notice, from a well-chosen point on this ridge, all that is going on in the crater, which is depressed from five to six hundred feet below the highest part of the mountain. It appears that the openings in the crater are subject to changes in their situation and number. When the German naturalist visited the place, he found three openings in the bottom of the crater. The central opening was evidently the principal orifice of the volcano. It was more than two hundred feet in diameter, and did not present any thing which deserves particular notice. Columns of vapor rose from it slowly and with great regularity, and the sides of its orifice were covered with numerous incrustations of sulphur of a deep-yellow color.

At no great distance from this opening was another. It was near the place on which the observer had placed himself; was somewhat more elevated than the great opening, but was only twenty feet in diameter. In this opening Hoffmann observed for a length of time the column of liquid lava alternately rising and sinking. It frequently rose to its very top. The melted matter did not answer the idea he had formed by reading the accounts of eruptions. He had expected to find a burning mass covered with flames, rising above the orifice. But there were no flames. It was a mass, shining with great brightness; and he compares it with the appearance of melted metals; for instance, with iron, running from a furnace in which it has been melted for casting, or with a mass of glass in a glowing fire. Spallanzani gives a similar description, and both agree with the account given of the lava by Sir William Hamilton, who, in 1766, had an opportunity of observing the matter at a place not far from the opening from which it had issued.

In looking attentively at the motion of this mass in the opening, Hoffmann was soon aware that it was subject to some variation. In general the column of fiery liquid remained about twenty or thirty feet below the orifice. It was evident that it maintained that position only by being supported by the expansion of the volumes of steam confined below, for its surface moved up and down very uniformly, and in regular intervals of one second's duration. Though the difference of level produced by these motions was not large, it proved evidently that the pressure originating in the gravity of the mass was constantly met by the force which the ascending vapor exercised on it. During these motions a peculiar noise was heard, which the observer compared to the popping noise produced by a current of air rushing through the opening in the inner door of a blast furnace. Every time the column of lava was raised in the chimney, a ball of white vapor, well determined and rounded, was seen emerging from the surface of the melted matter. As soon as the vapor had escaped the column sank again. The vapor at every escape detached from the surface of the mass some small pieces of lava, which were carried out of the chimney and thrown over its orifice, which at night added greatly to the picturesque beauty of the scene.

This was the common action, but from time to time, and mostly at intervals of a quarter of an hour, this process was interrupted, occasionally several times in succession, by a more active paroxysm of the volcanic powers. The column of lava, after having ascended higher than usual, was then suddenly arrested; the volume of smoke which had escaped from it, did not rise, but remained fixed; sometimes it seemed as if the smoke was again descending into the mass. At the same instant the observer felt a more or less violent concussion of the ground on which he was standing, and observed a perceptible wavering in the sides of the crater. It was evidently a slight shock of an earthquake, and it was immediately succeeded by a dull, rumbling noise, proceeding from the opening. Almost at the same moment, a large volume of vapor rose from its orifice with a shrill-sounding crash. This cloud carried off a whole layer from the surface of the melted matter, having broken it previously into numberless pieces. An intense degree of heat must have been evolved, as it was sensibly felt by the observer, though standing at a considerable elevation above the spot. The pieces of lava rose in divergent lines as they were carried upward, so as to form a girandole, and descended on the contiguous places like a shower of fire. Some pieces rose to an elevation of apparently more than twelve hundred feet, and passed over the head of the looker-on in a wide arc. When such a paroxysm had terminated, no lava was visible in the opening; it seemed to have disappeared entirely. But it soon became evident that this momentary state of quiescence was the effect of the column of lava having retired lower than before into the chimney. After a few minutes the shining matter again made its appearance in the orifice. By degrees it rose to its former level, and the usual state of the volcano was reëstablished.

This account of the German naturalist agrees with that of Spallanzani, but the Italian had an opportunity of observing another remarkable fact. One night, whilst he was watching the operations in the crater, the lava sank down without immediately rising again. The light, produced by the reflection of the red-hot matter which had previously illuminated all the objects within the crater, had scarcely disappeared, when numberless small columns of vapor made their appearance. They rose from the edges of the orifice and from the declivities and sides of the crater. Their emerging from the ground was attended with a hissing noise, which Spallanzani compares to the rustling noise produced by the bellows of a furnace. This continued for several minutes, and the sulphureous vapors rising from the steep declivity near him began to be very troublesome, when the burning mass suddenly rose from below, and shortly afterwards the volcanic process assumed its regular course. Spallanzani explains this phenomenon by supposing that whenever, by some accident, the consistency of the lava on the surface is so incrusted as to prevent the vapor from escaping through the mass, these vapors find their way out through the narrow rents in the sides of the mountain. As soon, however, as the lava has reacquired a greater degree of liquidity from the condensed heat, the vapors are again able to break through the mass, and to escape. The process then reassumes its regular course.

The third opening which Hoffmann observed in the crater of Mount Stromboli was more than one hundred feet lower than that in which he had observed the volcanic process going on in such a remarkable way. This third opening slowly and uniformly discharged a moderate quantity of red-hot lava, which ran down the declivities of the mountain in a narrow stream. Hoffmann considered it as only a lateral branch of the volcanic chimney, which terminated within the wide orifice, and thinks that the column of lava, whilst it rises and sinks in the large chimney, continually presses a portion of the melted matter into the lateral pipe, and that in this way a constant discharge of red-hot lava is maintained.

This account of the volcanic process in the crater of Mount Stromboli conveys to us an idea of the manner in which the same process operates in the intermittent volcanoes. There is certainly a great similarity between the permanently active volcano of Stromboli and the last-mentioned class of volcanoes. But the volcanoes which are constantly active assume in some instances a character so different in many particulars, that they can hardly be all comprehended under the same description. On that account we insert a short notice of two of them, of Mount Kraabla, in Iceland, and of the volcano of Kirauea, in Hawaii, one of the Sandwich Islands.

The bottom of Mount Kraabla is occupied by a circular pool of black water at least three hundred feet in circumference, from the middle of which a vast column of the same liquid is ejected, accompanied with a loud, thundering noise, and thick clouds of vapor and smoke. The surface of this pool may be about seven hundred feet below the highest part of the rim of the crater. Henderson describes the volcanic process in this pool in the following words: —

"Nearly about the centre of the pool is the aperture whence a vast body of water, sulphur, and bluish-black bolus is thrown up, and which is at least ten feet in diameter. The height of the jets varied greatly, rising on the first propulsions of the liquid to about twelve feet, and continuing to ascend, as it were, by leaps, till they gained the highest point of elevation, which was upwards of thirty feet, when they again abated much more rapidly than they rose; and, after the spouting had ceased, the situation of the aperture was rendered visible only by a gentle ebullition which distinguished it from the general surface of the pool. During my stay, which was upwards of an hour, the eruptions took place every five minutes, and lasted about two minutes and a half. I was always apprised of the approach of an eruption by a small jet that broke forth from a pool a little to the east of the great one, and which was evidently connected with it, as there was a continual bubbling in a direct line between them. None of its jets exceeded twelve feet, and generally they were not above five. Another bubbling channel ran a little way to the north-west of the principal opening, but did not terminate in a jet like the former. While the eruption continued a number of fine silver waves was thrown round to the sides of the pool, which was lined with a dark-blue bolus, left there on the subsidence of the waves. At the foot of the bank on which we stood were numerous small holes, whence a quantity of steam was unremittingly making its escape with a loud hissing noise; and on the west side of the pool was a gentle declivity, where the water ran out, and was conveyed through a long winding gully to the foot of the mountain."

It would seem that at no place is the communication between the interior and exterior of the globe so complete as on the Island of Hawaii, in the volcano of Kirauea, which must, therefore, be considered as the most remarkable of the volcanoes of the earth, and which doubtless will furnish us with a number of new facts, when its operations shall have been studied with the same attention and for such a length of time as those of Mount Vesuvius. It differs from other volcanoes in aspect, shape, and in the manner in which the ejected lava is disposed of.

The volcano of Kirauea is not found on the summit of a cone-shaped mountain, but in a depression which is more than a thousand feet below the level of the adjacent country, but which is still three thousand eight hundred and seventy-three feet above the sea. The circumference of this depression, according to the estimate, is between fifteen and sixteen miles. The sides of it are steep, at some places nearly perpendicular, to a depth of more than seven hundred feet, where they terminate in a ledge or plain. They are composed of volcanic matter, apparently a light red or gray kind of lava, vesicular, and lying in horizontal strata varying in thickness from one to forty feet. The ledge or plain at the base of this declivity consists of solid black lava; it is of irregular breadth, but completely surrounds the whole depression. Beneath this ledge the sides slope gradually towards the bottom of the crater, until they terminate at a second ledge; the perpendicular height of this slope is about three hundred and sixty feet; it consists of gray lava, which has assumed at some parts a white color from having been blanched by vapors. From this ledge to the bottom of the crater the descent is only forty-three feet.

The bottom of the crater at its lowest part is about three miles long from north-west to south-east, and nearly a mile wide. It contains two volcanic laboratories, an active and an extinct one. The first is called Great Kirauea, and the second Little Kirauea. They are divided from each other by a ridge of lava, level at its top, and about three hundred and seventy yards wide.

The depression called Great Kirauea, in which the activity of the volcano is concentrated, is about two miles long. Its bottom is covered with solid lava, except that a part of it is occupied by two lakes of liquid lava. The smaller one, situated towards the north, forms a circular basin three hundred and nineteen yards in diameter; the larger lake, near the south-west extremity, is eleven hundred and ninety yards long, of a heart shape, and a breadth between the lobes of about two hundred yards. Fifty-one conical islands, varying in size, and containing as many craters, rise either from the edge or from the surface of the lakes. Twenty-one of them constantly emit columns of gray smoke, and several of them continually vomit streams of lava from their fiery mouths, which roll in burning torrents down their outsides into the boiling mass below. A number of small craters in vigorous action are situated on the declivities with which the depression is surrounded.

The streams of lava which they emit also roll into the lakes, and mingle with the burning mass below. In this manner the two lakes are constantly supplied with the melted fluid.

The smaller lake is in a continual state of ebullition. The larger appears at times quiescent, with serpentine fiery streaks on its surface; but at other times the lava is thrown up to a fearful height. Shortly after the numerous vent holes have discharged their steam or slag, the lake for a short time becomes tranquil. Both lakes have a steady southerly current, the force of which Mr. Douglas was enabled to determine accurately by throwing blocks of lava on the stream, and noticing the time they took to pass a hundred yards; it is at the rate of three miles and nearly a quarter per hour. The south end of both lakes presents one of the most magnificent spectacles in nature — a vast caldron of lava in furious ebullition, sometimes spouting up to the height of twenty to seventy feet, rolling and tumbling in fiery waves, hurrying along, and finally precipitated down an elliptical fiery arch. The arch of the smaller lake, as stated by Mr. Douglas, has a width of a hundred and forty-two yards, with a maximum height of forty-three feet. In this awful arch the force of the lava is in some degree arrested by the escape of the gases or volcanic vapors, and large blocks are thrown back. Some of them are literally spun into a filamentous glass, which is carried by the wind all around the volcano. The sound issuing at the same time from the archway is beyond all comparison; that of all the steam engines of the world, says Mr. Douglas, would be a whisper to it.

On the lower ledge surrounding the crater is a tract five miles square, which seems to have been recently in a state of igneous fusion. In the process of cooling, the lava has apparently been broken up into immense ledges and rolled masses, like the breaking up of a great river of ice. These masses of lava are of every shape and form, from gigantic coils, like enormous cables, to threads as fine as human hair, which are carried by the wind a distance of many miles. On this tract are also dispersed numerous chimneys of various shapes, some of which emit scoria, smoke, or steam, while others are comparatively tranquil. Among them are three cones or bluffs of from twenty to twenty-five feet in height, and about one hundred and twenty yards in breadth at the base, with lateral doors, similar to those of a baker's oven, and into those, by kneeling on the edge, it is possible to peep and to witness a terrific vacuity and a red-hot atmosphere, while the volcanic vapor is at the same time discharged by a terminal vent hole.

The burning matter appears to be discharged from the lakes into the earth; but it has a subterraneous outlet into the sea, in latitude nineteen degrees, eleven minutes, fifty-one seconds north. The place is called, in the native language, Punahala, or "broken in." Near its vicinity many overflowings have taken place over a space of fourteen miles in length; in some of the steep chasms seventeen layers of lava may be counted. The whole eastern coast of Hawaii, through the district of Puna, is one entire sheet of lava.

The depression called Little Kirauea is of much smaller dimensions; it approaches more to a circular form. Its bottom is occupied by solid lava, which, however, does not appear to be every where quite cold. But it must have been long in a state of repose, for the declivities of the depression, which have a very gentle slope, are overgrown with bushes and trees. Among the trees some occur which have a hundred and twenty concentric rings or annual layers of timber. On the neck between the two depressions the ground opened in 1832, and discharged liquid lava for a period of three days into both depressions: this eruption was preceded by slight earthquakes.

Sixteen miles distant from Kirauea, and at an elevation of nine thousand seven hundred and ninety feet above it, is the crater of Mauna Loa. This may be considered as the summit crater of a mountain, of which Kirauea is a lateral one.

The form of Mauna Loa, a flattened dome, is its most remarkable feature. The idea of a volcano is so generally connected with the figure of a cone, that the mind at once conceives of a lofty sugar loaf ejecting fire, red-hot stones, and flowing lavas. But in place of slender walls around a deep crater, which the shaking of an eruption may tumble in, the summit of the Hawaiian volcano is nearly a plane, in which the crater, though six miles in circuit, is like a small quarry hole, the ancient orifice being not less than twenty-four miles in circumference.

A violent eruption of Mauna Loa took place in the year 1843, which is thus described by the Rev. Titus Coan, in a letter dated Hilo, Sandwich Islands, May 16, 1843:—

"On the 10th of January of the present year, just at the dawn of day, we discovered a rapid disgorgement of liquid fire from near the summit of Mauna Loa, at an elevation of about fourteen thousand feet above the sea. This eruption increased from day to day for several weeks, pouring out vast floods of fiery lava, which spread down the side of the mountain, and flowed in broad rivers, throwing a terrific glare upon the heavens, and filling those lofty mountainous regions with a sheen of light. This spectacle continued till the molten flood had progressed twenty or thirty miles down the side of the mountain, with an average breadth of one and a half miles, and across a high plain which stretches between the bases of Mauna Loa and Mauna Kea. After many weeks, in company with Mr. Paris, the missionary for Kan,—a station south of Hilo,—we penetrated through a deep forest, stretching between Hilo and the mountain, and reached the molten stream, which we followed to the top of the mountain, and found its source in a vast crater, amidst eternal snow. Down the sides of the mountain the lava had now ceased to flow upon the surface; but it had formed for itself a subterranean duct, at the depth of fifty or one hundred feet. This duct was vitrified, and down this fearful channel a river of fire was rushing at the rate of fifteen or twenty miles an hour, from the summit to the foot of the mountain. This subterranean stream we saw distinctly through several large apertures in the side of the mountain, while the burning flood rushed fearfully beneath our feet. Our visit was attended with peril and inconceivable fatigue, but we never regretted having made it, and we returned deeply affected with the majesty, the sublimity, the power, and the love of that God who 'looketh on the earth and it trembleth, who toucheth the hills and they smoke; whose presence melteth the hills, and whose look causeth the mountains to flow down.'"

As one of the most remarkable natural events, it may be observed, that volcanic eruptions sometimes occur which do not originate in volcanoes, and even in places where no volcanoes exist. These phenomena may therefore be called irregular volcanic eruptions. Such eruptions have taken place in level and low countries, as well as in mountain tracts. In 1783 an extensive mountain mass, in Iceland, called the Skaptaar Yökul, where no volcanic phenomena had been previously observed, was suddenly laid open by the subterraneous force, and the lava issuing from it deluged the adjacent country. A similar event occurred in the Island of Lanzarote, one of the Canaries, in 1730. The manner in which these eruptions were effected appears to bear a close resemblance to the opening of the lateral rents in the intermittent volcanoes. The surface of the country is broken open by the elastic vapors under ground, and thus a wide rent is formed, from which the volcanic matter is ejected. As, however, the rent is of irregular width, the subterraneous fluids direct their force in preference to those points where it is widest, and at such places cones of eruption are soon formed by the accumulation of scoria and other substances brought up by the elastic vapors. After some time, probably when some obstacle has arisen in the cone of eruption, the subterraneous forces widen the rent at some other place, and a new cone of eruption is formed. Thus it goes on until the elastic vapors cease to be active. These rents, however, are in general much more extensive than those formed by intermittent volcanoes. Sometimes they exceed ten miles in length, and have a great number of cones

Crater of Mauna Loa, as it appeared during the eruption of 1843.

of eruption, as was the case in the two eruptions just mentioned. On the rent in the Skaptaar Yökul more than twenty cones of eruption are found; and during the eruption in Lanzarote, twelve large ones were formed, besides a great number of smaller ones, situated close to the larger ones, and which are probably only their branches.

The Island of Lanzarote is very remarkable in this respect. One irregular eruption occurred in 1730, and another in 1824. The last eruption, however, did not occur at the same place where the rent had been formed in 1730. This is very remarkable, when it is considered that both rents run in the same direction, from east to west, and that they can hardly be more than two or three miles from one another. It will be asked, of course, Why did the earth not break open at the same place? Perhaps an observation made by Mr. Poulet Scrope respecting the lateral eruptions of intermittent volcanoes may account for this remarkable circumstance. This gentleman says that perhaps a new lateral rent is never formed in a volcano at a place where the mountain has been laid open before; and he thinks that the weak part of the mountain, which has once given way, has been strengthened by the lava which entered the rent, and there solidified. In this manner it has acquired a firmness better able to resist the pressure of the lava within the chimney than those parts of the mountain which have not been previously split. This observation appears to be very just, and to afford a satisfactory explanation for the facts stated respecting the two eruptions in Lanzarote.

The phenomena attending eruptions of this kind do not materially differ from those which accompany the eruptions of intermittent volcanoes, except that they are on a much larger scale, more impressive, and more terrific, and that sometimes they continue for a great length of time. The eruption in Lanzarote in 1730 lasted for more than five years and a half, beginning on the 1st of September, 1730, and terminating on the 16th of April, 1736, so that the inhabitants of the island were compelled to emigrate, and to take refuge on the Island of Gran Canaria. It is astonishing what immense masses of lava are emitted by these extraordinary phenomena. Sometimes they are spread over a hundred square miles and more. There are on the surface of our globe several places where immense tracts of country are covered with enormously thick layers of lava, without its being possible to discover whence the matter has issued. Philosophers find it, therefore, impossible to account for the origin of such lava. One of the most extensive fields of lava occurs in Patagonia, on both sides the River of Santa Cruz. It extends from the base of the Andes eastward over more than half the width of the continent, overspreading in that direction a country of more than a hundred miles in extent, while it has not yet been ascertained how far it reaches to the north and south. This immense layer varies in depth from a hundred to three hundred feet. As at present no active volcano exists in that latitude, within the range of the Andes, its origin remains in obscurity. It is probable that, at some remote period, an irregular volcanic eruption has taken place, either in the mountain chain itself, or along its base, and that this immense mass of lava has flowed from a rent of unusual dimensions.

It is a fortunate circumstance that these terrible phenomena are of rare occurrence, for they must be numbered among the most destructive operations of nature. All the active volcanoes in the world, during a whole century, do not cause as much damage as is sometimes produced by one of these events: the reason is obvious. The volcanoes and the effects of their eruptions are known in the countries in which they are found, and they are, besides, usually surrounded by at least a tract of some extent, unfit for cultivation. The streams of lava issuing from their tops or sides do not always extend to those parts which are cultivated, and then they do no damage at all. Whenever they reach the cultivated grounds they usually overrun only a few acres of land, or in some rare cases a square mile; but it is different with the irregular volcanic eruptions. They occur in places where no volcanoes are found, and commonly break out in the midst of a cultivated country, which is then overflowed by the lava to an immense extent. Tracts of many square miles are thus converted into useless wastes, and a large number of families are deprived of their property, their means of subsistence, and their homes. The loss of life is not generally great, but all other kinds of damage they cause are far more serious than those effected by earthquakes, and continue to be felt much longer; for the lava which has overrun countries which had previously attained some degree of cultivation, must in most cases be exposed for centuries to the effects of the atmosphere before it undergoes such changes as render it again available for cultivation. The lava which in 1730 was ejected on the Island of Lanzarote, covers a third of the island, or a space of more than a hundred square miles. Several flourishing and populous villages were formerly dispersed over that district. More than a hundred years have elapsed since the change was effected, and the whole tract is still a stony desert, on which no plants grow, and no animal finds subsistence; and in this state it may still continue for many centuries to come.

There is no record in history of any irregular volcanic eruption having taken place on the continent of Europe; but considering that in many places, as in the south of France, and in the countries bordering the Rhine, large tracts of country are covered with layers of lava, we may presume that such events have occurred before the historical period commenced. No part of the globe appears to be more frequently visited by these destructive catastrophes than the Azores, or Western Islands. Though four centuries have not yet passed since these islands were taken possession of by the Portuguese, the number of recorded eruptions of this description exceeds twelve. Most of them have occurred in the Islands of St. Michael and St. George, and in both have proved very destructive. The Canaries have also frequently been subjected to them, especially Lanzarote. It appears also that many of the eruptions noticed in the history of Iceland have been of this description. This is certainly the case respecting the eruption of the Skaptaar Yökul, which occurred in 1783. As this is one of the most remarkable events recorded in the natural history of our globe, the following account of this eruption will probably be acceptable, even if considered only as a specimen of the nature of these eruptions.

The Skaptaar Yökul, or Snow Mountain, for this is implied by the Icelandic term Yökul, is a mountain mass running from south-west to north-east, always surmounted with snow, and at its eastern extremity connected with other snow mountains. It lies about forty miles from the nearest sea. It was on the southern declivity, or that which faces the sea, that the earth opened in 1783. It appears that the rent formed during the eruption was about fifteen miles in length; for along such a space a number of conical hills, or craters of eruption, are still found, whose number probably falls not much short of thirty. On the declivity where the rent opened, two rather large rivers take their source, which fall into the sea at places about ten miles distant from each other. The western is called Skapta, and the eastern Kverfisfliot. By following the channels of these two rivers, the melted matter reached the low country which lies between the mountain and the sea. None of the Icelandic annals make mention of any eruption having previously occurred in these places.

The eruption was ushered in by earthquakes, which succeeded one another for eight days, from the 1st to the 8th of June, and which increased in violence. On the morning of the 8th a prodigious cloud of dense smoke darkened the atmosphere, and was observed to be continually augmented by fresh columns rising from behind a range of low hills, which hid the place of the eruption from the inhabitants of the plain; they soon, however, discovered that a tract of country in their vicinity was completely covered with ashes and other volcanic matter. The eruption had commenced, but as the opening in the ground was probably not large enough to give a vent to all the elastic vapors under ground which were striving to escape, the concussions of the earthquake continued to shake the country with great violence, and were accompanied by loud subterraneous reports, while the air began to be filled with vapor and gases, so charged with electricity as to produce unintermitting flashes of lightning, attended with the most tremendous peals of thunder. Meanwhile the heat by which the eruption was attended had begun to melt the ice on the nearest part of the Yökul, and as the waters of the river were greatly increased by the access of fresh volumes from under the ice, they overflowed the adjacent countries.

On the 10th the fire first became visible, when vast luminous jets were seen rushing up amidst volumes of thick smoke. The lava had issued from the openings and entered a glen, by which it ran to the valley of the Skapta River. When it reached the bed of this river a violent contention between the two elements ensued, attended by development of an amazing quantity of steam, which may easily be imagined, when it is stated that the river was dried up, and that the lava filled its bed in the space of twenty-four hours. The river runs between high rocks at this part, which rise to between four and six hundred feet above its level, and enclose a valley about two hundred feet wide. The lava not only filled up this valley, but overflowed to a considerable extent also the fields which were on the higher grounds. Several farms and hamlets were destroyed, and their pasture grounds and meadows buried forever under the lava. In the mean time the thunder, lightning, and subterraneous concussions were continued, with little or no intermission; and besides the splittings of the rocks and earth which the lava burned in its progress, the ears of the inhabitants were stunned by a tremendous roar proceeding from the volcanic orifices, which resembled that of a large caldron in the most violent state of ebullition, or the noise of innumerable bellows blowing with all their might into the same furnace.

Having filled up the valley of the Skapta River, the stream of lava reached the plain; there its progress was for some time arrested by an immense abyss in the bed of the river, into which it rushed with a great noise. In filling this cavity the lava had partly cooled, but an immense supply of new material overlaid the mass which had already cooled, rose to a prodigious height, and, precipitating itself over it, at length proceeded southward across the plain. Having buried a considerable portion of the plain, by which several farms and hamlets were destroyed, it rushed into some subterraneous caverns, and, during its progress under ground, threw up the crust either on one side or to a great height in the air. Where it proceeded below a thick, indurated crust, where there was no vent for the steam which escaped from the lava, the upper covering of the crust was broken to pieces, and thrown up with the utmost violence and noise to a height of nearly one hundred and eighty feet.

On the 18th another dreadful ejection of liquid and red-hot lava issued from the openings. During its progress through the channel of the Skapta it covered even the rocks on its sides which had towered above the reach of the former floods, and flowed down with amazing velocity and force over the masses that were cooling, so that the one stream was literally heaped over the other. In many places large pools of water had been formed near the lava which had filled up the channel of the river on the first discharge. The new burning stream reached them, put them into a violent state of ebullition, and caused them to overflow the adjacent country.

After having been reënforced by this supply, the melted matter continued to flow with considerable velocity over the plain, where it soon divided into two branches, of which one ran to the east and the other to the west: each of them destroyed several farms which stood in their way. It would, probably, have soon stopped, had not several new eruptions taken place between the 24th of June and the 13th of July, which sent forth such immense masses of burning fluid that they raised by several feet the layers formed by the former discharges, and were still sufficient to extend their devastations over countries containing many square miles which had not been reached by the last stream. When the lava at last ceased flowing, on the 20th of July, it was found that nearly the whole country between the Skapta and Kudafliot Rivers, whose beds are about twenty miles distant from each other, had been converted into a stony desert; and in this state it still remains. The length of this immense sheet of lava, from the place where it issued from the volcanic orifices to its termination on the banks of the Kudafliot and the vicinity of the sea, is probably not less than fifty miles, and its greatest breadth in the low plain between twelve and fifteen miles. The height of the masses of lava in the level country does not exceed a hundred feet; but in some parts of the Skapta channel it is not less than six hundred feet. It may be questioned whether all the lava which has flowed from Mount Etna and Mount Vesuvius within the historical period would, if put together, form such a volume as that which by the irregular volcanic eruption of the Skaptaar Yökul was ejected, and ran down the channel of the Skapta River in twenty-five days.

But even the ejection of these enormous masses of lava had not yet sufficiently disburdened the earth. By the efforts of the subterraneous forces the volcanic rent was continued farther to the east by a new splitting, and from these places, which were some miles east from the cones of eruption formed in June, a quantity of lava was discharged, which laid waste the valley of the Kverfisfliot and the contiguous plain. The day on which this eruption commenced is not stated; but on the 3d of August the inhabitants were informed of its having taken place by the same phenomenon which had been observed at the beginning of the previous eruption. An immense quantity of steam rose from the Kverfisfliot, and the heat which the water acquired in a short time showed clearly that the bed of the river had been entered near its source by the hot melted matter. In a short time the channel of the river was dried up; but its empty bed was soon filled with running lava to the very brink, and the low grounds were inundated on both sides by the volcanic mass. On the 9th of August it had already reached the point where the valley opens into the plain; then it appears that the velocity of the stream was greatly increased; for in the course of a few hours it had spread itself across the plain to a distance of nearly six miles. Its progress was slower afterwards; but as it received one or two considerable supplies of melted matter from the source, it continued to extend over the low country to the end of August, when it ceased, after having overrun a great part of the district. The mass of lava which by this eruption was poured into the valley of Kverfisfliot and the adjacent plain is about forty miles in length, and seven in width where it is broadest.

Some pains have been taken to ascertain the number of active volcanoes which are found on the globe. It is, however, difficult to obtain an exact result, as some are mentioned by one traveller as being extinct, while another may enumerate them among the still active volcanoes. This difference of opinion is easily accounted for when we remember that a great number of the intermittent volcanoes enjoy such long periods of repose that a century may pass between two eruptions. Besides, it sometimes happens that a volcano which has been extinct for centuries reassumes its activity. It must be also observed that some parts of the globe have not yet been visited by attentive and well-informed observers, and that for the accounts of the volcanoes existing in such unexplored regions we are obliged to rely on the narratives of unscientific reporters. The following statement of them is therefore only to be considered as an approximation to the truth, and one which is probably considerably below the actual number.

The number of active volcanoes thus estimated is about three hundred and twelve. By far the largest proportion is found in or around the Pacific Ocean. In the countries bordering on that great oceanic basin, and on the islands dotting its bosom, not less than two hundred and thirty-one are found, consequently more than three fourths of the whole existing number. The number of active volcanoes in that series of islands which, under the name of the Sunda Islands, stretch across the Indian Ocean, is sixty-five. In the Atlantic and the countries bordering on them only a few are found, — not more than fourteen; and in the centre of Asia, in the Thian-shan Mountains, only two.

CHAPTER XII.

Caverns. — The Table Land of Quito the Dome of an enormous subterranean Vault. — Crystal Caves. — Fingal's Cave. — Gurtshellir Cave. — Martin's Hole, and other natural Tunnels through Mountains. — Cave of Adelsberg. — Peak Cavern. — Portals of the Winds. — Cavern of the Gaucharo. — Stalactites. — Grotto of Antiparos. — Blue John Cavern. — Mammoth Cave. — Caverns in which Ice accumulates in Summer and melts in Winter. — Caverns containing immense Quantities of the Bones of Animals. — Mines remarkable for their great Depth and Extent.

When we reflect upon the manner in which the solid crust of the earth appears to have been formed, upon the powerful upheaving force by which its elevated sites have been raised, and the posterior agency of subterranean gases, volcanoes, and earthquakes, it is natural to expect chasms in the surface of tremendous depth — spaces also in the interior which have not been filled up with masses of stone similar to the materials of the earth itself, but by water, air, or vapor, with those cavities of grotesque and romantic appearance that are found in mountainous regions. There are few natural objects which have more awakened curiosity, or more strongly affected the imagination, than the hollow places, of various form and size, common in districts which have been subject to great physical disturbance. Their seclusion and gloom — their fantastic architecture — the effect of torch-light upon their numerous crystallizations — the augmentation of sound and its reverberations — together with their unknown extent in many cases — all these causes contribute to invest the cavities of the earth with exciting interest; nor is it strange to find them interwoven with the traditions and mythologies of unenlightened nations. On account of their sombre interior and strange

Dead Sea in the Mammoth Cave, Kentucky.

outline being adapted to impose upon an ignorant populace, and give effect to religious observances, the priesthoods of antiquity localized in caverns their false divinities, and celebrated sanguinary rites upon the natural altars found in their recesses. A cave, with a priestess seated upon a tripod at its mouth, pretending to inhale a vapor from the interior which inspired a knowledge of future events, the gift of Apollo, was the original Delphian oracle, reverenced by the mind of Greece, and resorted to by the proudest monarchs of the ancient world. The cavern, along with the deep forest, commended itself to the primitive inhabitants of Northern Europe by its mystery and gloom as an appropriate spot for the performance of a barbarous worship; and many local titles of such sites preserve the memory of their former uses. An instance of this we have in Thor's cave, or, as Darwin calls it,

"The blood-smeared mansion of gigantic Thor," —

a broad excavation on the face of a huge rock in the limestone district of Derbyshire, England, divided into two chambers, one beyond the other, with a detached stone at the farther extremity, where the light of day is very much subdued. But in India the largest use has been made of caverns for religious purposes, and immense pains have been taken with their adornment, extension, and architecture, at Elephanta, Salsette, and Ellora, where there are elaborately wrought temples constructed, probably out of small natural crevices in the rock. We shall now refer to a few of those cavities which are entirely the workmanship of nature, with whose form man has not intermeddled, and notice the principal phenomena which they exhibit.

That extensive cavities exist in the interior of the crust of the globe is evident from the phenomena of volcanoes and earthquakes. They are not accessible to observation, but the repeated tremblings of the soil in various places, and experiments made of oscillations of the pendulum, point to the conclusion that there are large underlying hollows at no great distance from the surface, of which the superficial land forms the roof. The table land of Quito, surrounded by the most powerful volcanoes upon the earth, and the remarkable plain of Jorullo, are supposed to be examples of this. Condamine believed that a considerable portion of the former district was to be regarded as the dome of an enormous vault; and Parrot has shown it to be highly probable, by a careful calculation, that a cavity of at least a cubic mile and a half exists beneath its surface. The rumbling noise, like that of distant thunder, which, on the testimony of Humboldt, usually precedes and accompanies the eruption of its volcanoes, affords evidence in favor of this supposition, and as an increase of the subterranean vacuity must be the necessary consequence of every outbreak, it is not at all an improbable event that the blooming landscape will ultimately fall in, and this piece of table land become an immense depression. The quantity of material scooped out of the interior of the earth by volcanic action is immense, and calculated to produce vacuities in which the largest mountains would have ample space. It has been estimated that Etna, in one of its last most important eruptions, — that of the year 1769, — threw out a mass of lava equal in volume to a cone five thousand eight hundred and twenty feet in height, and eleven thousand six hundred and forty feet in breadth, or nearly four times larger than Vesuvius. Fourteen such eruptions would produce a mass equal to Mont Blanc, reckoning from the level of the sea, and twenty-six such large eruptions have occurred since the twelfth century. In the year 1783, when the earthquake of Calabria occurred, the Skaptaar volcano, in Iceland, poured forth a stream of lava fifty miles long, between twelve and fifteen broad, and from one to six hundred feet in thickness, which must have been equal to six times the mass of Mont Blanc, and two and a half times that of Chimborazo.

From the discovery of America to the year 1759 the plain of Malpais, a volcanic district in Mexico, had remained undisturbed, and was covered with plantations of indigo and sugar-cane at the latter period. In the month of June a succession of earthquakes commenced, and on the night of September 28 a tract not less than from three to four miles in extent rose up in the shape of a dome; and six great masses suddenly appeared, having an elevation of from thirteen hundred and twelve to sixteen hundred and forty feet above the original level of the plain. The most elevated of these is the volcano of Jorullo, which is continually burning, the projection of which, with its kindred masses, must have created a considerable subterranean vacuity; and probably the whole dome-shaped plain of Malpais is hollow. Hence it is a common event, in countries subject to great volcanic activity, for portions of the surface to fall in, the subsidence frequently becoming the bed of a lake. A part of the forest of Aripas, in Caraccas, thus subsided in the year 1790; a lake was formed nearly half a mile in diameter, and from eighty to a hundred yards in depth; and for several months after, the trees of the forest remained green under the water. In the same year, in Sicily, at Santa Maria de Nisremi, a portion of the country three Italian miles in circumference sank thirty feet deep. Occurrences of the same kind appear to take place in the depth of the sea, the falling in of its bed being indicated on the surface of the waters by their sudden retreat and violent agitation on their return. A remarkable example of this phenomenon took place at Marseilles, June 28, 1812, when the water in the harbor suddenly sank, then rushed out with great rapidity, and returned with equal violence — a movement which was repeated several times, till the equilibrium was restored, occasioning considerable damage to the shipping. Instances of similar events are innumerable, which serve to prove the existence of cavities, both in the interior of the exposed crust of the earth, and those parts of it over which the ocean rolls.

To Humboldt we are indebted for a large amount of information respecting the cavities which appear upon the surface, the chief differences in their form, the beds in which they are found, and the causes which may have originated them. In the primary rocks caverns are relatively fewer than in the later deposits, while the oldest masses of the granite and gneiss formations are particularly destitute of them. The principal are wide fissures, sometimes of unknown depth, and those hollow passages which occur in Switzerland and Dauphiné, called crystal caves, owing to their walls being richly furnished with pillars of rock crystal. Similar vacuities occur in the gneiss of the Pine Mountain, in the neighborhood of Wiesenthal, but they are not important. In Sweden and Norway the granite presents fissures and caves of extraordinary extent, and hitherto perfectly unexplored — such as the cave of Marienstadt, the end of which is not known, and the enormous deep hole at Frederickstall, where a stone thrown in only gives the echo of its fall in a minute and a half or two minutes; an observation which, if well founded, would give, on the calculation of Perrit, a precipitous depth of fifty-nine thousand and forty nine feet, the highest estimate, or thirty-nine thousand eight hundred and sixty-six feet, the least; that is, from twice to three times the height of Chimborazo. It is the primitive limestone that supplies the most numerous examples of caves and grottos in the primary rocks; and if these yield in point of size to the later limestone formations, this arises from the inferior extent of the primitive limestone, rather than from its incapacity to form caves. In the transition mountains, and those of stratified structure, it is still the limestone in which the more extensive caves are found, of which those of the Hartz, the splendid caverns of Derbyshire, and those of the Carpathians, are well known. Caverns most frequently occur in the mountains of stratified limestone; and among these, one of the most modern formations, the Jura limestone, is particularly distinguished, and was therefore termed the cavern limestone by the early geologists. The celebrated caves of Franconia, the grotto of Notre Dame, between Grenoble and Lyons, the caves of Westphalia, and that of Kirkdale, in Yorkshire, England, occur in this formation. Next to the limestone in the stratified formations, the so called older gypsum, which contains salt, is the most abundant in caverns. They are of rare occurrence in the sandstone, have generally broad openings, but of no great extent. Such are the Cow-stall in Saxony, and a few caves in Bohemia.

In the volcanic rocks cavern formations are very common, and one of the most splendid examples in the world occurs in the basalt, a rock of comparatively modern igneous origin. This is the well-known Cave of Fingal, in the Island of Staffa, a small island on the western coast of Scotland, composed entirely of amorphous and pillared basalt. The name of the island is derived from its singular structure, Staffa signifying, in the language of the Norwegians,—a people who were early on this coast,—a staff, and, figuratively, a column. The basaltic columns have, in various places, yielded to the action of the waves, which have scooped out caves of the most picturesque description, the chief of which are the Boat Cave, the Cormorant Cave, so called from the number of these birds visiting the spot, and the great Cave of Fingal. It is remarkable that this grand natural object should have remained comparatively unknown, until Sir Joseph Banks had his attention accidentally directed to it, and may be said to have discovered it to the inhabitants of South Britain. This great cavern consists of a lava-like mass at the base, and of two ranges of basaltic columns resting upon it, which present to the eye an appearance of regularity almost architectural, and supporting an irregular ceiling of rock. According to the measurements of Sir Joseph Banks, the cave from the rock without is three hundred and seventy-one feet six inches; the breadth at the mouth, fifty-three feet seven inches; the height of arch at the mouth, one hundred and seventeen feet six inches; depth of water at the mouth, eighteen feet, and at the bottom of the cave, nine feet. The echo of the waves which wash into the cavern has originated its Gaelic name, Llaimh-binn, the "cave of music." McCulloch remarks, "If too much admiration has been lavished on it by some, and if, in consequence, more recent visitors have left it with disappointment, it must be recollected, that all descriptions are but pictures of the feelings of the narrator; it is, moreover, as unreasonable to expect that the same objects should produce corresponding effects on all minds, on the enlightened and on the vulgar, as that every individual should alike be sensible of the merits of Phidias and Raphael, of Sophocles and of Shakspeare. But if this cave were even destitute of that order and symmetry, that richness arising from multiplicity of parts combined with greatness of dimension and simplicity of style which it possesses, still the prolonged length, the twilight gloom half concealing the playful and varying effects of reflected light, the echo of the measured surge as it rises and falls, the transparent green of the water, and the profound and fairy solitude of the whole scene, could not fail strongly to impress a mind gifted with any sense of beauty in art or in nature, and it will be compelled to own it is not without cause that celebrity has been conferred on the Cave of Fingal." Caverns occur in modern porphyry in the neighborhood of Quito, and even in modern lavas, the ejection of which has taken place within the memory of man. Flinders has made us acquainted with caves in the lava of the Isle of France; and in the lava of Vesuvius of 1805, Gay-Lussac found several upon a small scale. But caverns of an enormous extent occur in the lava of Iceland, that of Gurtshellir, situated in the torrent which has flowed from Bald Yökul, being forty feet in height, by fifty in breadth, and nearly a mile in length. Beautiful black volcanic stalactites hang from the high and spacious vault, and the sides present a succession of vitrified horizontal stripes, a thick coating of ice clear as crystal covering the floor. Henderson, in particular, describes one spot, the grandeur of which surpassed all expectation, the light of the torches rendering it peculiarly enchanting. The roof and sides of the cave were decorated with the most superb icicles, crystallized in every possible form; while from the icy floor rose pillars of the same substance, assuming all the curious and fantastic shapes imaginable, mocking the proudest specimens of art, and counterfeiting many well-known objects of animated nature. A more brilliant scene, says Henderson, perhaps never presented itself to the human eye, nor was it easy for us to divest ourselves of the idea that we actually beheld one of the fairy scenes depicted in Eastern fable.

Among the forms under which caverns present themselves, Humboldt distinguishes only three principal kinds, which essentially differ from each other, notwithstanding all their apparent irregularities.

The first appear in the form of cracks or fissures, like empty veins of ore, of greater or less extent, but narrow and considerably prolonged, often penetrating far into the mountain, and only reaching the day at one end. Eldon Hole, in the Peak of Derbyshire, England, is an example of this class. This is a deep, yawning chasm, in the limestone strata, but no longer considered one of the wonders of the region, as its presumed unfathomable depths have been satisfactorily measured. In the reign of Queen Elizabeth, the Earl of Leicester is said to have hired a man to go down into it to ascertain its extent and form. The account of the adventure states, that he was let down about two hundred ells, and after he had remained at the length of the rope a while, he was drawn up again, with great expectation of some discoveries; but he came up senseless, and died within eight days in a frenzied condition.

Eldon Hole is a fissure about sixty feet long, twenty wide, and two hundred deep. In the Philosophical Transactions for the year 1781 there is an account of the descent of Mr. Lloyd, who was let down with a rope by eight men, and found the light sufficiently strong at the bottom to allow him to read print. He discovered a fissure in the rock at the bottom, through which a strong current of air proceeded; but as the aperture was nearly filled up with huge stones, he could not examine it. A former owner of the pasture in which the chasm is situated, having lost cattle by falling into it, made the attempt to fill it up, and threw down many loads of stones without any visible effect, some of which were probably those which choked the aperture reached by Mr. Lloyd. The whole extent and actual depth of Eldon Hole have not, therefore, been ascertained.

There is a second kind of caverns which are essentially distinguished from the first, by the circumstance that they reach the daylight at both ends, piercing through the rocks in which they are situated, and forming natural shafts. Their appearance is very remarkable when they occur on the top of isolated mountain peaks, or of independent masses of rock; and when they are so straight that the daylight appears through them, they present a very remarkable aspect, and have been designated by the name of transparent caverns. On this account, the so named Martin's Hole is particularly celebrated. It penetrates the Tschingel Peak, one of the highest mountains of the Dodi chain; and twice in the year, in March and in September, the sun appears as if through a pipe, and gives to the valley beneath a highly singular and pleasing light. A similar phenomenon has been described by Pontoppidan as occurring in Norway, where there is a perforation of the mountain of Torghatten, in Helgeland, of fifty fathoms in height, and a hundred fathoms in length, through which the daylight appears. Like phenomena present themselves at the hollow stone of Muggendorf; likewise in Saxon Switzerland, and a whole series of these perforations occur on the coast of the Island of Heligoland, and on the coast of New Zealand.

The third and most frequent form of caverns is unquestionably that in which there is a series of extensions of nearly similar height and direction, which are connected with each other by passages of greater or less extent. This is the form of the caverns of the Hartz, the Cave of Caripe, visited by Humboldt, of Antiparos, and of the Peak of Derbyshire. This is also the form of the more important caves of Franconia. The extent of these penetrations into the mountains, in particular of such as are situated in limestone, is often very extraordinary. In many of them the extremity has never been reached; and it appears from concurrent testimony, that some of them have been explored for more than a mile in length. The cave of Adelsberg, six miles from Trieste, is remarkable both for its length and height. Deep abysses, of five and six hundred feet, often occur in it; and in one of these, it was found necessary to give up the attempt to proceed farther. The entrance resembles a fissure in a huge rock caused by an earthquake. Here torches are always lighted to conduct visitors. The cavity itself seems as if divided into several large halls and other apartments. The vast number of pillars by which it is ornamented by nature gives it a superb appearance; for they are as white as snow, and have a kind of transparent lustre. The bottom is of the same material; so that a person may imagine he is walking among the ruins of some stately palace, amidst noble pillars and columns, partly mutilated and partly entire. From the top, sparry icicles are seen every where suspended; in some places resembling wax tapers, which, from their radiant whiteness, appear extremely beautiful. Here occurs that extraordinary animal the Proteus, in shape between a lizard and an eel, transparently white, with a tinge of rose color about the head. It adds, as Davy remarks, one instance more to the number already known of the wonderful manner in which life is produced and perpetuated, even in places which seem the least suited to organized existences — an animal to which the presence of light is not essential, living indifferently in air and in water, on the surface of the rock, or in the depths of the mud.

Of an analogous kind is the Peak Cavern in Castleton Dale, England, the approach to which is in the highest degree magnificent. The traveller passes through a chasm between two ranges of perpendicular rocks, having on his left a rivulet which issues from the cave, and pursues its splashing course over craggy and broken masses of limestone. A vast mass of rock suddenly appears before him, with the mouth of the cavern, which assumes the form of a depressed arch, a hundred and twenty feet in width, forty-two in height, and about ninety in receding depth. At the first entrance a spectator is surprised to find that a number of twine makers have established their residence and manufactory within this gulf; and their rude appearance and machines singularly combine with the sublime features of the natural scenery. After proceeding about thirty yards, the roof becomes lower, and a narrow passage is reached, where the blaze of day, which has been gradually softened into twilight, wholly disappears, and all further researches must be prosecuted by torch light. After penetrating twenty or thirty yards in a stooping posture, there is a spacious opening, beyond which is the margin of a small lake, called the First Water, the overhanging rock descending in one place to within twenty inches of its surface. The lake is crossed in a boat or skiff, partly filled with straw, in which the passenger lies down, and is conveyed to the other side, where a spacious vacuity opens, two hundred and twenty feet in length, two hundred feet broad, and in some parts one hundred and twenty feet high; but from the want of light, neither the roof nor the sides of this great cavity can be plainly discerned. Proceeding onwards by the side of the Second Water, there is a projecting pile of rocks, popularly called Roger Rain's House, on account of the water incessantly dripping from the crevices of the roof. Beyond this, another hollow opens, called the Chancel, where the rocks appear much broken, and the sides are covered with stalactical incrustations. Here the stranger is generally surprised by an invisible vocal concert, which bursts in wild and discordant tones from the upper regions of the cavern, where a group of women and children are stationed for the purpose, the inhabitants of some of the huts at the entrance. After leaving the Chancel, and passing the Devil's Cellar, and the Half-way House, the path leads beneath three natural arches to another vast concavity, termed Great Tom of Lincoln, from its resemblance to a bell. Here, under the influence of a strong light, the arrangements of the rock, the spiracles in the roof, and the flowing stream, produce a striking scene. From this point the vault gradually descends, the passage contracts, and at length leaves only room sufficient for the stream. The entire length of this great excavation is twenty-two hundred and fifty feet, and its depth from the surface of the mountain about six hundred and twenty. A striking effect is frequently produced by the explosion of a small quantity of powder, wedged into a crevice of the rock, the report of which rolls along the roof and sides, like a heavy and prolonged peal of overwhelming thunder. On returning from this dark recess, the effect of the light is singularly impressive. The rocks appear as if highly illuminated, and the plants and mosses upon them so vividly green, as to produce the impression that the sun must be shining brilliantly upon them, when the day is really dull and hazy. The Peak Cavern is thus an example of a succession of great chambers, connected together by narrow passages; and when we remember the soluble nature of the stone, and the stream which flows through it, there can be no doubt that, if not formed altogether by the action of water, it yet owes its present condition to that agency. A more extraordinary spot, perhaps, is in the neighborhood, at the foot of the Winnats, or Windgates, called also the Portals of the Winds, a deep and narrow inclined chasm, about a mile in length, the lower descent of which commands a fine view of the beautiful vale of Castleton. Here is the Speedwell mine, an artificial excavation, leading to a great natural cavern. After descending upwards of a hundred steps, and reaching the blackness of darkness, the visitor embarks upon a canal so narrow as to be able to touch the rock on both sides, and the ceiling above. Proceeding along this channel, which is not far short of half a mile in length, the guide pushing along the boat, an immense vacuity in the mountain is reached, and landing upon a ledge of rock, the scene becomes indescribably strange and appalling with the aid of a Bengal light. On the one hand there is an abyss of unknown depth, appropriately called the Bottomless Pit, into which the water from the level falls with a startling sound, and which swallowed up forty thousand tons of material in the excavation of the mine. On the other hand, an enormous cavity opens above, the ceiling of which no light can reach, for rockets have been here let off, and have given out their brilliant coruscations as freely as from the surface of the earth.

Humboldt describes a somewhat dissimilar but very remarkable cavern in the western world, in the province of New Andalusia, not far from the convent of Caripe, called the Cavern of the Guacharo — the name of a class of nocturnal birds which make it their abode. The exterior of the place was majestic even to one accustomed to the picturesque scenery of the Alps. He had visited the Peak Cavern, and was acquainted with the different caves of Franconia, the Hartz and Carpathian Mountains; and the uniformity generally observable in all these led him to expect a scene of a similar character in that which he explored in the new world: but the reality far exceeded his expectations; for, if the structure of the cave resembled those he had elsewhere witnessed, the majesty of equinoctial vegetation gave an individual character and indescribable superiority to the entrance of the Cavern of the Guacharo. The entrance is a vaulted arch eighty feet broad and seventy-two feet high; the steep rock that surmounts this opening is covered with gigantic trees, mixed with creeping and climbing plants and shrubs, brilliant with blossoms of the richest colors and the most varied forms. These form natural festoons, which hang from the mouth of the cave, and are gently agitated by the passing currents of air. Among them Humboldt enumerates a *dendrobium*, an orchideous plant, with golden flowers spotted with black, and three inches long; a *bignonia*, with a violet blossom; a purple *dolichos;* and a magnificent *solandra*, the deep orange flower of which has a fleshy tube four inches long. But this luxuriant vegetation was not alone confined to the exterior. The traveller, on following the banks of a subterranean stream into the grotto, beheld them, with astonishment, adorned for thirty or forty yards with the Praga palm tree, plantain-leaved heliconias, eighteen feet high, and arms that resembled trees in their size. It was not found necessary to light their torches till they had reached the distance of four hundred and thirty feet, owing to the continuous direction of the cavern, which allows the light of day to penetrate thus far; and when this began to fail, the hoarse cries of the nocturnal birds began to be audible from a distance. The shrill, discordant noise made by thousands of these birds, brought from the inmost recesses of the cave and reverberated from the arched roofs, formed an indescribable clamor. The Indian guides, by fixing torches to the ends of long poles, showed the traveller the nests of the birds, which were constructed in funnel-shaped holes, with which the roof of the grotto was pierced in all directions, and generally at about sixty feet high. Still pursuing the course of the river, the cavern preserved the same width and height to the distance of fourteen hundred and fifty-eight feet from the mouth. The traveller, on turning round, was struck with the singularly beautiful appearance which a hill covered with the richest vegetation, immediately fronting the entrance of the grotto, presented. This, brilliantly illumined by the sun's rays, and seen through the vista of the dark cave, formed a striking contrast to the surrounding obscurity; while the large stalactites depending from the roof were relieved against the luminous background of verdure. After surmounting, with some difficulty, an abrupt rise in the ground where the stream forms a small cascade, he found that the cave diminished in height to forty feet, but retained its original direction. Here a blackish mould was found, either brought by the rivulet or washed down from the roof by the rain water which penetrates the crevices of the rock; and in this he found seeds growing, which had been brought thus far by the birds, but so altered by the deprivation of light that the species of plant thus produced under such unfavorable circumstances could not even be recognized. It was found impossible to persuade the Indian guides to advance farther. The cries of the birds, rendered still more horrible by the contraction of the cave, had such an effect on their minds that they absolutely refused to proceed; and, to the regret of Humboldt, he was compelled to retrace his steps.

In Bolonchen, Yucatan, there is a remarkable cavern, from which the inhabitants obtain water four or five months in the year, when the wells of the village are dry. The entrance to this cavern is by a lofty and abrupt opening, under a ledge of overhanging rock. At the distance of sixty paces from the entrance the descent is precipitous for about eighty feet, and is accomplished by a ladder. A little farther advance leads to the brink of a great perpendicular descent, to the bottom of which a strong body of light is thrown from a hole in the surface, a depth of two hundred and ten feet. From the brink of this precipice the descent is made by a ladder between seventy and eighty feet long and about twelve feet wide, rudely constructed of the rough trunks of saplings, lashed together lengthwise, and supported by horizontal trunks braced against the face of the precipitous rock. In the large cavern at the foot of this ladder a village *fête* is annually held, at the opening of the wells in the *cueva*, which takes place on a day appointed by the municipality. The walls of the rocky chamber are dressed with branches and hung with lights, and the whole village come out with refreshments and music, the pastor at their head, and pass the day in dancing in the cavern, and rejoicing that when one source of supply fails another is opened to their need.

By a laborious descent from this great cavern, Mr. Stephens, to whom we are indebted for this information, reached a pool of water calculated to be at a depth of four hundred and fifty feet perpendicular height, and fourteen hundred feet distant from the entrance to the cave. There are seven water pools, several of which Mr. Stephens visited, reached by various passages diverging from the great cavern at the foot of the ladder.

Caverns, especially those which are situated in limestone, commonly present the formations called stalactites, from a Greek word signifying distillation or dropping. The manner of their production admits of a very plain and simple explanation. They proceed from water trickling through the roofs containing carbonate of lime held in solution by carbonic acid. Upon exposure to the air the carbonic acid is gradually disengaged, and a pellicle of lime is deposited. The process proceeds, drop after drop, and, eventually, descending points hanging from the roof are formed, resembling icicles, which are composed of concentric rings of transparent pellicles of lime, presenting a very peculiar appearance, and, from their connection with each other, producing a variety of singular shapes. These descending points are the stalactites, properly so called, from which the stalagmites are to be distinguished, which cover the floors of caverns with conical inequalities. These are produced by the evaporation of the larger drops which have fallen to the bottom, and are stalactites rising upwards from the ground. Frequently, in the course of ages, the ascending and descending points have been so increased as to meet each other, forming natural columns, a series of which bears a striking resemblance to the pillars and arches of Gothic architecture.

The amount of this deposition which we find in caverns capable of producing it is in fact enormous, and gives us an impressive idea of their extraordinary antiquity. The Grotto of Antiparos, one of the islands of the Grecian Archipelago, is particularly celebrated on account of the size and diversity of form of these deposits. It extends nearly a thousand feet beneath the surface in primitive limestone, and is accessible by a narrow entrance, which is often very steeply inclined, but divided by level landing-places. After a series of descents the traveller arrives at the Great Hall, as it is called, the sides and roof of which are covered with immense incrustations of calcareous matter. The purity of the surrounding stone, and the thickness of the roof in which the unfiltered water can deposit all impure admixtures, give to its stalactites a beautiful whiteness. Tall pillars stand in many places free, near each other, and single groups of stalagmites form figures so strongly resembling plants that Tournefort endeavored to prove from them a vegetable nature in stone. The remark of that intelligent traveller is an amusing example of over confidence: "Once again I repeat it, it is impossible this should be done by the droppings of water, as is pretended by those who go about to explain the formation of congelations in grottos. It is much more probable that these other congelations we speak of, and which hang downwards or rise out different ways, were produced by our principle, namely — vegetation." The sight of the whole is described, by those who have visited this cavern, as highly imposing. In the middle of the Great Hall there is a remarkably large and fine stalagmite, more than twenty feet in diameter and twenty-four feet high, termed the Altar, from the circumstance of the Marquis de Nointel, the ambassador from Louis XIV. to the sultan, having caused high mass to be celebrated here in the year 1673. The ceremony was attended by five hundred persons; the place was illuminated by a hundred large wax torches; and four hundred lamps burned in the grotto, day and night, for the three days of the Christmas festival. This cavern was known to the ancient Greeks, but seems to have been completely lost sight of till the seventeenth century. Some of the caves of France and Germany have a high reputation for the number and beauty of their deposits; but the finest examples are found in the Cave of Adelsberg, to which reference has been made. The stalagmites here have formed two bridges over the subterranean river, which are situated almost a mile apart from each other, the inner one of which hangs suspended from eighty to a hundred fathoms over the abyss. An American visitor graphically describes some of the principal objects: "We advanced with ease," he states, "through the windings of the cavern, which at times was so low as to oblige us to stoop, and at times so high that the roof was lost in the gloom. But every where the most wonderful varieties of stalactites and crystals met our admiring view. At one time we saw the guides lighting up some distant gallery far above our heads, which had all the appearance of verandas adorned with Gothic tracery. At another, we came into what seemed the long-drawn aisles of a Gothic cathedral brilliantly illuminated. The whimsical variety of forms surpasses all the powers of description. Here was a butcher's shop, which seemed to be hung with joints of meat, and there a throne with a magnificent canopy. There was the appearance of a statue with a bearded head, so perfect that you could have thought it the work of a sculptor; and farther on, towards the end of our walk, the figure of a warrior with a helmet and coat of mail, and his arms crossed, of the illusion of which, with all my efforts, I could not possibly divest my mind. Two stalactites, descending close to each other, are called, in a German inscription over them, with sentimentality truly German, '*the union of two hearts*.' The resemblance is certainly very striking. After passing the Hearts we came to the Ball Room. It is customary for the inhabitants of Adelsberg and the surrounding country to come on Whit-Monday to this grotto, which is brilliantly illuminated; and the part called the Ball Room is actually employed for that purpose by the peasantry. A gallery, very appositely formed by nature, serves the musicians for an orchestra; and wooden chandeliers are suspended from the vaulted roof. It is impossible for me to describe minutely all the wonderful varieties; the Fountains seeming, as they fall, to be frozen into stone; the Graves, with weeping willows waving over them; the Picture; the Cannon; the Confessional; the Pulpit; the Sausage Maker's Shop; and the Prisons. I must not omit mentioning one part, which, though less grand than many others, is extremely curious. The stalactites have here formed themselves like folds of linen, and are so thin as to be transparent.

Some are like shirt ruffles, having a hem, and looking as if they were embroidered; and there is one, called the Curtain, which hangs exactly in natural folds like a white and pendent sheet. Every where you hear the dripping as of a continual shower, showing that the mighty work is still going on, though the several stages of its progress are imperceptible. Our attention was so excited, that we had walked two hours without feeling the least fatigue, or being sensible of the passage of time. We had gone beyond the point where most travellers had stopped, and had been rewarded for it by seeing stalactites of undiminished whiteness, and crystals glittering, as the light shone upon them, like unnumbered diamonds."

Stalactical depositions vary in color according to the nature of the surrounding rocks, and Humboldt remarks in general that the formations occur more beautifully and completely in proportion as the caves are narrow and enclosed, since the deposition of crystals is less disturbed by the circulation of the surrounding air. On this account, those of the wide open Cavern of Caripe, which he explored, were far inferior to the stalactites of Adelsberg. In England the spot most remarkable for these formations is the Blue John mine, another of the celebrated places of the Peak, near its great cavern. This is a natural cavity, worked as a mine for the sake of obtaining the elegant fluor spar which gives its name to the site, and which is here found in small detached pieces in the limestone rock. Rude steps, leading downwards about sixty yards, conduct to a series of caverns and passages incrusted with depositions of lime, which have assumed a variety of interesting forms. In one instance, stalactites, of a delicate pearly yellow color, of fine texture, and fantastically varied one from the other, have grown downwards until they rested upon some shelf of a lower stratum, probably of earthy matter. Arriving at such a plane, the waters spread more widely around, forming a deposit, and connecting the former stems with an inferior tablet of similar composition. The earthy or mineral stratum having been by some chance removed, the fairy columns attached to their kindred floor now remain suspended in middle space. These are graphically termed the Organ. It is much to be regretted that a continental reproach against the English — that of their eyes being in their fingers — here receives an illustration of its truth. Some unprincipled and vagabond sight-seers have wantonly mutilated this rarity, and deprived it of its earlier proportions, for which cause the relics are now upbraidingly exhibited in a rude wooden cage. Here, as at Antiparos, the principal subterranean apartment is termed the Hall, a wide and lofty cavity, such as imagination conceives would be a fitting home for the romantic outlaws of Salvator Rosa, or the spurious banditti of Mortimer. In this spot, not a long time ago, a popular nobleman, who prosecuted adventurous researches in the most dangerous recesses of the mine, feasted a multitude of his friends, and made the wet rock resound to the toasts and sentiments imported from a more fashionable atmosphere. In a certain direction from this grand focus the visitor is led to a narrower and more irregular space, presenting a towering cupola, the grandeur of whose shivered sides can only be exhibited by drawing upwards, with cord and pulley, a round of lighted candles supplied by the conductor: these illuminate successively the varied and peculiar stages of the internal surface. The perpetual waters which trickle down have left a residuum of lime, which has been moulded, by accident, and by industrious and gentle operation, into a thousand free tresses and waving bands. The whole is fashioned by nature with less of the abrupt form which characterizes the congelation of fountain streams by cold, and presents a grotesque enamel of exquisite polish and gracefulness, giving to the artificial plain or colored lights uplifted within the conical abyss beautiful reflections from its unrivalled crystallized surfaces. Frequently, while attention is riveted to the precinct of gloom and awful solitude, a chant of voices is heard from the summit of the dome, accessible by hidden performers from other avenues of the mine. The fleeting and distant expression of sound, with the mournful intervals of the strain, seems like a song of captive spirits, obedient to the rigid discipline of some invincible gnome

The Mammoth Cave, in Kentucky, is celebrated for the beauty of its stalactites, and for its great extent, it being the largest yet discovered.* It contains two hundred and twenty-six avenues, forty-seven magnificent chambers or halls, twenty-three deep pits, several lakes, eight cataracts, and three rivers, one of which is three miles in length, and wide and deep enough to float a ship.

Audubon's Avenue, not far from the entrance of the cave, is more than a mile in length, fifty or sixty feet in width, and as many in height. The Gothic Avenue, so named from its resemblance to Gothic architecture, is two miles in length, and of great beauty. Cleveland's Avenue, which is three miles in length, its height varying from fifteen to seventy feet, is remarkable for the beauty of its stalactical formations. The Church, in which religious worship has sometimes been held, and which has a natural pulpit, behind which is a recess capable of accommodating an organ and choir, is one hundred feet in diameter, and sixty feet in height. The Ball Room is a splendid hall, furnished by nature with a beautiful gallery, and an orchestra large enough to accommodate a hundred musicians. The Star Chamber is a large apartment, arched on each side, the ceiling of which, when illuminated, appears as if studded with stars. The Temple is an immense vault, extending over an area of two acres, and crowned by a dome of solid rock, one hundred and twenty feet in height. The Mammoth Dome, which is four hundred feet in height, is an object of great beauty and magnificence. Croghan's Hall, nine miles from the mouth of the cave, is fifty or sixty feet in diameter, and is adorned with massive and beautifully colored stalactites. The Dead Sea is a sheet of water of considerable extent, apparently without any current, and is furnished with boats for the accommodation of visitors. Here fish are found which have no eyes, and hence are called *Pisces Bartimei.*

* See engraving opposite page 382.

A distinguished English author thus alludes to this cave, in a letter to a friend: "Last week I had the pleasure of exploring, with several other persons, the Mammoth Cave, in Kentucky. I make use of the term 'pleasure' in no conventional sense, but in its true and honest one, as significant of a happy feeling.

"I have described many things in my life, with, I believe, some force and capacity; but were you to offer me the world, I could not, either to my own or your satisfaction, describe what I have seen in the monarch of caves from which I have just come.

"I can but speak in the way of likeness or analogy. Well, then, I must say that in the Mammoth Cave is a cathedral in which any lord primate might be proud to preach, did not the solemnity of the place admonish all humanity to humbleness — a cathedral whose gigantic buttresses, and delicately-wrought friezes, quatre foils, &c., are respectively as bold and minute as any ever found in the great Christian temples of the upper world.

"There are portions of the cave called Arbors — a fit title; fanciful in their arrangement, and beautiful in their colors, they are fit for the reposing places of the prettiest fairies that ever danced in a ring beneath the moonlight. Then there are chambers of Cimmerian gloom — quite chaotic; but which, when they catch the reflection of light, display stalactites of brilliant hues, hanging as it were in mid air; and afar overhead a second firmament studded with stars.

"We are taken along a river named after, and like what the imagination may conceive of the fabled Styx. How silent is all upon the shores of this river! How appropriate it seems, as a flood running between two worlds! Then there are domes large and beautiful, avenues of miles' length, chambers, waterfalls, and recesses. Verily they must all be seen to be understood."

The temperature of caverns exhibits great diversities, dependent upon their extent and form, and that of the same cavern will greatly vary at different seasons. In those which are dry and deep, covered with a thick, stony roof, and withdrawn from the influence of the alteration of the external air by having only a limited opening, the temperature can vary but little, and will continue through the whole year at nearly the same degree of warmth which is peculiar to their geographical situation. Before the warmer air of summer has so penetrated the roof that the temperature of the cavern can be somewhat raised, the cooler air of the autumn and of the winter begins to penetrate; but before this lower temperature can establish itself, it is again overtaken by the warmth of the following spring and summer. The consequence of all this is a temperature subject to little alteration, but lower than the mean temperature of the surrounding atmosphere. The ancient Romans, hence, according to Seneca, were accustomed to erect their country seats in the vicinity of those natural cavities which abound about the capital, for the purpose of enjoying their refreshing chilliness in the summer season. It was in one of these volcanic caverns that Tiberius was nearly destroyed while at supper; for, during the banquet, the roof suddenly gave way, and buried several of his attendants beneath its ruins, when Sejanus threw himself upon the emperor to preserve him from the falling stones.

Many caverns, however, vary greatly in their temperature, and exhibit the apparently strange anomaly of being cold when the external air is warm, and warm when it is cold, in some instances carrying this contrast to the extreme, so as to be coated with ice amid the heat of summer, and affording a comfortable warmth amid the cold of winter. In the neighborhood of Czilicze, a village of Hungary, there is a cave in the transition limestone of the Carpathians which displays this phenomenon. The country in the vicinity abounds with woods, and the air is sharp and cold. The entrance of the cavern, which fronts the north, is eighteen fathoms high and eight broad; consequently, wide enough to receive a large supply of external air, which here generally blows with great violence; but the subterranean passages, which consist entirely of solid rock, winding round, stretch away farther to the north than has been yet discovered. In the midst of winter the air in this cavern is warm; but in summer, when the heat of the sun without is scarcely supportable, the cold within is not only very piercing, but so intense that the roof is covered with icicles of great size, which, spreading into ramifications, form very grotesque figures. When the snow melts, in spring, the inside of the cave, where its surface roof is exposed to the sun, emits a pellucid water, which immediately congeals as it drops, and thus forms the above icicles, and the very water that drops from them on the sandy ground freezes in an instant. It is even observed that the greater the heat is without, the more intense is the cold within, so that in the dog days all parts of this cavern are covered with ice, which the inhabitants use for cooling their liquors. The quantity of ice is so great that a narrator estimates that it would require six hundred wagons to remove it in a week. In autumn, when the nights grow cold and the heat of the day begins to abate, the ice in the cavern begins to dissolve, so that by winter no more ice is seen. The cavern then becomes perfectly dry, and has a mild warmth. At that season it is the haunt of swarms of flies, gnats, bats, owls, and even of hares and foxes that resort hither as to their winter retreat, and remain till the return of spring. An instance almost as singular occurs at Besançon, in a grotto which extends three hundred and sixty-four feet into the rock, the mouth of which, like that of Czilicze, is towards the north, and covered with vegetation. During the whole summer this cavern contains masses of ice, which melt away in October and November.

This apparently anomalous phenomenon is supposed to be capable of being explained by the relation which subsists between the moisture in these caverns and the external air When it is hot and dry outside, as in summer, evaporation takes place, and by this means a considerable degree of warmth is withdrawn from the enclosed air, the vapors making their escape through the openings, and through fissures in the roofs. The greater the exterior temperature, the more vigorously the evaporation is carried on, producing a degree of cold in the interior which may sink beneath the freezing point, just as in the greatest heat we can most readily freeze water if we surround it with ether. On the contrary, the more the warmth and dryness of the external air are diminished, as in winter, the less will be its capability to promote evaporation in the cavern; the warmth contained in the air will no longer be absorbed, and the ice which has been produced must melt. The cooling in these caverns, however, so as to sink below the freezing point, can only occur where there is a certain relation, which but rarely subsists, between the openings and the evaporating surface of the interior. If the opening is too large, too much warm air is introduced, and the temperature of the interior is thereby much more increased than it can be diminished by evaporation. If it is too small, the vapors cannot withdraw themselves fast enough, and the evaporation is lessened, because the surrounding air is saturated with moisture. The ice caverns, therefore, are comparatively rare; but, in addition to those named, there is a cave at Vesoul, in France, where a stream flowing through it is frozen over in summer, and clear of ice in winter. Mr. Murchison, in the course of some recent geological surveys in Russia, met with a freezing cavern near the imperial salt works at Iletski, to the south of the Ural Mountains, situated at the southern base of a hillock of gypsum, one of a series of natural hollows used by the peasantry for cellars or stores. The cave in question is, however, the only one in the district which possesses the singular property of being partially filled with ice in summer, and of being destitute of it in winter. "Standing on the heated ground and under a broiling sun, I shall never forget," he remarks, "my astonishment when the woman to whom the cavern belonged unlocked a frail door, and a volume of air so piercingly keen struck the legs and feet, that we were glad to rush into a cold bath in front of us to equalize the effect." Three or four feet within the door, and on a level with the village street, beer and quash were half frozen. A little farther the narrow chasm opened into a vault fifteen feet high, ten paces long, and from seven to eight feet wide, which seemed to send off irregular fissures into the body of the hillock. The whole of the roof and sides were hung with solid, undripping icicles, and the floor was covered with hard snow, ice, or frozen earth. During the winter all these phenomena disappear; and when the external air is very cold, and all the country is frozen up, the temperature of the cave is such that the Russians state they could sleep in it without their sheepskins.

There is another circumstance of high interest disclosed by the interior of many caverns — the occurrence of extinct animals of the ancient earth; on which account these receptacles have obtained the name of zoolites, or bone caverns. This phenomenon prevails in almost every country of Europe, and also of America, and has obtained of late years, particularly by the investigations of Dr. Buckland, who has made it the subject of his peculiar study, a high degree of importance, on account of the light which it throws upon the ancient condition of the earth, and the changes which the surface has undergone. His researches into the condition of a cave discovered in 1821, at Kirkdale, in Yorkshire, are highly valuable, and deserve a notice here. Its mouth had long been choked up with rubbish, and overgrown with grass and bushes, but was accidentally found by some workmen. The cave is situated on the older portion of the oölite formation, on the declivity of a valley. It extends, as an irregular, narrow passage, two hundred and fifty feet into the hill. There are a few expansions, but scarcely high enough to allow a man to stand upright. The sides and floor were found covered with a deposit of stalagmite, beneath which there was a bed of from two to three feet of fine sandy and micaceous loam, the lower portion of which, in particular, contained an innumerable quantity of bones, with which the floor was completely strewn.

The greatest part of them were very well preserved, and still retained a great portion of their natural gluten, in consequence of the peculiar nature of their investiture. The animals to which they belonged were the hyena, bear, tiger, and lion, elephant, rhinoceros, hippopotamus, horse, ox, deer of three species, water rat, and mouse, belonging wholly to extinct species, and the same with those with which we are acquainted in the steppes of Asia. The most plentiful of all were the remains of the hyena; and from the amount which he saw, Buckland estimated the number of the individuals interred here to be between two and three hundred. The animal must have been one half larger than the living species, in its structure resembling the hyena of the Cape. The bears, which were less abundant, belonged to the large cavern species, which, according to Cuvier, was of the size of the large white bear, and about eight feet in length. The elephants were the Siberian mammoth. Of the stags the largest was of the size of the moose deer. Of the ox two species were distinguished, and its bones were most frequent, next to those of the hyena. All these bones lay irregularly strewed one with another, but those of the largest animals were in the most remote and narrowest corners, into which they never could have penetrated while living. The teeth, and the hard, marrowless bones of the extremities, as well as those of the fore and hind feet, were uninjured; these were so numerous that they must have belonged to a much greater number of individuals than could be estimated as belonging to the other bones. Many of the bones bore marks which exactly corresponded with the form of the incisor teeth of the hyena, and the broken horns of the stag were evidently marked by gnawing. These facts warranted the conclusion, that the hyenas must have lived for a long time in this cave, and have dragged the bones of the larger animals, particularly the oxen, into this den, as their prey. The supposition was confirmed in the most striking manner by a variety of other facts. Dr. Buckland found that bones which he caused to be gnawed by living hyenas had exactly the same appearance as those found in the cavern, and the teeth and harder bones were thrown aside by them. He even found in great abundance excrements of the hyena, which offered the closest resemblance to those of the living animal. From the facts described, it appears that the Kirkdale cave was for a long series of years a den inhabited by hyenas, who dragged into its recesses the other animal bodies whose remains are there commingled with their own, some great catastrophe causing an inundation in this region which destroyed the whole race.

Similar zoolitic caverns occur in the following places in England: 1. Kent's Cavern, in the limestone of North Devon, about a mile from Torquay. It is said to be nearly six hundred feet long, varying in width from two to seventy feet, and in height from one to six yards. The bones of extinct species of animals are found buried in a mass of mud, covered over with a crust of stalagmitic formation. From certain appearances in this cavern, it seems to have been in former times the habitation of man, perhaps the bandit's home. 2. Cave near the village of Hutton, in the Mendip Hills. This is a series of cavernous chambers found by the laborers in working for ochre, which occurs in fissures of the mountain limestone. In the first chamber, about twenty feet square and four high, a large stalactite depends from the roof in the centre, and beneath a stalagmite rises from the floor, nearly touching it. The bones from this cavern are those of the elephant, horse, ox, deer, bear, and hog. 3. Cave at Balleye, near Wirksworth. Bones and molar teeth of the elephant were discovered here in a cavity of mountain limestone by the lead miners, mentioned in the following record of a workman: "In sinking for lead at Baulee, within two miles of Wirksworth, A. D. 1663, they came to an open place as large as a church, and found a skeleton reclining against the side, so large that his brain pan would have held two strike of corn, and so big that they could not get it up without breaking it. My grandfather having a share in the said mine, they sent him a tooth weighing four pounds three ounces. — George Mower." Some of these remains are still preserved. 4. Dream Cave, near Wirksworth. This was likewise discovered by the miners in pursuing a vein of lead. After sinking about sixty feet through solid mountain limestone, they came to a large cavern filled with argillaceous earth and stony fragments. Here were found the remains of a rhinoceros, in a high state of preservation. They belonged apparently to the same individual, and formed probably an entire skeleton, though several parts were wanting, having been separated from the rest through the subsidence of the mass in which they were embedded into an underlying hollow, owing to the workmen disturbing the site. Bones of deer and fragments of horns were found in the same spot, all of which are now deposited in the Oxford Museum. 5. Cave on Derdham Down, near Clifton; a fissure which contained fragments of stone and stalagmite, with bones incrusted with stalactic matter, among which was a fossil joint of the horse. 6. Caves at Oreston, near Plymouth. Several caverns were discovered in removing materials for the construction of the breakwater from a hill of transition limestone. They contained bones belonging to a species of rhinoceros, the tiger, hyena, horse, ox, wolf, and deer. 7. Cave of Crawley Rocks, near Swansea. This cavity was accidentally intersected in working a quarry. It has now been entirely cut away. Various parts of the elephant, rhinoceros, hyena, ox, and stag were found in it. 8. Caves of Paviland. Two cavities occur in a lofty cliff of limestone facing the sea on the coast of Glamorganshire, which the waves reach in considerable storms. The remains of an immense number of animals of extinct species have been found in them.

It is clear from these facts, that anciently, as Dr. Buckland remarks, "extinct species of hyena, tiger, bear, elephant, rhinoceros, and hippopotamus, no less than the wolves, foxes, horses, oxen, deer, and other animals which are not distinguishable from existing species, had established themselves from one extremity of England to the other, — from the caves of Yorkshire to those of Plymouth and Glamorganshire, — whilst the diluvial gravel beds of Warwickshire, Oxford, and London show that they were not wanting also in the more central parts of the country; and M. Cuvier has established, on evidence of a similar nature, the probability of their having been spread in equal abundance over the continent of Europe. But it by no means follows, from the certainty of the bones having been dragged by beasts of prey into the small cavern at Kirkdale, that those of similar animals must have been introduced in all other cases in the same manner; for, as all these animals were the antediluvian inhabitants of the countries in which the caves occur, it is possible that some may have retired into them to die; others have fallen into the fissures by accident, and there perished; and others have been washed in by the diluvial waters. By some one or more of these latter hypotheses we may explain those cases in which the bones are few in number, and not gnawed, the caverns large, and the fissures extending upwards to the surface; but where they bear marks of having been lacerated by beasts of prey, and where the cavern is small, and the number of bones and teeth so great and so disproportionate to each other as in the cave at Kirkdale, the only adequate explanation is, that they were collected by the agency of wild beasts." In Germany the zoolitic caverns are much more numerous and important than in England. There is a remarkable example on the north-east border of the Hartz Mountains, called Bauman's Höhle, after an unfortunate miner, who, in the year 1670, ventured into it alone in search of ore; and, after having wandered three days and nights in its solitude and darkness, at length found his way out, but in such a state of exhaustion that he died almost immediately. It is a suit of natural chambers in a bed of transition limestone, the floor of which is composed of a thick crust of stalagmite, beneath which lies an accumulation of several feet of mud mixed with bones and pebbles. But the caves of Franconia are by far the richest and most beautiful of this class. They lie on the north-east extremity of the chain of the Jura, between Nuremburg and Baireuth, in the valley of the Wiesent, a tributary stream of the valley of the Maine. The most important is the Cave of Gailenreuth, situated in a perpendicular rock, its mouth being upwards of three hundred feet above the bed of the river, consisting of an aperture seven feet high and twelve broad. An open fissure in the rock, like the shaft of a mine, extends from the cave to the table land above. The floor consists of stalagmite lying over a bed of slime, which contains the animal remains. The cave has two chief chambers, the roof of which is abundantly hung with stalactites. The visitor descends to a considerable distance, by a ladder of rude construction, from the first to the second chamber, where he sees the breccia of bones, pebbles, and loam, and the artificial extension of the cavern by the removal of it. Almost all the bones belong to the bear of the caverns, and are admirably preserved. Those of a species of cat, resembling the American jaguar, have also been discovered, and those of the hyena; but the latter are of rare occurrence. In conformity with the habits of the bear, the remains of prey, dragged in, are almost entirely wanting. There are two neighboring caverns of the same class; those of Zahnloch (teeth-hole) and Küloch. The latter is supposed to contain animal matter equal to at least twenty-five hundred individuals of the cavern bear; and allowing an annual mortality of two and a half, it follows that here we have the history of a thousand years; for probably these animals retired to the solitude of this spot upon the approach of death, as is the well-known custom of many creatures. The bone caverns in Europe decisively prove that, previous to a great inundation in bygone time, animals inhabited these districts known not to have lived there from the earliest records of human history — the rhinoceros, elephant, and hyena, now, and for ages past, exclusively confined to more southern latitudes.

There is another class of caverns remarkable for the development of irrespirable gas, which often renders the access to them dangerous. They are of two kinds—those in which the gas is produced by the surrounding rocks, and those in which it proceeds from the interior of the earth. The first class are principally caves of gypsum. The gypsum is not, however, the cause of the phenomenon, the component parts of which are not susceptible of any decomposition from the air. There is commonly fetid limestone intimately mixed up with it, which forms connected wavy stripes, and even single beds of considerable thickness. This earthy limestone, which is penetrated with bitumen, and often very clayey in its composition, has the property of giving out all its carburetted hydrogen in the air; and in every case where caves exist in it, its presence, on account of its connection with gas, is offensive and much dreaded. In the limestone caves of the sandstone formations, on the contrary, there commonly prevails a very pure air. The development of irrespirable gases from the interior of the earth, which, penetrating through fissures, collect in caves, is a constant result of volcanic activity. The chemical processes continually going on in volcanic regions must produce the liberation of great quantities of gas, which are connected with the world above by these chimneys of the perpetual forge. Caverns of this nature occur, therefore, only in the neighborhood of volcanoes, or at points where volcanic processes may be supposed to be going on beneath. The gases so developed are almost entirely the carbonic and sulphuric acids. Among the most important of the grottos which give out carbonic acid, there is the Grotto del Cane at Naples, in the neighborhood of the Lake of Agnano, near Puzzuoli. It was known to the ancients, and is mentioned by Pliny, who refers to it as one of a class of excavations called, in his time, "Charon's ditches." Its size is very unimportant—ten feet deep, four feet broad, and nine feet high. The carbonic acid collects itself on the soil in a bed of about six inches deep, and, on account of its specific gravity, does not mingle with the atmospheric air. Its actual height may be clearly ascertained by lighting some candles, which, when they reach its surface, are extinguished at once. Small animals falling in are speedily suffocated; and it takes its name from the dogs which are placed in it by way of experiment. The cave and its neighborhood appear to have undergone some considerable changes; for, from Pliny's reference to the mephitic gas, it would seem to have been fatal to human life, which is not possible now, owing to the small height of the stratum, unless an individual threw himself upon the surface of the floor. According to some ancient accounts, bubbles were constant upon the Lake Agnano close by, occasioned by the escape of gas, of which there is no appearance now; so that the quantity of deadly air exhaled has been much reduced, if dependence may be placed upon these authorities. A similar instance, on a much larger scale, is seen in the crater of the extinct volcano of St. Leger, or of Neyruc, in the south of France, on the banks of the Ardêche, amid the great number of volcanic remains of that region. This crater exhibits a cultivated, and in part inhabited, district, which is surrounded, like an amphitheatre, by the ancient walls of volcanic debris. Its soil is one vast sieve for the ascent of carbonic acid. Perforations have been made in it to facilitate the emission of the gas, and guide it from the fields, to which its contact is very injurious. The height of the bed of gas, over the ground of these holes, has been found to be, in the most favorable circumstances, about one foot and a half. Changes of weather have the most important influence on it; and in violent rains the whole mass of gas is absorbed. The quantity of this gas, which issues from the soil of the whole neighborhood, has a very striking influence on the health of the inhabitants who work in these fields; and if the proprietors do not yearly clear out these perforations, their harvest is lost by means of the poisonous vapors. Another example occurs near Pyrmont, where there is a cavern of mephitic gas, named Dunsthohle, which exhibits the same phenomena as the Dog Grotto near Naples; and of a kindred kind is the extraordinary valley in the Island of Java, called by the natives Guevo-upas, (poisoned valley,) described at page 298.

In addition to the cavities which are the handiwork of nature, immense subterranean caverns have been formed by the industry and enterprise of man.

The demand for the mineral treasures of the earth, and especially its coal, created by the advance of civilization, has caused the undermining of its surface upon an extraordinary scale in modern times, and some of the English mines date their origin from the era of the ancient Britons. This is the case, as the name imports, with Odin's mine, at the southern foot of Mam Tor, in Derbyshire. A horizontal gallery, nearly a mile in length, leads to the vein of ore that is now worked, which varies in thickness from two or three inches to as many feet. Beautiful crystallizations of blende, barytes, calcareous spar, and selenite are found in this extensive excavation, as well as the curious and dangerous mineral called slikensides. "The effects of this extraordinary mineral," says Mr. Rhodes, "are not less singular than terrific. A blow with a hammer, a stroke or a scratch with a miner's pick, are sufficient to rend those rocks asunder with which it is united or imbodied. The stroke is immediately succeeded by a crackling noise, which is sometimes accompanied with a sound not unlike the mingled hum of a swarm of bees; shortly afterwards an explosion follows, so loud and appalling that even the miners, though a hardy race of men, and little accustomed to fear, turn pale and tremble at the shock. This dangerous combination of matter must, consequently, be approached with caution. To avoid the use of the common implements of mining, a small hole is carefully bored, into which a little gunpowder is put and exploded with a match, which gives the workmen time to withdraw to a place of safety, there to await the result of their operations. Sometimes not less than five or six successive explosions ensue, at intervals of from two to ten or fifteen minutes; and occasionally they are so sublimely awful that the earth has been violently shaken to the surface by the concussion, even when the discharge has taken place at the depth of more than one hundred fathoms."

The celebrated salt mines of Wiliescki, Poland, are also very ancient, having been worked since 1251. The entrance to these mines is by six shafts, of four or five yards in diameter; their greatest depth is nearly eight hundred feet, and the subterraneous excavations extend upwards of three miles. Various structures are formed in the body of salt itself. We find there a stable, chambers, and chapels, all the parts of which, including pillars, altars, and statues, are of pure salt. The number of persons employed in these mines is from twelve hundred to two thousand.

When a mine is opened, a shaft like a well is sunk perpendicularly from the surface of the ground, and from it horizontal galleries are dug at different levels, according to the direction of the metallic veins, and gunpowder is used to blast the rocks when too hard for the pickaxe. When mines extend very far in a horizontal direction, it becomes necessary to sink more shafts for ventilation, as well as for facility in raising the ore. Such is the perfection of underground surveying, that the work can be carried on at the same time from above and below, so exactly as to meet; and in order to accelerate the operation, the shaft is worked simultaneously from the different galleries or levels of the mine. In this manner a perpendicular shaft was sunk two hundred and four fathoms deep, about nineteen years ago, in the Consolidated mines in Cornwall; it was finished in twelve months, having been worked in fifteen different points at once. In that mine there are ninety-five shafts, besides other perpendicular communications under ground from level to level: the depth of the whole of these shafts, added together, amounts to about twenty-five miles; the galleries and levels extend horizontally about forty-three miles, and twenty-five hundred people are employed in it; yet this is but one of many mines now in operation in the mining district of Cornwall alone.

The infiltration of the rain and surface water, together with subterranean springs and pools, would soon inundate a mine, and put a stop to the work, were not means employed to remove it. The steam engine is often the only instrument adequate to the accomplishment of this object; and the produce of mines has been in proportion to the successive improvements in that machine. In the Consolidated mines already mentioned there are nine steam engines constantly pumping out the water; four of these, which are the largest ever made, together lift from thirty to fifty hogsheads of water per minute, from an average depth of two hundred and thirty fathoms. The power of the steam engines in draining the Cornish mines is equal to forty-four thousand horses — one sixth of a bushel of coals performing the work of a horse. The largest engine is between three hundred and three hundred and fifty horse power; but as horses must rest, and the engine works incessantly, it would require a thousand horses to do its work.

Mines in high ground are sometimes drained to a certain depth by an adit or gallery, dug from the bottom of a shaft in a sloping direction to a neighboring valley. One of these adits extends through the large mining district of Gwennap, in Cornwall; it begins in a valley near the sea, and very little above its level, and goes through all the neighboring mines, which it drains to that depth, and, with all its ramifications, is thirty miles long. Nent Force Level, in the north of England, forms a similar drain to the mines in Alston Moor; it is a stupendous aqueduct, nine feet broad, and in some places from sixteen to twenty feet high; it passes for more than three miles under the course of the River Nent to Nentsbury engine shaft, and is navigated under ground by long, narrow boats. Daylight at its mouth is seen like a star at the distance of a mile in the interior. Most of the adits admit of the passage of men and horses, with rails at the sides for wagons.

The ventilation of mines is accomplished by burning fires in some of the shafts, which are in communication with the others, so that currents of air flow up one and down the others. In some cases fresh air is carried into the mines by streams that are made to flow down some of the shafts. Were this not done, the heat, which increases with the depth, would be insupportable; ventilation diminishes the danger from the fire damp; for, even where Sir Humphry Davy's safety lamp is used, accidents happen from the carelessness of the miners.

The access to deep mines, as in Cornwall, is by a series of perpendicular or slightly-inclined ladders, sometimes uninterrupted, but generally broken at intervals by resting-places. It is computed that one third of a miner's physical strength was exhausted in ascending and descending a deep mine. They are now drawn up by the steam engine.

The greatest depth to which man has excavated is nothing when compared with the radius of the earth. The Eselschacht mine, at Kuttenberg, in Bohemia, now inaccessible, which is thirty-seven hundred and seventy-eight feet below the surface, is deeper than any other mine. Its depth is only one hundred and fifty feet less than the height of Vesuvius, and it is eight times greater than the height of the Pyramid of Cheops, or the cathedral of Strasburg, and more than seventeen times greater than the height of Bunker Hill Monument. The Monkwearmouth coal mine, near Sunderland, England, descends to fifteen hundred feet below the level of the sea, and the entire depth from the surface is sixteen hundred and eighty feet. A pair of ropes, used in this mine for elevating the coal from the bottom to the top of the shaft, weigh five and three fourth tons, and cost five hundred and fifty pounds.

The salt works of New Saltzwerk, in Prussia, are twenty-two hundred and thirty-one feet deep, and nineteen hundred and ninety-three feet below the level of the sea. Mines on high ground may be very deep without extending to the sea level: that of Valenciana, near Guanaxuato, in Mexico, is sixteen hundred and eighty-six feet deep, yet its bottom is fifty-nine hundred and sixty feet above the surface of the sea; and the mines in the higher Andes must be much more. For the same reason the rich mine of Joachimsthal, in Bohemia, twenty-one hundred and twenty feet deep, has not yet reached that level.

In descending into deep mines, the temperature becomes warmer in proportion to the distance from the surface of the earth. By experiments made at hundreds of places in Europe and America, both in mines and Artesian wells, the heat has been found to increase at the mean rate of one degree for every forty-five feet. At this rate, water would boil at the depth of a little more than a mile, and all rocks would be melted at the depth of sixty miles. Shall we, therefore, conclude that all the internal parts of the earth are actually in an incandescent, melted state? Many of the ablest geologists have not seen how they could escape this conclusion, especially when they see how it explains the spheroidal figure of the earth; also the phenomena of active and extinct volcanoes; the protrusion of the unstratified rocks; the numerous elevations of mountains and continents that have taken place, and the fact that a tropical climate once prevailed in the northern regions of the globe, even to the arctic circle. It has been proved by the profound mathematical researches of Baron Fourier, that even though all the internal parts of the earth, below the depth of eighteen or twenty miles, are five hundred times hotter than boiling water, — that is, in a melted state, — it would not increase the temperature at the surface more than one degree in two hundred thousand years, and consequently would not sensibly affect the climate. It would be presumptive to say that this doctrine of internal heat is as well established as the Newtonian doctrine of gravitation; yet every candid mind will acknowledge that it bears the strongest marks of probability, and that it lacks but little of being placed among the settled principles of science.

Still more certainly demonstrated is another related conclusion, viz., that the whole globe in early times was in a melted state, and has been slowly cooling ever since. It is certain that its internal parts are now at a higher temperature than the surface, and that the planetary space around the earth is as low as 70° below zero on Fahrenheit's scale. The laws of heat show, therefore, that the process of refrigeration must be now going on, and however little heat now escapes, it increases as we run backward through past ages, until we reach a period when it must have been great enough to have melted all known substances. That such a state of things once existed, the character of the rocks demonstrates. It is agreed on all hands that all the unstratified formations were once melted, and almost equally unanimous is the opinion that the stratified rocks, whether crystalline or sedimentary, were derived chiefly by abrasion from the unstratified. The spheroidal figure of the earth, exactly such as would be taken by a fluid globe revolving with the velocity of the earth, confirms this conclusion; and so do the facts as to the tropical and ultra-tropical character of the organic remains in the older rocks in high latitudes. Original fluidity and subsequent refrigeration are seemingly the only theory that will explain the elevation and subsidence of continents and mountain ranges. Moreover, the slow passage of worlds from a liquid and even a gaseous to a solid state, seems to be a law of the material universe. The evidence, therefore, appears to be overwhelming, to prove the early igneous fluidity of the earth, and scientific men will not long hesitate, if some of them now do, to place this among the demonstrated verities of philosophy.

A careful examination of all the rocks in the earth's crust, accessible to man, results in the conclusion, that the whole crust of the globe — at least several miles thick, and probably to its centre — has undergone an entire change, and most of the rocks several changes, since their creation. The unstratified rocks, which probably form the whole of the interior of the globe, have been melted, as all admit. The stratified class, lying above the unstratified, have been worn from the latter, and then deposited in water. Afterwards, they have been solidified by heat, and some of them so nearly melted as to become crystallized, constituting the metamorphic rocks. The loose materials now covering the surface have also been subsequently worn off by atmospheric and aqueous agencies, from whatever rocks were exposed. Probably no particle in the earth has now the form in which it was originally created. How different this from the common views of the earth's condition!

Another conclusion, forced upon the practical geologist, is, that the continents of our globe have, for long periods, and most of them several times, been beneath the ocean, and have been subsequently elevated from thence, or the waters have been drained off. At least two thirds of these continents are covered by rocks, thousands of feet thick, abounding in the remains of sea animals and plants, which evidently lived near where they are now found.

The number of species which have been found in the rocks is not less than thirty thousand; and, with the exception of a few near the top of the series, chiefly in clay and marl, they are different, often widely, from those now living on the globe; and hence the conclusion seems irresistible, that the fossil species must have lived and died before the present races had a being.

To accumulate materials, with their fossil contents, several miles thick, must have required immense periods of time. The fractured and upturned condition of most of the older rocks proves that they have been elevated by some internal force, acting vertically or laterally, to form continents. But in some places the strata, especially the newest, have never been disturbed, and in such cases it seems most probable that the waters have been drained off. Again, we have evidence often of the subsidence of the same continent that had long been above the waters, and then a second emergence. Nay, three, and even more vertical movements of this kind are sometimes shown by the geological monuments. In the tenth chapter of this volume we have abundant evidence that existing continents are now experiencing similar changes, in some places rising, and in others falling, yet so slowly as to be unnoticed, except by the most careful observation.

These vertical changes have not been effected without causing a vast amount of erosion at the earth's surface. While the continents were below the ocean, this work was aided in high latitudes by enormous icebergs, charged with bowlders, and driven by the currents along the surface, grinding down its salient parts, and sweeping along the abraded materials, even hundreds of miles from their original beds. The grooves and polished surfaces thus produced still remain in such countries as the northern parts of the United States, Scotland, and Scandinavia, wherever the rock has not been decomposed, and the huge bowlders lie every where strewed along the course of these ancient icebergs.

As the continents rose, lakes and rivers would be formed, whose currents would bring together and accumulate those large deposits of sand and gravel, which show themselves in the form of old beaches, ridges, and terraces, which can be found at least two thousand feet above the present ocean, and which attest unequivocally the former presence of the ocean, and the gradual drainage of the land.

The amount of abrasion by these various causes has been very great. In Great Britain,—in South Wales, for instance,—nearly ten thousand feet in thickness have been worn away. Indeed, it is a moderate estimate to say that more matter has been swept into the ocean from England and Scotland than now remains above the waters. The same is doubtless true in regard to the United States, although the observations here have not been so accurately made.

How deeply interesting to every ingenuous mind must it be to trace out on the earth's surface the marks of these stupendous and wonderful changes! They lie scattered along every man's path; yet how few have an eye open to see them! How many would prefer the baseless visions of romance to these mementos of the earth's wonderful history!

www.ingramcontent.com/pod-product-compliance
Lightning Source LLC
LaVergne TN
LVHW020933110826
845150LV00004B/846

9781425552688